THE
ONE YEAR®
BOOK OF
Devotions
for
Kids
#2

Tyndale House Publishers, Inc., Wheaton, Illinois

Stories written by: Katherine Ruth Adams, Susan F. Arcand, Esther M. Bailey, Carol Baker, Evelyn J. Behrens, Teresa M. Beverly, Judith K. Boogaart, Janet L. Boulter, Kathy A. Brand, Julie J. Brooks, Wanda E. Brunstetter, Jean A. Burns, David C. Carson, Jane K. Chase, Susanna B. Chenoweth, Karen E. Cogan, Mildred P. Colvin, Rosalie J. Currier, Carol A. DeCesare, Becky L. Decker, Mary L. DeMott, Douglas G. DeVries, Karen R. Ditthardt, Harriett A. Durrell, Sandra E. Dusa, Corrine Canavan Fifield, Dean A. Fowler, Linda Lee Gerard, Katherine F. Gibson, Brenda K. Good, Ruth M. Hamel, Mary E. Hanks, Myrina D. Harris, Diane K. Hesselberg, Beth R. Hoppers, Rebecca R. Howell, Clara E. Hustus, Vera M. Hutchcraft, Lyn Jackson, Christie P. Kehn, Margaret M. Keiffer, Nance E. Keyes, Dorothy R. King, Bonnie L. Kinne, Phyllis I. Klomparens, Daryl B. Knauer, Linda E. Knight, Pamela J. Kuhn, Sherri L. Kuyt, Donna A. LeBlanc, Joyce R. Lee, Glenn G. Luscher, Richard S. Maffeo, Linda M. Magoon, Blanche Manos, Hazel Marett, Tanya K. Marshall, Ruth K. McQuilkin, Lenora McWhorter, Valarae C. Murphy, Emilia M. D'Andrea Nichols, Emma L. Noll, Matilda H. Nordtvedt, Della R. Oberholtzer, Bill K. O'Conner, Linda J. Opp, Ellen C. Orr, Mary Rose Pearson, Richelle J. Pfeiffer, Judith A. Philip, Cynthia Y. Powell, Tait E. Powell, Margaret M. Primrose, Elizabeth A. Raum, Victoria L. Reinhardt, Janet E. Rhine, Deana L. Rogers, Darlene Minkler Root, Nathan Runyon, Shelley L. Russwurm, Alan A. Sawyer, Charissa S. Schalk, Heidi J. Schmidt, A. J. Schut, Elzina A. Scott, Maria I. Sellers, Marilyn J. Senterfitt, Sheri Shaw, Marie Shropshire, Debra W. Smith, Sam L. Sullivan, Lois A. Teufel, Kimberley J. Tracey, Trudy M. Vander Veen, Debra A. VanDyke, Cindy M. VanSchalkwyk, Rebecca L. Velez, Geri Walcott, Lyndel F. Walker, Linda M. Weddle, Carolyn E. Yost, Pauline O. Youd, Carol J. Zileski. Authors' initials appear at the end of each story. All stories are taken from issues of *Keys for Kids,* published bimonthly by the Children's Bible Hour, P.O. Box 1, Grand Rapids, Michigan 49501.

The One Year is a registered trademark of Tyndale House Publishers, Inc.

Scripture quotations marked NKJV are taken from The New King James Version. Copyright © 1979, 1980, 1982, Thomas Nelson Inc., Publishers.

Scripture verses marked TLB are taken from *The Living Bible,* copyright © 1971 owned by assignment by KNT Charitable Trust. All rights reserved.

Scripture quotations marked NIV are taken from the *Holy Bible,* New International Version®. Copyright © 1973, 1978, 1984 by International Bible Society. Used by permission of Zondervan Publishing House. All rights reserved. The "NIV" and "New International Version" trademarks are registered in the United States Patent and Trademark Office by International Bible Society. Use of either trademark requires permission of International Bible Society.

Scripture quotations marked KJV are from the *Holy Bible,* King James Version.

Library of Congress Cataloging-in-Publication Data

The One year book of devotions for kids.
     p.   cm.
    Includes Indexes.
    Summary: A collection of devotions for each day of the calendar year, including readings, illustrative stories, memory verses, and questions to internalize the messages.
    ISBN 0-8423-5088-8 (#1-pbk.)
    ISBN 0-8423-4592-2 (#2-pbk.)
    1. Devotional calendars—Juvenile literature. 2. Children—Prayer books and devotions—English. [1. Devotional calendars. 2. Prayer books and devotions. 3. Christian life.]
    BV4870.064   1993
    242′.682—dc20   93-15786

Printed in the United States of America

03 02 01 00 99 98 97 96
9   8   7   6   5   4   3   2

Table of Contents

Introduction

Introduction

For many years Children's Bible Hour has published *Keys for Kids,* a bimonthly devotional magazine for kids. Their fine ministry to parents and children has been much appreciated over the years, and Tyndale House is proud to present this new collection of stories from *Keys for Kids.*

The One Year Book of Devotions for Kids #2 has a full year's worth of stories that illustrate the day's Scripture reading. Following each story is a "How about You?" section, which asks children to apply the story to their lives. There is also a memory verse for each day, usually taken from the Scripture reading. We have quoted the memory verses from the New International Version, the King James Version, the New King James Version, and *The Living Bible.* However, you are free to have your children memorize the verses as they appear or use whichever Bible translation your family prefers. The devotion ends with a "key," a two- to five-word summary of the lesson.

The stories in this devotional are geared toward children between the ages of eight and fourteen. Kids can enjoy these stories by themselves as they develop their own daily quiet time (with any degree of parental involvement), or the stories can be used as part of family devotions. Like the many stories in the Bible that teach valuable lessons about life, the stories here will speak not only to children but to adults. They are simple, direct, and concrete, and like Jesus' parables, they speak to all of us in terms we can understand.

This book contains a Scripture index for both daily readings and memory verses as well as a topical index. The Scripture indexes are helpful if you want to locate a story related to a passage that you want to emphasize. The topical index is included because of concerns that arise unexpectedly in any family—such as moving, illness, or the loss of a friend or family member. We hope you will use this book every day, but the indexes are here so you will not feel locked into any one format. Please use any story any time you feel it relates to a special situation in your family.

The Secret (Read Acts 4:13-20)

"Please tell me the secret," Don begged Gary during recess. "What makes them jump?"

Gary was holding several Mexican jumping beans in his hand. At first they were still. Then one moved. "It's my secret," Gary said. "I'm not telling anyone."

"Mom," said Don when he got home, "Gary had some Mexican jumping beans at school, but he wouldn't tell me what makes them move. He said it's a secret."

"It's not a secret," Mom said. "Mexican jumping beans are three-celled bean pods that house moths. The jumping is caused by the moth larvae moving inside."

1

JANUARY

"That was driving me crazy all day," said Don, "and it shouldn't have been a secret at all. I wish I had a secret to keep from him. Then he'd know how it feels."

"I think you're already keeping something a secret from him," replied Mom. "Just like something in that bean pod made it jump, there's something in you that makes you choose to do the things you do. But you haven't told Gary what that is, have you?" Don looked at her in surprise. He didn't think he had any secrets. "When you refused to make fun of the new boy at school, what was the reason you gave Gary?" asked Mom.

"I told him I didn't feel like it," said Don.

"And when you collected the canned goods for the needy, what reason did you give Gary?" Mom asked.

"Well . . . I said I just felt like it," said Don.

"And when we prayed for Daddy to get well and he had a miraculously quick recovery, what did you tell Gary about that?" Mom asked.

Don shrugged. "Nothing," he said.

"Then I would say you're keeping a secret from Gary," Mom told him. "And it's far more important for him to know your secret than it was for you to know his." Don still looked puzzled, so Mom explained. "It isn't supposed to be a secret that Jesus is your Savior and that his love in your heart urges you to do the things you do," she said. "You know Gary's secret. Go tell him yours." *N.E.K.*

HOW ABOUT YOU?

Are you keeping it a secret that Jesus is your Savior? It should never be a secret that you are a Christian. Tell others the wonderful news.

MEMORIZE:

"For we cannot help speaking about what we have seen and heard." *Acts 4:20,* NIV

 Don't Keep Jesus a Secret

Walking the Beam (Read Proverbs 4:20-27)

2

JANUARY

Rhonda balanced carefully on the balance beam. Even though the basement floor was cushioned with a gym mat, she hated to slip off the narrow beam. "This is hard!" she moaned, after taking a few steps. "I'll never be good enough for the gymnastics team."

"Focus," Mother said gently. "You need to concentrate and focus your eyes on that picture you put up."

Rhonda lifted her foot carefully while staring at the picture placed on the wall across the room, but she still wondered if her foot would land back on the beam or if Mother would have to catch her. When she glanced at her mother, she tilted to the left and then swayed to the right. She tried to regain her balance but toppled to the floor.

"Every time I lose my focus, I get totally off track," Rhonda said. "I wish I could keep my eyes from wandering."

"Don't we all," Mother agreed. Rhonda stepped onto the beam again, wondering just what Mother meant. After all, she was the only one on the balance beam. "We need to practice two types of balance—one for gymnastics and one for life," continued Mother. "For example, I recently heard someone say, 'I'm really worried about my math test. I studied hard, and I prayed that I would remember the facts, but what if I fail?'"

Recognizing her own words from before school that very day, Rhonda turned and looked at Mom—and fell from the beam. "Oops!" exclaimed Rhonda, hopping back up.

"'I know I should read my Bible, but there's a really good show on TV tonight,'" murmured Mom softly.

This time, Rhonda recognized her thoughts, if not her actual words. She turned toward the clock to see if it was time for the TV program. "Oops!" she said, as her feet once again slipped off the balance beam.

"Just like losing focus means you lose your step on the balance beam, losing a dedicated focus on God allows us to become easily distracted and lose our step from the peaceful, righteous path that God has for us," Mother said. *N.E.K.*

HOW ABOUT YOU?

What draws your attention away from God? School activities? Friends? TV? These may all be fine, but don't make them the most important part of your life. Put God first—talking to him in prayer—and then carry thoughts of him into your other activities. Ask him to help you focus on him and live as you should.

MEMORIZE:

"Let your eyes look straight ahead, fix your gaze directly before you." *Proverbs 4:25,* NIV

 *Focus on God*

The Lost Dollar (Read Luke 11:9-13)

3

"Bobby, will you come here, please?" called Mother. Bobby put his red truck down and hurried to the kitchen. "I need you to run an errand for me," said Mother. "Take this money across the street to Sally's house, please. Her mother is going to buy some bread for us when she goes to the store."

Bobby put on his coat and pulled the collar up around his neck. Mother helped him pull on his fuzzy blue mittens. Then he took the dollar she handed him and started out the door.

Mother stood at the window and watched while Bobby crossed the street. Just as he reached the other side, a strong gust of wind took the money from Bobby's mittened hand. The dollar bill landed somewhere in the hedge in front of Sally's house. Bobby hurried over to the hedge. When Mother saw him sit down there and bury his face in his hands, she quickly put on her coat and went to help him.

"What's wrong?" asked Mother as Bobby looked up.

"I'm sorry, Mom. I lost the dollar," said Bobby. "It should be right in these bushes, but I can't find it."

"I'll help you find it," said Mother, "and let's pray that God will help us, too. We can do that while we look." She smiled at Bobby. "You can talk to God anywhere and anytime, you know. He always listens."

They began to search, and a few minutes later Bobby exclaimed, "Look! God answered our prayers. The dollar is stuck right here in the leaves!" *M.S.*

HOW ABOUT YOU?

Do you think to pray throughout the day whenever you need God's help? You can call upon him anytime and know that he hears you. It doesn't matter where you are or what your problem is. God isn't concerned about your physical position when you talk to him. He just wants you to remember to pray.

MEMORIZE:

"Ask, and it shall be given you; seek, and ye shall find; knock, and it shall be opened unto you." *Luke 11:9,* KJV

 *Keep Praying*

God's Address (Read Ephesians 2:11-22)

4

"What are you doing with the phone book, Missy?" asked Mom.

Jeff, who was helping with the dishes, took a plate and dried it. "She must be looking up somebody to call," he said. He snickered. "Of course, that's kinda hard when you can't read yet."

Mother smiled. "Five years old is a bit young to start calling people anyway, honey," she said.

"Hey, Missy," said Jeff as he put a plate in the cupboard, "you got a boyfriend you're going to call?"

Missy looked up. "No," she said, "I'm not calling anyone. I'm looking up an address."

"I thought you had our address memorized," said Mother.

"Yeah, Missy," said Jeff. "It's 445 Alice Aven—"

"I know our address!" interrupted Missy.

"Just whose address are you looking up?" asked Dad.

"I'm trying to find God's address."

Jeff exploded with laughter. "Missy, you're goofier than I thought," he said. "God doesn't have an address! You're wasting your time looking in there."

"Now, I just wouldn't be too sure about that, Jeff," said Dad. He pulled out a chair and sat down next to Missy. "Would you like me to help you?" he asked. Missy slid the telephone directory toward her father. "Well, let's just see now," said Dad. He riffled through the pages. "It should be several different places." He ran his finger slowly down the page, then stopped. "Yep!" he said. "Just as I thought. It's here all right."

"See!" exclaimed Missy, giving Jeff a triumphant look.

"What? This I've got to see," said Jeff. He walked to the table and peered over his father's shoulder. "Wait a minute!" he exclaimed. "You're pulling our legs. That's our address!"

Dad sat back and smiled. "Sure, it's our address. But God lives with us in our lives and in our home—that makes it his address, too." Dad closed the phone book. "Hopefully anyone who enters our house will be able to tell right away that God lives here." *A.J.S.*

HOW ABOUT YOU?

Does God live at the same address as you do? Does he live in your home . . . in your room? If you've accepted Jesus, he should be in every part of your life—at church, at school, and at home.

MEMORIZE:

"As for me and my house, we will serve the Lord."

Joshua 24:15, KJV

 Include God in Everything

The ID Badge (Read Matthew 10:32-38)

5

As Karen and her mother studied the menu at the restaurant, they noticed a group of people wearing badges. "They must all belong to some club," observed Karen.

Just then another man with a badge entered the restaurant and looked around briefly. He joined the group and introduced himself to them.

"Those people over there with identification badges are all councilmen from other cities," explained the waitress when she came to take orders from Karen and her mother. "There's a joint meeting in our town today."

When their food came, Karen and her mother bowed their heads and prayed before eating. Then Karen said, "Mom, it's easy to ask the blessing in a restaurant, but is it really so important to do that at school? I know the kids will make fun of me."

Mother thoughtfully pointed to the group of people wearing badges. "That man located his group by looking for the badges," she said. "Praying before a meal is something like that. It's one way we can be identified as Christians."

The next day, Karen sat apart from the others in the lunchroom. She looked around fearfully. Then, taking a deep breath, she bowed her head and thanked God for her food. Soon Linda, a classmate, joined her. "You must be a Christian," said Linda. "Well, I am, too, but I . . . I've been embarrassed to pray in front of the kids. Can I eat with you at lunch? We could pray together."

"Sure," agreed Karen. She grinned. "I 'wore my badge,' and I found another member of the club right away, didn't I?" At Linda's puzzled expression, she added, "I'll explain while we eat." *M.R.P.*

HOW ABOUT YOU?

Do the kids at your school know you're a Christian? A simple way to help identify yourself as God's child is to pray before eating—even at school. Wear your Christian "badge" proudly! You may be surprised to find there are other Christians in your school, too.

MEMORIZE:

"I am not ashamed of the gospel of Christ."

Romans 1:16, NKJV

 Show You're a Christian

On the Line (Read Ephesians 5:1-8)

"Did you see the pants Ronny wore today?" asked Brenda, holding the phone close to her mouth. "He looked like a real geek."

"His whole family is geeky," replied Danielle. The girls giggled. "What about Lynn—that new girl?" continued Danielle. "Did you notice that when she laughs she snorts like a hog?"

"Gross," Brenda said with a laugh. "Maybe she grew up on a pig farm." Just then the phone made a rasping sound. "What's that?" Brenda asked.

"Oh, pardon me, girls." Brenda's mom's voice interrupted them. "I was going to make a call from the den and didn't realize you girls were using the phone. I'll wait till you're finished." Brenda heard the click as Mom hung up.

"Where were we?" asked Danielle.

"I don't know, but I just thought of something," gasped Brenda. "What if Mom heard us talking about Ronny and Lynn? What if she heard the nasty things we said?"

"She didn't," said Danielle confidently. "We would've known it."

"Yeah. Well, I better go anyway," replied Brenda, so the girls said good-bye.

"Mom, we're off the phone," Brenda told her mother after they had hung up. She hesitated. "Did you hear what we were saying when you picked up the phone?"

"I know your conversations are private," replied Mom.

"But did you hear the things we were saying?" repeated Brenda. "I mean, if I knew you were listening, I wouldn't have said some things."

Mom raised her brows. "I didn't hear you," she said, "but does the fact that you're worried about it mean you were saying things that shouldn't be said? You need to remember that even though I don't hear, every time you're on the phone the Lord is on the line with you." *N.E.K.*

HOW ABOUT YOU?

Do you participate in conversations that you would be embarrassed for certain people to hear? Remember that the Lord hears every word that comes out of your mouth. He even knows your words while they are still thoughts. Be careful what you say.

MEMORIZE:

"Do not let any unwholesome talk come out of your mouths."

Ephesians 4:29, NIV

 *Speak Kindly*

Hidden Crystals (Read 1 Samuel 16:6-11)

Becky watched eagerly as Mrs. Sanders held up an ugly old stone. "This looks like an ordinary rock, doesn't it?" said Mrs. Sanders. Then she turned it around. The rock had been cut open, and the class could see beautiful, sparkling crystals on the inside. "This kind of stone is called a geode," said Mrs. Sanders as she picked up a box and handed it to a boy sitting in the front of the class. "When the box comes around to you, you may each take out a piece to keep."

7

JANUARY

Becky was delighted. She would never have guessed from looking at the ugly outside of the rock that the inside would sparkle so prettily. She selected one of the pieces, then turned and handed the box to Clara, who sat behind her. Becky didn't like Clara much. Clara had big, crooked teeth and was not very pretty. *She's almost as ugly as the outside of the geode,* thought Becky.

As Becky was running down the school steps at the end of the day, someone bumped her. Her books tumbled down the stairs, and papers scattered everywhere. Whoever bumped her didn't even stop.

Becky was picking up her belongings when she heard a voice. "Here, let me help you." Becky looked up and saw Clara kneeling beside her, gathering loose papers.

"Thanks," mumbled Becky. She was so surprised that she couldn't think of anything else to say as they gathered the rest of her things.

"Oh! Here's your stone!" exclaimed Clara. She picked up the piece of geode from the bottom step and handed it to Becky. "It's pretty, isn't it?"

As Becky took the stone, she thought about how people could be like the geode—not very pretty on the outside, but beautiful inside. Like Clara. "I have a rock collection at home, Clara. Would you like to come over to my house and see it?" invited Becky.

Clara smiled. "Sure," she said. *J.K.C.*

HOW ABOUT YOU?

Do you choose your friends by how they look? Do you ignore people who are overweight or have big ears or a crooked nose? God looks at the inside, the part that's important. Be more like him; don't judge what's inside people just by looking at the outside. Get to know them.

MEMORIZE:

"Stop judging by mere appearances, and make a right judgment." *John 7:24,* NIV

 Don't Judge by Appearance

Tips from Tippy (Read Psalm 105:1-5)

8

JANUARY

Joey watched as Uncle Stan put a bone right in front of Tippy. "No, Tippy! No!" Uncle Stan commanded the puppy. "Look at me!" Tippy looked straight at his master's face, then glanced down at the bone he wanted so very much. "Tippy, no! Look at me!" repeated Uncle Stan. Tippy raised his eyes and gazed again at his master, ignoring the bone.

"Why do you want Tippy to look at you?" asked Joey.

"If he looks at me rather than the bone, I know he'll obey me," replied Uncle Stan. He patted and praised Tippy and gave him some doggie treats. "Tippy reminds me a little of how we should act when we're tempted to do wrong," Uncle Stan told Joey. "If we keep our eyes on our Master, Jesus Christ, we'll be far more likely to obey him. But if we look at what is tempting us, it will be easier to give in to temptation."

"I don't get what it means to keep our eyes on Jesus," Joey said. "We can't really see him."

Uncle Stan smiled. "Well, let's see. . . ." he said. "I'm thinking of that tennis competition you participated in a few weeks ago. You worked so hard to be in shape—you even gave up desserts so that you'd be ready when it was time to play. Why did you do that?"

"I wanted to win the trophy," said Joey, grinning. "And I did!"

Uncle Stan nodded. "Would you understand what I meant if I said you had your eyes on the trophy?" he asked. Slowly Joey nodded. "You couldn't really see it, but you kept thinking about it. In much the same way, we keep our eyes on Jesus by thinking about him and what he'd want us to do. For example, if we think about Jesus and how he feels about certain TV shows, we'll turn them off. But if we forget about Jesus, we may keep watching, even though it displeases him. The same could be said about wrong books or videos or improper activities," added Uncle Stan. Again Joey nodded. He decided that from now on, he'd "look" at Jesus, his Master. *C.E.Y.*

HOW ABOUT YOU?

Do you keep "looking" at your Master, Jesus Christ? That's the thing that will keep you from giving in to temptation. His strength can keep you strong to fight against every temptation you'll ever meet.

MEMORIZE:

"Seek the Lord, and his strength: seek his face evermore." *Psalm 105:4,* KJV

Look to Jesus

The Plumb Line (Read Amos 7:7-9)

"Dad, the wallpaper in the corner of my room isn't on straight," observed Jerry. "Look—the blue stripe starts right next to the wall at the top, but it's not next to the wall at the bottom."

"You're right," agreed Dad. "Maybe the wall isn't straight. Let's find out." He took a ball of thick string and tied a little metal ring to the end of it for a weight. Then he handed Jerry a ruler and climbed on a chair so he could hold the string next to the ceiling. Slowly he unwound the string until the little ring reached the baseboard. Although Dad held the string next to the wall at the ceiling, it swung away from the wall at the baseboard. "The weight of that ring makes the string hang down straight, and that shows that the wall actually is crooked," said Dad. "Measure the distance between the string and the wall to see how far off it is."

Jerry took the ruler and set to work. "About an inch," he reported, "and we wouldn't even have noticed it if it weren't for the stripe on the wallpaper."

"Right," said Dad, "but the plumb line tells the truth."

"The plumb line?" asked Jerry. "Is that what you call that string with the ring on it?"

Dad nodded. "Maybe you'd like to hear what the Bible has to say about a plumb line," he suggested. "When it's time for devotions today, we'll look it up." He smiled at Jerry. "When God was going to judge a nation for its evil ways, he always used some sort of measuring device to show them their sins," he added. "Some of the prophets called the Law and the Commandments the plumb line."

"I can see why," said Jerry. "That would show if they measured up to God's standard."

"Do you think God uses a plumb line with us today?" asked Dad.

"Yep." Jerry nodded. "And I bet I know what it's called," he added. "The Bible." *P.O.Y.*

JANUARY
9

HOW ABOUT YOU?

How do you measure up to God's "plumb line"? The Bible tells you how God wants you to live. Don't just read it—apply it to your life to check and see if you're doing the things that please God.

MEMORIZE:

"Thy word is a lamp unto my feet, and a light unto my path."

Psalm 119:105, KJV

 Study the Bible

Who's Paralyzed? (Read Ephesians 4:17-24)

10

JANUARY

"Grandma, I'm sorry you can't do everything you used to do," said Cody. He wasn't sure what a stroke was, but he knew that was what had made his grandmother different several months ago. "I've been praying that you'll get all better."

"Me, too," said Grandma, "but I knew this old body would give out sooner or later—it happens to the best of us, you know." Grandma always had a smile, even though she couldn't walk very well and her left arm hung loosely at her side. "But did you know that lots of people in the world are paralyzed, and some of them don't even know it?" she added.

Cody was surprised. "How could they not know?" he asked.

"Well, you see, sin works like a stroke sometimes—it paralyzes," said Grandma. "Sometimes a person just keeps on doing something wrong until it doesn't 'hurt' anymore." She took a pair of scissors from a nearby table and gently poked her left arm with the sharp point. "He loses the feeling of guilt, just like I've lost the feeling in my arm. And unless the feeling comes back, he may remain in sin until it's too late to change." *S.L.S.*

HOW ABOUT YOU?

Have you noticed that the more often you do something wrong, the less concerned you are about it? You may even get to thinking that the wrong thing is right. Don't play with sin. Don't continue it long enough for your conscience to become paralyzed. When you're tempted to do something wrong, get away from it quickly.

MEMORIZE:

"Avoid every kind of evil."

1 Thessalonians 5:22, NIV

 Don't Be Paralyzed by Sin

The Same Old Thing (Read Psalm 119:127-135)

Robbie watched as his sister Brenda put on her coat, ready to leave for the children's rally at their church. "Too bad you have a bad cold and can't come, too," said Brenda.

Robbie shrugged. "Oh, well," he said, "Dr. Walters is just going to talk about Noah. It's the same old thing."

"God's Word is never just the 'same old thing,'" Mother reminded him as she and Brenda left.

It is the same old thing, Robbie said to himself. *I'm glad I don't have to go.* He turned on the TV set.

11

JANUARY

"The Lions and Bears game?" asked Dad. "That's a delayed broadcast, isn't it? You know who won."

Robbie nodded. "Yeah," he said, "but I like football."

The game ended, and Robbie was looking through some old baseball magazines when Mother and Brenda came home. "What shall we have for supper?" asked Mother.

"Pizza!" said Robbie promptly.

"Again?" asked Mother.

"Sure," replied Robbie. "I never get tired of pizza."

As they ate, Brenda told Robbie how much she had enjoyed the meeting. Robbie wasn't impressed. "I already know all about Noah," he told her. "Ask me anything."

"How big was the ark compared to a football field?" asked Brenda. "And how much food did Noah have to gather?"

"Well . . ." Robbie didn't know the answers.

"You say the story of Noah is the 'same old thing,' but a replayed football game is exciting to you," observed Dad.

"And you never get tired of pizza," said Mom.

"Or those year-old baseball magazines," added Brenda.

"How come you're ganging up on me?" protested Robbie.

Dad smiled. "We just don't want you to think of the Bible as being the 'same old thing,'" he said. "There are new facts and lessons to be learned, even from familiar stories."

Robbie thought about it, and Brenda grinned at him. "You would have liked Dr. Walters," she said. "We bought a tape!"

"Thanks," said Robbie. "I'll listen. I promise." *L.W.*

HOW ABOUT YOU?

Do you complain about hearing the "same old thing" in church? Do you use it as an excuse not to learn about the Lord? One special thing about the Bible is that no matter how many times you've heard a lesson, there is still more you can learn.

MEMORIZE:

"The grass withers, the flowers fade, but the Word of our God shall stand forever."

Isaiah 40:8, TLB

 God's Word Is Always New

Static Cling (Read Psalms 19:12-14; 139:23-24)

12

JANUARY

Rose's sweater crackled with static as she pulled it over her head. She wet a comb to tame her flyaway hair and hurried downstairs for breakfast. "Why are you giggling?" Rose asked her brother as she took her seat at the table.

Brian pointed at Rose's back, and Mom and Dad chuckled, too. "There's a pink sock stuck to your back!" said Brian.

"Oops!" said Mom, removing the sock from Rose's sweater.

"I'm glad you noticed that," said Rose. "It would've been embarrassing if I went to school looking like that."

After breakfast, Dad reached for the family Bible. "Let's read a few verses before you leave for school," he said. "We've removed the item sticking to your clothes. Now let's do a little spot-checking to be sure we aren't letting sin stick around in our lives."

"I don't have any sin stuck in my life," stated Rose confidently.

"Are you sure?" asked Mom.

"What about the way you shove stuff under your bed when Mom tells us to clean our rooms?" asked Brian with a smirk. "You do it all the time."

"How would you know?" asked Rose. She was embarrassed. "Besides, I don't really consider it sin when I do that—after all, I clean it up later." She scowled at Brian. "What about tattling?" she added.

"If we're not careful, sin can sneak up and attach itself to us without our realizing it," said Dad. "It's there as clear as your sock was, but somehow we don't see it. That's why each of us must come before God daily and ask him to show us what's wrong in our lives."

N.E.K.

HOW ABOUT YOU?

Do you regularly ask God to reveal your sin to you so that you can get rid of it? Don't cling to sin or allow it to cling to you. Be willing to be taught and made aware of it through God's Word or through his like pastors, teachers, or parents.

MEMORIZE:

"Search me, O God, and know my heart: try me, and know my thoughts." *Psalm 139:23,* KJV

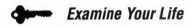 *Examine Your Life*

No Mirage (Read 2 Timothy 3:14-17)

Looking up from her book, Sara said, "The girl in this book is always seeing mirages. Are there really such things, Dad?"

"Sure," replied Dad. "A mirage is an optical illusion. For instance, a thirsty person in a desert might think he sees a lake or stream up ahead, but the water really isn't there."

13

JANUARY

Sara want back to her book. Just then her little sister Jana came toddling into the room, banging two toys together. "Play with me?" she asked.

Sara scowled. "Can't you see I'm trying to concentrate on this book?" she snapped. "Now get out of here." Jana's lip quivered, and she toddled back out of the room.

Then the sounds of voices and laughter came floating into the room as Sara's brother Dan and his friends talked about the latest basketball game. "Can't you guys pipe down?" yelled Sara angrily. "You sound like a bunch of squealing pigs."

Dad put down his paper and looked sternly at Sara. "Sara, you've been rude to both your sister and brother this evening—and I've noticed you acting like that a lot lately. You have to change your ways," he said.

"But, Dad, they drive me crazy," objected Sara.

"Then it's a perfect time to start practicing the command of God that we read in devotions today," Dad told her. "Remember it?"

Sara pouted as she shook her head. "I forgot," she mumbled.

Dad frowned. "What was that word you asked about—*mirage?* Well, I'm afraid you treat the commands in the Bible as if they're a mirage," he said. "You see them, but you act as if they're not really there. They are real, and God intends for us to put them into practice—so listen again. The verse we read was Philippians 4:5: 'Let your gentleness be evident to all.' This command is not a mirage, Sara. We need to be gentle with others in every way, including our speech."

Sara sighed. She knew Dad was right. "I . . . I'm sorry," she said. "I'll honestly try to do better and to be more polite." *C.E.Y.*

HOW ABOUT YOU?

Do you read and hear God's commands without obeying? His commands are no mirage. They're real, and he wants you to obey them. Sometimes the hardest place to be gentle and polite is in your own family. If you really desire to please him in this, ask God to help you, and he will.

MEMORIZE:

"Let your gentleness be evident to all. The Lord is near."

Philippians 4:5, NIV

 **Be Gentle**

The Unseen Helper (Read Psalm 121:1-8)

14
JANUARY

Crash! Robby bolted upright in bed. "I am not drunk!" his father's voice thundered from downstairs. "Give me my keys."

Robbie crept to the top of the stairs and saw his father stagger toward Mom. Mom was holding the car keys behind her. "It's not safe for you to drive," Mom said.

"I don't care!" roared Dad. "Give me those keys!" He made a grab for her. She spun away, tossing the keys behind the upright piano. "Whad'ya do that for?" Dad bellowed. He grabbed Mom by the shoulders and shook her.

Robby shuddered as his mother cried out. He knew he needed to get help, but he was too scared to move. As he stood shaking, his eyes fell on a picture of snowcapped Pikes Peak. What was it their next-door neighbor, Mr. Simms, said when he gave Robby the picture? Something about hills and help from the Lord. *Oh God, I need help,* Robby prayed. *My mom needs help. Show me what to do.*

Robby opened his eyes. He could see the front door at the bottom of the stairs. His father's back was toward him. Robby tore down the stairs. His fingers fumbled with the dead bolt. Robby jerked the door open, dashed down the walk, and raced onto the Simms's porch.

Robby pounded on the front door, and soon the porch light flickered. Mr. Simms opened the door. "My dad," Robby wheezed. "He's drunk, and he's hurting my mom."

"Call the police, Ida," Mr. Simms said to his wife. Minutes later, a policeman helped Robby's father into the back seat of a cruiser.

"What will happen to Dad?" Robby asked Mr. Simms.

"The police will take him to House of Hope. Your dad will get help there for his drinking problem," Mr. Simms assured Robby. "You did a brave thing tonight, Robby."

"I had help," Robby told him. "The picture of Pikes Peak reminded me of that Bible verse about help coming from the Lord. I asked God to help me and my mom."

"That's the best help a guy can have," said Mr. Simms. *H.J.S.*

HOW ABOUT YOU?

Are you afraid when people you love are out of control? Do you worry about frightening situations? Remember that God, who created our world with a word, is here to help. Ask him for wisdom and courage.

MEMORIZE:

"I will lift up my eyes to the hills—From whence comes my help? My help comes from the Lord, Who made heaven and earth." *Psalm 121:1-2, NKJV*

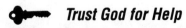 *Trust God for Help*

The Big Stain (Read Isaiah 1:16-20)

15

JANUARY

Adam's eyes widened in horror as his elbow knocked the ink bottle off the desk, sending it crashing. Blue ink spread in a growing circle across his grandparents' dinette floor. Adam jumped down from his chair and quickly bent to pick up the ink bottle. *What am I going to do?* he wondered. *I've got to clean this up before they see it.*

Adam rushed into the utility room, grabbed some rags, and filled a small bucket with water. Coming back into the dinette, he began scrubbing . . . and scrubbing . . . and scrubbing the ink blob. But his efforts didn't help much. In fact, they seemed to make things worse. What used to be only a small spot on the floor was now a very, very large ink spot. *Oh! This is not going to work!* Adam thought to himself. He knew he would have to tell his grandparents.

Grandma frowned when she saw the stain, but she knew it had been an accident. She quickly asked Grandpa to get cleaner from the garage, and soon all trace of the ink was gone.

"You know, Adam," Grandpa said as they washed their hands with the special soap they had used to clean the floor, "maybe we can both learn a good lesson from what just happened."

Adam looked up at him. "Not to fool around with ink, huh?" he asked.

Grandpa smiled. "Well, yes," he said, "but I was thinking of an even more important lesson. The Bible tells us we're all stained by sin, and no matter how hard we try, we just can't clean it ourselves." Grandpa dried his hands and continued. "But the Bible also says that Jesus died for us, and his blood can cleanse us completely of all of sin's dark stain."

Adam finished washing and looked at his hands. They were completely clean. "I needed soap to clean the floor and my hands, and I need Jesus to clean my heart, right?" he said.

Grandpa smiled and put his hand on Adam's shoulder. "Right," he said. "That's exactly right." *R.S.M.*

HOW ABOUT YOU?

Have all your sins been washed away? You can try to clean your heart and life by being good or doing good things, but it won't work. Only Jesus can make you completely clean. Ask him to cleanse your heart from sin.

MEMORIZE:

"Though your sins be as scarlet, they shall be as white as snow." *Isaiah 1:18, KJV*

 Let Jesus Make You Clean

Swords and Things (Read 2 Corinthians 10:3-6)

16

JANUARY

Kenny was in trouble for sure. His teacher, Mr. Hancock, had called his name, but he had been too preoccupied to hear. Mr. Hancock walked over, picked up Kenny's notebook, and thumbed through it. "I'll see you after class," he said.

When the bell rang, Kenny nervously approached his teacher's desk. Mr. Hancock took Kenny's notebook and turned to some drawings Kenny had made. They were all pictures of swords and daggers in rather peculiar settings. Some had what seemed to be rays of light coming from the sword. Others had an eye on the hilt of the sword with some odd writing. "What are all these?" asked Mr. Hancock.

"Swords," Kenny replied.

"I can see that. But what do they mean? Isn't it unusual just to draw swords?" asked Mr. Hancock.

"They're like the ones in a video game I play," said Kenny. "See . . . these swords all have special powers."

"Kenny," Mr. Hancock said, "it's bad enough that you weren't paying attention in class, but it *really* disturbs me to see what has been occupying your thoughts. You are giving a man-made object power that only belongs to God. That's what idolatry is."

"It's just a game," objected Kenny. "I know they don't really have powers."

"At this point you do," acknowledged Mr. Hancock, "but many people have opened the door for Satan to work in their lives by letting their thoughts be occupied with things just like this. The Bible says we are to 'cast down imaginations, and every high thing that exalts itself against the knowledge of God.' You see, even things we think about—or imagine—can have real spiritual power. That's why we have to be so careful about what occupies our thoughts." *D.C.C.*

HOW ABOUT YOU?

Have you been playing games that are not pleasing to God? Such games usually give God's power to some man-made object. This is from Satan—he has always wanted God's power. Decide today that you will not become involved in anything that gives God's power to something other than God.

MEMORIZE:

"Casting down imaginations, and every high thing that exalteth itself against the knowledge of God, and bringing into captivity every thought to the obedience of Christ."

2 Corinthians 10:5, KJV

 Don't Let Satan Control Your Mind

Way to Win (Read Proverbs 6:4-11)

Timothy sat at the kitchen table, reading a magazine. "Did you memorize today's verse?" asked his sister Shana. "This is the last week of the contest, you know."

"Aw, I won't win anything anyway," Timothy mumbled. "It's too hard."

"Better hurry," advised Mother. "It's almost time to leave for church, and you still need to feed Riley, too."

17

JANUARY

At the mention of his name, Riley got his dish and dropped it at Timothy's feet. "Just a minute, boy," said Timothy.

"Timothy!" said Mother. "Get going!"

Timothy went to his room. Riley got his bowl, followed Timothy, and again dropped it at Timothy's feet. Timothy halfheartedly looked over his verse. Then he went back to the kitchen and picked up the magazine again. *CRASH!* Riley again dropped his dish. Timothy laughed. "You don't give up, do you, Riley?" he said. "OK, I'll feed you."

Mother smiled. "We should all be a little more diligent, like Riley," she said.

"Diligent?" asked Timothy. "What's that?"

"It's what you just said—keeping at something and refusing to give up," explained Mother.

But the prize wasn't a pencil. It was a trip to Chicago, and Shana was one of the winners. "Mrs. Morris is going with us," she said excitedly on the way home. "I can't wait!"

"It's not fair," grumbled Timothy. "Shana gets everything!"

"Shana worked very hard at that contest," said Dad.

"Right," agreed Mother. "She showed as much diligence as Riley. Riley wanted his breakfast and was willing to keep after you until he got it. He didn't get lazy and give up."

Dad nodded. "You only memorized three or four verses. That's not giving your best," he told Timothy. "That's not the way to win."

Timothy felt a little foolish—he hadn't expected to learn a lesson from his dog! *I wonder when the next contest starts?* he thought. *Next time I'm going to do my very best. L.M.*

HOW ABOUT YOU?

Do you sometimes give a halfhearted effort at something and then become upset when you don't get rewarded? Do you complain because things "aren't fair," when actually it's your complaining that is unfair? The Lord tells us to be diligent—to give our best in all that we do.

MEMORIZE:

"Be careful to do what is right in the eyes of everybody."

Romans 12:17, NIV

 Work Diligently

The Perfect Spot (Read Ephesians 4:29-32)

18
JANUARY

"I know I shouldn't have called Sarah a cheater," Mandy told her mother as they drove down a mountain road toward town. "But it made me so mad when she got an A on her spelling test and I only got a C."

"Well then, why don't you call and apologize?" suggested Mother.

"Oh, Mom," whined Mandy, "that's so hard. I think I'll just wait a few days and see if I don't get a good chance to make friends with her again."

Mother frowned. Suddenly she slowed the car and turned down a side road. "I heard this is a shorter way to get to town," she said. "Let's try it." For a short distance the road was good, but then the pavement ended and the road became muddy.

"I think we should go back," Mandy said finally.

"I think you're right," agreed Mother. "We'll just have to drive a little farther until we find a place to turn around."

They went on, and soon Mandy saw a big, open space up ahead. "You can turn around there," she told her mother.

Mother slowed down, but she shook her head. "No," she said, "I think I can find a better spot."

As they drove farther, Mandy motioned with her arm. "How about right there?" she asked.

But Mother passed it by, too. "I'm trying to find the perfect spot to turn back," she said.

"Mother!" protested Mandy. "If you ask me, the first possible spot is the perfect spot!"

Mother grinned. "Actually, I think so, too," she said, as she slowed down and turned into a narrow path off the road. "I guess we'll turn around right here. Waiting for a perfect spot was foolish, wasn't it?" she asked. "We made a mistake in coming this way, and the first chance to correct that mistake was the best chance. That's true when we make other mistakes, too—like when we need to apologize for something. It's foolish to wait for a perfect time to do it." *C.C.F.*

HOW ABOUT YOU?

Do you find it hard to apologize? Do you put it off instead of doing it right away? Remember that God does not want you to hold on to your anger. Apologize, and you'll feel much better.

MEMORIZE:

"Be kind to each other, tenderhearted, forgiving one another, just as God has forgiven you because you belong to Christ."

Ephesians 4:32, TLB

 Seek Forgiveness

A Piece of Clay (Read Isaiah 45:6-13)

19 JANUARY

Jon held the headless clay animal in his hand. "Look, Mom!" he wailed. "How can I take this to school without a head?" He opened his other hand slowly. In it was a clump of deformed clay, hard and crusty. "This was going to be his head," he mumbled. "I forgot to put it back in the container!"

"I'm sorry, Jon," said Mother, "but it's too late to do anything about it now. It's time you hopped into bed— you need your rest."

"My project is due tomorrow, so now all this work was for nothing!" Jon said with a groan. He dropped the materials onto his dresser, pulled back his covers, and slid beneath the sheets.

Mother glanced at the Bible that lay on Jon's dresser next to the school project. "Do you still read your Bible before you go to sleep?" she asked.

Jon sighed. "Sometimes," he said, "but I've been so busy lately. Besides, I don't understand it very well." He pulled the covers up to his chin. "Do you think there's much point in kids reading it?" he asked. "Wouldn't it be better to wait till I'm older and can understand it better?"

Mother picked up the hardened lump of clay. She held it out toward Jon. "We're a lot like this clay," she said.

"We are?" asked Jon.

Mother nodded. "The Bible compares us to clay that God can shape," she said. "But if we want God to shape us, we need to stay pliable. One way to do that is to spend time with his Word—the Bible."

Jon looked down at the hardened clay. "So if I wait till I'm older to start reading my Bible, I might get hard—sort of like this clay," he said.

"That could happen," Mother agreed. "Older people who have kept their distance from God often seem more hardened and less open to God's shaping."

"Well, . . . hand me my Bible then, OK?" said Jon. "I don't like this hard old stuff." *A.J.S.*

HOW ABOUT YOU?

Are you willing to be shaped by God's hand? Do you regularly read the Bible and pray for the Holy Spirit to guide you in understanding? Spend time with God each day to allow him to shape you into the person he wants you to be.

MEMORIZE:

"As the clay is in the potter's hand, so are you in My hand."

Jeremiah 18:6, NKJV

 Let God Shape You

Filling a Space (Read Leviticus 19:17-18; Matthew 5:43-48)

20

Josh walked straight from school to the building where his mother worked as a dental assistant. Josh arrived and plopped himself down on one of the chairs in the waiting room, letting his book bag slide to the floor beside him. He was glad school was out. What a day it had been! He gave his book bag an angry little kick. Mom noticed.

"What's the trouble, Josh?" Mom asked as they started home.

"I don't like Brian," said Josh. "In fact, after what he did at school today, I think I hate him!"

"Hold it!" exclaimed Mom. "*Hate* is not a word I like to hear. What happened?"

"Brian threw a huge wad of paper and hit Stacey on the back of her head. Since I sit right behind Stacey, she told Mrs. Cramer I did it. I said I didn't do it, but Mrs. Cramer made me stand in the hall for the whole period. Brian should have admitted he did it, but he just let me stand there. After school he tried to apologize, like that would do any good. It was too late then!"

Mom looked thoughtful. "Sounds like you need a filling, Josh," she said.

"A filling!" exclaimed Josh. "Who's talking about teeth? Besides, I just had some fillings, and now my teeth are fine!"

Mother smiled. "When you had the cavities, what did the dentist do?" she asked.

"Well . . . he drilled out the decay and filled the space with a special material," replied Josh. "But what about Brian?" Josh was anxious to get back to his problem.

"I was thinking of the problem with Brian," said Mom. "Brian was wrong, but I think you need to drill the decay—which is hate—out of your heart and fill the space with forgiveness."

"Drill out hate?" asked Josh. "How can I do that?"

"Well," began Mom, "you need to use a much more powerful tool than a dentist's drill. You need to use the tool called prayer. With God's help, you can get rid of the hate and forgive Brian." *D.R.K.*

HOW ABOUT YOU?

Do you find it hard to forgive? It's not easy, but with God's help it can be done. Ask God to give you a forgiving spirit. It will make you a happier person, too.

MEMORIZE:

"Pray for those who persecute you!" *Matthew 5:44,* TLB

 *Get Rid of Hate*

Open Ears (Read 1 Samuel 3:1-10)

21

"We had a new girl in Sunday school today," announced Yvonne one Sunday noon. "Her name is Jane, and she's deaf. She has to read lips."

Mother nodded. "I met her mother," she said. "The family moved here so Jane can attend the special class for the deaf in your school." Mother set a casserole on the table. "I read recently that 4 million people in our country are completely deaf," she added. "And even more than that can't hear as well as they should."

"How terrible!" Yvonne exclaimed. "I think deafness must be the worst thing in the world. I'm glad I'm not deaf."

"Oh, now, I can think of a lot of things that would be much worse than being deaf, but I do agree that we should all be thankful for two good ears," said Dad. After a moment he added, "Sadly enough, some of us who have two good ears are deaf in another way—we're spiritually deaf."

"Spiritually deaf? What does that mean?" asked Yvonne.

"Some people don't listen to God," explained Dad. "I'm afraid there are more people in our country who are spiritually deaf than there are people with physical hearing problems. Even Christians often don't hear God as well as they should. After they accept his gift of salvation, they neglect Bible study and prayer life. They quit listening—they don't keep their spiritual ears open."

Mother nodded. "Let's all be especially aware of that in this coming year," she said. "Let's not become hard of hearing when there's something God wants to tell us." *M.S.*

HOW ABOUT YOU?

Are you hard of hearing—spiritually, that is? Be sure to read your Bible and pray every day. As you saw in today's Scripture, the boy, Samuel, was ready to listen to the Lord; you should be, too. Ask the Lord to help you never to turn a deaf ear to him.

MEMORIZE:

"I am listening carefully to all the Lord is saying." *Psalm 85:8*, TLB

 *Listen to God*

Beautiful Music (Read 1 Corinthians 12:11-14)

22
JANUARY

"Is the stereo fixed already, Dad?" asked Nathan.

Dad smiled. "Try it," he suggested.

Nathan pressed down one of the buttons on the stereo, but all he heard was a loud *bzzzzzzzzz*. He tried another button. More of the buzzing sound. "Nope, it's not fixed yet," he said, peering at the mass of colored wires in the back of the set. "It looks awful complicated back there."

"All it takes is some fine-tuning," said Dad. "Watch." After carefully connecting several wires, Dad looked at Nathan. "Try it now," he said. Nathan did, and beautiful music began coming from the speakers.

"That was as easy as one-two-three!" exclaimed Nathan.

"The wires just had to be properly connected," said Dad as he put the back panel in place. Picking up his tools, he added, "You know, Son, all these wires remind me of the body of Christ—Christians. By ourselves, we all make some sound, something like that buzzing sound you heard. But it's when we're together, in tune with one another, that we make beautiful music." *L.E.K.*

HOW ABOUT YOU?

Do you sometimes think you don't need other believers? Do you think you don't need to go to church as often as you used to? It's true that God can use you, all by yourself, but very often you're more effective as you work together with others who know the Lord.

MEMORIZE:

"You are the body of Christ, and each one of you is a part of it." *1 Corinthians 12:27,* NIV

 Believers Need Each Other

Thin Ice or Thick (Read Acts 16:25-32)

Patrick couldn't believe his ears when Grandpa pulled out some photos and began to tell the family about his recent fishing trip to Minnesota. "You mean you really drove right out on the ice, Grandpa?" he asked in disbelief.

"Yes, indeed," Grandpa replied. "I drove out on it, camped on it, and fished through a hole in it."

"But you always warn me about walking on the river in the winter!" exclaimed Patrick.

23

JANUARY

"That's true," admitted Grandpa. "When your father was your age, he nearly died because he trusted the ice on the river. But I was in no danger. The difference between the lake and the river was the thickness of the ice." He hesitated and tugged at his beard.

Patrick's father laughed. "Go ahead, Dad," he told Grandpa. "It's obvious that you want to say something about our spiritual lives."

Grandpa chuckled. "Well, now that you mention it, it does remind me of our walk with Christ," he said. "Pat, no matter how much faith your father had in the river ice, it would not hold him up. On the other hand, even if I had stepped onto the lake ice doubtfully, it would still have supported me because, in spite of my feelings, it was thick and strong."

Patrick nodded thoughtfully.

"Our *feelings* are not so important as *what we trust in.* Some people feel very good about themselves. They feel sure that their church membership or their good works will get them to heaven. But those things are like thin ice—they won't hold. Other people know they're sinners. Still, they know God says he loves them and that Jesus died to save them, so they put their trust in him. Jesus is like the thick, strong ice. When your trust is in him, you're safe."

"Even though sometimes I hardly *feel* like a Christian?" asked Patrick. "Like . . . maybe when I've done something wrong. But God says I am one because I've accepted Jesus as my Savior, right?"

"Exactly!" agreed Grandpa. "Your faith may be weak, but Jesus is strong and always supports and keeps you." *S.F.A.*

HOW ABOUT YOU?

Are you trusting in Jesus? Don't trust the "thin ice"—the good things you can do. Trust in Jesus and what he has done for you. If your faith is in him, you're safe—even though that faith may sometimes be weak. If you haven't done so before, won't you trust him today?

MEMORIZE:

"Believe on the Lord Jesus Christ, and you will be saved."

Acts 16:31, NKJV

 Put Your Faith in Jesus

The Old Made New (Read Psalm 103:8-14)

24
JANUARY

One day, Chris went with his grandpa to an automobile museum. "Aren't these old cars funny-looking, Grandpa?" said Chris.

Grandpa smiled. "Well," he said, "they were mighty stylish in their day, you know." He pointed to one of the cars. "There's one like my father drove when I was about your age. It came in any color you wanted, as long as it was black."

Chris laughed. "Some of these old cars look brand-new!" he exclaimed, peering through the window of one of the cars. "This one doesn't look like it's ever been out of this building."

"Oh, but it has," said Grandpa. "It's very old, but it's been restored. Worn out parts have been replaced, and the old paint has been removed and replaced with bright, shiny, new paint." After a moment he added, "It's kind of like what Jesus does for us. He restores our souls."

"Jesus doesn't make us *look* different," said Chris.

"Well," said Grandpa, "we might wear a smile instead of a scowl when we're restored. But I was thinking about how he changes us inside—how he takes all our sin away when we confess it to him, and he makes us clean again. I guess you could call him the Divine Restorer." *S.L.S*

HOW ABOUT YOU?

Do you need to be restored? When you're sorry for your sin and confess it, God will restore you and make your heart clean again.

MEMORIZE:

"He restores my soul."

Psalm 23:3, NIV

 Jesus Restores His Children

The Magnifying Glass (Read Psalm 34:1-8)

25

"Magify, oh, magify . . ." sang Kimmy as she and her big brother, Jack, walked up to their grandfather's house.

"Hi, Grandpa," said Jack as they went into the house. "What are you doing? Reading the paper?" Grandpa nodded.

"What's that?" asked Kimmy, pointing to Grandpa's hand.

Jack knew what it was. "It's a magnifying glass," he said.

"That's right," said Grandpa. "This makes the letters look bigger so I can see them better. Here . . ." Grandpa motioned for them to come close. "Try it out."

"You know what, Grandpa?" asked Kimmy. "Last Sunday a lady sang a song about a magifying glass."

Jack laughed. "The word is *magnify,* not *magify,*" he informed his sister. "And it wasn't about a magnifying glass. She sang, 'Magnify the Lord.'" He paused. "But what does that mean, Grandpa?" he asked. "To magnify something means to make it bigger, but we can't make God bigger!"

Grandpa smiled. "When I use this glass to read, the letters seem bigger to my eyes, but they're not really bigger, are they?"

Jack thought about that. "But I still don't see what it means to magnify the Lord," he said.

"Well, I think we magnify God when we block out the things that distract us and just focus on him. Then we get to know him better and get a better glimpse of how great he really is. We feel his presence close to us. Does that make sense to you?"

As Jack slowly nodded his head, Kimmy called out, "Look!" She was holding the magnifying glass over a cartoon in the paper. "Look how big Bugsy's whiskers are!"

"I think Kimmy has just pointed out another way we magnify the Lord," said Grandpa. "She's the one looking at that cartoon, but even from here we can see something of what she sees. When we magnify the Lord, we hold him up and praise him, and it helps other people get a glimpse of how great he is, too." *H.M.*

HOW ABOUT YOU?

Do you spend a little time each day thinking about how great God is? If you do, you'll soon begin to think about him more, even when you are busy, and people around you may begin to notice him, too.

MEMORIZE:

"O magnify the Lord with me, and let us exalt his name together." *Psalm 34:3,* KJV

 *Magnify the Lord*

Pain in the Neck (Read Genesis 19:15-17, 25-26)

26

JANUARY

Whitney turned her head and looked out the car's back window. If she squinted, she could just see their old house. "I don't want to move," she said as tears ran down her cheeks. "I want to stay in Greenwood with my friends."

Mother put a hand out and gently turned Whitney's face toward her. "I'll miss my friends, too," she said, "but Dad has a new job, and we have to move." Whitney pulled away. She wanted to look at Greenwood as long as she could. "Let's sing," suggested Mother. Whitney didn't feel like singing. She went on pouting and turning her face back toward the familiar, old town.

"We're family, Whitney," said her father. "We'll help each other." Whitney pretended she didn't hear him.

When they stopped for lunch, Whitney wanted to stay in the car, but she was hungry. She stomped into the restaurant and slid into the booth. "Did you see the circus wagons when you drove into town?" asked the waitress who came to serve them.

The girl in the next booth piped up. "Did the clowns wave to you?" she asked Whitney. "They waved to us." But Whitney had missed the clowns.

"Whitney, do you remember the story about Lot's wife?" asked Mother. "When God called her to a new place she didn't want to go—she kept looking back. And because she looked back, she turned into a pillar of salt. She couldn't help her family anymore. She couldn't make friends."

Mother put her arm around Whitney and drew her close. "Dad and I need you, honey," she said. "We need your friendship and your smile. All we saw this morning was the back of your head."

Whitney rubbed her neck. She had missed the circus wagons and the clowns. She had a heavy feeling in her chest, but she hoped she wouldn't miss any other exciting things. And she didn't want to hurt her parents either. "Well," she said, "I'm glad I didn't turn into a pillar of salt." Then she smiled. "But I sure got a pain in my neck." *R.M.H.*

HOW ABOUT YOU?

Are you cheerful when there are changes you don't like? Are you a good family member when things don't go your way? Sometimes it's hard to understand God's plan, but you need to trust him at all times.

MEMORIZE:

"I trust in the mercy of God forever and ever." *Psalm 52:8,* TLB

 Accept Changes Cheerfully

A New Story (Read Mark 5:18-20)

27

JANUARY

"I'm so happy about this, Brian." Mother gave him a big hug. "The decision to accept Jesus is the most important one you'll ever make." Brian felt happy, too—it was good to know he was part of the family of God along with his parents, grandparents, and his friends at church. Of course, his friends at school . . . Brian's smile disappeared like snow on a sunny day. His two school buddies—they didn't even go to church. The three boys had been together since first grade, and their teacher often referred to them as "the three musketeers." There was Pete, the practical joker, and Mike, the storyteller. Of course, they all liked to tell funny stories—and some of them were not the kind you'd want to tell your mother! *Will Mike and Pete still want to be my friends when they find out I'm a Christian?* wondered Brian.

The next morning, Brian fooled around while he was getting ready for school. Maybe he shouldn't tell his buddies what had happened. "Your egg is getting cold, Brian," said Mother.

Brian slumped into his chair and took a few bites of toast. "I'm not very hungry," he said.

"Well, it's time for you to go," said Mother.

At school Brian shuffled to his seat just as the bell was ringing. Pete waved and pointed to a plastic spider he had put on the shoulder of the girl in front of him. Brian pretended not to see him. Good old Pete; he'd do anything for a laugh. But Brian didn't feel like laughing.

At noon, he was unusually quiet as the boys ate their lunches. "Hey, Brian, know any new stories?" Mike asked. Then he poked him in the ribs and added, "I've got one that will knock your socks off!"

Brian squirmed and took a big breath. Suddenly he knew this was the right time to tell them. "Yeah, guys, I have a brand-new story." He spoke quickly before he lost his nerve. "You'll never guess what happened last night. . . ." *D.M.R.*

HOW ABOUT YOU?

Are you afraid to talk to your friends about Jesus? Some children grow up in homes where the Bible is not read. They may just be waiting for someone to tell them what it means to be a Christian. Wouldn't you like to be that person?

MEMORIZE:

"Go home to your family and tell them how much the Lord has done for you, and how he has had mercy on you."

Mark 5:19, NIV

 Tell Your Friends about Jesus

Mine Again (Read Hebrews 9:11-15)

28

"Mom, can I have some money for the 'lost and found' auction today?" asked Joel as he ate his breakfast. Mom nodded. Joel's school was going to auction off any unclaimed items remaining in the lost-and-found box during the noon hour.

That noon, most of the school children gathered in the auditorium. Joel watched as they bid on scarves, mittens, and sweaters. But when the auctioneer—the principal—held up a pair of gym shoes, Joel sat up straight. He realized they were a pair he thought he had left at his grandmother's house! So Joel decided to buy them back. Back and forth the bidding went. He wondered if he'd have enough money. After bidding his last cent, he held his breath, but no other bid came, and the shoes were his.

Back home, Joel grumbled a little. "The shoes are mine again," he said, "but they really were always mine. It doesn't seem fair that I had to buy them back. They cost me all my money!"

Dad nodded. "I can understand how you feel," he said, "but you know what? Your experience is a good example of what God has done for us. He made us, you know, so in a sense everyone belongs to him. But just like your shoes, mankind got lost—lost in sin. And just like your shoes, we had to be bought back, too."

"That's right," agreed Mom. "And just like it took all you had to buy them back, it took all Jesus had. He left the glory of heaven and gave himself to die so that we could be brought back to God." She smiled at Joel.

"I guess maybe that's where the comparison ends," said Dad with a grin. "Your shoes didn't have a choice—they had to come home with you whether they wanted to or not. But we have a choice. We can accept what Jesus did for us and go to live with him someday, or we can refuse it. It's up to us."

"Yeah," said Joel thoughtfully, "but who'd refuse it?" *H.M.*

HOW ABOUT YOU?

Have you accepted what Jesus did for you? He paid a great price to save you from your sins and offer you a home in heaven. Accept him now if you haven't already.

MEMORIZE:

"You were redeemed . . . with the precious blood of Christ."

1 Peter 1:18-19, NIV

 Jesus Paid to Save You

Questions (Read Proverbs 2:3-9)

29

JANUARY

Although Kevin had prayed and prayed for Grandma to get well, she didn't seem to be improving. Seeing him frown, his twin sister, Jenny, asked, "What are you thinking about?"

Kevin hesitated. "About Grandma," he said. "I've just been wondering if God really hears us when we pray."

"Of course he does! I can't believe you're questioning God," scolded Jenny. "Better not let Dad hear you do that!"

"Do what?" Dad asked as he joined them. "Come on, you two. Out with it."

"Well," muttered Kevin, looking at his feet, "sometimes I don't understand things about the Bible and about God. I have questions. Jenny says it's wrong to have questions."

"It is when they're about God," declared Jenny. "Kevin doesn't think God will answer our prayers about Grandma."

"Oh, I see," said Dad. "Well, actually, it's OK for Kevin to have questions."

"It is?" exclaimed the twins.

"It's by asking questions that we learn," explained Dad. "For example, Jenny, you made macaroni and cheese for dinner last night, right?" Jenny nodded. "How did you learn to do that?" asked Dad.

"She asked Mom a ton of questions," Kevin chimed in. "Like 'How much water?' 'What temperature?' 'For how long?' You saw Mom do it a million times, Jenny, but you didn't seem to know anything when you tried to do it."

"Doing it on your own is harder than it looks," replied Jenny. "But I could do it now."

Dad nodded. "I bet you could. You've watched Mom and me try to follow God and live for him, and you've imitated what you've seen us do. But as both of you start following God yourselves, you may have questions. Don't be afraid to ask them, even if they're hard ones. Your questions will help you really know what you believe so you can love and follow God on your own. Now . . . let's hear your question once again, Kevin. . . ." *S.S.*

HOW ABOUT YOU?

Are there things you don't understand? Times when you wonder if God is there? It's OK to ask questions. Ask your parents, Sunday school teachers, or any Christian adult you feel you can talk to. Also ask God to help you understand, and look to his Word for answers.

MEMORIZE:

"Call to Me, and I will answer you, and show you great and mighty things, which you do not know." *Jeremiah 33:3, NKJV*

 *Ask and Learn*

Finished (Read John 19:28-30)

30

JANUARY

"Yummmm! Pie!" exclaimed Eric, coming into the kitchen where his mother and sister Jana were working. He looked longingly at the fluffy, yellow mixture Jana was stirring.

"Go away," said Jana. "This isn't finished."

Eric left, but the smell of lemon followed him. When he came back later, Jana had poured the lemon filling into the pie shell. "Can I have a piece?" he asked.

"No," Jana told him. "The filling is still hot."

Some time later, Eric again eyed the pie on the cupboard. "Can I have a piece now?" he asked.

"Not yet," replied Jana. "I baked the pie for dessert tonight. Besides, it's lemon *meringue* pie, and it doesn't have any meringue yet. It isn't finished."

Eric checked back one more time before dinner. "It's finished," Jana told him, "but I told you—it's for dessert."

They did have the pie for dessert. Eric carefully scooped up and swallowed every crumb on his plate. "Now the pie is really finished," he said, patting his tummy. "It's all gone."

When it was time for devotions, Dad read from the Gospel of John. "Some of the words I heard around here this afternoon reminded me of Jesus' words on the cross," he said. "The words *It is finished* are the ones I'm thinking of. A couple of times I overheard Jana tell Eric that the lemon pie was not finished yet. Finally, she said it was finished, but even then it didn't do Eric any good. Why didn't it?"

"Because I didn't get to eat it yet," replied Eric promptly.

Dad smiled. "Jesus came into the world to take the punishment for our sin," he said.

"Because they won't accept him as Savior," suggested Jana after a moment.

"That's right," said Dad. "To receive the benefit of the finished pie, we had to take it for ourselves and eat it. To receive the benefit of Christ's finished work, we have to take it for ourselves, too."

H.M.

HOW ABOUT YOU?

Have you accepted what Jesus did for you? He finished the task of purchasing your salvation, and he offers it to you right now. Accept him today.

MEMORIZE:

"God laid on him the guilt and sins of every one of us!"

Isaiah 53:6, TLB

 Accept Jesus' Finished Work

Faster than a Telegram (Read Psalm 139:1-3, 13-16)

Ding dong! Nathan looked up at the sound of the doorbell. "Please answer the door, Son," his mother called out. She and Melissa, Nathan's sister, were putting the finishing touches on his birthday cake.

"Mom! There's a clown at the door!" squealed Nathan a moment later. "Come and see! Hurry!"

"Well, well, Mr. Clown, what brings you here?" asked Mother, coming into the room, a smile on her face.

"Hi, there!" said the clown. "You must be the Bennett family. "I'm 'Kevin the Clown,' and I'm looking for a Master Nathan Bennett who is six years old today!"

"Wow! That's me! I'm Nathan!" exclaimed Nathan in astonishment.

"Here, Nathan. These are for you," said the clown, holding out a huge bunch of brightly colored balloons. "And now I have a singing telegram for you." The clown began to sing. "Happy Birthday to you! Happy Birthday to you! God bless you today—and all the year through!" Nathan, Melissa, and Mother clapped to show their approval and appreciation.

Later Nathan told his father all about it. "That clown knew it was my birthday today," he said, still amazed at what happened.

Dad smiled. "Isn't that something!" he said. "I guess someone told him about you. But you know what? There's someone who knew it was your birthday today without being told. In fact, he knew it was going to be your birthday today even *before* you were born. Do you know who that one is?"

"I know!" Nathan exclaimed. "You're talking about Jesus!"

"That's right, Nathan," agreed Dad. "He knows all about you, and he loves for you to keep in touch with him. Best of all, you don't even need a phone or telegram to do that. You can just pray—just talk to him—at any time." *L.E.K.*

HOW ABOUT YOU?

Do you wonder if God thinks about you? Do you wonder if sometimes he's too busy to know what's happening to you? Not God! You're always in his thoughts, and you're someone very special to him. He'll never forget you or be too busy to meet your needs!

MEMORIZE:

"**You are familiar with all my ways.**" *Psalm 139:3,* NIV

 God Knows All about You

Messed-Up Money (Read 2 Corinthians 5:14-21)

1

FEBRUARY

"Oh, no," groaned Jenny. "I just can't get it to balance."

"What are you doing?" asked her mother.

"I'm counting the money for Young Conqueror Club." Jenny pointed to the money on the table. "We're saving to buy a VCR for church. I've been elected treasurer, and Miss Schmidt gave me the money to keep until tomorrow after school when we'll put it in the bank. This paper says I'm supposed to have $27.75, but I only have $22.25. I've counted it six times!"

"Let me count and see if I get the same thing," Mother suggested. She did, and her total was the same as Jenny's.

"What if I get blamed for the missing money?" moaned Jenny. "Miss Schmidt trusts me!"

The telephone interrupted the conversation, and Jenny answered it. She talked a few minutes. Then she hung up the phone and turned to her mother with a big smile. "Whew! That's a relief," she said. "That was Miss Schmidt, and she was calling to apologize. We spent some money for our party, and Miss Schmidt meant to change the total, but it slipped her mind. She said we used $5.50 for the party, so that leaves $22.25—just what's here."

"Oh, good!" exclaimed Mom. "I'm glad you were able to reconcile the money with the record."

"*Reconcile?*" asked Jenny. "What does that word mean? I hear it in church a lot."

"It means to settle an account—to bring back into harmony. The money you actually had did not add up to the amount you were required to have, so those two amounts had to be reconciled," explained Mom. "And, yes, you do hear that word in church, because as a sinner, you did not have the righteousness God requires of you. You and God had to be reconciled. That happened when you accepted Jesus as your Savior—that's when you received the righteousness God requires."

"Oh, I see," Jenny said, smiling. "I think that's neat—and from now on, reconciling my club account will remind me that I'm reconciled to God." *L.W.*

HOW ABOUT YOU?

Are you reconciled to God, or is your sin still separating you from him? Accept Jesus as your Savior and get in harmony with the Lord.

MEMORIZE:

"We implore you on Christ's behalf: Be reconciled to God."

2 Corinthians 5:20, NIV

 Be Reconciled to God

Half Darkness (Read Romans 12:1-2, 21)

"Mommy, I can't see anything," Katie wailed, when Mother turned off the bedroom light. "My new night-light isn't bright enough!"

"Now, Katie, you know it takes a minute for your eyes to get used to the dark," said Mother. She sat down on the bed and brushed the curls off Katie's forehead.

"I can see better now," said Katie. "I can see my pictures on the wall and my rocking horse."

"Good," said Mother. "Let's pray together, and then you can go to sleep."

When they finished praying, Katie opened her eyes. "Now I can see even better," she said. "It looked so dark at first, but now it's almost as light as when the big light is on."

"God made our bodies to adjust gradually to many things," said Mother. "It's like that with our minds, too. Our thoughts often gradually adjust to things—good or bad."

"They do?" Katie didn't understand.

Mother nodded. "Take TV, for example," she said. "There are good programs you may watch, but some of the things on TV are neither really good nor terribly bad. They're sort of 'half-dark,' like your room. If you watch those things instead of taking part in good, wholesome activities, you could get used to that kind of half darkness, too."

"I usually have more fun playing with my friends anyway," said Katie, "but Angie always wants to watch TV when I go to her house."

"What fun thing can you interest her in?" asked Mother.

"I could take my new game over," said Katie. "Or maybe we could come here and make cookies!"

"I like both your ideas," said Mother. "Those are good ideas to keep yourself in the light." *P.O.Y.*

HOW ABOUT YOU?

It's easy to sit and let the world give you its thoughts. But the world's viewpoint is not God's viewpoint. You need to keep your body and mind active with games, reading, and hobbies. Daily Bible study and prayer help you tell which activities please God and which please Satan.

 Don't Watch Too Much TV

MEMORIZE:

"Don't copy the behavior and customs of this world, but be a new and different person with a fresh newness in all you do and think. Then you will learn from your own experience how his ways will really satisfy you.

Romans 12:2, TLB

Rings and Things (Read Matthew 25:14-29)

3
FEBRUARY

Sarah ran all the way home from school. "I'm not going to sing in the school recital," she told her mother. "I missed some notes, and the kids laughed. I'm not going to stand up there and look like an idiot. I'm never going to sing again."

"That's too bad," said Mother. "God gave you a lovely voice." She looked thoughtful for a moment, then she slipped a beautiful ring from her finger—one she had gotten from Dad just the night before to celebrate their wedding anniversary.

"Why are you taking your new ring off?" asked Sarah.

"Mrs. Knapp and Benji were over this morning," Mother replied. "Benji said it looked just like a plastic ring he got from a gumball machine. I don't like having it made fun of, so I figure if I keep it in its box and don't wear it anymore, that won't happen."

"But, Mom," objected Sarah, "Benji's just a little kid—he doesn't know anything about rings. Your ring is beautiful! And think how disappointed Dad will be if you don't have it on when he comes home."

"Well, I guess my feelings are more important than his," declared Mother.

"Mom!" exclaimed Sarah. "How can you say that! You know how hard Dad worked to buy you that ring!"

Mother looked at the ring. "Would it be accurate to say your father 'blessed me' with the ring and I shouldn't worry about what anyone says about it?" she asked. Sarah just looked puzzled. "Our heavenly Father blesses us with gifts, too," continued Mother.

Sarah stared at her. "Oh, so that's what this is all about!" exclaimed Sarah. "You're showing me that God gave me a talent for singing, so I should use it no matter what other people say."

"That's exactly right," Mother said with a smile. She slipped her ring back on. "Just as your father will be disappointed if I don't use my gift, God will be disappointed if you don't use yours." *C.C.F.*

HOW ABOUT YOU?

Did you read today's Scripture? The talents discussed there are different from the abilities God gave you, but the principle is the same. Don't throw aside your abilities just because someone teases you as you're developing them. Use the talents God gave you, and never be ashamed of them.

MEMORIZE:

"Every good and perfect gift is from above, coming down from the Father of the heavenly lights." *James 1:17*, NIV

 **Use God's Gifts**

Enough Love (Read 1 John 4:16-20)

4

FEBRUARY

"Grandma, I love you, but I miss Mother so much," Judy said as she entered the utility room where Grandma was taking towels from the dryer. "I wish she could have come home from the hospital today."

"I know, honey, but remember, she'll be here tomorrow," encouraged Grandma. "And just think—she'll bring your brand-new brother." Grandma closed the dryer and gave Judy a hug before she began to fold the towels.

"I know." Judy hesitated, then she added, "But Grandma, I'm worried about something." She looked down at her feet. "I . . . I wonder if Mother still loves me. I mean . . . as much as she did before the new baby came."

"Why, of course she does, honey," Grandma said promptly. "Why did you think she might not?"

Judy frowned. "Oh, I don't know. I just keep wondering about it."

"Well, Judy, let me ask you about something," said Grandma. "I know your dad promised you that when the baby is a little older, you'll all take a trip back to Springdale, where you used to live. Why do you want to go back there?"

"Nancy lives there, and she's my very best friend!" Judy answered.

"But you moved from there three months ago," replied Grandma, "and you have *new* friends now."

"But Grandma, I didn't forget Nancy when I got new friends," Judy said. "Don't you understand?"

"You mean you still love her?" asked Grandma. Judy nodded. "Then why do you think your mother will stop loving you?" asked Grandma with a smile. "She has enough love for you and your baby brother, just as you have plenty of love for Nancy and your new friends."

Judy smiled. Then she gave Grandma a big hug. "I think I understand now," she said. *M.S.*

HOW ABOUT YOU?

Do you sometimes wonder if your parents love you as much as they love your brothers and sisters? Are you jealous of some member of your family? God's love can help you overcome that jealousy. Or perhaps you wonder if God loves some people more than others? He doesn't. He loves everyone equally.

MEMORIZE:

"**We love him, because he first loved us.**" *1 John 4:19,* KJV

 ***God Loves You***

The Other Daniel (Read Daniel 1:8, 11-15)

5

FEBRUARY

"I don't like chicken," Daniel told Grandma. She put some on his plate anyway. "Don't give me any green beans or carrots," he begged.

"I'll only put a little of each on your plate," said Grandma.

Daniel scowled. "Can I have some pop?" he asked.

"Milk is better for you," replied Grandma. "Now bow your head while I thank Jesus for our food." Daniel bowed his head, but he wasn't thankful.

Daniel played with his food. "I think this stuff's icky," he announced. Grandma frowned, but she didn't beg him to eat it. When she was finished, she got an apple for each of them. "Don't you have any ice cream?"

"You haven't eaten enough good food for us to have ice cream today," Grandma told him.

"I hate apples," whined Daniel.

"I'm afraid you have the wrong name," Grandma said quietly. "The Daniel in the Bible ate food that made him strong. He knew that God made his body and that keeping it healthy is a way to give the Lord glory." She put the food away without another word.

It was dark before Grandma had dinner ready. Daniel could hardly wait. She gave him the lunch he had refused earlier. "We can't throw food away," she said.

"Yuck!" said Daniel, but he tasted the chicken anyway. It was better than he thought. He ate all of it. The carrots and beans were all right, too. He drank the milk and looked at the apple. "Did the other Daniel like apples?" he asked.

"I don't know," said Grandma.

"I guess he ate them anyway," said Daniel. He took a bite of apple. He was surprised at how good it was. "Now am I like the other Daniel?" he asked.

"Yes," said Grandma with a smile. "I'm proud of you, and I believe God is pleased, too." *M.M.P.*

HOW ABOUT YOU?

Do you drink milk and eat the fruits and vegetables your body needs? Or do you snack on chips, pop, and sweets instead? Remember that God made you and wants you to treat your body as his property.

MEMORIZE:

"Honor God with your body."

1 Corinthians 6:20, NIV

 **Eat Healthful Food**

The Best Buy (Read Philippians 3:12-16)

6

FEBRUARY

"These are just what I want!" exclaimed Alyce, admiring the shoes she was trying on. "Can I get them?"

"OK," said Mother, "if you're sure. Otherwise we can look a little—this is our first stop—and you're spending your own money for this, you know." But Alyce was sure. She not only bought the shoes—she decided to wear them.

In another store, Alyce pointed at a display. "See . . . there are some more shoes almost like the pair I just bought." She looked at them more closely. "These cost less," she said. "Maybe I should have gotten them instead."

"Too late now," said Mother.

Still later, they saw the same shoes on sale. Alyce was mad. "I should have waited," she moaned. "I could have saved some money."

Alyce pouted so long that Mother became annoyed. "Look," she said, "you found the shoes you wanted, and you got them. Even if you made the worst possible bargain, it's too late to do anything about it, so you'll be happier if you don't compare anymore. OK?" Alyce agreed, and they didn't look at shoes again that day.

Back home, Alyce showed her shoes to her father. And she just couldn't help telling him about the money she could have saved if she had just waited! "But Mom says to forget about that and enjoy my shoes," she finished.

Dad nodded. "That's good advice," he agreed. "Next time, remember that it might pay to shop around a little, but as far as this purchase is concerned, there's no use fretting over it." After a moment he added, "All of life is like that, really. It doesn't help to wish we had done something differently. True, we should consider past mistakes and learn from them so that we don't repeat them, but thinking too much about them just makes us unhappy."

Mother nodded. "Worrying about what's done doesn't change anything," she said. "Instead we should confess our mistakes to God and leave them with him. And we should ask him to help us in the future." *H.M.*

HOW ABOUT YOU?

Do you keep fretting over things you can't change? Over times you failed to witness, obey, or help someone? Learn from those mistakes, but then put them behind you. God wants you to look forward and serve him with joy in the future.

MEMORIZE:

"Forgetting what is behind and straining toward what is ahead, I press on toward the goal."

Philippians 3:13-14, NIV

 Don't Dwell on Past Mistakes

Not Boring (Read Revelation 21:1-14, 22-27)

7

Nathan watched little Nikki out of the corner of his eye. The baby blinked, then nodded, and finally her eyes closed as she snuggled back in her car seat. When he was sure she was asleep, he spoke softly across her to his mother. "You know, Mom, I keep thinking about Pastor Ryan's sermon yesterday," he said, "but sometimes I'm not sure I want to go to heaven very soon—not for a long, long time."

Mother glanced at him. "Why do you say that, Son?"

Nathan squirmed. "Well, I know preachers always say it will be so great, but all that music and singing sounds boring to me," he confessed. "I like church, but I don't think I'd like it all the time. I'd miss baseball and hamburgers and TV. This is a great world right here!"

Suddenly Nikki jumped in her sleep and cried out. As Mother reached to pat her, she looked thoughtful. "Do you suppose Nikki was thinking something just like that a few months ago?" she asked.

"Huh?" Nathan was puzzled. "She's only two months old!"

"Yes, but she was alive before she was born, you know," replied Mother. "Maybe she liked being right where she was then."

"Well . . . I doubt it," said Nathan. "She was in the dark and couldn't even move much before she was born."

"True," agreed Mother, "but she was warm and comfortable and never hungry. I imagine she might have thought her life was very good. Maybe if someone had had a way to ask her if she wanted to be born and be part of a brand-new world, she might even have said, 'No, I'd rather stay here.'"

"Well, then she'd have missed out on an awful lot," declared Nathan.

"I agree," said Mother. "Sights, sounds, and tastes we couldn't even begin to describe to her. Things she would have to experience for herself to understand." She smiled at Nathan. "I'm sure it's that way with heaven, too, Son. It's more fantastic than we can imagine and better than we can understand down here." *S.F.A.*

HOW ABOUT YOU?

Are you afraid that heaven won't really be much fun—that it might even be boring? Remember that the God who created you and all the things that give you pleasure here is responsible for heaven as well. We may not know everything we will experience there, but we can trust that it won't be a disappointment.

MEMORIZE:

"They were living for heaven. And now God is not ashamed to be called their God, for he has made a heavenly city for them."

Hebrews 11:16, TLB

 Heaven Will Be Great

God's Ocean Liner (Read Psalm 23:1-6)

8

Ten-year-old Jonny, chin in his hands, stared gloomily at the TV. Huge tanks rolled through city streets in a far-off country. People with frightened faces huddled together, while others shouted and shook their fists. *If God loves the world,* Jonny thought, *why do people fight and kill each other? If God cares about little sparrows, can't he do something to make people be nice to each other?*

"Hi, Son. Any good news tonight?" Jonny felt Dad's warm hand on his shoulder as his father sat down.

Jonny shook his head. "It's pretty bad, as usual." Then he put his thoughts into words. "Do you ever wonder if God knows what's going on? And if he does, can't he stop it?"

Dad thought for a moment. "Jonny," he said, "maybe a story will help you understand. Just suppose an ocean liner leaves New York bound for London, England. There are many passengers on board, and they're not locked in their cabins nor chained to the railings. They're completely free to do whatever they want. Some choose good, pleasant things like playing games, eating, or reading; others make bad choices, like gambling or drinking. All the while, the big ship carries them steadily toward England, because the man who owns the ship has planned its destination, and nothing can change that." Dad paused.

"Go on," urged Jonny.

"Well, think of the ship as the earth and the ship's owner as God, who keeps the world on a steady course over the sea of time," said Dad. "God allows people the freedom to choose, even though they sometimes make bad choices. But the Bible assures us that God is in command of his world, and it gives us hope for the future. God knows and cares for each one of us."

Jonny sighed. "Yeah, but I guess I still get scared thinking about war and fighting."

Dad nodded. "It can be scary," he agreed, "but your heavenly Father loves you and is in control of this 'ship'—his world. You can count on him to do what's right." A fatherly hug emphasized the words. *P.I.K.*

HOW ABOUT YOU?

Do you feel afraid when you see scary news on TV? God isn't afraid, and he knows how it will all end. Remember that. He wants you to obey his Word and trust him for the future.

MEMORIZE:

"Fear not, for I am with you. Do not be dismayed. I am your God." *Isaiah 41:10,* TLB

 *Trust God*

No Power, No Music (Read Acts 1:7-9; 2 Timothy 1:6-7)

9

"Can I skip Bible study group tonight?" asked Randy as he got up to help clear the supper table. "I didn't have time to do my lesson this week, and I know Pastor Frank really doesn't like it when that happens."

"Well," said Randy's mother, "I'm glad Pastor Frank expects you to study on your own, but I think you should go to the Bible class even if your lesson isn't done."

"I don't know, Mom," said Randy doubtfully. "I've been thinking about quitting, anyway. I just don't have the time to do those assignments every week."

Mother frowned as she turned on the radio. "Hmmmmm," she murmured after a moment, "I wonder why this radio isn't working." She turned the dial and clicked the power button. "I wanted to listen to some music while I wash the dishes."

Randy looked at the radio. He turned the dials. Then he noticed the cord lying loosely across the counter. "Here's your trouble, Mom," he said with a laugh. "The radio wasn't plugged in. You've got to have power to run this thing, you know. No power, no music."

"Oops!" Mother laughed, too, as she set the dial. "That radio reminds me of you," she said as she began to run water into the kitchen sink.

"What do you mean?" asked Randy.

"Well," said Mom, "you say you want to live a Christian life—you even say you want to witness to others. But we get power to live for Christ and to witness by plugging into the Word, by spending time in worship and in prayer, and by spending time with other Christians. So when you don't do those things, you're like an unplugged radio—powerless. Like you said, 'no power, no music'—or in your case, no witness. If you really want to do what you say, the Bible study group can help you."

Randy sighed, but he knew his mother was right. "Mom," he said as he went to get ready for Bible study, "you knew all along that the radio was unplugged, didn't you?" *L.F.W.*

HOW ABOUT YOU?

Are you doing the things that keep you plugged into your "power source"? Things like reading your Bible, attending church and Sunday school, and learning your memory verses? Put God first so you will have his power.

MEMORIZE:

"**For God is at work within you, helping you want to obey him, and then helping you do what he wants.**" *Philippians 2:13,* TLB

 Spiritual Power Comes from God

A Deal! (Read 1 Corinthians 11:23-26)

10

Winifred and Carrie had been friends for a long time. They lived on the same street and had gone to the same kindergarten and first grade. Now Winifred's family was moving away. On their last day together, they played at Carrie's house while Winni's parents packed. But they didn't have much fun. "I can't play," Carrie finally said. "I keep thinking about tomorrow and the day after tomorrow. Who will I play with then?"

"I know," said Winifred. "I wish I didn't have to go."

Carrie's mother called them in for a last lunch together: the last juice, the last carrot sticks, the last sandwiches. The girls were sadly thinking about their coming separation.

"I know what we can do," said Carrie thoughtfully as she picked up her peanut butter-and-jelly sandwich. "We can make a deal. Whenever we eat peanut butter-and-jelly sandwiches, we can think of each other and remember the things we did together and remember that we're friends."

"Yeah!" agreed Winni. "Good idea!" She grinned at her friend. "It's like at church," she added. "That's what Jesus did with his friends at their last meal together. He didn't give them any present to remember him by. But he told them they should often share bread and wine together—like they did at that last supper—and think about him and what he did and remember that he would come back. That's why we have Communion."

Carrie nodded. "So you want to do it?" she asked. "Is it a deal?"

Winni smiled and hugged her friend. "Deal!" she said. "I won't forget!" *M.D.H.*

HOW ABOUT YOU?

Have you thought about what the Communion service means? Use the quiet time during the service to remember that Jesus loves you and died for you. Remember him as you would remember a friend who has left you for a while. After all, Jesus *is* your friend—your very best friend!

MEMORIZE:

"And he [Jesus] took bread, and gave thanks, and brake it, and gave unto them, saying, 'This is my body which is given for you: this do in remembrance of me.'" *Luke 22:19,* KJV

 Always Remember Jesus

Shane's Offering (Read Mark 12:41-44)

11

FEBRUARY

"See what I brought for the offering." Shane waved a five-dollar bill in the air. The other children in the Sunday school class glared at him because he always bragged about how much he gave. "You're all jealous," he said in a sing-song voice.

When it was time to take the offering, the students placed their money in a globe that was cut open to serve as a bank. Most of the students gave their gifts quietly and sat down, but Shane proudly displayed his five-dollar bill, waving it as if it were a flag. "I came ready!" he said loudly. He snickered as another student dropped in some coins. "Is that all you're giving those poor, starving kids?" His voice was loud. "A measly nickel or two? I gave five bucks."

"Whose money was it?" Deborah asked.

"Whadda ya mean?" asked Shane. "My dad gave me that money." He grinned. "He's got plenty more."

"Well, I helped my grandma with some work yesterday," said Deborah softly. "She paid me for doing it, and I just wanted to give it for the missionaries. It wasn't my dad's money; it was mine." No one said a word, but they all knew that Deborah's attitude toward giving was the one that pleased the Lord. *M.E.H.*

HOW ABOUT YOU?

Are you willing to give God your own money? Or will you only share what your parents hand you on Sunday mornings? How about your time? Are you giving God a portion of each day? He's pleased when you do.

MEMORIZE:

"I don't want to offer to the Lord my God burnt offerings that have cost me nothing."

2 Samuel 24:24, TLB

 *Give of Yourself*

Jimmy's Grandparents (Read 1 Peter 4:12-16)

Jimmy watched Grandpa Walker climb into the car and then back slowly down the driveway and out into the street. "Mom," said Jimmy, "how come Grandpa still goes to see Grandma at the nursing home every day? You said yourself she doesn't talk to him anymore."

12
FEBRUARY

"Well, even though Grandma's been sick a long time, your grandpa still loves her and wants to be with her," explained Mother. "Even if she doesn't recognize him now."

"Well, I feel sorry for him!" Jimmy blurted out. "He sure doesn't have any fun. Adam's grandparents take him to play miniature golf and stuff. Adam said they're buying an RV, and maybe he can go on a trip out west with 'em."

"Are you really sorry for Grandpa, Jimmy, or for yourself?" Mother's question brought a hot pink to Jimmy's ears, and he was embarrassed by the direct look she gave him. "Listen, Son, things don't always turn out the way we might like," she said. "Your grandparents would have enjoyed having the kind of life that Adam's grandparent's have, but Grandpa knows Jesus has good reasons for permitting one that's far different."

"But it seems so unfair," Jimmy complained.

"Think of it like this," suggested Mother. "When Grandpa willingly gives up the so-called fun things of life and shares Grandma's suffering, it's a way of sharing in the sufferings of Jesus. The Bible says there are special blessings for people who do that."

Jimmy couldn't remember much about Grandma, but he really did love his kind, gentle grandpa, and he was sorry for being envious of Adam. "I'm going to share with Gramps, too," he said. "I'll make a special card for him to take next time he goes to see Grandma. Would Jesus like that?"

"I'm sure he would, and so would Grandpa," said Mother. "Maybe Grandma will smile when he shows her." *P.I.K.*

HOW ABOUT YOU?

Are you envious when other kids' relatives bring great presents to them but yours do not? This can be a wonderful opportunity to show God's love to the special people in your family as you accept them for who they are, not for what they do for you.

MEMORIZE:

"I will walk in my house with blameless heart." *Psalm 101:2,* NIV

 *Appreciate Your Family*

First Steps (Read Galatians 6:1-6)

13
FEBRUARY

Scott banged the back door shut and slammed his books on the table. Then he went into the living room and, with a scowl, flopped down heavily on the sofa. "What's wrong?" asked Mother as she bounced baby Mindy on her knee.

"It's my new friend, Chad," replied Scott. "When he became a Christian, he said he'd give up smoking. But this afternoon I saw him smoking with a couple of his old buddies behind the school building."

Mother put Mindy down on the carpet. "You'll have to be patient with Chad," said Mother. "He just became a Christian a few weeks ago. Until he gets to know Jesus better, he's bound to make a few mistakes."

Scott sighed as he watched Mindy playing happily with a pile of blocks on the floor. She knocked the blocks together, then crawled to the coffee table and pulled herself up. Scott chuckled, for the moment forgetting his anger toward Chad. "I think you're showing off," he said to Mindy.

As if on cue, Mindy held on to the table and took a few steps around it. She looked at Mother and smiled. Mother held out her hands. Mindy took one shaky step and fell into Mother's arms. Scott clapped his hands. "All right, Mindy!" he exclaimed. "You took your first step!"

Mother stood Mindy in front of her and let go. Mindy reached out, took one small step, and fell to the floor. She looked startled for a moment, and then her whole face puckered up. "Don't cry, Mindy," said Scott as he picked her up. "They're just your first steps." He stood her up beside the table again. "Everything new takes a little practice," he added.

"Like being a Christian," said Mother. "Your friend Chad is taking his first steps as a Christian. In the beginning, it's easy to stumble and fall." Scott thought about this for a moment. "Maybe you could give Chad a helping hand," suggested Mother as she reached out to catch Mindy, who was taking another step. *J.A.P.*

HOW ABOUT YOU?

Do you know someone who says he's a Christian but doesn't "act like one"? Perhaps that person needs to learn how to walk with God. Instead of criticizing, pray for him. Encourage him to attend Christian functions and to avoid sinful things. Be a good example as he takes his first steps in the right direction.

MEMORIZE:

"If someone is caught in a sin, you who are spiritual should restore him gently."

Galatians 6:1, NIV

 Help Weaker Christians

Two New Hearts (Read Psalm 51:10-17)

The blue station wagon parked in Eric's driveway meant that Aunt Dee was here. Maybe she had brought Grandma home from the hospital—the doctor had said she might come home today. Grandma had been near death when the doctor said they needed to find a donor heart soon. Even after the heart transplant, it had looked like her body might reject the new heart, but now she was doing better.

14

FEBRUARY

Eric rushed into the house. He was delighted to learn that Grandma *was* home, and she was anxious to see him. "How are you doing, Grandma?" Eric asked after he gave her a gentle hug.

"I was just thanking the Lord for both of my new hearts." Grandma's eyes sparkled as they often did when she was about to share a secret.

"But Grandma, you just got one new heart," said Eric. He knew Grandma would have an explanation, and he wondered what it was.

"In the hospital, yes. But I got my first new heart when I was about your age," replied Grandma. Eric thought he knew what she was talking about, but he waited for her to go on. "When I asked Jesus to come into my heart and cleanse me from sin, it was just as though he gave me a new heart," Grandma told him. "I'm thankful for the new heart the doctors gave me, but I'm even more thankful to Jesus for dying so that I could have a new heart spiritually."

Eric nodded. "I have a new heart spiritually, too, don't I?" he said.

"You do if you've accepted Jesus as your Savior," Grandma told him. "Have you done that?"

Eric nodded again. "Yes, I have, Grandma," he said with a grin. "We both have new hearts." *E.M.B.*

HOW ABOUT YOU?

Do you have a new heart? You can. Not a new physical heart, but a new spiritual one. Maybe you've thought about accepting Jesus as your Savior, but you've been putting it off. Why not accept the new heart God offers you right now?

MEMORIZE:

"Rid yourselves of all the offenses you have committed, and get a new heart and a new spirit." *Ezekiel 18:31,* NIV

 Accept a New Heart from God

Proper Programming (Read Romans 13:12-14)

15

FEBRUARY

"Our computer isn't working right," Janet complained to her father, and she explained what she wanted it to do. "I heard you tell Uncle Bob a computer could do that," she said.

Dad smiled. "Yes, but *our* computer won't do that because I've never programmed it to. Without the right instructions on the inside, the computer won't do anything," he said. Then he sat down at the keyboard and began to type. "I'll write a program to tell the computer what you want. It responds only to what it has been told." Soon he stood up. "Try it now," he suggested, and he told her which keys to use.

The new program worked. The computer did just what Janet wanted. "Wow, Dad!" she said. "That's amazing!"

"Not really," her father replied. "It's a basic law of computer science that you can only get out what you've put in. If you put garbage in, you get garbage out. If you put good stuff in, you get good stuff out. Just like life."

"Like life?" asked Janet. "What do you mean?"

"I mean that your life becomes what you make it, too," replied Dad. "Your mind is something like a computer. It's a fabulous database that stores everything you put into it. And it responds to the instructions you give it. If you store away good things, your mind responds with good thoughts and actions. If you store up a lot of junk, that's what your mind gives back to you, and you act accordingly. What you put into your mind determines what response comes out in your life. In a way, you're programming, or writing, your own future right now by what you put into your mind and life." *B.K.O.*

HOW ABOUT YOU?

Are you storing up thoughts and ideas that will help you later on? What kind of future are you programming yourself for? Things like good books (especially the Bible), good friends (especially Christians), and good programs (those with Christian morals and values) will help prepare you for a wholesome future.

MEMORIZE:

"For as he thinks in his heart, so is he." *Proverbs 23:7,* NKJV

 Get Help from God

A Diamond in the Rough (Read Romans 5:1-5)

16

FEBRUARY

Jenny dropped her book bag on the corner of her grand-mother's kitchen cupboard. She shook her head when Grandma offered her peanut-butter cookies and milk. "No, thanks, Gram," she said. "I don't feel like eating." She sighed. "Nothing is going right! You even prayed with me that I'd pass my math test and that I'd make a friend this week, but it didn't do any good. Oh, Gram, I just want to go back to Hickory Falls!" A tear slipped down her cheek. "I hate it here," she added.

Grandma handed Jenny a tissue. Then she slowly twisted the diamond ring off her finger. "Do you know anything about diamonds?" she asked, holding the treasured ring out to Jenny.

Jenny took the ring. "Well, I know they're beautiful and valuable," she said. "And they come from mines, and it takes a long, long time to make one." She tried the ring on her finger and held it up in the light. "Oh, look at it sparkle!" she added.

Grandma nodded. "Diamonds don't look like this when they come from the ground," she said. "It takes an expert stonecutter a long time to very carefully cut and polish them."

"Oh, yeah. I remember studying that in school," said Jenny. "He uses very sharp tools, and one slip can cause a diamond to shatter and be ruined."

"That's right! And did you know that we are like diamonds in the rough, Jenny?" asked Grandma. "God is the Master Stonecutter. Although the tools he uses sometimes seem painful to us, he uses them to make us strong and beautiful. And he never makes a slip. If we trust him, he'll never allow us to be shattered."

As Jenny continued to admire the diamond, Grandma placed the cookies on the table. This time Jenny thoughtfully reached for one. *J.R.L.*

HOW ABOUT YOU?

Have you been disappointed when you asked God to help you pass a test or hit a home run and it didn't happen? Do you think he doesn't seem to care if you don't have a friend? Trust him anyway, and let the Master Stonecutter turn you into a jewel.

MEMORIZE:

"My God, I trust in thee: let me not be ashamed, let not mine enemies triumph over me."

Psalm 25:2, KJV

 Trials Strengthen You

The Dollhouse (Read Ephesians 6:1-4)

17
FEBRUARY

"Hi, Grandma!" exclaimed Tanja as she stepped off the bus. "I'm glad I can spend the weekend with you."

Grandma put Tanja's luggage in her car, and they began the drive to the farm. "How is everything at home?" asked Grandma. "Are you and your stepmother getting along?"

"We did at first, but now I don't like her," replied Tanja.

"Oh, that's too bad," said Grandma. After a moment she added, "You know, Tanja, the Bible says you should honor your parents. That means your stepmother, too."

"Well, since she doesn't honor my mother, I'm not going to honor her," declared Tanja stubbornly.

"Your mother died before your father met Monica. What do you think she's doing wrong?" Grandma asked.

"She's changing everything," Tanja told her. "Mom had our house just perfect, but Monica's moving furniture and pictures all around. It's not fair. First I lost my mother, and now I'm losing my home." Then Tanja changed the subject.

After dinner, Grandma took Tanja up to the attic. "Your mother wanted you to have this when you were old enough, Tanja," she said.

"Her dollhouse!" Tanja exclaimed. "I love it!" She danced around, clapping her hands in delight. She began to take out all the dolls and furniture. "Guess what, Grandma," she said. "I'm going to paint the girl's room lavender and make the old-fashioned parlor into a recreation room."

"Really?" asked Grandma. "Your mother liked it the way it was. Don't you think your plans dishonor her?"

"I don't see how," protested Tanja. "I'm just . . . Grandma, you gave me this dollhouse today because of Monica, didn't you?"

Grandma nodded. "God blessed you with wonderful Christian parents, and now you have a lovely Christian stepmother," she said. "I was hoping this might help you realize that."

Tanja slowly arranged the dollhouse family in their kitchen. "And I should remember that when Monica changes the furniture, she doesn't do it to dishonor my mother at all." *R.K.M.*

HOW ABOUT YOU?

Do you have stepparents, or perhaps step-grandparents? Do you show them respect as you should? Honor them as parents. This is pleasing to the Lord.

MEMORIZE:

"Honor your father and mother." *Exodus 20:12,* TLB

 Honor Parents and Stepparents

The Decision (Read Psalm 1:1-6)

Barry sat quietly in the chair, staring out the window as his father read the note he had brought home from his teacher. "Do you want to talk about this?" Dad asked softly after he had laid the letter aside.

Barry wondered how he could tell him. "I . . . I started to walk away from the guys when I saw that the magazine they were reading had dirty pictures in it," he began. "But they started saying stuff like, 'Come on and have some fun,' and 'Don't be a nerd,' and 'Be a man'—stuff like that." Barry took a deep breath and sighed. "So I guess I went back and looked at the pictures with the rest of them until Mrs. Thomas saw what we were doing and took us to the principal's office." He looked at his father. "I'm awfully sorry, Dad."

18
FEBRUARY

"How do you think the Lord felt when you did that?" his father asked softly.

Barry shrugged. "Sad, I guess."

For a while his father sat quietly. Finally he said, "What would you say if some of your friends made up jokes about your sister or your mother and told them, just to have some fun?" asked Dad. "Would you join them?"

"Of course not!" Barry replied.

"You care about your mom and Suzy too much to want to hurt them, don't you?" asked Dad, and Barry nodded. "But what if your friends called you names because you didn't want to go along with their fun?" persisted Dad.

"Too bad!" Barry thought he knew what Dad was getting at.

Dad looked at him and smiled a little. "It's easy to say no when someone you care about will be hurt by what you do, isn't it?" Barry felt his cheeks grow warm. He understood what his father was really saying. "Barry," Dad said softly, "if we cared about Jesus like we ought to, a lot of what goes on in our lives would probably be changed. It just shows us how much we need him to help us love him more and more." *R.S.M.*

HOW ABOUT YOU?

Do you love the Lord enough to say no when your friends ask you to do something wrong? Why not ask God to help you stand for him?

MEMORIZE:

"Blessed is the man who does not walk in the counsel of the wicked." *Psalm 1:1, NIV*

 Say No to Sin

Unknowing Witness (Read 1 Corinthians 3:5-10)

19

"Yes, Pastor Williams." Dad was speaking into the phone. "Uh-huh . . . yes. Well, praise the Lord!" After finishing his conversation, Dad called out, "Hey, everyone! Guess what happened!"

Karen and Mother came around the corner into the kitchen. "What?" asked Karen.

"Karen, do you remember when you and your Sunday school class went to eat pizza last month after your roller-skating party?" asked Dad. Karen nodded, and Dad continued, "Pastor Williams just told me a man came into his office today who had been in the pizza shop when you all walked in."

"Really?" asked Karen. "How did he know who we were?"

"He saw the church name on the van you were using that night," explained Dad. "Anyway, he said he had been annoyed to see all you young people come in because he was afraid you'd be too rowdy. But you weren't. And when you all bowed your heads to thank the Lord for the food, the man said he was suddenly reminded of the days when he was a youngster in Sunday school."

"That's great!" said Mother.

Dad nodded. "This fellow told Pastor Williams he went home that night and couldn't stop thinking about how he had strayed away from the Lord, and now he wants to come back to Christ. Isn't that wonderful?"

"In other words, you kids were being a witness without even knowing it!" exclaimed Mother.

"Yes," agreed Dad, "the seed of God's Word was planted in that man's life a long time ago. You kids watered it, and 'God gave the increase.'"

Karen was delighted. "Do you mean we watered it just by thanking God for the pizza and behaving ourselves?" she asked.

Dad nodded. "That's right, honey. You never can tell how God will use even the smallest act of faithfulness on our part to bring glory to himself." *R.S.M.*

HOW ABOUT YOU?

Do you witness by your life and actions? A friendly word, a kind act, a prayer over your food in a restaurant? God can use you in many ways to bring souls to himself. Ask God to help you be faithful and fruitful for him.

MEMORIZE:

"I planted, Apollos watered, but God gave the increase."

1 Corinthians 3:6, NKJV

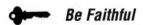 *Be Faithful*

Ambush (Read 1 Peter 5:5-11)

"Look at Kitty crouching under the bushes," said Nikki.

"She sees the doves feeding on the patio," said Dad. "She's going to ambush them." Just then the cat sprang toward the birds. The doves quickly flew away, and the cat was left to smell the empty birdseed shells.

"I'm glad they got away," said Nikki. "They're pretty smart. I think they know there's a cat in this yard, so they watch out for him while they eat."

20
FEBRUARY

Dad nodded. "We should be so smart," he said. Seeing Nikki's surprised expression, he explained. "That cat reminds me that Satan likes to hide and then spring out at us when we least expect it. We need to watch out for the traps he sets to lead us into sin."

The next day Nikki called to Dad. "Come see what Kitty's doing now."

Dad laughed when he saw Kitty, her tail up, slowly walking across the patio towards the doves. "I think she's trying to pretend she's their friend and won't hurt them," he said. Again the birds flew away when Kitty got too close. "That's another lesson from Kitty," added Dad. "Satan pretends he's our friend, too. But he's still trying to fool us into following him and disobeying Jesus."

"Those birds are smart," said Nikki.

Dad nodded. "God gave them instinct," he said. "It's their natural ability to watch for danger and fly away from it."

"I wish we had instinct about Satan," said Nikki.

"If we belong to Jesus, we have something even better," Dad told her. "We have his Holy Spirit living within us to guide us, to warn us of danger, and to help us know how to escape." *P.O.Y.*

HOW ABOUT YOU?

Do you know when Satan is trying to get you to do something wrong? You can protect yourself by reading your Bible, obeying your parents, and asking God to help you. When the Holy Spirit makes you uncomfortable about something, pay attention to the warning and avoid the things that are wrong.

MEMORIZE:

"Test everything. Hold on to the good." *1 Thessalonians 5:21*, NIV

 **Don't Trust Satan**

Is It a Secret? (Read Mark 8:34-38)

21

FEBRUARY

Kirsty and her brother, Nathan, walked home from Bible Club. "Wouldn't it be exciting to live like the early Christians and meet in secret in homes and caves?" asked Nathan.

"I think it'd be more dangerous than exciting," said Kirsty as she switched her Bible to her other hand. "They were often thrown into jail or put to death. They had to meet in secret to stay alive. She waved to a girl on the other side of the street. "Hi, Brooke," Kirsty called.

"Hi," responded Brooke. "I just got out of my gymnastics class. What have you been doing?"

"Oh, just hanging out," said Kirsty with a smile. "See you in school tomorrow."

A little later, a boy on a bicycle stopped to chat with Kirsty and Nathan. After he went on, Kirsty recalled the conversation she and Nathan had begun. "I'm glad we don't have to be secret Christians anymore," she told her brother.

"It looks to me like you are one," said Nathan.

"What are you talking about?" asked Kirsty.

"You didn't tell Brooke you were coming from Bible Club," said Nathan. "Why not?"

"Are you kidding?" Kirsty stepped around a broken section of sidewalk. "Brooke is the most popular girl in my class. If I do anything she doesn't like, nobody else will like me either."

"And I noticed you hid your Bible under your jacket when Travis stopped to talk," said Nathan. "Why did you do that?"

"Well, Travis is the biggest blabbermouth in my class," replied Kirsty. "He'd tell everybody that I go to Bible Club. The other kids would make fun of me."

Nathan shook his head. "Sounds to me like you're ashamed of being a Christian."

Kirsty's face turned red. "I . . . I guess you're right," she admitted. "I should try to be a better witness."

"Me, too," confessed Nathan. "If the early Christians were willing to die for him, I guess the least we can do is put up with a little teasing." *R.K.M.*

HOW ABOUT YOU?

Are you a secret Christian? It's not easy to tell other boys and girls about Jesus, is it? Ask God to help you be strong enough to speak up for him.

MEMORIZE:

"**I am not ashamed of the gospel.**" *Romans 1:16,* NIV

 Don't Be a Secret Christian

No Fairy Tales (Read 2 Timothy 3:14-17)

David sat with the driver's manual in his hand. He waved it as Dad came into the room. "Howie knows all the rules, so he's ready to take the test for his driver's permit this Saturday," David reported, grinning. "I've been helping him. He promised to treat me to ice cream after he gets his license and you let him take the car."

22

FEBRUARY

"Oh, I see," said Dad. "Well, that will take a little time, you know. After Howie gets his permit, he still has to learn to drive, and he has to pass his driver's test, too." He smiled at his son. "By the way," added Dad, "I hope you're not forgetting your own lessons. Have you studied your Sunday school lesson this week?"

"I'll do it right now," replied David. He frowned. "I have a problem though. My friend Chuck says some of the stories in the Bible are only myths, so then how do I know which ones to believe?"

"You do have a problem," said Dad. He thought for a moment. "Let me ask you something," he said. "After learning all those rules for driving a car, do you suppose Howie will pick out just a few that he likes to obey and ignore the rest of them?"

David grinned. "He'd better not," he said, "or he'll be in trouble. He'll get lots of tickets."

Dad nodded and picked up the evening paper. He showed David a picture on the front page. "This is what happened when a driver ignored a stoplight," he said.

"Wow!" said David. "Those cars are a mess!"

"When you start picking out what you want to believe in the Bible, your Christian life is going to be a mess, too," said Dad. "All the driving rules are to be believed and obeyed. All of the Bible is, too." *H.A.D.*

HOW ABOUT YOU?

Do you have friends or classmates who try to tell you the Bible contains fairy tales? Do they make you doubt the Bible? Jesus rebuked the devil by quoting Scripture. That's a good way for all of us to answer. Try quoting the following verse when someone tells you parts of God's Word are false.

MEMORIZE:

"Every word of God is flawless; he is a shield to those who take refuge in him." *Proverbs 30:5,* NIV

 The Bible Is God's Word

Flying in Formation (Read Ephesians 4:1-6)

"Well, if that's the way you're going to be about it, I'll just find someone else to do my science project with," Jeff angrily told Nathan and Tom. He crossed his arms, turned, and walked away from the boys.

23
FEBRUARY

At dinnertime that evening, Jeff was still angry. "Those guys just won't listen to me," he grumbled. "They want to change the whole project, and they don't care what I say about it. I'll find someone else to do my science project with."

"Hmmm," murmured Dad. "I take it you can't fly in formation?" he asked with a frown.

"Huh?" grunted Jeff. "What are you talking about?"

"Remember when we went to see the navy's flying team perform at the air show last summer?" asked Dad. Jeff nodded. "Do you remember how far apart those six jets flew?" continued Dad.

"About three feet, I think," replied Jeff. "That really takes some teamwork! When one of them moved, they all moved." His eyes sparkled as he remembered the thrill of watching the shiny blue-and-yellow jets.

Dad nodded. "Flying in formation certainly does take teamwork," he agreed. "Doing a good job on any team project does, and that includes your science project. It's true that the other boys should listen to your ideas, but you should also listen to theirs, shouldn't you?"

"Well . . . maybe," Jeff admitted slowly. He sighed. "Yeah, I guess you're right, Dad. If we're all going to fly in the same formation, we need to work together." He smiled. "I better call Tom and ask him about their idea."

"Well, while we're on the subject of teamwork," Mother said quickly as Jeff started to get up, "let's remember that the most important team of all is God's team. We all need to work together for his glory."

Jeff grinned. "And you're afraid I forgot the special youth service tonight, right?" he asked. "Well, I didn't, and while I'm talking to Tom, I'll ask him to come, too." *D.K.H.*

HOW ABOUT YOU?

Do you sometimes ignore ideas that are not your own? Do you have a hard time working as part of a team? Remember that God wants Christians to work together in unity. If you're not working together, it will be more difficult to accomplish your goal.

MEMORIZE:

"Behold, how good and how pleasant it is for brethren to dwell together in unity!"

Psalm 133:1, NKJV

 Work Well with Others

The Right Instructions (Read Psalm 119:105-112)

"This isn't working!" exclaimed Billy.

Mother looked up. "What isn't working?" she asked.

"I can't figure out this math problem," replied Billy.

"Let's take a look at it together," Mother suggested as she glanced at his figures. "Are you sure you're using the correct method?"

24
FEBRUARY

Billy nodded. "Jimmy's the smartest guy in our class," he said, "and today he showed me how to do these fractions."

"Hmmm," murmured Mother. "Well, let's look up the chapter in your textbook anyway—just to make sure."

"OK," said Billy reluctantly. He opened his math book and found the chapter they were studying.

"Now," said Mother, "try it one more time, following those instructions step-by-step."

Billy started again. Soon he found the correct answer. "I was leaving out a step!" he exclaimed. "Thanks, Mom."

Later that evening, Dad asked Billy to read the Scripture passage for family devotions. Billy sighed. "Dad, why can't I read the devotional story?" he asked. "Some of the words in the Bible are too hard for me to read."

"The stories can help us understand the Bible passage," said his father, "but they're not God's Word. The Lord wants us to read his Word. If we ask him, he'll help us understand it. Your mother and I will help you with the hard words."

"Billy, what happened when you were doing your homework today?" asked his mother.

"What do you mean?" Billy asked.

"You couldn't get the correct answer by using Jimmy's instructions, could you?" asked his mother.

"No," replied Billy, "but when I followed the book, I got it."

"Exactly," said Mother. "That's an example of why we need to read God's Word and follow his instructions. People make mistakes and may point us in the wrong direction, but God's Word has no mistakes. I guess you could call it our textbook for life." *S.L.R.*

HOW ABOUT YOU?

Is the Bible hard for you to understand? Keep on reading God's Word anyway! Your parents, teachers, or pastor can help you understand it, but ask God to help, too. Life's answers are found in the Bible.

MEMORIZE:

"Thy word is a lamp unto my feet, and a light unto my path."

Psalm 119:105, KJV

 The Bible Is Life's Textbook

The Real Thing (Read Hebrews 13:7-9)

25

FEBRUARY

"Guess what?" exclaimed Dad, as the family was eating dinner one evening. "Today someone tried to give me a counterfeit twenty-dollar bill for some groceries."

"Counterfeit?" Mom was surprised.

"What does *counterfeit* mean?" asked Susan.

"It means fake," Billy, her older brother, told her. "Pass the ketchup, please."

"Yes, it means fake," Dad answered, as he passed the ketchup across the table to Billy. "Counterfeit money looks like the real thing, but it's not."

Susan picked up her hamburger and started to eat. "How can you tell it's not real?" she asked between bites.

Dad thought for a moment before he answered. "Well, sometimes it takes an expert," he began, "but I do handle a lot of money everyday in the store, don't I?" Susan nodded. Her father owned the grocery store, and she often saw him at the cash register. "Well, after handling so much money every day, you get somewhat used to the real thing. And so, even though it doesn't happen very often, when a fake bill turns up, it often stands out." Dad took a sip of his lemonade and then continued, "When the man gave me the counterfeit bill today, it just didn't feel right, and when I looked at it more closely, I was quite sure it was phony."

"Wow!" said Billy. "Just like the FBI!"

Dad laughed. "Well, not quite. But I am thankful I caught it; otherwise we'd have been out twenty dollars." After a moment he added, "You know, now that I think of it, what happened today is a little like our Christian faith."

"What do you mean?" Susan looked puzzled.

"If we spend a good amount of time reading the Bible, we learn what it really teaches," explained Dad. "Then when someone comes along with a counterfeit teaching, we won't accept the phony message quite so readily—even though it may sound a lot like the real thing."

"That's right," agreed Mom. "When we're very familiar with God's Word, we won't be so easily fooled. *R.S.M.*

HOW ABOUT YOU?

It's very important to know what the Word of God teaches. Do you read your Bible every day? Do you listen carefully in Sunday school and church? Do you pay attention during your family devotions? Ask God to help you to study and understand his Word.

MEMORIZE:

"Do not be carried away by all kinds of strange teachings. It is good for our hearts to be strengthened by grace."

Hebrews 13:9, NIV

 Study the Bible

Fruit Roll (Read Galatians 5:16-23)

26

FEBRUARY

The pocket of Nanci's red sweater bulged. She didn't want Miss Allen to notice, so she slipped into the classroom without her usual "Good morning" and took her seat. She quickly removed a big orange from her pocket and hid it behind the big box of crayons inside her desk.

The morning dragged. Usually Nanci liked reading class, but not today. She could not keep her mind on the story. But Mike had said the class should wait until time for math. When Miss Allen turned to the chalkboard, he would give the signal.

Excitement really built up after recess. Everyone kept looking at Mike. When he put his hand in his desk, Nanci covered her mouth. She didn't want Miss Allen to see that she was giggling. She reached inside her desk, too, and took hold of the orange.

At last Miss Allen had her back to the class. Nanci drew a long breath as Mike yelled, "Fruit roll!" In a flash Nanci's orange was rolling down the aisle with lots of others. The room became noisy, and Miss Allen looked puzzled. "It's for you," Mike said, pointing to the fruit.

"Oh," said Miss Allen in surprise. "How thoughtful of you! Thanks, class."

That afternoon Nanci told her mother about the fun they'd had. "Miss Allen said she'd never heard of a fruit roll," said Nanci. "She got oranges, grapefruit, some tangerines, and even a lemon. She liked it—and then she let us play Fruit Basket Upset until lunchtime."

"Good," said Mother. "I was sure you'd enjoy it." She smiled at Nanci. "Did you know that you should have a fruit roll every day?" she asked.

"Every day?" exclaimed Nanci.

Mother nodded. "I'm thinking of the fruit of the Spirit," she said. "It's quite a list. Love, joy, peace, patience, kindness, goodness, faithfulness, gentleness, and self-control should be 'rolling' from your life each day. I don't know if our heavenly Father chuckles the way you did about the fruit roll, but I'm sure he's happy when he sees his fruit in you." *M.M.P.*

HOW ABOUT YOU?

Is a "fruit roll" a regular part of your life? As a Christian, you should be showing the fruit of the Spirit each day. Ask God to help you display these characteristics in your attitudes and actions.

MEMORIZE:

"But the fruit of the Spirit is love, joy, peace, patience, kindness, goodness, faithfulness, gentleness and self-control." *Galatians 5:22-23, NIV*

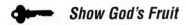 **Show God's Fruit**

One, Two, Three! (Read John 10:30; 14:16-20, 26)

27

FEBRUARY

"Pastor Banks says he's going to preach about the Trinity, so he asked me to practice this song for this coming Sunday," Kelsey announced, showing her mother some music. "I don't even know what the Trinity is," Kelsey added.

"Well, the word *trinity* isn't found in the Bible, but the idea of God in three persons is found in several places," said Mother. "It means that God the Father, Jesus the Son, and the Holy Spirit are three persons, yet they are one God."

Just then the doorbell rang. Aunt Lila, Mother's sister, had come to ask for help with her bookkeeping, so Kelsey practiced her song while Mother and Aunt Lila worked.

Aunt Lila had just left when Dad hurried into the room. "Hon, could you help me?" he asked Kelsey's mother. "A button just came off this shirt. Could you please sew it on for me?" Mother gladly agreed.

As Kelsey waited, she frowned as she thought about what Mother had said about the Trinity. But by the time Mother bustled into the room again, a smile replaced the frown.

Mother reached for her Bible. "Now," she said, "let's see if I can think of an example to help you understand the Trinity."

Kelsey laughed. "I think I've got the idea," she said. "I think you're a good example."

"Me?" exclaimed Mom, looking puzzled.

Kelsey nodded. "You're just one person," she said, "but you're Aunt Lila's sister, Dad's wife, and my mother! As a sister, wife, and mother, you do different things for all three of us, but you're still just one you! One, two, three—simple as it can be!" *L.A.T.*

HOW ABOUT YOU?

The doctrine of the Trinity is a little hard to understand, isn't it? None of the examples we can think of are perfect. However, God's Word teaches this important doctrine. Each person of the Trinity is distinct, yet they're all one God. Don't worry if you don't understand it perfectly. Just believe it because God said it.

 God Is Three-in-One

MEMORIZE:

"God the Father chose you long ago and knew you would become his children. And the Holy Spirit has been at work in your hearts, cleansing you with the blood of Jesus Christ and making you to please him."

1 Peter 1:2, TLB

The Juice Catastrophe (Read Proverbs 15:13-16)

28
FEBRUARY

Jeff and Katie had spent a day with their grandparents, and they were telling their parents all about it. "Guess what happened," said Katie, giggling. "Grandma mixed up a glass pitcher of orange juice. And when she picked it up—"

"The bottom of the pitcher fell out!" finished Jeff.

"Oh, dear!" exclaimed Mom. "That's a strange thing to have happen! It must have made an awful mess."

"It did," Katie said. "Juice splashed all over the floor and up onto the cupboards, too. And there was juice all over Grandma."

"You should have seen the look on her face," added Jeff. "She kept holding on to the pitcher and staring at it. But then she started to laugh. Grandpa was in the living room, and he came to see what was going on."

"I thought he'd get upset when he saw the big mess, but he didn't," said Katie, giggling some more. "He got a big grin on his face, and then he said, 'Well, Arlene, I knew you didn't like that pitcher, but you didn't have to go this far to get rid of it, did you?' Then we all laughed until our stomachs hurt."

Dad chuckled. "That's the way your grandparents are," he said. "They can usually take a tough situation and find the humor in it. Grandpa loves to quote the verse from Proverbs that says a cheerful heart is like good medicine."

Katie nodded. "Cleaning up all that sticky juice didn't seem so hard while we were laughing," she said.

"I'm going to try to be just like Grandpa and Grandma," declared Jeff.

"Good!" said Mom. "You can start right now. I . . . ah . . . I have to tell you—your favorite T-shirt somehow got in with the wrong batch of clothes today. It turned pink!" *L.J.O.*

HOW ABOUT YOU?

Do you get upset when inconvenient things happen to you? If you try to find some humor in the situation, you'll enjoy life a lot more. Of course, some things are too serious to laugh about, but God wants us to enjoy the life he's given us.

MEMORIZE:

"A cheerful heart is good medicine, but a crushed spirit dries up the bones."

Proverbs 17:22, NIV

 *Enjoy Life*

Blueberry Blizzard (Read Proverbs 15:1-4)

1

Ashley looked in horror at the Blueberry Ice Cream Blizzard spreading over the table. "I wish I was an only child!" she yelled. "Why can't you leave my stuff alone, Kristen?"

"I didn't mean to spill it," said Kristen. Her lower lip was trembling. "I just wanted a taste."

Mom appeared at the table with paper towels. "Here, Kristen," she said. "Big girls clean up their messes."

"No . . . wait," said Ashley. "We've got to put it back in the cup."

"I don't see how," said Mom.

Ashley grabbed a spoon and tried to scoop up the creamy purple drink. It was no use. "I bought this with my own money," she sputtered, "and you had no business touching it, Kristen."

"I . . . I'm sorry," murmured Kristen.

"You're going to buy me another one the next time we're at the mall," Ashley informed her.

"But I don't have enough money," wailed Kristen.

"Then save up," growled Ashley, glaring at her. "I wish I didn't have a little sister."

"Go to your room, Kristen," said Mom. "We'll talk about this later." After Kristen left, Mom turned to Ashley. "I'm sorry this happened," she said, "but it's no excuse for saying unkind things to your sister."

Ashley looked up from wiping the counter. "It's not fair," she complained. "Kristen always messes with my stuff, and you're lecturing *me.*"

"Kristen is only trying to be like you. It hurts her to hear you wish she wasn't around."

"Well, . . . I was mad," mumbled Ashley. "I didn't mean it."

"We can get mad and still watch what we say," replied Mom. "When we don't, words can pour out and make a big mess. And taking words back is even more difficult than putting that Blueberry Blizzard back in a cup. But I think you'd better try, don't you?" Ashley sighed, but she nodded as she threw the towels away. Then she headed for Kristen's room to apologize. *D.W.S.*

HOW ABOUT YOU?

Are you careful not to say angry, thoughtless words? Sometimes it's hard not to let them spill out, but it's impossible to take them back once they've been said. Don't displease God with your tongue. Ask him for help in controlling it.

MEMORIZE:

"May my spoken words and unspoken thoughts be pleasing even to you, O Lord my Rock and my Redeemer."

Psalm 19:14, TLB

 Control Your Tongue

A Much-Needed Push (Read 1 Thessalonians 5:11-22)

Lucy and Matt helped their dad load groceries into the car. "I hope it stops snowing soon," said Matt, as he closed the trunk. Hearing the sound of spinning tires, he looked around to see who was stuck.

"Let's give that driver a hand," said Dad, and the three walked across the snow-covered parking lot to a gray car. An elderly man inside rolled down the window. "I don't think you're stuck too bad," said Dad. "Try not to race the engine, and we'll give you a push." As the man stepped on the gas, the others pushed. The car moved easily, and the driver went gratefully on his way.

2

MARCH

"That reminds me of what our Sunday school teacher said a few weeks ago," Matt said as they walked back to their car. "She said that sometimes people get stuck in life and just spin their wheels."

Dad nodded. "I guess there are times when we all need a little push in the right direction," he said, as they started for home. "Can you think of some ways we might give that kind of help to someone?" Dad grinned. "Besides giving them a shove when they're stuck in the snow, that is?"

No one spoke for a few minutes. Then Lucy had a suggestion. "I know," she said. "Matt gave me a push when he helped me with my homework the other day."

"Good," said Dad. "And you gave me a push when you told me your friend's parents enjoyed my Sunday school class. I was getting a little discouraged about that."

As they turned into their driveway, Matt had one more idea. "I guess Mom gave me and Lucy a push when she made us take a time-out from fighting," he admitted.

Dad smiled. "I think you're right," he said. *G.G.L.*

HOW ABOUT YOU?

Can you "give someone a push"? Can you give a little help or a word of encouragement to someone who seems to be "spinning his wheels"? God is pleased when we encourage and help one another.

MEMORIZE:

"Encourage one another and build each other up."

1 Thessalonians 5:11, NIV

 *Help Others*

No More Teasing (Read Luke 6:31-36)

3

MARCH

Beth wished she didn't have to walk past the house on the corner, but that was the only way home from school. *Well, maybe Josh is already inside,* she thought. *Maybe he won't tease me today.* But then she saw him sitting on his porch.

"There she goes—ol' too-tall walking on sticks," called Josh. He laughed loudly, and Beth blushed. She was tall and thin and sensitive about it.

When she reached home, her mother could see that she was upset. "What's the matter, honey?"

"Josh always makes fun of me when I walk past his house." Beth's voice quivered. "I'll get even with him one of these days."

Mother looked thoughtful. "I can understand why you're upset," she said, "but I was just thinking. . . . Remember when I scolded you last week for something you hadn't done? You didn't get angry with me. Instead, you explained what had happened and handed me some wildflowers."

Beth smiled. "And then you gave me a hug," she said.

Mother nodded. "Maybe you didn't even realize that you were responding the way God says you should, but you were," she said. "I was wrong, but I'm not sure how I would have reacted if you had gotten angry in return. As it was, your explanation and flowers were a soft answer to my anger. You see, when you do something kind for someone who doesn't deserve or expect it, that often changes that person's attitude. Maybe it would work with Josh."

"Well, maybe," said Beth. Then she grinned as she added, "But I don't think he'd like flowers."

Mother smiled. "No, but there's a baseball card in one of the cereal boxes. Why don't you offer that to Josh tomorrow?"

The next day Beth walked right up to Josh and handed him the card. He stared at her. "I'll save the next one for you, too," she promised.

Josh didn't say a word, but the following day Beth was almost past his yard when he called out, "Hey! Thanks for the card." The taunting stopped. *K.E.C.*

HOW ABOUT YOU?

When someone is unkind to you, do you take God's advice? He wants you to treat your enemies with kindness, just as you treat your friends. By the way you act, you show others what it's like to love Jesus and just a little of what it's like for Jesus to love them.

MEMORIZE:

"A gentle answer turns away wrath, but harsh words cause quarrels." *Proverbs 15:1,* TLB

 Return Unkindness with Love

Loaves and Fishes (Read John 6:5-13)

"We had my favorite Bible story today," Robby said, as he helped his mother and older brother Mitch set the table for Sunday dinner. "The one about the boy with the loaves and fishes. I wish I could be like that boy and share my lunch with Jesus."

"You know, Robby," said Mitch, as he filled the water glasses, "I always liked that story, too, but I never could figure out why a little boy would be carrying five loaves of bread. Do you know, Mom?"

4

MARCH

"Well," said Mother, as she placed the salad bowl on the table, "you're thinking of our modern-day loaves of bread. In Bible times they were probably smaller and flatter. The little boy might have been carrying loaves about the size of our hot-dog rolls."

"Then what about the fish?" asked Mitch. "Wouldn't fresh fish smell bad after being in the hot sun for hours?"

"Probably," agreed Mother. "Maybe the fish were smoked or dried."

Robby brought in the salt and pepper shakers. "I still want to be like that boy," he said.

"You can," Mitch told him. "Just start carrying five loaves of bread and two tins of sardines around with you."

"Don't let your funny brother discourage you," Mother advised. "Christians have lots of opportunities to share."

On Wednesday, Robby and his class were on the way to the cafeteria when he noticed that a new boy in his class looked very unhappy. "What's the matter, Terry?" Robby asked.

"I forgot my lunch," mumbled Terry, "and I don't have money for the cafeteria. Mom says we haven't got money to spend like that. But I'm hungry."

"You can share my lunch," suggested Robby. "This is pizza day, so we can split it and all the other stuff, OK?" Terry nodded happily. *R.K.M.*

HOW ABOUT YOU?

Do you ever share with your classmates when they forget their lunch or lunch money or when they lose their pencils or need paper? Do you share at home with your brothers, sisters, and parents? Ask God what you should share. He may want you to share your time and talents as well as your money and possessions.

MEMORIZE:

"Let us not love with words or tongue but with actions and in truth." *1 John 3:18,* NIV

 Share with Others

A Sad Condition (Read Ephesians 4:17-24)

5

MARCH

Bert jumped from seat to seat in the back of the school bus. He laughed and joked with the boys who were harassing some girls. He joined in the teasing and laughed loudly when a few of the boys made gestures at the passing cars. Soon the bus driver pulled to the side of the road and scolded the boys. Bert felt ashamed, and when he found out his parents would be notified, he felt even worse.

That evening, Bert expected to get it from his parents, but nothing was said. He was glad when the evening news came on TV and Dad's full attention was given to it. The news broadcast showed a young man who had been found wandering the streets. He couldn't remember anything from his past—he couldn't even remember his own name. The newscaster asked that anyone with information notify the police and identify the man.

"How can that be possible?" Bert asked. "People forget some stuff, but not everything."

"Authorities believe this man is experiencing amnesia," explained Mom. "They think maybe something traumatic took place, and the man's brain reacted by blocking everything out."

"Oh, that's so sad!" exclaimed Bert's sister.

"But can a person really forget who he is?" asked Bert again.

"We were wondering that very thing this afternoon when your bus driver called," said Dad, looking at him sternly. "Do you know what she called about?"

"She . . . uh . . . she reported my behavior on the bus, I guess," mumbled Bert.

"Exactly," replied Dad. "Apparently you forgot who you were this afternoon. You are a Christian. But today you didn't display Christlike behavior."

"It sounds like you were suffering from spiritual amnesia," added Mother. "That is a very sad condition indeed!" *N.E.K.*

HOW ABOUT YOU?

Do you remember who you are? If you've accepted Jesus, you're a child of God—a member of his family. Don't act as if you suffer from spiritual amnesia. Remind yourself of who you are and act accordingly.

MEMORIZE:

"For now we are all children of God through faith in Jesus Christ." *Galatians 3:26,* TLB

 Remember You're a Christian

Joey's New Toy (Read 2 Peter 1:2-8)

"But, Mom," Joey pleaded as he and his mother sat at the kitchen table, "it didn't cost much." He had come home with the electronic game he'd seen advertised in the paper, and he was afraid his mother was going to make him return it.

"We've talked about this before," Mom replied. "You spend your hard-earned paper-route money on things you play with for a few days and then hardly use again. Why didn't you wait awhile before buying this?"

6

MARCH

"But, Mom, this is different," Joey insisted. "I really want this game."

Mom sighed. "OK," she said. "It's your money—you earned it. But I think you'll be sorry."

Joey was elated. "Wow!" he exclaimed. "Thanks a lot, Mom!" He was glad his mother had given in.

Joey's excitement over his new game soon fizzled. It wasn't as much fun as he had expected.

"I haven't seen you playing with your new toy lately," Mom said one evening after dinner. Joey fidgeted with his napkin. "What happened?" she pressed gently.

"Nothing," mumbled Joey without looking up. He glanced at her. "Are you mad at me for buying it?"

Mom smiled. "Joey, I'm not angry with you," she said, "but I think God can teach both of us something through this."

Joey was puzzled. "Both of us?"

Mom nodded. "Yes, both of us," she said. "You wanted that game so much you didn't ask my advice—and wouldn't listen when I gave it. But there have been times when I also wanted something very much and went ahead without asking God for his guidance. Other times I've ignored what I knew he wanted me to do." Joey looked at his mom. So she had made this kind of mistake, too! "Let's pray that God will teach us both an important lesson in patience, shall we?" suggested Mom. Joey smiled and nodded.

R.S.M.

HOW ABOUT YOU?

Are you sometimes impatient? Do you get angry if your parents say no when you want them to say yes? How about when God says no? He knows what will make you truly happy. Trust him to do the right thing for you.

MEMORIZE:

"Giving all diligence, add to your faith . . . patience."

2 Peter 1:5-6, KJV

 *Be Patient*

Payback Time (Read Matthew 6:1-4; Luke 14:12-14)

7
MARCH

Renee looked at the bright pink envelope that had come in the mail. "I bet this is an invitation to Samantha's birthday party," she said. Then she nodded. "Yep," she said with a sigh.

"You don't look very happy about it," observed Mom. "I thought the reason you had Samantha over one day was because you hoped to get paid back with an invitation to that fantastic party she's throwing. We talked about that, remember?"

"What you mean is, you scolded me about that," said Renee. "Well, I got paid back, all right, but now I'm sorry I did. Samantha's not really the type of person I want for a friend, and neither are the other kids she invited to her party."

"That's the problem with planning your own reward," Mom said. "Sometimes it backfires."

"What do you mean?" asked Renee.

Mom explained. "Jesus said that when we do things for people, we shouldn't do it with the idea of having the favor returned. When they pay us back, that just might be our whole reward. But if we do something for somebody who can't possibly pay us back, the Lord himself will bless us with heavenly rewards."

"Really?" asked Renee thoughtfully. A moment later she added, "Then maybe I should have Jean over. Her dad's been laid off from work for a long time. She wears old clothes, and she can't afford to do things with the kids. I'm sure she couldn't pay me back." Renee looked at her mother. "Can I have her over after school tomorrow?" she asked. *K.R.D.*

HOW ABOUT YOU?

When you do something for someone, is it with the idea that you can get something out of it? That's not God's way. He promises heavenly rewards to his children who do things for others without thinking of themselves.

MEMORIZE:

"Store up for yourselves treasures in heaven."

Matthew 6:20, NIV

 Work for Heavenly Rewards

<u>B</u> Is for Bears (Read 2 Kings 2:23-24; James 3:5-10)

8

MARCH

"Mr. Herschel looks so funny," said Abby. She snickered. "His ears are so big—all he'd have to do is flap them, and he'd fly away."

Seth laughed. "Yeah, if his big feet didn't hold him down," he said. "He must wear size twenty-four!" Grandma paused, her coffee cup halfway to her mouth. Mr. Herschel had been a Sunday school teacher for years. Did they mean him? "And Mrs. Pritchard!" continued Seth. "She wears the same dress every Sunday!" Abby nodded, and Grandma nearly dropped her cup. Did they mean Molly Pritchard, who had often taken her to the doctor's office when everyone else was busy? The one who often brought shut-ins meals?

"*Ahem.*" Grandma cleared her throat. "Your conversation brought something to mind," she said. "When I was a girl, I had an ABC Bible story book. I can remember the story for only one letter—*B*. It was called '*B* Is for Bears.'"

"Tell us the story, Grandma," begged Abby and Seth.

"Well, it's not a nice story," Grandma told them. She paused. "These bears were not the cute, cuddly kind," she said. "They were huge, shaggy beasts with sharp fangs. Some young men were running. They looked terrified, and some had fallen down."

"Ugh!" exclaimed Abby. "I never heard of anything like that in the Bible!"

"It's not a story we really like to tell," said Grandma. "You've heard of Elisha? Well, some rude young men ran after him, mocking and yelling, 'Go up, you baldhead!' God didn't like them making fun of his servant, so he sent the bears. You see, to ridicule God's servants is like striking God." She looked directly at the children as she added, "Mr. Herschel and Mrs. Pritchard are God's servants."

Abby's face turned red. "I'm glad they didn't hear us," she said.

"Me, too," Seth agreed.

"I heard you. God heard you," Grandma reminded them. "I think you'd better ask him to forgive you. And next time you're tempted to speak disrespectfully, remember the bears." *B.L.K.*

HOW ABOUT YOU?

Do you remember to speak only kind words about others even if they aren't present to hear you? Remember that God always hears. He may not send bears your way, but he does care, and he does punish. Be wise. Speak gracious, kind words.

MEMORIZE:

"**The words of a wise man's mouth are gracious, but the lips of a fool shall swallow him up.**" *Ecclesiastes 10:12,* NKJV

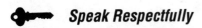 *Speak Respectfully*

Decision Time for Dan (Read Proverbs 4:20-27)

9

MARCH

On his way home from school, Dan glanced at a large, brightly colored picture of a young man and a girl huddled on a black motorcycle. The movie it advertised was being shown at the theater he and his friends passed each day. It was also the one to which he had been invited by his friend Bernie. Dan could tell from the ad that it wasn't going to be a "good" movie, and he wished he hadn't been invited. In his heart a voice seemed to whisper, *Just this once won't hurt. If the movie isn't any good, you can just ignore it and enjoy the pop and popcorn.* But at the same time, he sensed a warning voice: *Don't go.*

Dan walked slowly toward home, but he turned quickly when a car stopped beside him at the curb. It was his father. "Hi, Son!" called Dad. "Need a ride?"

"Sure! Thanks, Dad." Dan tossed his books into the backseat and climbed in.

"Is something wrong?" asked Dad.

"Oh, it's just one of those pizza-movie deals my friends have for their birthdays," explained Dan with a sigh. "The party sounds like fun, but I know it's a bad movie, so I'll tell Bernie I'm not going." He looked out the window to conceal the unexpected tears that welled up in his eyes.

"Son, there's no way to make this easy," said Dad, "but I'm glad you're taking a stand now, while you're young." He paused, then said, "This kind of situation always reminds me of something I heard long ago. Suppose you were on a train that was moving toward a broken bridge. You don't know exactly how far away that bridge is. Should you get off right away, or take a chance and stay on for a while?"

"Get off," replied Dan promptly. "That bridge might come up quicker than you think."

Dad nodded. "It's better to make the move right away than to wish later that you had. It's like that with many decisions in life. Make right choices now, before it's too late." *P.I.K.*

HOW ABOUT YOU?

When you have a hard decision to make, do you ask Jesus for wisdom and courage to do the thing that will please him? He will keep you from bad choices as you trust in him.

MEMORIZE:

"Choose you this day whom ye will serve." *Joshua 24:15,* KJV

 Choose to Do Right

Grumpy Glen (Read Philippians 4:7-9)

Glen slammed the kitchen door and stomped across the room. "I'm not playing with Fred anymore!" he said loudly.

Mother, who was making cookies, turned to face Glen. "Why are you so grumpy today?" she asked.

"Fred won't let me play with his new puppy," whined Glen. "He's so selfish!"

"I'm sorry Fred is being unkind, but you were grumpy this morning during breakfast, too," Mother reminded him.

10

MARCH

Glen wrinkled his nose. "We had oatmeal, and I don't like oatmeal," he said.

"Oatmeal is good for you," Mother told him.

"I'd rather have scrambled eggs," grumbled Glen. He pulled out a kitchen chair and nearly sat on Goldie, the cat. Goldie was curled up on the soft chair cushion, purring loudly. "You're in my chair," Glen complained, as he moved the cat to the floor. Goldie looked up at him and purred even louder; then in one swift movement she was in his lap. She laid her furry head on his knee and purred contentedly. "What are you purring about, Goldie?" asked Glen.

"I think she has a happy heart," said Mother. Glen gave Mother a questioning look. "Goldie is a happy cat," Mother explained. "Even though you took her chair, she's happy to see you, so she's in your lap purring instead of sulking or running out of the room."

Glen scratched Goldie's ear as Mother continued, "You need a happy heart like Goldie's," she said. "If we think about happy things, it makes us feel better. Bad thoughts make us grumpy."

Glen grinned. "I could think about Goldie and how she tickles my nose with her furry tail," he said.

Mother nodded. "Yes, and the very best thing to think about is how much God loves you. Just remembering that he loves us so much that he sent Jesus to us should make us feel glad."

Glen hugged Goldie, who was still purring loudly. "It is more fun to be happy than grumpy, anyway," he decided. *W.E.B.*

HOW ABOUT YOU?

Are your thoughts happy ones? Do you think about things that are pure and lovely? The next time you feel sad or grumpy, think about all God has done for you. That will help you to have a happy heart.

MEMORIZE:

"The Lord has done great things for us, and we are filled with joy." *Psalm 126:3,* NIV

 Have a Happy Heart

Jillian's Cross (Read Psalm 3:1-8)

11

Jillian woke up with a start and lay trembling in her bed. *What was that noise?* she wondered as she pulled the blankets closer around her. Then she remembered something, and she quickly reached over to her bedside table and felt around for her little, white ceramic cross. Picking it up, she felt a sense of relief, and she held it close. *Now I'm safe. Nothing can hurt me when I hold my cross,* she thought. Jillian relaxed and happily went back to sleep.

The next morning at breakfast, Jillian told her mother what had happened. "I sure am glad Aunt Jenny gave me that cross for my birthday!" she finished.

"Well, honey, I'm glad you were comforted when you held that cross," said Mother. "But you do know that your little ceramic cross doesn't really protect you, don't you?"

"It doesn't?" asked Jill.

Mother shook her head. "Do you know what the cross stands for?" she asked.

"Sure." Jillian nodded. "Jesus died on the cross for my sins," she answered.

"You're right," said Mother. "The cross is to remind you of what God did for you. But it's only a symbol. Let it remind you that Jesus is always with you. When you're afraid or in trouble, he will comfort and help you. It's good to respect the cross and know how special it is, but if you trust in it, you're really making it an idol. Be sure to put your trust in Jesus, not in the symbol, OK?"

Slowly Jill nodded. "OK," she agreed with a smile. *J.J.B.*

HOW ABOUT YOU?

Are you sometimes afraid? Do you have some object that you like to hold when you're afraid? Remember that an object—even a cross—is only a symbol. A cross is a reminder of Jesus' death for our sins. He is the only one who gives real peace. Ask him to help you stop being afraid.

MEMORIZE:

"Whenever I am afraid, I will trust in you." *Psalm 56:3,* NKJV

 *Trust God, Not Things*

Extraordinary Tea (Read John 15:4-11)

Aunt Jan was brewing herbal tea when Emily stopped in to see her one Sunday afternoon. Emily gladly sat down in the homey kitchen and sniffed the air. "Orange blossom tea—my favorite," said Aunt Jan with a smile. She pointed to a plate of cake. "Help yourself," she invited. Quietly Emily helped herself to the lemon cake. Aunt Jan raised her brows. "Why so silent today, honey?" she asked. "You're usually so bubbly, and you talk my ears off."

12
MARCH

Emily looked up at her aunt's pleasant face. "I was just thinking," she said. "Our Sunday school lesson was about abiding in Christ, but I didn't really get what it means." She smiled at her aunt. "Maybe you can explain it better," she suggested.

Aunt Jan leaned back in her wooden chair and thought. "Tea," she said, after a few moments.

"Tea?" Emily echoed.

"Yes, tea," Aunt Jan repeated. "When we first accept Christ, it's something like putting that tea bag into hot water. As new Christians, we are like weak tea. Just as the water is slowly transformed into stronger tea, we should slowly become stronger Christians—our lives should become more and more like Christ's. The tea becomes so much a part of the water that you can't say, 'This is tea, and that's water.'" She smiled at Emily. "When Jesus abides, or lives, in us and we in him, he becomes so much a part of our lives that others see his characteristics when they spend time with us." *C.M.V.*

HOW ABOUT YOU?

Is Christ a part of your life? Are you becoming more and more like him? Do you let his truth show in you? Let Jesus fill your life by spending time with him, listening to his voice, and obeying his Word. Let others see Jesus in you.

MEMORIZE:

"If anyone loves me, he will obey my teaching. My Father will love him, and we will come to him and make our home with him." *John 14:23,* NIV

 Let Christ Be Seen in You

Already Filled (Read 2 Corinthians 5:14-17)

13

MARCH

Russ wished he could escape from the scene while his father was examining his report card. Dad would not object to the Bs and Cs, but he was going to be disturbed by the note from Mrs. Blair saying that Russ had gotten into trouble again. Actually, the note disturbed Russ, too.

"What's the problem, Son?" asked Dad. "Why do you keep doing things you know are wrong?"

"I don't know, Dad. It just seems to happen," murmured Russ. "Roger James starts acting up, and then without thinking I join in."

"Do you ever pray for God's help?" asked Dad.

"Yes," mumbled Russ. Actually, he didn't do much praying in advance, but at least he always prayed for forgiveness when he got into trouble.

Dad thought for a moment, then said, "I have an idea." He took a glass from the cupboard and went out to his workshop. When he came back, the glass held some dirty-looking liquid. "Suppose this is the only glass in the house, and you want a drink," said Dad. "Will you just pour water into the glass?"

"Of course not." Russ knew that Dad had something specific in mind, but he didn't know what. "The glass is already full of dirty-looking stuff."

"Show me what you would do," said Dad.

Russ hesitated, then he emptied the glass, washed it out with soap, filled it with water, and then took a drink of the water.

"Good," Dad said. "Maybe your problem is that you've been trying to put righteousness on top of a heart that is already full."

"I don't get it."

"Have you asked God to cleanse your heart from sin?" Russ squirmed. For as long as he could remember, he had been taught that Jesus was the Savior, but he had never asked Jesus to forgive and save him. "Before asking God to help you do right, you need to ask him to cleanse your heart from sin," continued Dad. "Then he'll be ready to help you." *E.M.B.*

HOW ABOUT YOU?

Do you have trouble doing right? Is it because your heart is already full of sin? Wouldn't you like to ask Jesus to cleanse your heart so he can fill it with his righteousness? If you haven't asked Jesus to save you, you can do it now.

MEMORIZE:

"Therefore if any man be in Christ, he is a new creature: old things are passed away; behold, all things are become new." *2 Corinthians 5:17,* KJV

 God Requires a Holy Heart

Upside Down (Read 2 Timothy 3:13-17)

"Claudette!" exclaimed Jeanie. "What are you doing?" She stood and watched as her friend tumbled over after standing on her head. Claudette had been braced against her bedroom wall.

Looking up from the floor, Claudette smiled. "I think I was doing yoga," she explained. She pulled herself up to a sitting position and tucked her legs under her. "I was meditating."

14
MARCH

"Oh, no! Not another fad," groaned Jeanie. "I thought you were a Christian."

"I know, but sometimes I don't feel in touch with God," said Claudette. "I was just trying another way of feeling close to him."

Jeanie groaned again. "Last week you were 'playing' with a Ouija board," she said accusingly.

"Well, I wanted to get some answers about some things," said Claudette. She hurried to add, "I was just doing it for fun, though."

"The week before that you were trying to find someone who could read tea leaves," Jeanie reminded her. Claudette just shrugged. "Anyway," said Jeanie, "I came over to see if you could help with my math. I brought my book."

"Sure," agreed Claudette, but then she laughed as she glanced at the book Jeanie was holding up. "But if you want help with math, what are you doing with your English book?" she asked.

"Oh, no!" moaned Jeanie, "I brought the wrong book." Then she sat up straighter. "You can laugh," she added, "but you're even worse. I may be trying to learn math from an English book, but you're trying to find out how to live by getting into everything but the Bible!" She pointed to Claudette's pile of books. "I'll go get my math book, and why don't you get rid of those." *H.A.D.*

HOW ABOUT YOU?

Are you looking to the wrong places and the wrong things to find answers for Christian living? Doing yoga, playing with a Ouija board, or reading horoscopes may seem harmless, but the Bible warns against such things. God has all the answers for a Christian, and he gives them to you as you study his Word.

MEMORIZE:

"Turn away from godless chatter and the opposing ideas of what is falsely called knowledge." *1 Timothy 6:20,* NIV

 Study God's Book

The Master's Call (Read John 6:35-40)

15

"Mom, Sheba won't come!" wailed Lee. "When I call her, she just yips and runs in circles or runs the other way. Look!" Mom watched as Lee called to Sheba, his four-month-old puppy. Sure enough, Sheba barked and began racing around the kitchen, running in circles and coming close to Lee, but always dodging away at the last moment. Finally, exhausted, she lay in a corner, panting. Lee looked at her and sighed. "Disobedient dog!" he mumbled.

"You're right," agreed Mom, "but I have a suggestion that might help. Try offering her a reward to encourage her to come. I think we have some dog biscuits on the porch shelf. When you call her, ignore her silly antics. When she comes, praise her, pet her, and give her the biscuit. Eventually she'll get tired of wearing herself out for nothing. She'll learn she needs to come to get her reward."

"OK," agreed Lee. "It's worth a try."

Several days later Lee called excitedly, "Look, Mom! Watch Sheba now!" Mom turned to watch as Lee called to his puppy. "Sheba, come!" The puppy stopped chewing on her dog toy, looked at Lee, and cocked her head. Lee repeated the command. "Come, Sheba!" He held out a dog biscuit. Sheba quickly walked to Lee. She stood silently beside him and stared at the biscuit but remained still. "Good girl, Sheba!" Lee rubbed her head and gave her the biscuit, which she ate eagerly.

"Wonderful!" exclaimed Mom.

Lee beamed. "She's real smart," he said. He knelt and hugged the happy pup.

Mom smiled. "She is smart to come to her master," she agreed. Looking wistful, she scratched behind Sheba's ears. "If only everybody in the world would come to the Master . . . wouldn't it be wonderful?"

Lee looked up, startled. "You mean—come to Jesus?"

Mom nodded. "Those who come to Jesus share in the greatest reward of all—eternal life." *S.B.C.*

HOW ABOUT YOU?

Have you come to Jesus? He wants you to come and receive the eternal life that he is offering. It's wonderful, and it's free—but you must come. Do so today.

MEMORIZE:

"Come to Me, all you who labor and are heavy laden, and I will give you rest."

Matthew 11:28, NKJV

 Answer Jesus' Call

Blind Salamanders (Read 1 Corinthians 12:13, 18-25)

16
MARCH

"Hey, Dad, look at this ugly, white lizard," called Daniel as he peered into a tank in the reptile house at the zoo. "It doesn't have any eyes." The lizard crawled off its rock and slid into the pond in its tank.

Daniel's father stepped up beside him. "Actually, that's not a lizard," said Dad. "It's a Texas blind salamander. *Proteus anguinus.*" He opened his zoo brochure to the reptile section. "It says the Texas blind salamanders are born with tiny, sightless eyes, but they lose them as they mature. They live in complete blackness in underground caves and eat fungi and bits of plants and insects that wash into the caves in the spring floods." Daniel studied the salamander. It was easy to understand why God hadn't given it eyes. Living all its life in darkness, there was nothing for it to see.

Daniel pointed. "Look! It's got little feathery wings on the sides of its head," he said.

Dad looked at the brochure again. "Those are gills," he said. "Blind salamanders spend most of their time underwater and breathe through gills, like fish." As Dad leaned forward to get a better look, he dropped the brochure. Daniel snatched it before it landed on the ground and handed it back to his dad. Dad smiled. "Thanks, Daniel," said Dad. "That was quick."

Daniel shrugged. Catching the brochure was easy. But he began to think about what God had—and hadn't—given him. Daniel had always been small, with thin arms and bony knees. He didn't have a big, strong build, but he did have good coordination. Maybe God hadn't given him big muscles because he didn't need them.

He watched the little, white salamander swim contentedly in the pond. It didn't have big muscles, either. *J.K.C.*

HOW ABOUT YOU?

Do you wish you were taller, prettier, or better at sports? Do you feel as if you aren't as talented or as smart as other people? Remember, God has created everyone with special gifts and abilities. Each person is different, and each person is valuable in God's eyes—including you!

MEMORIZE:

"Those parts of the body that seem to be weaker are indispensable."

1 Corinthians 12:22, NIV

 You Are Special

Turn It Off (Read Colossians 3:1-8)

17
MARCH

"Mom, what is that smell?" Courtney asked when she got home from school.

"It's that trash in the garage," replied Mom. "Dad forgot to haul it to the landfill before he left on his business trip."

"Can't we take it ourselves?" asked Courtney.

Mom shook her head. "Dad took the truck, so we can't haul it. But we'll keep the kitchen door closed, and that will help a lot. Besides, your nose will get used to it." She opened a cupboard door and took out a scented candle. "Here, light this," she said. "That might help cover the smell, too."

Courtney lit the candle and then sat down to watch a TV program. After hearing girls at school discuss how interesting it was, she'd recently begun watching it. At first she had been shocked by the things that she saw and heard. But she soon got so caught up in the story lines that the wrong activities didn't seem so bad.

Courtney was soon involved in the program and didn't notice Mom standing nearby. "Is this the program you've been watching so often lately?" Mom asked, startling Courtney.

"Yes," Courtney admitted uncomfortably. "But it's usually better than this," she added quickly when she saw that there was a scene that she was sure Mom wouldn't approve of. "Besides, the story is so interesting, I just ignore the bad stuff."

Mom frowned. "Maybe you're just getting used to the bad stuff," she said. "You can get used to trash, you know—like the stuff in the garage. Do you notice it so much now that you've been around it awhile?" Courtney sniffed the air. She could barely smell it. "You can try to cover up the smell and ignore it, and you can even get used to the smell," continued Mom, "but it's still trash. And so is that scene I just saw on your program."

Courtney sighed. "I suppose so," she admitted.

"Well, at least we don't have to wait for Dad to come home before we can get rid of this trash," said Mom. "Turn it off." *K.R.A.*

HOW ABOUT YOU?

Have you allowed yourself to get used to wrong things in the TV programs you watch, the music you listen to, or the books you read? Don't allow your spiritual "nose" to get used to trash. If it wouldn't please God, turn it off!

MEMORIZE:

"Finally, brothers, whatever is true, . . . noble, . . . right, . . . pure, . . . lovely, . . . admirable—if anything is excellent or praiseworthy—think about such things." *Philippians 4:8,* NIV

 Don't Get Used to Evil

Cracked Glass (Read 2 Corinthians 4:6-10)

"Hi, Mom! I'm home!" shouted Alyssa as she came bounding in the back door after school.

"Hello, honey!" greeted Mother. "How was your day? Did you learn anything interesting?"

"Did we ever!" exclaimed Alyssa. "Mr. Knight, our science teacher, poured some really hot water into two glasses. One glass had a spoon in it, and the other one didn't. The glass without the spoon cracked. Mr. Knight said the other glass didn't crack because the metal spoon helped absorb some of the heat and kept the glass from breaking."

18
MARCH

"Hmmm, that's interesting," murmured Mother. "I hope he was holding the one that broke over the sink!"

Alyssa laughed. "He was," she said. Then the smile faded from her face. "You know what?" she asked. "Karen Holmes's little brother fell down their basement stairs last night, and he was still unconscious this morning. They've got so many other problems, too. Her mother has a broken leg, you know, and her grandma is awful sick—she might be dying! And now this!"

"Oh, that's too bad," sympathized Mother. "Let's be sure to pray for them. And would you like to help me fix a meal to take over there?"

Alyssa nodded. "I just don't see how they can stand it," she said. "I don't think I could."

"Well, they know the Lord. Without him, I don't know how anyone does stand it," agreed Mother. "Your science experiment today is a good example of what God does for us. The glasses represent our lives, and the hot water represents the problems and difficulties that sometimes seem to surround us. The spoon represents the Lord Jesus. He's the one who helps absorb our trials. It's his constant love and care that keeps our spirits from 'cracking.'"

L.E.K.

HOW ABOUT YOU?
Do you sometimes feel surrounded by problems and difficulties? Does stress make you feel as if you're going to "crack" sometimes? Give your fears and your life to Jesus. He's the one who will give the strength you need to endure.

MEMORIZE:
"Cast all your anxiety on him because he cares for you."
1 Peter 5:7, NIV

 Give Your Anxiety to God

Quilts and Sweaters (Read Luke 6:43-46)

19

MARCH

"I think Mom is being unfair. She won't let me buy that tape I want," said Rachel as, for the tenth time, she rearranged colorful quilt squares on her grandmother's coffee table. She studied the design. "There! I think I've got it. What do you think, Gram?"

Her grandmother looked it over. "I like it," she answered. "That will make a pretty patchwork pillow."

"What is it with Mom?" continued Rachel. "Does she think that if I listen to rock groups I'll do drugs or something?"

Just then the door flew open, and Grandpa whirled in with a gust of wind. Whoosh! Several of the squares for Rachel's pillow blew around the room. "Oh, Grandpa! Look what you've done!" exclaimed Rachel. "It took me all morning to get those arranged just right." She gathered the squares and tried to put them back in place. "I can't remember which one was where," she moaned. Grandpa hastily apologized.

Grandma picked up the yarn in her lap and began to crochet. "Rachel," she said, looking thoughtful, "do you think rock music glorifies the Lord?"

"Oh, come on, Gram," whined Rachel. "What does it hurt? I go to Sunday school and church and everything. Listening to rock music isn't going to change me."

"I see," said Gram. "You've divided your life up into nice little squares, like those quilt pieces. Some of the pieces belong to Jesus, and other pieces don't." Rachel frowned as she adjusted the pieces on the table once again. "When the wind blew, some of your quilt squares flew all over the floor," continued Grandma. "And when problems or temptations blow into your life like that wind, all your neat little life-squares could blow apart." She held up the sweater she was making. "Now, this whole sweater is made from one long strand—it can't blow apart," she added. "And you need Jesus to be the 'yarn' that runs through your whole life, honey—through every part of it, not through only certain squares. Then nothing can ever blow you away!" *J.R.L.*

HOW ABOUT YOU?

Is Jesus Lord of the music you listen to and the programs you watch? Is he Lord of the language you use when you're at school as well as when you're at home or in church? Don't divide your life into little squares and give him only some of them. Make Jesus Lord of everything.

MEMORIZE:

"So why do you call me 'Lord' when you won't obey me?"

Luke 6:46, TLB

 Make Jesus Lord

Clean Again (Read Isaiah 1:16-19)

20
MARCH

"Mommy! Mommy!" screamed Amy as she ran into the house. "My nose is bleeding!"

Mother quickly rinsed a washcloth in cool water to hold on her daughter's nose. While she gently wiped away the smeared blood, Amy's tears continued. "T-T-Tommy B-Bentwater punched me," she whimpered. "Just 'cause I wouldn't g-give him my candy b-bar." Amy's sobs stopped as she suddenly noticed something on her sleeve. "Oh, no, Mommy! Look!" she exclaimed. "I got blood on my new shirt!"

"Yes," said Mother, "and that will stain if I don't wash it out with cold water right away." She helped Amy change her shirt, and then Amy watched Mother make the stain disappear.

"Did Tommy sin, Mommy?" Amy asked.

"He certainly did," replied Mother.

"Does that mean he won't go to heaven now?" asked Amy.

"No," answered Mother. "If Tommy believes that Jesus died for his sins and has asked him into his heart, he'll go to heaven."

"But, Mommy! He sinned!" protested Amy.

Mother nodded. "Yes, but we're all sinners, honey," she said. "It's sort of like the stain on your new shirt. Pretend that the stain is a sin you committed—like hitting your brother or calling him a name. Well, when I washed that stain out, your shirt became clean again. Jesus died on the cross to wash away your sins, and when you ask forgiveness, you become clean again, too!"

Amy was silent for a moment. "But what if Tommy doesn't ask God to forgive him?" she asked, a little concerned.

"If Tommy trusts in Jesus, all of the sin he'll ever commit is washed away by Jesus' blood," Mother assured her. "But that doesn't mean he can just go on sinning. If he's really saved, he won't want to sin. But if he does, God will make him feel bad about it. Let's trust God for that. Let's just make sure our own lives are pure and clean before the Lord." *V.L.R.*

HOW ABOUT YOU?
Does it worry you that you do wrong things even though you're a Christian? Well, it shows that the Holy Spirit is not allowing you to be comfortable in your sin. But don't go on worrying. Talk to God about it. Confess your sin to him, and ask him to help you live a pure life.

MEMORIZE:
"Though your sins be as scarlet, they shall be as white as snow; though they be red like crimson, they shall be as wool." *Isaiah 1:18*, KJV

 Ask God's Forgiveness

Leftover Chocolates (Read Ecclesiastes 11:7–12:1)

"How about going to Sunday school with me tomorrow, Doug?" Paul asked his new friend. "I think you'll like it."

Doug shook his head. "No way," he said emphatically. "I don't want anything to do with religion."

Paul was a bit taken aback. "But . . . don't you want to go to heaven someday?" he asked timidly.

Doug shrugged. "There's plenty of time to worry about that," he said. "Right now I want to have a good time."

Paul didn't say anything more then, but he was determined to witness to Doug every chance he got. One day something his pastor said gave him an idea.

Paul knew Doug loved caramels. So he took some money from his piggy bank and bought a box of chocolates. "I bought some candy for you," he told Doug. "It has lots of caramels in it."

"Really?" exclaimed Doug. "Where is it?"

"At home," said Paul. "I'll bring it one of these days." After that he gave the same answer whenever Doug asked him about the chocolates. And every day Paul opened the box and ate some of the caramels.

Finally Paul gave the box, which now contained only a few pieces of candy, to Doug. "Oh boy! Thanks a lot!" Doug exclaimed. But when he opened the box, he frowned. "Where are all the caramels?" he asked. He looked at Paul. "Did you eat them?" Paul nodded. "Well . . . uh . . . thanks for these, anyway," muttered Doug.

Paul grinned. "I just wanted to show you how you're treating God," he said. "See, you said you'd think about God someday—after you've had a good time. You want to give God a leftover life, just like I gave you leftover candy."

Doug stared at the chocolates for a long moment. And when Paul repeated the invitation to come along to Sunday school, Doug slowly nodded his head. *M.R.P.*

HOW ABOUT YOU?

Have you trusted Jesus as your Savior? If not, when do you plan to do so? Each day you put off salvation is one more day that you live to please yourself instead of God. Jesus gave his best for you when he died on the cross. Don't give him a leftover life.

MEMORIZE:

"I tell you, now is the time of God's favor, now is the day of salvation." *2 Corinthians 6:2,* NIV

 Accept Christ While Young

Harmonious Music (Read Romans 12:3-10)

On a bright, sunny Saturday morning, Marci and her parents were driving through town when Marci pointed at a sign in a yard. "Estate Sale," she read. "Can we stop?" They stopped, but Marci didn't see anything too interesting until they walked into a room that looked like a library. In the corner was a tall object covered with a sheet on which was tacked a sign: "Not for Sale." Marci, being a curious girl, lifted the sheet, and to her surprise she saw a tall, stately harp. She gave a little gasp; she loved harp music.

22
MARCH

What a variety of strings there were! Some were as delicate as a hair, while others were thick and strong. Some were spiraled, some grooved, some smooth. Certain strings were bright red, others black, silver, or gold.

A young woman who was supervising the estate sale smiled at Marci. "This harp belonged to my mother's great-aunt," she said. "Now I'm going to take it home so my daughter can learn to play." She touched the strings gently. "When it's tuned and repaired, this harp will make beautiful music again."

That night Marci studied her Sunday school lesson. "Will you help me with this question?" she asked her dad. "I'm supposed to explain what the church is and give an example. You know, like many grains baked into one loaf. But I can't use that one; I need one of my own."

"Well, let's see." Dad thought for a minute. "Maybe you could use that beautiful harp you saw today," he suggested.

Marci grinned. "Hey, yeah!" she exclaimed. "Many strings make one instrument like many people make one church."

Dad nodded. "Each string is different—each is designed to sound its own individual note. Yet when each string is in tune with the others, the harp gives beautiful, harmonious music!"

"Some strings needed to be repaired," remembered Mom. "And sometimes we need to help repair members of the church who are broken with sin or sorrow. We must not let their music be silenced." *T.M.V.*

HOW ABOUT YOU?

Have you thought about how each member of God's church is different? That's as it should be—don't expect them all to think or act just like you. But do help them whenever you can. And keep in tune with those around you. Ask Jesus, the Master Musician, to help you "harmonize your music" with that of others.

MEMORIZE:

"We, being many, are one body in Christ." *Romans 12:5,* NKJV

 Christians Should Live in Harmony

Mark's Problem (Read Romans 8:14-17; 1 John 3:1-2)

23
MARCH

"Why are Daddy's golf clubs by the door?" asked Mark.

"Mom's selling them," answered his sister, Ashley.

"Selling them?" Mark's voice rose. "Daddy will want them when he comes back."

"Stop dreaming," said Ashley. "He's not coming back."

"He is so," said Mark. "Besides, I want to use the clubs when I grow up."

"Well, Mom needs the money," said Ashley with a shrug. Mark rushed to his room and slammed the door. Daddy seemed farther away than ever.

The following day, Mark went to play at Bobby's house. "Guess what?" said Bobby. "Dad gave me his old toy train!"

"Neat!" exclaimed Mark. "I guess your mom won't ever sell it."

Bobby gave him a strange look. "Of course not," he said.

Bobby's dad helped the boys put the train together, and Mark was having fun. But it made him jealous to watch Bobby with his dad. Suddenly Mark picked up a piece of track and threw it. Then he banged his fists on the carpet.

Bobby's father put his hand gently on Mark's shoulder. "Would you like to talk about it?" he asked quietly.

"No!" yelled Mark. Then he changed his mind. "Mom's selling Dad's golf clubs," he said with a sob.

"I'm sorry," said Mr. Jones, "and I think I understand. You see, my parents also divorced when I was about your age. I thought Dad would come back home, but he never did."

"My dad *will* come home," insisted Mark. He wished he could believe that.

"He may, but it would be somewhat unusual," said Mr. Jones. "I know the emptiness you feel, but let me tell you about Someone who loves you and can fill that empty place." Mark looked up at him, a question in his eyes. "Let me tell you about Jesus," continued Mr. Jones. "If you'll accept Jesus into your life, God will make you his child. He will be your heavenly Father, and he'll always be with you. You can talk to him anytime, anywhere. Then things like golf clubs won't matter quite as much." *M.M.P.*

HOW ABOUT YOU?

Have you asked the heavenly Father to make you his child? You need him whether or not you live with an earthly father. If you've not done so, ask him today to come into your life.

MEMORIZE:

"There is a friend who sticks closer than a brother."

Proverbs 18:24, NIV

Be God's Child

Eternal Life (Read John 14:1-6)

"Grandpa," said Jennifer, as she climbed up onto her grandfather's lap for her nightly Bible story, "would you rather live a long time or only a short time?"

Grandpa laughed. "Well, I don't know anyone who wants to die."

"I know somebody who's going to," Jennifer said softly.

"Really?" asked Grandpa. "Somebody old or somebody young?"

24
MARCH

"Somebody six," replied Jennifer. "Today we found out that Darcy has AIDS."

"I see," said Grandpa solemnly. "That's why your mother went to school today, isn't it?"

Jennifer nodded. "All the moms and dads did."

"Is Darcy going to stay in school?" Grandpa asked.

"As long as she can," said Jennifer.

"What do the other kids think?" asked Grandpa.

"Some are afraid to sit by her or to eat with her," replied Jennifer, "but the school nurse says you can't get AIDS just by being around her."

"And how do you feel about it?" asked Grandpa gently.

Jennifer began to cry. "I feel bad when people stare at her," she said. "She can't help it. I wish God would make her all better."

"So do I," said Grandpa. He held Jennifer close for a minute. Then he said, "What does Darcy say?"

Jennifer wiped her eyes. "She says her mommy told her everybody is going to die sometime, and only God knows when. She loves Jesus and knows he has already made a special place for her in heaven. She said her grandma and grandpa are even up there waiting for her to come."

Grandpa nodded. "I'm thinking about the question you asked me," he said. "Length of life is not nearly so important as what happens to you after you die. Rather than live a long life and not know where I'll go when I die, I'd choose to live a short life and know I'll be forever in heaven in the special place Jesus prepared for me. Just like Darcy." *P.O.Y.*

HOW ABOUT YOU?

Do you know where you'll go when you die? You can. Invite Jesus into your life, and then you can live with him now, every day. And then when you die—or when he comes again—he will take you to live in heaven, in the place he has made especially for you.

MEMORIZE:

"I am going there to prepare a place for you." *John 14:2,* NIV

 Live Forever with Jesus

God's Variety World (Read Acts 10:28-35)

25

MARCH

"What color should I use next, Patty?" asked Aunt Edith as she tied off the yellow yarn she was crocheting with.

"Use this purple one!" said Patty eagerly. "This is the prettiest afghan you've ever made."

"I call it the variety afghan because it has so many different colors and stitches," said Aunt Edith.

While her aunt crocheted, Patty told her about some of the students at her school. "Juan's from Mexico," she said, "and sometimes he forgets to speak English and starts talking in Spanish. Some of the kids laugh at him. They say he should go back to school in Mexico." Then she told about Chan and how the kids teased him because of the strange lunches he brought. "Waleed is different, too," she added. "He was born in Jordan, and he just doesn't seem to fit in."

"Maybe those children think you and the other kids who were born here are different," suggested Aunt Edith as she held up the afghan she was making and looked at it thoughtfully. "Patty, if God were making an afghan, do you think he'd use a rainbow of colors, or would he use only one?" she asked.

"Well . . ." Patty hesitated. She had never been asked such a strange question. "I guess, since he used so many colors in nature, he'd do the same in an afghan."

Aunt Edith smiled. "I think so, too," she agreed. "I can make a variety afghan, but only God could make our beautiful variety world. He used many different colors and stitches when he made flowers and animals—and people!"

Patty was quite sure she knew what Aunt Edith was thinking. "You mean like those kids at school that get teased?" she asked.

Aunt Edith nodded. *T.M.B.*

HOW ABOUT YOU?

Do you accept others just the way they are? Remember, God made and loves each person. Learn to enjoy his creativity as you learn to enjoy what makes each person unique.

MEMORIZE:

"**God does not show favoritism but accepts men from every nation who fear him and do what is right.**" *Acts 10:34-35,* NIV

 **Be Kind to Everyone**

How May I Help You? (Read 1 Chronicles 28:2-6, 9)

26

MARCH

Tom loved to go to Grandpa's muffler shop. Sparks flew when torches cut through metal. Then old mufflers came off, and shiny new ones went on with a loud buzzing noise as the air gun tightened bolts. When Grandpa answered the phone, he'd say, "How may I help you?"

At home, Tom played muffler shop with his younger brother and sister, Ted and Jodi. When Ted called Tom on the toy phone, Tom answered, "How may I help you?" Then Ted brought his bicycle in for repair, and Jodi rode her tricycle in for a new muffler.

One evening Tom, Ted, and Jodi were all ready to play muffler shop when their dad said, "Time to get dressed. Our church families take turns visiting the people at the nursing home, remember? Tonight is our turn."

Tom groaned. "Why do we have to go there?" he asked. "Those old people are no fun. Can't we skip it?"

Dad shook his head. "They look forward to our visits," he said. "They especially like seeing children—it brightens up their whole day just to have you there."

"Well, it doesn't brighten my day to go there," grumbled Tom.

Suddenly, Dad changed the subject. "Tom, how does Grandpa answer the phone at the muffler shop?" he asked.

"He says, 'How may I help you?'" replied Tom.

Dad nodded. "I've heard you answer the same way when you have a pretend shop going here at home," he said. "It's a good way to show that you're willing and eager to help someone. But it's too bad that we sometimes give customers a better answer than we give God."

"What do you mean?" asked Tom.

"Well, the Bible teaches us that God wants those who love him to serve him willingly," explained Dad. "He'd like us to say to him, 'How may I help you, Lord?' Tonight I think he'd answer, 'You can serve me by bringing cheer to those at the nursing home—willingly, without grumbling.'"

Tom looked thoughtful. Then he headed to his bedroom to change clothes. *C.E.Y.*

HOW ABOUT YOU?

Are you eager to serve the Lord in any way he wants? Even when he wants you to do something you don't want to do? He looks in your heart and sees when you serve him with a happy and willing heart.

MEMORIZE:

"Worship and serve [God] with a clean heart and a willing mind." *1 Chronicles 28:9*, TLB

 Be a Willing Worker for God

Champ and the Cactus (Read Matthew 18:1-6; 19:13-14)

27

MARCH

"Rowf! Rowf!" A big, brown dog stood eye-to-eye with baby Leah. They were separated by a pane of glass. "Champ! Naughty dog!" scolded Grandma. "Get away from the window!"

Little Leah and her older sister, Sarah, were visiting Grandma, and they were fascinated by the big, friendly dog. Leah sturdily pressed herself against the window, and Sarah asked, "Is Champ a naughty dog, Grandma?"

"Not usually, but he can be rough and noisy," replied Grandma. "That's why he stays outdoors when you're here. He would surely knock Leah down."

A loud shriek interrupted them. Leah, tears streaming down her cheeks, held out a hand. "Oh, dear! She touched the cactus plant. I should have moved it." Grandma cuddled Leah and spoke soothingly. "There, there, honey. That mean old cactus is covered with prickers, isn't it?"

"Is the cactus mean, Grandma?" Sarah's expression was puzzled as she looked at the plant.

"Well, not actually, Sarah." Grandma's voice had a smile in it. "God made cactus plants prickly, but they won't hurt us as long as we stay away from them."

"But Leah got too close to the cactus, didn't she?" Sarah persisted. "And I know she'd walk right up to Champ, too."

Grandma nodded. "When she's bigger, she'll learn that dogs can bite and a cactus is prickly," she said, "but until then, we have to protect her. You see, Sarah, that's one reason God gives us mommies, daddies, grandmas, and teachers. He knows children need grown-ups to love and teach them and show them the right things to do."

"Yep," Sarah agreed, then quickly added, "but I'm five, so I already know what to do!"

"There are things that can hurt even big girls like you, honey, and God wants to protect you, too," said Grandma.

"Mommy told me about stuff like that," Sarah announced. "Like asking her if I can cross the street or riding my bike only as far as the corner—and lots of other stuff. I remember it, too."

"Good for you, Sarah," said Grandma. "Good for you!" *P.I.K.*

HOW ABOUT YOU?

Who did God provide to care for you? Parents? A grandma or grandpa? Foster parents? Teachers? Jesus loves boys and girls, and he has given many different people the job of caring for them. Obey and learn from those God has provided to take care of you. Thank God for them.

MEMORIZE:

"Jesus said, 'Let the little children come to Me, and do not forbid them; for of such is the kingdom of heaven.'"

Matthew 19:14, NKJV

 God Cares for You

Burned-Out Barn (Read Ephesians 2:19-22)

It was early Saturday morning when Tim and his grandfather arrived at the farm. There had been a fire the week before, and all the buildings now lay in ruins. As they walked about the littered yard, Gramps told Tim about his boyhood in this very place.

28

MARCH

"This was where the springhouse stood," said Gramps. "My mother stored eggs and butter here because it stayed cool inside—a little like a refrigerator." Tim enjoyed listening to his grandfather's long-ago memories, and it made him sad to see the charred ash heap that was all that remained of the little building. The jagged, burnt trunk of a large tree, which had evidently shaded the springhouse, was close by. Gramps continued speaking. "This is where my father hung a rope swing for us boys. When I pumped really hard, I could get high enough to see way down to the south pasture."

Next, Tim and his grandfather circled a rectangular stone foundation that outlined the shape of the old barn. "Not much left to see," murmured Gramps.

Tim shook his head. "At least we can see where it was," he said. "Stone doesn't burn, does it?"

"That's right," agreed Gramps. "The old barn is gone—nothing left but the foundation, is there? Not even fire could destroy that. It reminds me that when we put our trust in Jesus for salvation, he becomes the foundation for our lives." He smiled at Tim. "Nothing can destroy that foundation, either," he added. "Nothing at all . . . ever!"

Tim's hand rested against the rough stones of the barn's foundation. It felt firm and strong, even as a puff of wind swirled a small cloud of ashes into the air. "I'm glad Jesus is the foundation of my life, Gramps," he said quietly. *P.I.K.*

HOW ABOUT YOU?

Is Jesus the foundation of your life? Is he your Savior? When you accept him as Savior, he becomes the foundation for all the rest of your life. Accept him today. It's the most important decision you will ever make.

MEMORIZE:

"No one can ever lay any other real foundation than that one we already have—Jesus Christ." *1 Corinthians 3:11,* TLB

 Make Jesus the Foundation of Your Life

Burned-Out Barn (continued from yesterday)

(Read 1 Corinthians 3:9-15)

29
MARCH

Late Saturday afternoon, Tim and his grandfather drove slowly away from the farm, down the gravel country road, and toward the highway. They were both tired and dirty after poking around in the rubble of the fire-charred farm buildings in search of anything of value that might remain. In the trunk of the car were the few things they had found—a tin box containing an assortment of tools, a belt buckle still attached to a shred of leather, a rusted iron vise, and a blue china pitcher.

"Not much left," Gramps had said with a sad smile. "Just some building foundations and a few odds and ends that wouldn't burn." After a moment he added, "I trust God will find that my life has more of lasting value than these old buildings did. You remember we said that when we accept Jesus as Savior, he becomes the foundation of our lives?" Tim nodded. "Well, after accepting him, our part is to do our best to live in a way that pleases him—to build on the foundation he provides," said Gramps.

"Like building on top of the stones!" Tim said quickly.

Gramps nodded. "The Bible says the things we do will be tested, as by fire," he said. "Those that are pleasing to God will remain. The things we do to please ourselves will be gone. We need to be careful how we build!" *P.I.K.*

HOW ABOUT YOU?

What materials are you building with? Are you careful to please God in your attitude? Do you obey quickly and cheerfully? Do you tell others about Jesus? Are you honest? These are just a few ways to build with "gold, silver, and precious stones." God will reward the actions and attitudes that please him.

MEMORIZE:

"If what he has built survives, he will receive his reward."

1 Corinthians 3:14, NIV

 Please God in Actions and Attitude

For the Love of Skipper (Read Ephesians 4:1-2, 32; 5:1-2)

30

MARCH

"It's not that I don't love you and Mom," Beth said to her parents. "It's just that all adopted kids wonder why their mothers gave them up."

Her father nodded. "Actually, we don't know much more than you do about your birth mother," he said. "All we were told, besides medical information, was that your mother asked that you be placed in a Christian home and that your first or middle name be Elizabeth."

Beth's sister Carla burst into the room. "Beth, you've got to do something about that overgrown puppy of yours," she declared. "He just chewed up my shoes."

Dad sighed. "We should have known that Skipper would grow too big for our small house," he said. "He needs a large area to run. Don't you think it's time to find him a new home, honey?" he asked.

Skipper pranced into the room carrying one of Beth's socks. "Oh, Skipper," cried Beth as she knelt down beside him, "I love you too much to give you up."

"Love sometimes means sacrifice, Beth," Dad told her. "Don't you think Skipper would be happier with more room to run and grow?" Reluctantly, Beth agreed.

A friend who worked at the animal shelter promised he'd find a good home for Skipper. So a few days later Dad drove Beth and Skipper to the shelter. When they got there, Beth gave Skipper one last hug before he was led away. She was then given a form to fill out. It took Beth a long time to fill it out because her eyes kept blurring over with tears.

On the way home, Beth said, "You were right, Dad. Love does mean sacrifice. When I was filling out that form, I realized that eleven years ago my birth mother must have filled out a form something like that for me."

Dad nodded. "Just as you want a better life for Skipper, she may have wanted a better life for you."

"And you know what else I think?" asked Beth. "I think she prays every night that I'm in a wonderful Christian home. And I am!" She gave Dad a big hug. *R.K.M.*

HOW ABOUT YOU?

Has someone sacrificed to give you a happier life? Be grateful. Are you also willing to sacrifice for family or friends? Do you love God enough to give up your desires in order to please him? That's not an easy choice, is it? Ask God for the strength to make the right sacrifices. You will be blessed when you do.

MEMORIZE:

"It is more blessed to give than to receive." *Acts 20:35,* KJV

 Love May Mean Sacrifice

Grandma's Hot Pads (Read Psalm 119:9-11, 105, 165)

31

MARCH

"What are you doing, Mom?" asked Angela as she and her brother Mark came home from school.

"Grandma needs some hot pads, so I thought maybe you and Mark could make some for her birthday," replied Mother with a smile. She showed the children some small hand looms and strips of material. "I'll show you how to do them," she added.

"Oh, I know how to do those!" exclaimed Angela. "I learned in school. It's fun." She insisted that she didn't need any help, so Mother turned her attention to Mark.

Mark watched carefully as Mother showed him what to do. First, he fitted a neat row of red loops between two sides of the loom. Then he used a hook to start blue rows going the opposite way. Over and under the red loops he went with the hook. He checked with Mother every now and then to make sure he was getting it right.

"How are you doing?" Mother asked Angela after a while.

Angela sighed. "I thought I knew how to do these," she said, "but this one isn't turning out right. I guess I forgot some of the things we learned."

Mother looked at what Angela had done. "Do you want to take most of that apart and start over?" she asked.

Angela nodded and began to pull it loose. Mother showed her what she needed to do, and after that Angela let Mother check each row.

That night Angela was reading an exciting mystery story when Mother suggested they all read a Bible story together since it was almost bedtime. "Oh, Mother," whined Angela, "can't I finish this book instead of listening to a Bible story tonight? I know them all anyway."

"Remember the hot pads?" asked Mother. "It's easy to forget what we have learned if we don't keep checking. And the things we learn in God's Word are not things we can afford to forget."

Angela sighed, but she closed her book. Then she grinned. "Oh, well," she said, "my favorite stories really are the ones in the Bible anyway." *M.M.P.*

HOW ABOUT YOU?

Do you think you know all the Bible stories and the lessons they teach? As you read God's Word each day, he will teach you new things from familiar stories. Remembering what the Bible says and obeying it are very important.

MEMORIZE:

"I will not forget Your word."

Psalm 119:16, NKJV

 Keep Reading God's Word

Who's Being Fooled? (Read John 10:7-15)

As sleepy-eyed Sara came into the kitchen, her brother Matt glanced at her mischievously, then looked out the window. "Snow on the ground!" he exclaimed. "How can there be snow on the ground at this time of the year?"

"Huh?" grunted Sara. She ran to see.

"April Fool!" Matt chuckled in delight. "Got ya!"

"Ohhhh!" groaned Sara, but she grinned at her brother as they sat down to eat.

At the dinner table that evening, Sara and Matt talked about April Fools' jokes that had been played at school. Dad smiled. "I hope nobody carried the jokes too far," he said.

"Nobody did," Sara assured him, "and we only do stuff like that one day." She paused, then added, "Most of us, anyway. Then there's Donna who fools people every day—especially grown-ups. They think she's such a great Christian. She always plays up to them, especially to our Sunday school and Kid's Club teachers."

"And to Pastor Smith," put in Matt.

"You should see the way she acts at school," Sarah said. "None of the kids like her—she's so sneaky. Whenever somebody loses money or a pencil or something, nine times out of ten Donna shows up with it later. Of course, she always has an explanation of where she got it. Today she was all smiles and sweetness to Mrs. Potter. But when Mrs. Potter's back was turned, Donna stuck out her tongue at her. She's always doing stuff like that."

"Careful now," cautioned Dad. "Are you sure you're not exaggerating? I've always thought Donna seemed to be a very nice girl." Mother nodded her agreement.

"See what I mean?" grumbled Sara. "She's even got you two fooled."

"Well, even if what you say is true, she hasn't fooled everybody," Dad said. "There's one who can never be fooled. God knows exactly what is in her heart—and what's in each of our hearts."

"Hey, that's right," said Matt with a grin. "He can't be fooled on April Fools' Day or any other day of the year." *H.M.*

HOW ABOUT YOU?

Are you fooling someone into thinking you're a Christian although you've never accepted Jesus as Savior? You may fool your parents. You may fool your pastor and teachers. You may fool your classmates. But you can never fool God. If you haven't truly trusted Jesus, do so today.

MEMORIZE:

"The Lord knows those who are really his." *2 Timothy 2:19*, TLB

You Can't Fool God

Bee without a Stinger (Read 1 Corinthians 15:20-26, 54-57)

2

APRIL

"Yikes!" yelled Jonathan, as he ducked quickly. A bee buzzed by, barely missing his head. He watched carefully as the bee settled on a garden flower before moving on.

"That bee was so close to your head, he almost gave you a buzz cut," joked Dad as he came up behind Jonathan. But Jonathan didn't laugh. He had something else on his mind. "Dad," he said, "can I ask you something?" He hesitated. "Grandma died weeks ago, but I'm still sad about it," he said at last. "Is that bad? I mean, Christians are supposed to be happy all the time, aren't they?"

Dad put his hands on Jonathan's shoulders. "It's very natural to feel sad," he said. "We loved Grandma very much, so we miss having her around us, and that makes us sad." Dad turned Jonathan toward him. "Death is an awful thing that began when sin entered the world. But for Christians, death is not the winner. So even while we're sad, we can feel good about the fact that death can't really hurt us."

Jonathan looked up. "What do you mean it can't hurt us?" he asked.

"I mean that since Grandma loved God and accepted Jesus as her Savior, she is now free of death and will be living in joy forever," replied Dad. "Let's see . . . how can I explain it?" He thought for a moment, then asked, "Why were you afraid of that little bee that flew by a few moments ago?"

Jonathan snorted. "Because it has a stinger, and I could have gotten stung," he said.

Dad nodded. "Would you still have been afraid if the bee didn't have a stinger?"

"No," said Jonathan, "at least not as much."

Dad smiled. "That's how it is with Christians," he said. "Death is like a bee without a stinger. It is still scary, but it can't really hurt us. After all, Christians will live with God forever."

Jonathan took a step backward as the bee zoomed by again. "I see what you mean," he said, "but I think I'll keep away from that bee until it loses its stinger!" *A.J.S.*

HOW ABOUT YOU?

Has someone you loved died? Do you feel sad when you think about that? There's nothing wrong with feeling sad. Even Jesus cried when his friend Lazarus died. Just remember that God gives victory over death and takes away the sting.

MEMORIZE:

"O death, where is thy sting? O grave, where is thy victory?"

1 Corinthians 15:55, KJV

 Jesus Takes Away Death's Sting

Take Up Your Cross (Read 1 Peter 2:19-25)

3
APRIL

Donna leaned out the car window to watch a line of people walking along the side of the road. Accompanied by a police escort, several children and adults followed a man who was dressed to look like Jesus. He was wearing what looked like a crown of thorns and carrying a large cross upon his back. "One of the local churches must be reenacting what happened on Good Friday many years ago," said Mom as she slowed the car at the policeman's signal.

Donna looked away; it was hard to look at the scene, thinking about what really happened, about what Jesus did for sinners. But her eyes were drawn back when she heard a man in a car call out something. "Hey! You're nuts!" the man hollered. He honked his horn and then hollered some more. The man portraying Jesus didn't even look up. He and the crowd of followers continued their solemn journey.

"That kind of thing, and much worse, really happened as people mocked and scorned Jesus many years ago," Mom said, "but Jesus kept on going, too. He was committed to doing the will of his Father."

"It must've been hard," observed Donna.

"I was thinking about how you sometimes get teased because you go to church or because you stand up for what you know to be right," Mom said. "You need to keep going on and doing the Father's will, too."

"Sometimes I feel like going along with the kids even when I know it's wrong," admitted Donna. "But being left out of their fun or putting up with mean things they say doesn't amount to much compared to what Jesus did for me, does it?"

"No, it doesn't," agreed Mom. "Each of us needs to 'take up his cross,' bearing whatever is necessary to follow Jesus. Nothing should stop us or hold us back from doing the Father's will."

N.E.K.

HOW ABOUT YOU?

Are you ever rejected or teased because of what you believe? Jesus knows that pain and understands what you are going through. Ask him to help you to continue to do right in spite of those who are unkind to you.

MEMORIZE:

"Then He said to them all, 'If anyone desires to come after Me, let him deny himself, and take up his cross daily, and follow Me.'" *Luke 9:23,* NKJV

 Follow Jesus Daily

Invalid Request (Read 1 John 5:13-15)

4
APRIL

Nan's mother helped her get started typing party invitations on her word processor and then went back to her cooking. Nan enjoyed doing it. But then something unexpected happened. "Mom!" she called, "something's wrong!" Mother came and looked over her shoulder. "See?" Nan pointed to two words at the top of the screen. "It says 'INVALID REQUEST.' What does that mean?"

"It means you pressed a wrong key—one that asked the word processor to do something it's not programmed to do," explained Mother. "Here, I'll get you going again." Mother helped Nan, and soon the invitations were nicely printed.

The next few days Nan prayed and prayed that God would let her party be the best ever. But it wasn't. It stormed the day of the party; Lynne, Nan's best friend, was sick and couldn't come; and Patty spilled punch on the carpet and went home in tears! "What a flop!" moaned Nan when the last guest had left. "All summer I've been hearing how neat Gina's party was, and I wanted mine to be better. I even prayed it would be."

Mother paused in picking up plates and looked at her daughter in surprise. "You prayed that your party would be better than Gina's?" she repeated.

"Well . . ." Nan looked a little embarrassed. "It's just that I hoped the girls would say they liked mine best and stop bragging about hers."

Mother looked thoughtful. "Nan," she said after a moment, "do you remember the invalid request you made on the word processor? When you did that, you didn't get what you asked for. Now, I certainly don't mean to insult God by comparing him to a word processor, but I'm afraid your prayer, too, was an invalid request."

Nan sighed. "You mean I shouldn't have prayed for a good party?"

"It was OK to pray for a good party, Nan," Mother said, "but perhaps you were asking in the wrong way, for the wrong reasons. God's Word says that when we pray that way, we probably won't get what we ask for." *T.M.V.*

HOW ABOUT YOU?

What do you ask for when you pray? Will your requests bring blessing to others and honor to God? If not, they may be invalid requests that God will not answer. Try to ask him only for things he approves of. The Bible will help you find what those things are.

MEMORIZE:

"When you ask, you do not receive, because you ask with wrong motives, that you may spend what you get on your pleasures." *James 4:3*, NIV

 Pray with Right Motives

Trapped (Read Proverbs 22:3-8)

Diane was surprised when her new friend Sherri lit a cigarette and inhaled. She didn't know what to say when Sherri offered it to her, saying, "Here. Your turn."

Should I pretend to smoke to please Sherri? she wondered. *Maybe there would be no harm in just putting the cigarette in my mouth.* But she knew she should not let anyone persuade her to do something she knew was wrong, so she slowly shook her head. "No thanks," she said.

"Oh, you're such a goody-goody," grumbled Sherri. "You might as well go home!" So Diane got up and slowly walked out the door. Once outside, she wondered if she had done the right thing.

On her way home, Diane stopped by her Aunt Carrie's house. "Why the glum look, sweetheart?" asked Aunt Carrie.

Diane hesitated. "Well, I do have a question," she said. "What's so bad about smoking—not all the time, but just once in a while with a friend?"

Aunt Carrie looked thoughtful. Then she pointed to a fly batting against the window pane. Over and over, the fly banged into the window, trying to escape. "Maybe that trapped fly has a lesson for you," Aunt Carrie said. "It probably wanted to come into the house for warmth and food. Now that it's in, it can't get back out, can it? So what do you suppose will happen to it?"

Diane made a face. "I bet it'll get swatted," she suggested.

"Yes." Aunt Carrie nodded. "People who try habit-forming substances like tobacco, drugs, and alcohol often get trapped just like that fly. They can't stop even though they want to," she said. "Doctors tell us that these things will hurt our bodies, and God tells us that we reap what we sow. If we sow bad habits, we will reap the bad results of those habits."

Buzzing loudly, the fly dashed itself against the window, then crawled around the pane, trying to get outside. Diane spoke thoughtfully. "Thanks for the lesson, Mr. Fly. I needed that," she said. "I'll never put a cigarette in my mouth. I don't want to get trapped." *C.E.Y.*

5
APRIL

HOW ABOUT YOU?

Are you tempted to do something wrong because someone wants you to? You're the one who will be hurt by your action. Trying a cigarette, drugs, or alcohol is not worth the cost that you'll pay in the end. Decide beforehand that you won't give in.

MEMORIZE:

"He who sows wickedness reaps trouble, and the rod of his fury will be destroyed."

Proverbs 22:8, NIV

 Bad Habits Trap You

Not a Copy (Read Psalm 139:13-18)

6

APRIL

Arthena sat at the kitchen table, carefully finishing her book report for school. "When this is finished, I get to use the copy machine at school to make copies of my report for everyone in class," she said. "That way we'll all have twenty-five book reports in a folder to use as guides in selecting books to read."

At school the next day, the school secretary showed Arthena how to use the copy machine. Soon warm copies filed out of the machine. Each one looked as if it were the original.

When Arthena handed the reports to her teacher, Mrs. Peters said, "Thank you, Bonnie."

"I'm not Bonnie," Arthena replied firmly. She didn't like it when people confused her with her older sister, but it happened quite often. Out on the playground later, Arthena complained to her friend Pat. "My teacher called me Bonnie again," she said. "She thinks we're alike, but we're really very different."

"You think *that's* bad," Pat said. "Not only do I get called my sister's name, I even get called my brother's name sometimes. And people assume that because Ann and Ned are good in sports, I should be, too."

"It seems like some people think God used a copy machine when he made us," Arthena said. "A bunch of identical copies, hot off the press!"

"Yeah," agreed Pat. Then she grinned and added, "But my mom says I shouldn't worry about people mixing me up with my relatives. She said the God of the whole universe knows me as Pat—the important person he created to be the only me. No copies here. I'm the original." *N.E.K.*

HOW ABOUT YOU?

Are you sometimes called by your sister's or brother's name? Do you get compared to other people? Remember that God never confuses your identify. He made you a very special creation, and you are the only one just like you. In God's eyes, you are a very precious, special person.

MEMORIZE:

"I will praise thee; for I am fearfully and wonderfully made." *Psalm 139:14,* KJV

 God Made You Special

Remote Control (Read Luke 17:11-19)

7

APRIL

"I sure hope we get remote-control cars for our birthday," said Frank as he and his twin brother Johnny walked home from school.

"Me, too," agreed Johnny, "but with Dad out of work, you know we won't." He kicked at a stone on the sidewalk.

"Oh, don't be so sure," replied Frank. "When Aunt Elizabeth called last week, she asked what we wanted, so I told her we wanted the cars. Who knows—she might come through with them."

When the boys got home, they saw that there was a package waiting for them—a package from Aunt Elizabeth. Could it be? It was! A remote-control car! Well, sort of. "A remote-control . . . oil truck?" said Johnny. "Not a *car?*"

"You mean we have to *share* it?" asked Frank in disbelief. He didn't like that idea at all.

For a little while the boys took turns playing with the truck as they figured out how it worked. Then Johnny spoke. "It's hard to work—it's really tricky to back it up with that trailer," he said. "I really didn't expect it to be like this."

"What did you expect?" asked Mother.

"I thought each of us would get one," said Frank.

"I didn't," said Johnny. "I didn't really expect to get a remote-control car at all." He looked thoughtful. "I suppose we really should be thankful to have this one."

"I agree with that," said Mother firmly. "Let's see how many things you boys can think of that you like about it."

"Well, . . . it's a nice red color," said Frank at last.

"And it might be fun to learn how to back it up with that trailer," suggested Johnny. He brightened. "Maybe even more fun than an ordinary car."

"How about writing a thank-you note to Aunt Elizabeth?" she suggested. "Just include all the things you can think of that you like about it. And while you're at it," she added, "don't forget to thank God for Aunt Elizabeth. She's been very good to you." Frank and Johnny grinned and nodded. *T.E.P.*

HOW ABOUT YOU?

If you're given something that isn't exactly what you want, do you grumble and complain? Or do you stop and think of something you like about it and then thank the giver? Be sure to do that. Most of all, be sure to thank God for those who love you enough to give something to you.

MEMORIZE:

"Always be thankful."

Colossians 3:15, TLB

 Disappointed? Be Thankful Anyway

Remote Control (continued from yesterday)

(Read Matthew 8:5-10, 13)

8
APRIL

One afternoon, as Frank and Johnny played with their remote-control truck, their little sister Ami was amusing herself by hopping around the living room on a hobbyhorse. "Mommy," she said suddenly, "I wish I had a remote-control hobbyhorse. One that would go up and down, up and down all by itself."

"Yeah, that'd be neat!" agreed Johnny, who was watching.

Mother laughed. "You'll have to invent one when you grow up," she suggested.

"But I want one now!" insisted Ami.

Just then Mother had an idea. "Get on your hobbyhorse, and when I give the command, do whatever I say," she told Ami. "For instance, if I say to go left, you go left; or if I say to go right, you go right. No wires required; it's remote control! Do you get it?"

Ami nodded. "And if you say 'stop,' I stop. Right?"

"That's right," said Mother. "Here we go! Go straight ahead! Turn left! Turn left again! Go right! Back up! Go forward! Stop!" Ami hopped up and down according to her mother's instructions. Soon the boys joined in, too. They took turns giving and receiving instructions all afternoon.

That evening before Mother tucked them in, she read them a Bible story about a centurion who wanted Jesus to heal his servant. "Don't even come," said the centurion. "Just say the word, and my servant will be healed." And that's just what Jesus did; he was so pleased with the man's faith. When Jesus simply spoke the word, the servant was healed at that moment.

"Mom!" exclaimed Johnny. "I didn't know there was remote control in the Bible." *T.E.P.*

HOW ABOUT YOU?

God made the world and everything in it, and he's in complete control of it. Let him have "remote control" of your life, too. Then you never need to be afraid of what will happen. You can trust him—he knows what is best.

MEMORIZE:

"Let them know that you, whose name is the Lord—that you alone are the Most High over all the earth." *Psalm 83:18*, NIV

 God Is in Control

No Wicked Thing (Read Psalm 101:1-7)

As the TV show ended, Nan turned the TV off. Julie looked at her older sister in surprise. "I always watch the next show," Julie said.

Nan smiled. "Let's go get an ice cream cone instead," she suggested. On the way to the ice cream parlor Nan asked, "What did you think of the show we just watched?"

Julie shrugged. "Well, it's usually OK. It's one Mom lets me watch."

"Yeah, but did you notice that the story was based on lying?" asked Nan. "One lie led to another until it got so ridiculous that in the end they had to tell the truth."

Julie laughed. "They lied in the first place to keep out of trouble," she said, "but they shouldn't have bothered. When the truth came out, they never did get in trouble anyway."

"No, but they should have," said Nan.

After getting their ice cream, the girls sat on a park bench as they licked their cones. "There's one more thing that bothers me about a lot of movies or TV shows," said Nan. "Some of the kids in them are pretty rude—like in the movie last night. And after we watched it, I noticed that you . . . well, you sort of copied the way the kids in the movie talked."

"I . . . I . . . ," Julie sputtered. "Well . . . maybe I did a little." She scowled at her big sister. "You're acting like . . . like you're my grandmother," she grumbled.

Nan squeezed Julie's shoulder. "I just wanted you to think about how the stuff you watch affects you. I have the same problem," she said.

"You do?" asked Julie in surprise.

"Sure," answered Nan. "There are lots of shows I won't watch because I don't want that junk in my mind—immorality or violence. But when my college friends all watch them, it's really hard not to."

"I guess so," agreed Julie.

"A verse in Psalms says, 'I will set nothing wicked before my eyes,'" added Nan. "I quote that verse a lot, and it helps."

Julie nodded. "Maybe I better learn it, too," she said. *R.J. C.*

9 APRIL

HOW ABOUT YOU?

Think about how TV influences your thoughts and actions. Have you ever found yourself copying the actions of TV characters even though you know you shouldn't? It's easy to do. One way to avoid it is to "watch what you watch when you watch TV."

MEMORIZE:

"I will set nothing wicked before my eyes." *Psalm 101:3, NKJV*

TV Influences You

Staying Afloat (Read Daniel 4:29-37)

10
APRIL

Jonathan burst through the front door and slammed his textbooks on the kitchen table. "I'm going to have the best report in the class," he announced. "I'm the smartest guy in my grade. I've gotten the top score on our spelling tests for three weeks running. Math is so simple, it's pathetic. And most of the kids write the dumbest essays." Mother frowned as Jonathan headed for his room.

Later that evening, Dad and Jonathan played a game of Ping-Pong. "I'll have you begging for mercy with my alley slam shot," boasted Jonathan with a laugh.

Dad grinned. "Well, you might, Jon," he said, "and then again, you might find you have bitten off more than you can chew. Which reminds me, I know just the thing you should write about for your next report."

"What's that?" asked Jonathan.

"The sinking of the *Titanic*," replied Dad.

"That big ship?" asked Jonathan.

Dad nodded. "It was one of the greatest passenger ships of all time," he replied. "It was elegant—crystal chandeliers, even a ballroom with its own orchestra. You might say it was the pride of its era. Everyone thought the ship was unsinkable. Only problem was. . . ." Dad's voice trailed off.

"It sank, didn't it?" asked Jonathan. "Sounds interesting, but why do you think that's such a good topic for me?"

Dad twirled his paddle. "In some ways, I'm afraid you're a little like the *Titanic*, Son," he said. "You see, it's a good thing to strive for excellence. But you need to be careful. Just as an iceberg tore a hole in the *Titanic*, pride can shipwreck you. God is the source of all our talents and abilities, and when we get puffed up and put others down, God can't bless our lives."

Jonathan hit the ball into the air a few times with his paddle. "I guess I see what you mean," he said slowly. Then he grinned as he added, "But I still can't resist an alley slam shot!" He slammed the ball toward Dad's side of the net, and the battle was on!

C.P.K.

HOW ABOUT YOU?

Do you strive to be number one, not caring whose feelings you hurt in the process? Do you take all the credit for every good grade, every victory, every prize you win? God is the source of all good gifts. Give him the glory and ask him to help you walk in love.

MEMORIZE:

"Proud men end in shame, but the meek become wise."

Proverbs 11:2, TLB

 **Don't Be Proud**

Chocolate Pudding (Read Hebrews 5:12-14)

Jody watched his baby sister suck greedily on her bottle of milk while he ate chocolate pudding. "Can I give Sarah some of my pudding?" he asked.

Mother smiled. "No, I'm afraid not," she said. "Sarah is just a baby, and the chocolate might give her a tummy-ache."

"But all she ever has is milk!" exclaimed Jody. "Yuck! I bet she's tired of that."

"Babies always begin with milk; you did, too," Mother told him. "Then, a little at a time, we added cereal, vegetables, fruit, and finally meat—and, of course, chocolate pudding." Mother smiled at Jody. "We fed you very carefully," she added, "and look at what a big strong boy you've become."

Jody grinned and sat up a little taller as Mother added, "Did you know, Jody, that Daddy and I are 'feeding' you God's Word in much the same way?"

"You are?" asked Jody. He looked surprised.

Mother nodded. "A little at a time, we're giving you more and more of his Word," she said. "When you were just a little older than Sarah, we began reading to you from a baby's Bible storybook. Then we read from the Bible storybook Grandma bought for you, and we also read some of the easier stories right out of the Bible itself. Now you're beginning to read your own Bible. We want you to love God's Word."

Jody grinned. "As much as I love chocolate pudding?" he asked.

"Yes," agreed Mother. "And even more than that!" *J.L.B.*

11
APRIL

HOW ABOUT YOU?

Do you love God's Word? Do you read your Bible and feed on his words? Or are you still a "baby" Christian, depending on someone else to feed you? To grow up to be a mature Christian, you need to learn to read God's Word for yourself and "feed" your soul every day.

MEMORIZE:

"Grow in spiritual strength and become better acquainted with our Lord and Savior Jesus Christ." *2 Peter 3:18*, TLB

 Read God's Word for Yourself

Stubborn Leaves (Read Colossians 3:8-14)

12

APRIL

"I think that tree must be confused," Joy said, pointing to an oak tree along the bike path where she was riding with her father. "Half of its leaves are green, and half are brown. It can't decide whether it's spring or fall. The green leaves are crowded right up against some dead ones that are all wrinkly and brown."

"Those are last year's leaves," Dad said, stopping his bike under the tree. "This kind of oak is very unwilling to let its leaves drop in the fall. Even strong winter winds can't tear them from the branches."

"They sound pretty stubborn," Joy said. "Since they're ugly and useless, why don't they just let go?"

"I don't know," said Dad. "Maybe they're a lot like the ugly and stubborn habits that cling to us."

At once Joy thought of the trouble with her brother, and she was sure Dad was remembering it, too. The night before, Mom and Dad had once again scolded her for teasing her younger brother. "It's a bad habit you've gotten into," they had said, "and it must stop!" But first thing this morning, she had called Tim a baby. As a result, they had a big fight, with Joy saying a lot of mean, ugly words. When scolded, Joy had replied, "I can't help it! I try to get those bad words out of my mind, but they just won't leave!"

Joy and Dad got back on their bikes. "Those old brown leaves do fall eventually," he said.

"How?" Joy wanted to know. "What makes them fall?"

"The new leaves," Dad replied. "As they grow and cover the tree, they simply push the old ones off."

Joy knew what Dad was really telling her. "You mean," she said, "that if I'd start saying nice things to Tim, the mean and ugly words would drop off, right?"

Dad nodded. "God doesn't tell us just to get rid of sin," he said. "He tells us to replace unkind deeds with good ones, angry words with loving ones. That's the only way to deal with stubborn habits in our lives." *T.M.V.*

HOW ABOUT YOU?

Do you work very hard to push bad habits away from you? Do you replace them with good things? If you're tempted to say something unkind, change the subject or even make a little joke. Try pushing anger away with kindness, and replace put-downs with praise.

MEMORIZE:

"Put off . . . the old man; . . . put on the new man which was created . . . in true righteousness and holiness."

Ephesians 4:22, 24, NKJV

 Kindness Removes Anger and Hate

In the Dog Pen (Read Romans 10:9-13)

"Sure I'm a Christian," Paul told Mr. Nelson, his neighbor, as the two of them put out fresh food and water for Spot and Ginger. The dogs belonged to another neighbor, Mrs. Smith. Paul and Mr. Nelson were helping her by caring for her dogs while she was in the hospital. "I've been a Christian all my life, I guess," continued Paul. "I go to church all the time."

13

APRIL

"I know you do," said Mr. Nelson, "and that's very important." He turned off the water hose and sat down on the ground beside the dogs as Paul started for the gate.

Paul turned back toward Mr. Nelson. "What are you doing?" he asked. "We're finished here, aren't we?"

"Yes, but I'm thinking of trying an experiment," said Mr. Nelson. "Maybe I'll stay here with the dogs tonight. If I sit in the dog pen long enough, I'll become a dog just like Spot and Ginger, won't I?"

Paul laughed. "What's the joke?" he asked. "Who'd want to be a dog? Besides, sitting in the dog pen and living with dogs doesn't make you a dog."

"That's true," said Mr. Nelson, getting up. "And sitting in the church building doesn't make you a Christian."

"But I . . . ah . . . my folks had me baptized," said Paul weakly.

"Living with dogs doesn't make you a dog, and living with Christians doesn't make you a Christian," repeated Mr. Nelson.

"I guess that's true," Paul said, frowning. "So just what does make you a Christian then?"

Happily, Mr. Nelson told him. *S.L.S.*

HOW ABOUT YOU?

Do you think showing up at church is all it takes to be a Christian? Or that belonging to Christian parents means you are also a Christian? That's not what the Bible says. The Bible says you, personally, must believe on Jesus. Do that today.

MEMORIZE:

"Believe on the Lord Jesus and you will be saved." *Acts 16:31,* TLB

 Only Jesus Saves

Luke's Answer (Read Proverbs 4:20-27)

14

APRIL

"Let's see," said Dad one evening as he spread out a map on the table. "We've decided to go to Montana on our vacation, but we haven't decided whether to go through the Black Hills or through the Rockies."

Luke squirmed in his chair. He had other things on his mind. At school, Billy had cornered him on the playground. "Look what I got," Billy had said as he held out his hand and showed Luke some pills. "They make ya feel real good, and for a price, I'm willing to share them with you, Luke."

Luke hadn't known what to say. He knew it would be wrong to experiment by taking even one pill! Drugs were not something the Lord would want him to do. Yet, instead of giving a strong no for an answer, he had stumbled over his words. "Well . . . no, I . . . ah . . . my dad would get mad if he ever found out," he had muttered. "I . . . ah, better not."

"Come on," Billy had coaxed. "Your dad won't find out." Luke hadn't taken any, but he couldn't forget the incident. And he knew Billy would be after him again.

"Well, which way do you think we should go?" asked Dad.

Luke shrugged. "We can decide later, can't we?" he asked. "We aren't leaving on our trip for a month."

"That's true," said Dad, "but we do want to make the most of our vacation time. I'll send for brochures, and we may want to make some reservations. It helps to plan ahead."

Exactly, Luke thought. *That's my problem. I know drugs are wrong, but I've never thought about what I would say if someone offered me some. I haven't planned ahead!*

That night Luke wrote in his notebook: "Answers I will give when someone tempts me to do wrong. (1) No, thank you. I'm not going to take drugs. (2) No. I'm a Christian, and I know drugs are wrong. (3) No, I don't want to do that. (4) No. God wouldn't want me to."

Luke scratched his head as he thought about more answers.

L.W.

HOW ABOUT YOU?

Have you prepared what you will say if someone asks you to do something you know is wrong? The Bible says you are to "ponder the path of thy feet." To "ponder" means to think about or prepare for. Think about what you'll say if someone tempts you to do some wrong thing. Be prepared!

MEMORIZE:

"Ponder the path of thy feet, and let all thy ways be established." *Proverbs 4:26,* KJV

 Plan Responses to Temptation

Squeaky Hinges (Read Numbers 14:1-4; 1 Corinthians 10:10-12)

15
APRIL

"Don't forget to take out the trash, Shelly," said Mother, coming into the kitchen.

Shelly scowled. "Aw, I hate taking out the trash," she complained. "Tony gets the easy stuff to do, while I have to tramp around the house collecting smelly old garbage."

"You chose to take care of the trash as your job for this month," Mother reminded her. "You said you were tired of dusting and folding laundry and that Tony always got the easy jobs, like emptying the trash." Shelly muttered to herself, but she started collecting the trash.

The back door squeaked loudly as Shelly's brother pushed it open and stepped into the room. "Tony, quit going in and out," whined Shelly crossly. "That squeaky door is driving me crazy."

Tony only grinned and turned back toward the door. "I think I left something outside," he teased. "I'll be back in a minute." He swung the door back and forth, and Shelly covered her ears. "I don't think this door wants to work anymore," said Tony.

Mother smiled. "Maybe not," she agreed. "Maybe it doesn't like its job anymore, so its hinges have become loud and squeaky to let everyone know." She paused, then added, "Those hinges remind me of the Israelites after they left Egypt. The Israelites complained a lot, even though God was good to them and supplied all their needs." She looked at Shelly. "Some people are still like that today."

Shelly sighed. "You mean me, don't you," she said. She hesitated, then added, "I'm sorry."

Just then Dad opened the squeaky door and came in. "I guess it's about time for me to oil those hinges," he said.

Mom smiled and nodded. "We need to apply the 'oil' of contentment to our lives," she said, putting an arm around Shelly's shoulder. "Instead of complaining, we are to be content with whatever God has for us." *M.I.S.*

HOW ABOUT YOU?

Do you complain about things you're asked to do? Washing the dishes? Baby-sitting your little sister? Mowing the lawn? Instead of murmuring, praise God for all he has done for you and be glad that you're able to work for his glory.

MEMORIZE:

"I have learned to be content whatever the circumstances."

Philippians 4:11, NIV

 ***Work Contentedly***

Rooted in Faith (Read Romans 5:1-5)

16
APRIL

Sarah and her family were enjoying the spring Saturday afternoon. Her younger brother and sister played on the swings while Sarah and her mom dug in the flower garden. Nearby, Sarah's dad tightened screws on the lawn mower. It was time to cut the grass for the first time that year.

Mom sighed as she looked out across the lawn in front of their new house. "Just look at all those dandelions!" she exclaimed. The yellow flowers had popped up everywhere. They were pretty all right, but Sarah's family appreciated their beauty more in the woods behind the house than on the front lawn.

Soon the mower roared to life. Sarah and Mom watched as the dandelions began to disappear. When Dad turned off the mower, Sarah said, "The dandelions will be back, won't they, Mom?"

Mom nodded. "I'm afraid so," she said. "They have long, tough roots, and when the top of the plant is cut down, it simply grows back again."

Mom paused, then continued. "You know," she said, "as I watched Dad mow, it occurred to me that we Christians sometimes feel cut down by things that happen in our lives—things like disappointments and sadness. But our roots are deeply planted in Jesus Christ. If we care for them as we should and 'nourish' them daily through prayer and Bible study, we can come out of our troubles whole and maybe even stronger—just like those dandelions!" *D.R.K.*

HOW ABOUT YOU?

Do you take care of your Christian roots daily with prayer and Bible study? If not, begin now to set aside some time each day to read your Bible and pray. It will make you stronger and better able to spring back when troubles come.

MEMORIZE:

"Just as you trusted Christ to save you, trust him, too, for each day's problems. . . . Let your roots grow down into him and draw up nourishment from him." *Colossians 2:6-7,* TLB

 God's Word and Prayer Strengthen You

The Other Dog (Read Luke 12:15-21)

17
APRIL

Jimmy put down the wood for the campfire and hurried to see why Samson, his puppy, was barking. The little dog stood at the edge of the stream looking down into the clear water. "What is it, Samson?" asked Jimmy, and he also looked down. He began to laugh.

Just then Dad came up. "What has Samson found, Jimmy?" asked Dad.

"Himself!" cried Jimmy. Sure enough, Samson was barking fiercely at his own reflection in the water! "Silly dog!" exclaimed Jimmy. "Come on to the tent. I'll get you a treat." The magic word was *treat,* and Samson immediately left the "other dog" and scurried to the tent. Soon he had his treat and was stretched out near the stream. He watched for the other dog out of the corner of his eye.

"Do you know the old fable of the dog and the bone?" asked Dad. "As the dog carried his bone across a bridge, he saw another dog in the water below and bristled."

"Just like Samson!" exclaimed Jimmy.

"Yes, and the dog wasn't going to let that other dog get his bone," continued Dad, "so he began to bark to chase that dog away. Of course, his bone fell into the water. The greedy dog ended up with nothing."

The fire was ready, and Mother brought out the skillet. "Greed makes us want to hold on to things," she observed, as she put some bacon into the pan, "but we really can't keep them in the end. Besides, *things* aren't the true measure of happiness."

Dad nodded. "When Jesus comes into your heart, you are the richest person alive," he added. "Too bad more people don't realize that."

Samson ran up, begging for another treat. Jimmy threw him one, and Samson hurried to his spot in the warm morning sun. He continued to watch the stream, just in case that other dog wanted a treat, too. *M.J.S.*

HOW ABOUT YOU?

Are you concerned about having the things all your friends have? Do you want money, a new CD player, or maybe a new bike? Things of this world last for only a little while. The love of Jesus is a precious treasure that lasts for all eternity. Make sure Jesus is in your life—be rich in God's sight.

MEMORIZE:

"What is a man profited, if he shall gain the whole world, and lose his own soul?"

Matthew 16:26, KJV

 Jesus Makes You Rich

Going in Circles (Read 1 John 2:15-17; 3:1-3)

18

APRIL

Oh, how Sandra wished she hadn't looked at the "dirty" pictures in Jennifer's magazine! But the other girls had looked at them, and Sandra didn't want to be different. She felt terrible now, though—as if her mind wasn't clean. How could she concentrate on her science report with all these awful thoughts going through her mind? Oh no! Mr. Lewis was calling on her right now!

Picking up her report, Sandra walked to the front of the classroom. Swallowing the big lump in her throat, she began. "My report today is on the processional caterpillar. These caterpillars are called 'processionaries' because they always follow a leader, doing exactly what he does."

Sandra gulped. She had been like that when she looked at the pictures. Taking a deep breath, she went on with her report. "Henri Febra, a French naturalist, proved this by putting a number of these caterpillars on the rim of a big stone jar in his garden. Each caterpillar thought the one ahead of him was the leader and followed him faithfully. For seven days those caterpillars crawled around the rim of the jar, going in circles. They just kept following the leader, who wasn't really a leader at all."

I don't want Jennifer to be my leader, thought Sandra.

"Finally, one of the caterpillars decided to strike out on his own to find food, and right away the rest followed him," continued Sandra. She finished the report and took her seat.

Sandra didn't even hear the next report on katydids. She was thinking about the caterpillars who blindly followed their leader and about the one that became a leader. *Jesus, forgive me for looking at those pictures,* she prayed in her heart, fighting back the tears. *Help me to be like the caterpillar that dared to strike out on his own. Help me to lead other girls to do right things instead of following Jennifer to do wrong ones.*

Sandra felt so much better after she had prayed. She knew God had forgiven her. He would help her to do right. *M.H.N.*

HOW ABOUT YOU?

Do you follow the leader or follow what God says in his Word? Dare to be different. Don't do something that is wrong just because you don't want to be different from the other kids. Be a leader for the Lord.

MEMORIZE:

"If sinners entice you, do not give in to them." *Proverbs 1:10,* NIV

 Dare to Be Different for God

The Rusty Old Skates (Read John 6:5-13)

19
APRIL

Rick stared at the rusty skates in disgust. What he really wanted was a new skateboard. But maybe the old skates would still roll. He put them on his shoes and fastened the straps. He was trying to skate when Andy, one of the neighbor boys, came along with his skateboard. Andy laughed as he pointed to the skates. "Did you get those from the city dump?" he asked with a sneer. "Can't your dad buy you a skateboard?"

"Well, no, he can't," replied Rick.

"Too bad. We could have had fun together," said Andy. "'Bye. See you later."

As Andy took off on his skateboard, Carol, another neighbor, walked up. "I heard him," Carol told Rick. "I wanted a skateboard, too, but Mom said no. I'd be glad if I just had a pair of old skates like yours."

"You would?" asked Rick. "Do you want to try one of these? We can each use one skate and have races. It will be more fun than playing alone."

After a while, Andy coasted down the street to meet them. "Let me race, too," he begged.

Rick shook his head. "A new skateboard against old skates wouldn't be fair," he said.

"Well, I could race one of you with a skate. The other one could play with my skateboard," suggested Andy. "We could take turns." And that's just what they did.

Dad smiled when Rick told him about the good time they had. "You sound a lot happier about the skates than you did when I gave them to you," he said.

"I am," answered Rick. "I almost told you to throw them in the trash. But I shared them with Carol. Then Andy shared his new skateboard with us."

"Good!" approved Dad. "I'm glad to hear that. Even more important is the fact that Jesus is pleased when you share what you can. And you know what? It generally makes you happy, too."

M.M.P.

HOW ABOUT YOU?

Do you share even when you don't have much to offer? Or do you leave the sharing to people you think have more? The boy in today's Scripture reading didn't have much, but God used and blessed what he gave. He'll do the same for you. Ask God to help you be the first to share.

MEMORIZE:

"Whenever we can we should always be kind to everyone."

Galatians 6:10, TLB

 Share What You Have

Golf Balls and Birdseed (Read Matthew 6:31-34)

20
APRIL

Peter's fingers itched to play the new video game his friend Joey had gotten the day before. He was getting ready to go to Joey's house when he heard his mom say, "Peter, don't forget that we promised to help clean out Mrs. Jordan's garage today. Don't run off until it's done."

"Do I have to help?" groaned Peter.

"We promised," said Mom firmly. "We've been praying for God to help Mrs. Jordan with her bad back. One way God can help her is by using us."

"Why can't God use somebody else for a change?" grumbled Peter. "Don't I ever get to do what I want?"

"I want to show you something, Peter," Dad said. Dad led the way to the garage. "Bring me a couple of those empty jars." Peter did so, and Dad took off the lids. "These jars are like your life," he said. "We'll fill one with golf balls. The golf balls are the things God wants you to do. Can you name some of the balls?"

"Going to church?" guessed Peter. "And studying the Bible?"

Dad nodded. "Yes, and helping other people," he said.

"And praying, and doing what you and Mom tell me to." With each idea, Peter dropped another ball into the jar. Soon it was filled.

"Now we'll fill the other jar halfway up with birdseed," said Dad. "It will stand for all the neat things you like to do."

"Like riding my bike and playing video games," said Peter. Dad nodded and Peter poured birdseed into the jar till it was about half full.

"Now, try moving the golf balls into the jar that's already partly filled with the things you want to do," said Dad.

Peter tried. Only a few balls fit. "They won't go," he said.

"Now put the birdseed into the jar filled up with seeking God," instructed Dad. Peter's eyes grew wide as a lot of the birdseed poured into the jar, right along with the golf balls.

"You see, it really matters what comes first," said Dad, "in life, as well as in the jars." *R.R.H.*

HOW ABOUT YOU?

What things have first place in your life? The things that you like to do? Or the important things that God tells you to do? If you put God first, he finds room in your life for many other things. But if you put your desires first, there won't be room for God.

MEMORIZE:

"But seek first the kingdom of God and His righteousness, and all these things shall be added to you." *Matthew 6:33,* NKJV

 *Put God First*

Smell of Sin (Read Psalm 34:11-16)

"Mom, may I have another cookie?" asked Jimmy, as he sniffed the air.

"No more now, Jimmy," answered Mother. "You've had enough. You can have a couple for dessert after dinner tonight."

"OK," said Jimmy, but he looked longingly at the cookies as they cooled on the counter. They smelled so good and tasted even better. He was still standing there, sniffing the cookies, when Mother came back to take another panful from the oven. "The more I smell these cookies, the more I want one," moaned Jimmy. "Can't I have just one more?"

21
APRIL

Mother shook her head. "It would be easier to wait if you'd go play instead of standing there smelling them," she said. "Remember the verse you learned last month at Bible Club?"

"Which one?" asked Jimmy. "I've been learning a lot of verses."

"The one about getting away from evil," answered Mother.

"'Turn from evil and do good,'" quoted Jimmy. "Is that the one you mean?"

Mother nodded. "Maybe you should practice what that verse says," she suggested.

"But cookies aren't evil," protested Jimmy.

"No, they aren't," agreed Mother, "but if you stay around the cookies long enough, you might eat one, and disobedience is evil."

With a sigh, Jimmy left the kitchen and went to his room. He was working on a model plane when his mother called him to get ready for dinner. "You were right, Mom," he said as he sat down at the table. "The cookies quit bothering me as soon as I got away from them."

"Good," said Mother. "That will work with all kinds of evil. If you get away from it, you won't be so tempted." *P.J.K.*

HOW ABOUT YOU?

Do you have trouble saying no to wrong things? Do the kids at school want you to cheat on your homework, or "sneak a smoke"? Stay away from the wrong crowd and find some good friends. Stay away from places where you're tempted to do wrong things. Then you'll be less likely to give in.

MEMORIZE:

"Turn from evil and do good."

Psalm 34:14, NIV

 *Avoid Temptation*

In Control (Read Galatians 5:16-25)

22

APRIL

Rain sprinkled the road as Barry rode his bicycle down the street. He and his family were new in town, and he was eager to make friends. So when Alan had invited him over, Barry had jumped on his bicycle and started out in spite of the rain. Alan was one of the most popular boys at school, and that made Barry especially excited about the invitation.

As he rode, Barry was thinking so much about making new friends that he wasn't paying attention to the road. He didn't see the patch of wet, slick leaves until the front wheel of his bicycle started to twist and slide. Barry tried to straighten the wheel, but he crashed to the ground.

Slowly and painfully, Barry freed himself from a tangle of wheel spokes and bike frame. His pants were torn, and one knee was scratched and bleeding. His knee ached as he walked his bike the remaining distance to Alan's house.

Alan greeted him at the door. "Guess what!" Alan said. "My parents went out of town for the weekend." Shouts and laughter burst out behind Alan. "Come on in and meet the guys." Alan introduced Barry to several boys who were seated on the couch and the floor. "Look what we have," Alan said. "Beer." He held a bottle out for Barry.

Barry stared at the bottle but didn't reach for it. He felt a tightness in his chest. He knew his parents didn't like drinking, and he was sure God didn't, either. He knew it would be wrong for him to take the bottle. "You do drink beer, don't you?" asked Alan. "Everybody does."

Barry frowned. "Why do you drink?" he asked.

"It's cool," said one boy.

"It's relaxing," said another.

Alan grinned. "It makes me feel wild and out of control," he declared. The other boys laughed and howled.

Barry looked down at his torn pants and felt his stinging knee. "No thanks, Alan," he said as he turned away. "I'd rather be in control. I've been out of control enough today." *D.B.K.*

HOW ABOUT YOU?

Do you know young people who drink? Are you pressured to drink to be popular? When others tempt you, remember to ask God for strength to "stay in control."

MEMORIZE:

"But the Lord is faithful, and he will strengthen and protect you from the evil one."

2 Thessalonians 3:3, NIV

 *Don't Drink*

Poisonous Beetles (Read Jeremiah 9:3-9)

Carl had just moved to the country, and he and his new friend Andy followed Mr. Peterson, Andy's dad, to the barn. "Do you know how to ride a horse?" Andy asked.

"Oh, sure," lied Carl. Actually, he'd never been on a horse, but he didn't want Andy to know that.

Andy led the way to a stall. "Here's my horse, Firebrand," he said.

23

APRIL

"Why don't we saddle Firebrand and Star," suggested Mr. Peterson, "and you boys can go for a ride."

"Oh no," Carl said quickly. "I can't. I mean . . . I've got to get home. Mom's sick." He added a lie to cover the first one.

"Oh. That's too bad," said Mr. Peterson. "I'll stop by and see how she's feeling."

"No, it's OK." Carl had to lie again. "The doctor said she can't have visitors."

"Hey, look!" Andy pointed to a black beetle crawling on the floor. "That's not a blister beetle, is it?" he asked.

His dad looked closely at the bug and shook his head. "No," he said, "that's just a black beetle."

"What's a blister beetle?" asked Carl.

"Blister beetles are small and look harmless, but they're poisonous to horses," explained Mr. Peterson. "Where there's one, there are always more. If a horse swallows as few as five, they'll kill him." He turned toward the door. "Well, Carl," he said, "I hope you'll come back when you have time to ride. And I hope your Mom feels better."

As they all walked toward the house, Carl thought that the lies he'd been telling were like blister beetles. They were small and didn't seem very dangerous, but where there was one, there were more, and together they could be deadly. Besides, he was a Christian, and he knew it hurt God when he lied. Carl realized he had to stop telling lies before he got into real trouble. He stopped in his tracks. "Wait," he said. "My mom isn't r-really sick. I . . . I just didn't want to admit that I've never ridden a horse. I'm sorry."

J.K.C.

HOW ABOUT YOU?

Do you tell little lies to cover up the truth or to impress your friends? Remember, one lie often leads to more lies. All lies are sinful. Ask God to help you to be honest, even in little things.

MEMORIZE:

"A false witness shall be punished, and a liar shall be caught." *Proverbs 19:9,* TLB

 *Tell the Truth*

A Hole Is a Hole (Read James 2:8-13)

24
APRIL

Lindsay twirled in front of the mirror. "Oh, I love my new dress," she told her mother, who was folding laundry. "I can hardly wait to wear it when I sing at church Sunday."

Mother smiled. "It should be an interesting service," she said, "since so many of the young people are taking part. It would be a good time to invite new people. Have you met any of the kids from the new family down the street yet?"

Lindsay nodded. "Sara's my age."

"Maybe you could invite her," suggested Mother. "Maybe she'd like to get involved in a youth group."

Lindsay shook her head. "She wouldn't want to come. She's . . . done things. She talks about things like smoking."

Mother raised her brows. "Well, Jesus said he came to save sinners—that it's not the people who are well who need a doctor, but those who are sick," she replied. "It sounds like Sara really needs to know Jesus."

"But, Mom, smoking isn't even the worst thing she talks about," said Lindsay. "She sounds hopeless to me."

"Did Jesus forgive you?" asked Mother.

Lindsay nodded. "Yes, but I've never done the things Sara's done," she said.

Mother held up a sock with a huge hole. "Would you like to wear this with your new dress next Sunday?" she asked. Lindsay laughed and shook her head. "How about this one?" asked Mother, holding up a sock with a small hole.

"Mother!" protested Lindsay. "I don't want to wear that sock, either. A hole is a hole, even if it's a little one!"

Mother smiled. "A hole is a hole," she agreed, "and sin is sin. In the book of James, God says if you commit any sin, it's the same as committing all sins."

"But no one is perfect," said Lindsay.

"Jesus is," said Mother. "That's why he came to die for us. Anyone can be made whole by Jesus as he heals the 'holes' that sin has made—whether they are big or small." *S.S.*

HOW ABOUT YOU?

Do you think some people are beyond God's forgiveness because of what they've done? Perhaps you think you're too bad to be forgiven. That's not true. All sin is the same to Jesus. It's all forgivable. Accept him today and be made whole.

MEMORIZE:

"Mercy triumphs over judgment!" *James 2:13,* NIV

 *All Sin Is Forgivable*

Why Must It Hurt? (Read Luke 12:6-7; Romans 8:18-25)

25
APRIL

One day, Andrew saw a dead rabbit along the roadside. *Why do little rabbits have to die?* Andrew thought. Later he winced at the sight he saw on television—many water animals dying due to an oil spill. *Why does this have to happen?* wondered Andrew with a sigh.

That afternoon, Andrew visited old Mr. Mason, who was crippled with arthritis. Sometimes Andrew helped Mr. Mason with chores, or sometimes the two just talked. Andrew climbed the steps and took his usual place in a green lawn chair. After they talked a few minutes, Mr. Mason shifted in his chair, then groaned. "Ohhh! I shouldn't have moved," he said. "My hips are so sore today. As a matter of fact, so are my back and shoulders."

Andrew frowned. It made him sad to see Mr. Mason hurt so much. "Why are you frowning, Andrew?" Mr. Mason asked kindly.

"Well, everything seems wrong," explained Andrew. "Animals and you and other people are all hurting." He sighed. "Where is God? Doesn't he care?" Andrew asked.

"Good question," said Mr. Mason. Then he smiled and pointed to sparrows splashing in a birdbath. "See those little birds?" he asked. "The Bible says we're worth even more to God than the sparrows, but even they are not forgotten by God. Not one falls to the earth without God knowing and caring."

"But if God cares," said Andrew, "why does he allow so much suffering?"

"Well, Andrew, nature is suffering and groaning in agony from the effects of sin entering the world," explained Mr. Mason. "But God has done something about it. He sent his dear Son, Jesus, to save us from eternal suffering. And someday, when all Christians are up in heaven, God is going to destroy sin from the world. No suffering or death will be in the new world, and those who trust in Christ can live in that beautiful place." He smiled. "Actually," he added, "I think my suffering here makes me look forward to heaven even more than I normally would." *C.E.Y.*

HOW ABOUT YOU?

Do you wonder why there is suffering in the world? Do you wonder if God cares? The Bible says that God cares so much that he sent his only Son to die for the world. Someday God will destroy all sin. Suffering will be gone, and everyone who believes in Christ will be happy forever with God.

MEMORIZE:

"The sufferings of this present time are not worthy to be compared with the glory which shall be revealed in us."

Romans 8:18, NKJV

 Sin Causes Suffering

Running Rough (Read Acts 2:42-47)

26
APRIL

"What's wrong with the car, Daddy?" asked five-year-old Kevin as the family drove to their hillside home after a church service in the village. "It's jerking."

"It's the spark plugs, I think," his father answered. "It sure is running rough."

"Are we going to make it home?" Kevin peered through the window at the trees lining the steep drop at the side of the road.

"Sure, we'll make it," his older brother Nick said, yawning. "We always do."

The car bucked as it slowly climbed the hill. The road ahead was the steepest part of the trip home, and Dad pushed the accelerator pedal to the floor, but the car refused to speed up. Dad shook his head. "I must say I'm annoyed with myself for not taking proper care of our car," he said. "It's a long walk uphill. I should have taken it to the garage when I first noticed it wasn't working properly."

"What will happen if you don't get it fixed?" Kevin asked.

"It will get even worse," Nick told him. He was wide awake now. "Just like us, it needs regular checkups," he added with a grin. "Like Pastor Baker said this morning—have a checkup every day, and if you see a trouble spot, take care of the problem before it gets worse."

"Did he mean our car?" Kevin asked, puzzled.

Nick laughed. "No, silly. He meant we need to check every day to see if we're doing what Jesus wants us to do, and then do something about it right away if we're not."

Dad smiled as they finally reached their driveway. "Well, I hope you'll remember this lesson about what happens if you don't get those regular checkups," he said, "because I don't intend to give you another lesson on the subject. This car goes to the garage to be fixed tomorrow!" *E.M.D.N.*

HOW ABOUT YOU?
Do you think once a week—Sunday—is often enough to tend to your spiritual life? If you don't want to be "running rough," you'd better tend to it every day. Read your Bible and examine your life to see if it's pleasing to God. Talk with him daily.

MEMORIZE:
"They received the message with great eagerness and examined the Scriptures every day." *Acts 17:11,* NIV

 Get Spiritual Help Each Day

Just an Earthworm (Read Luke 16:10-13; 1 Corinthians 4:1-2)

27
APRIL

It was a warm day, and Dad had just finished rototilling the family garden plot. "Look at that dirt!" exclaimed Emily. She had her shoes and socks off in no time. Rolling up her pants legs, she flashed a smile at her Dad. "Can Tim and I walk in it, Dad? Please?"

"I suppose," said Dad with a smile. "You know, you ought to be able to find some earthworms in there." In no time, Tim and Emily were enjoying the feeling of the soft, warm earth between their toes.

"Hey, look!" shouted Emily. "Here are two worms!" She held one up and quoted a poem she heard at school. "'I fry, I stew, I bake, I boil, but I never stop eating that good old soil!'" She waved a worm under her brother's nose.

"Hey, cut it out!" squealed Tim.

"OK, you guys," said Dad, smiling as he knelt beside them. "That's enough of that. But you know what? God has something to say to us through this worm. And your little poem was on the right track, Em."

"It was?" The children were surprised.

Dad nodded, "You see, the earthworm labors faithfully," he said. "As he passes the soil through his body, he receives nourishments, and the castings he leaves behind improve the soil quality. Millions of acres of the earth's topsoil are loosened, or plowed, in this way. Even though we don't see him working, he faithfully labors in his hidden places."

"But, Dad, a worm doesn't decide to be faithful," objected Tim. "It just does what earthworms do. Besides, what does that have to do with us?"

"Well, we *can* choose to be faithful," replied Dad. "And sometimes God asks us to be faithful in the hidden places, where no one notices and no one is there to praise us. In those times, our love for God will help us do what is right."

Emily smoothed the dirt over the worms. "Thanks, faithful friends," she said. "Keep working so we can have some good sweet corn!" *C.P.K.*

HOW ABOUT YOU?

Are you faithful in doing your chores even if no one is watching? God sees even into the hidden places. He will reward you.

MEMORIZE:

"A faithful man shall abound with blessings." *Proverbs 28:20,* KJV

Be Faithful

God Bless Mommy

(Read Genesis 45:4-8, 15; Jeremiah 29:11-13)

28

APRIL

Shawna turned off the light and crawled into her bed. How she wished someone would tuck her in and kiss her good night! A picture she had made with special paints at Bible school glowed in the dark. In the picture, Jesus held two children on his lap. One was a little girl with her head against his chest. Under the picture, painted in gold letters, was one word: *Come.* Her teacher had explained that Jesus loved her and invited her to come to him, and Shawna had done that. But she still was often so very lonely and hurt.

Pulling the blankets over her head, Shawna sobbed and then prayed in a whisper. "Dear Jesus, help Mommy not to beat me and Donnie anymore. God bless Daddy, Grandma, Grandpa, Donnie, and Friskie." Shawna paused. She thought about the story she'd heard at Bible school—about Joseph. He was treated very badly by his brothers, who wanted to kill him. But many years later Joseph and his brothers were joyfully weeping and hugging each other. Because Joseph prayed and put his trust in God through many years of pain, things were made right. Shawna continued her prayer. "Bless Mommy, too. And please help me to love her even when she's mean to me. Amen."

Shawna looked at the blue pinch marks on her arms and bruises on her legs. She stroked them gently. Looking at the picture again, she pretended she was the little girl on Jesus' lap and he was rubbing away her hurts. *S.E.D.*

HOW ABOUT YOU?

If you're being beaten or mistreated, talk to a parent, teacher, or pastor about it. Ask Jesus every day to watch over you, and pray that God's love, through you, will change that person's heart.

MEMORIZE:

"All who are oppressed may come to him. He is a refuge for them in their times of trouble."

Psalm 9:9, TLB

God Changes Hearts

Owl under Siege (Read Romans 5:1-5)

Chris quietly held his fishing pole as the morning sun turned the sky purple, then pink. His granddad cast his line from the other end of the boat. The bait landed with a small plop in the water. All was silent except the chorus of crickets.

29

APRIL

Then a loud squawk split the misty air. Chris jumped. The sound came again. "What was that?" asked Chris.

Granddad pointed to a tall, dead cypress across the bayou. A lone owl sat perched on the top, his silhouette dark against the sky. A large crow circled him, squawking with each pass. "What's that crow's problem?" asked Chris.

"There's no telling," said Granddad. "The owl might be sitting too near the crow's nest. Or that crow could just be pestering the owl—they're like that sometimes."

Chris watched as the black bird swooped again and again, its harsh cries filling the swamp. Only the owl's head moved. "I wish that crow would go away," said Chris. "Can it hurt the owl?"

Granddad shook his head. "Not likely," he said. "The good Lord gave owls what they need to protect themselves—strong wings and sharp talons. If the crow gets too close, he'll come out on the short end, and he knows it. Watch how he stays at a safe distance."

"Yeah, but if I were the owl, I couldn't just sit with that noisy thing swooping around," said Chris. The racket was getting on *his* nerves. "I'd have to fight or fly away—or something."

Granddad chuckled. "Maybe that old owl knows the crow will get tired after a while and go bother someone else," he said. "We could learn a lesson from him. When things trouble us, we tend to get all excited. Sometimes we just need to trust the Lord and be patient." *D.W.S.*

HOW ABOUT YOU?

Even when you're minding your own business, trouble may come your way. Don't panic; trust Jesus. His power and protection are yours. Let others see his patience in you.

MEMORIZE:

"In this world you will have trouble. But take heart! I have overcome the world."

John 16:33, NIV

 Be Patient and Trust God

Lost Opportunity (Read Colossians 4:1-6)

30

Jerry was troubled; he didn't know how to answer his friend Bill. "How can you say God loves me after what he let happen to my family?" Bill had demanded as they left school for the day. Bill's parents were involved in a divorce, and his family was torn apart. *If only I read my Bible more, I'd know how to answer him,* thought Jerry.

Suddenly, there was a loud explosion behind the boys. Turning around, they saw smoke and flames billowing out of one of the school's science room windows. A crowd quickly formed, mostly junior high students trying to see what was going on.

"Oh, why didn't I bring my camera to school today," moaned Jerry. "The most exciting thing that will happen all year, and I forgot my camera!" He was the photographer for the school newspaper. "Find out what happened, Bill," he shouted as he started down the street. Jerry raced home, flew up the stairs to his room, snatched the camera from his desk, and dashed back to school after a hurried explanation to his mother.

By the time Jerry got there, Bill had already left, and most of the excitement was over. "It looked more serious than it was," someone told him. Nevertheless, Jerry halfheartedly took a few shots, all the time mentally kicking himself for not having his camera with him before. *I could have had great pictures,* he thought, *but now they're almost useless.*

As Jerry started for home, his thoughts again turned to Bill's problem. *What can I say to Bill?* he wondered. Then a thought struck him. *I wasn't prepared to answer such a difficult question, just like I wasn't prepared to get a great picture when the explosion happened. Well, from now on I'm going to keep my camera handy. And from now on I'm going to study my Bible more faithfully so I'll be prepared for any spiritual "explosions."* E.C.O.

HOW ABOUT YOU?

People can ask some very difficult questions concerning God. It's up to the Christian to be prepared to answer them at any time. The only way to be prepared is to spend time in God's Word and in prayer every day. Do you do that?

MEMORIZE:

"Make the most of your chances to tell others the Good News. Be wise in all your contacts with them." *Colossians 4:5,* TLB

 Be Prepared to Witness

Rainy Day Blues (Read Psalm 119:137-144)

"Another rainy day! Aren't we ever going to have sunshine again?" exclaimed Dottie, as she flung her books down on the table.

"Rain is what makes the garden grow," said Mother. She smiled at her daughter. "This might be a good time to do your Sunday school lesson," she suggested. "You haven't done that yet, have you?" Dottie shook her head and reluctantly went upstairs.

As Dottie finished her lesson, she glanced out the window. "The rain has almost stopped!" she exclaimed. "Good! We've had enough." She got up to put her lesson book and Bible away. "And I've had enough of these, too," she mumbled to herself. "All we do in this family is go to church, study the Bible, and pray." She blushed when she saw Mother glance her way. Had Mother heard?

"Come with me to the garden and let me show you something," said Mother, and they put on their raincoats and boots. Mother picked up a small shovel, and they headed for the garden. "You think we've had a lot of rain," said Mother, "but look at this." She plunged the shovel into the dirt and turned it over. The ground was muddy on top, but the dirt was dry a little way down.

"I thought it would be muddy clear down to China!" exclaimed Dottie. "I guess we do need more rain."

Mother smiled. "This reminds me of us as Christians," she said. "Sometimes we think we've taken in so much of God's Word that we don't need any more." Now Dottie was sure Mother had heard her grumbling. "And yet," continued Mother, "we're really 'dry' down deep because, although we go to church, we really don't listen. Although we take a few minutes to read a verse and say a hurried prayer before we go to sleep, we don't think about what God is saying to us." Dottie knew what Mother said was true. As they headed back indoors, she made up her mind that she would read her Sunday school lesson again, and this time she'd really think about what God was teaching her. *C.E.H.*

HOW ABOUT YOU?

Are you taking just time enough to snatch a hurried look at your Bible and mumble a few words in prayer before you sleep? Do you tune out your pastor and Bible teachers? Don't do that. Listen carefully to what God wants to say to you. Don't be a dry Christian.

MEMORIZE:

"Your word is very pure; therefore Your servant loves it."

Psalm 119:140, NKJV

 Seriously Think about God's Word

The Groundhog (Read 1 Samuel 12:20-25)

"Dad, look!" called Robbie. He was standing at the front window, waiting to be picked up for baseball tryouts. "There's the groundhog again."

Dad went to see. In the fall they had often seen the groundhog, but when the weather became cold, he had disappeared. Dad had explained to Robbie that the groundhog was hibernating for the winter—taking a long sleep. Now the animal had again become active. They watched until the groundhog went behind a tree.

"There's Joe and his mom," said Robbie, as a car pulled into the driveway. He said good-bye and ran out the door.

That evening Robbie told his parents about the team. "We'll be practicing every night after school," he said.

Dad raised his brows. "What about Boy's Club at church?" he asked.

"I'll only miss two weeks," replied Robbie. "Oh . . . uh, Coach says we need to practice this coming Sunday morning to get ready for our first game."

"Sunday morning!" exclaimed Dad.

"Just this once," said Robbie. Then he added, "Well, . . . this time and . . ." He hesitated. "Well, see, the coach invited the team on a weekend fishing trip after baseball season ends. I can go, can't I?"

Dad frowned. "Remember our hibernating groundhog?" he asked after a moment. Robbie nodded. "Well, some people hibernate spiritually during the summer," Dad told him. "They're involved in church activities all winter, but when the weather gets warm, they neglect the Lord. Fishing, swimming, ball games, and camping all take the place of studying the Bible."

"And you don't grow by hibernating," added Mother. "In fact, we've noticed that the groundhog is a lot thinner now than he was when he disappeared last fall, remember?"

"We don't want to be hibernating Christians," said Dad. "You'd better tell Coach you'd like to play ball, but you won't be able to if it interferes with church activities, OK?"

With a sigh, Robbie agreed. *L.W.*

HOW ABOUT YOU?

Do you hibernate spiritually? Are you involved in church activities during the winter but then drop out when the weather turns warm and ball games, picnics, and swimming take priority? You need to learn about the Lord during the summer, too. You need to be spiritually strong at all times.

MEMORIZE:

"Do not turn away after useless idols. They can do you no good, nor can they rescue you, because they are useless."

1 Samuel 12:21, NIV

 Don't Hibernate from God

A Time to Tell (Read Matthew 18:1-6, 10)

Dara sat at her desk, staring out the window at the playground. Startled to attention by her teacher's voice, she quickly turned around. "What?" she asked. "I . . . I didn't hear you."

"Dara, please pay attention," said Mrs. Davis with a sigh. "I asked you to begin reading on page twenty-six."

Flushing deeply, Dara opened her third-grade reader and began flipping pages.

When class was over, Mrs. Davis quietly approached Dara as she gathered up her books. "Dara, is there something wrong?" asked Mrs. Davis. Dara looked down at her shoes and shook her head. Mrs. Davis studied her for a moment. "Are you having trouble at home?" she asked.

Dara felt her throat burning, and tears came to her eyes. "I don't know what to do!" she sobbed.

Mrs. Davis put an arm around Dara. "It's OK to cry," she said. "Do you want to talk about it?"

Dara wiped her eyes and slowly began to tell her teacher what had happened to her over the weekend. "I don't know how to say it," she said. "Someone . . . someone scared me."

"What did they do to scare you?" Mrs. Davis asked.

Tears streamed down Dara's face. "He . . . he touched me."

Mrs. Davis's voice was serious. "Dara, did he touch you someplace private?" Dara nodded, and Mrs. Davis continued. "That was very wrong, but it isn't your fault," she said. "Will you tell me who it was?"

Dara's lip quivered. "He's . . . he's my grandfather!"

"Dara," Mrs. Davis said, "have you told anyone else about this?"

"No." Dara shook her head. "I didn't think anybody would believe me."

Mrs. Davis smiled. "I believe you," she said. "This is a hard thing to have to do, and I know you're scared, but we must call your parents about this. I'll do what I can to help you, OK?"

Dara sighed, smiled weakly, and nodded. *K.J.T.*

3
MAY

HOW ABOUT YOU?

Have you been hurt by someone you trusted? Are you afraid to tell anyone? God cares! Ask him to help you tell a parent, a teacher, a pastor, or an adult friend. God will be there to help heal you, love you, and protect you. You can always bring your deepest pain to him.

MEMORIZE:

"Cast all your anxiety on him because he cares for you."

1 Peter 5:7, NIV

 Get Help When You Need It

Wilderness Cure (Read Matthew 6:25-34)

4
MAY

"This state park we're camping at is really nice, isn't it, Joel?" asked Dad as they walked along a wooded path.

"Huh? Oh, yeah," mumbled Joel. But he hadn't really noticed—he'd been too busy worrying. The company Dad worked for was going out of business, and Dad was looking for a new job. *What if we run out of money for food and clothes?* Joel wondered. He was so distracted by his thoughts that he didn't pay attention to where he was walking.

"Joel, watch out!" warned Dad as Joel wandered off the path. Joel stopped and looked down. He was standing in a patch of low bushes. "You're in poison ivy," Dad told him.

"Poison ivy!" moaned Joel. He quickly returned to the path. "Now I'll be itching all weekend!"

Dad smiled. "Maybe not," he said. "I think I see something that might help you."

"There's medicine for poison ivy in the middle of the woods?"

"Sometimes God provides for us in surprising ways," Dad said with a smile. He pointed to a tall plant with yellow, spotted, horn-shaped flowers. "There," he said.

"That's touch-me-not, isn't it?" asked Joel. "Mom has some growing by the house."

"That's right," replied Dad. "It's also called jewelweed." Dad broke off some leaves, crushed them in his hand, and rubbed them over Joel's bare legs. "That ought to stop your poison ivy reaction."

"Really?" asked Joel. He hoped Dad was right.

Back at their campsite, Mom cooked dinner on the grill, and later they watched the sun set over the lake. "So how are your legs?" asked Dad when they were ready to go to bed that night.

"My legs?" asked Joel. Then he remembered—the poison ivy! He looked at his legs. "Wow! The poison ivy isn't doing anything. That jewelweed really worked." As he thought about that, it occurred to him that if God could provide a poison ivy cure in the woods, he certainly could provide for Joel's family as well. Joel realized he truly didn't need to worry. *J.K.C.*

HOW ABOUT YOU?

Do you sometimes worry about having enough money, especially if one of your parents is out of work? Do you worry about how your family will be able to buy food or pay the rent? Remember, God will provide everything you need. Trust him, and don't worry.

MEMORIZE:

"My God shall supply all your need according to his riches in glory by Christ Jesus."

Philippians 4:19, KJV

 **Don't Worry**

Friendship Seeds (Read Galatians 6:7-10)

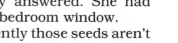

5
MAY

"I will *never* talk to that girl again!" said Cindy, plopping down in the grass at the side of the garden.

"Who? And why not?" asked Grandpa without looking up. He was planting a row of carrots.

"Marcy, the new girl," replied Cindy. "I'm tired of trying to make friends with her."

"Has she made any friends at school?" Grandpa asked.

Cindy shook her head. "She's too rude. She just ignores everybody," she said. Cindy jumped up and began to uncoil the long, green garden hose.

"What are you doing with that?" asked Grandpa.

"I'm going to water my flowers," Cindy answered. She had planted a little patch of marigolds near her bedroom window.

"Oh, why bother," said Grandpa. "Apparently those seeds aren't growing anyway." He fanned his face with his hat. "You put them in ten days ago," he added, "but I don't see anything happening. They must be duds."

"Grandpa, it takes time," protested Cindy. "You just watch. Any day now they're going to be sticking their little green leaves up out of the ground." She grinned. "I think you just need to have a little more faith—we've been studying faith in Sunday school."

"So why don't you have faith in the 'friendship seeds' you've been planting around Marcy?" asked Grandpa.

Cindy's mouth fell open. "Friendship seeds?" she asked. But she knew what Grandpa meant, and she knew he was right. Each time she had tried to make friends with Marcy it was like planting seeds of friendship. And Cindy knew you couldn't always see something growing at first—not even friendship.

Cindy dropped the hose. "See you later," she called as she ran across the wide yard toward Marcy's house. "I'm going to give my 'friendship seeds' a little water. I'm going to invite Marcy to our Sunday school picnic." *T.M.B.*

HOW ABOUT YOU?

Do you become angry when no one responds to your efforts to reach out to them? Or do you keep on being kind, no matter how you're treated? Sometimes people don't respond to kindness overnight, but God says to continue your acts of love and friendship. They're a lot like seeds. Trust God to make them grow.

MEMORIZE:

"Let us not get tired of doing what is right, for after a while we will reap a harvest of blessing if we don't get discouraged and give up." *Galatians 6:9,* TLB

 Sow Seeds of Kindness

The Spark Plug (Read Matthew 5:33-37)

6
MAY

Jason pulled the rope on the lawn mower. He pulled it again. And again. But no matter how many times Jason pulled the rope, the lawn mower would not start. Finally he sat down on a lawn chair with a disgusted look on his face. "This isn't my day," he grumbled as his father came out of the house. "First, Mr. Bradley bawled me out, and now the mower won't go." He glanced up—he hadn't meant to tell Dad about Mr. Bradley. He hurried to explain. "Honest, Dad, I didn't do anything very bad. I just used a few words that Mr. Bradley called mild oaths."

"I see," Dad said as he went over to the silent mower. "I think you and this piece of machinery may have the same problem."

He got out his toolbox and removed the spark plug from the mower. "Look at this, Jason. What do you see?" Dad asked.

Jason glanced at the spark plug. "Looks OK to me," he began, "and . . ." He looked closer. "Oh," he said, "there's a little dirt right here." He pointed to the end of the spark plug.

"Watch this," said Dad. He cleaned the carbon off the spark plug and carefully inserted it back into the mower. "Now try to start it."

The mower started on the first pull. "Thanks, Dad!" exclaimed Jason. "You wouldn't think such a tiny bit of dirt could stop a great big lawn mower! Next time I have trouble, I'll check the spark plugs." He started to push the mower along the edge of the sidewalk.

"Wait a minute, Son." Dad stopped him and turned the mower off. "Always remember that just as a little carbon on a spark plug can damage the performance of the lawn mower, a little bad language can damage a Christian's testimony for the Lord." Dad patted Jason's shoulder. "I know it's hard not to talk like the other guys do," he added, "but language can stall a Christian's witness before he even gets started."

"Right, Dad." Jason nodded and turned to his task of cutting the lawn. *R.K.M.*

HOW ABOUT YOU?

Do you think using a few bad words or mild oaths won't hurt your Christian witness? Think again. Both saved and unsaved kids are listening to you. There are always popular expressions around that don't contain vulgar meanings or profanity. Use them instead.

MEMORIZE:

"Don't use bad language. Say only what is good and helpful to those you are talking to."

Ephesians 4:29, TLB

 Don't Use Bad Language

A Weighty Problem (Read John 5:2-9)

7

MAY

At the sound of footsteps, Becky tried to hide the bag of potato chips. She was too late, though, because Mom was already in her room. "Becky, Mrs. Martin called and wondered if you would baby-sit Freddie on Saturday night," said Mom.

"Sure." Becky nodded. "The money can help me get that red plaid outfit sooner." In another week or two Becky figured she would have enough money for it.

"If you keep eating junk food, Becky, you may not be able to wear the outfit when you get it." Mom's words were gentle, but they added to Becky's guilt.

"I know, Mom," said Becky with a sigh. "I stopped at the drugstore to get some paper. I wasn't going to buy any snacks, but I saw someone eating potato chips, and I just had to have some."

Mom reminded Becky of their visit to the doctor, who had explained how important it was for Becky's health to get rid of her excess weight and keep it off. Becky agreed that she needed to discipline herself, but she always reasoned that she would indulge her appetite just one more time. "Would you like to pray about this, Becky?" Mom asked now.

Becky nodded. She wondered how much good it would do, though, because she often prayed about her weight problem.

After praying, Mom gave Becky a hug. "Sometimes it helps to keep a special Scripture in mind as you deal with a problem," she said. "I'm thinking of the Scripture that tells about Jesus healing the man at the pool of Bethesda. Before Jesus healed him, he asked him if he wanted to be healed."

"That seems like a strange question," said Becky.

"At first it does," agreed Mom. "But think about it—do you really want not to eat junk food?" Becky nodded. She still thought it was a strange question.

On Saturday evening, Mrs. Martin showed Becky what snacks were available. Later, when Becky was about to open the cookie jar, she imagined Jesus saying to her, "Do you want to be healed?" Then she chose an apple instead. *E.M.B.*

HOW ABOUT YOU?

Do you have a bad habit you'd like to get rid of? Overeating? Gossiping? Bad thoughts? Are you willing for God to take away the pleasure that your bad habit gives you? When you really want to be healed, Jesus will help you.

MEMORIZE:

"**Do you want to be made well?**" *John 5:6, NKJV*

🗝 *Desire Healing*

Columbia Hill (Read James 1:2-6, 12)

8
MAY

"Not again!" groaned Randy at the end of a busy afternoon. "I delivered groceries to Mrs. Jensen just this morning."

"Sorry, Randy, but she forgot a few items that she needs," said Mr. Brown, owner of Brown's Grocery Store.

"But she lives way up on Columbia Hill!"

"I know," Mr. Brown replied, "but she's forgetful. She's also one of our best customers—probably because we still offer free delivery."

Randy packed the groceries into his basket carrier and set out on his bike for the last delivery of the day. At the foot of the hill, he took a deep breath and began to pedal furiously. Halfway up, he got off his bike and pushed it the rest of the way. Then, after delivering the order to a grateful Mrs. Jensen, he coasted down the hill and headed home.

During dinner that evening, Randy was unusually quiet. "Tired out, Son?" asked his father.

Randy nodded. "Look, Dad," he said, "I think I'll quit my Saturday delivery job."

"Why is that?" asked Dad. "I thought you liked your job."

"It would be OK if it weren't for Columbia Hill," Randy told him. "Sometimes I have to climb it twice a day."

"Well, it's your decision, but don't make up your mind too quickly," said Dad. "After all, you'll be confronted with 'Columbia Hills' all your life. Learn to climb them now, and then you'll be strong enough to tackle life's bigger problems."

"I don't see how Columbia Hill can help me when I get older."

"Columbia Hill is your big problem right now," his father explained, "and the only way to solve it is to climb it. Doing that instead of running away strengthens you in a number of ways. Throughout your life you'll have other problems. The only way to solve them is to ask God's help and then face them squarely, too. As you do so, you grow spiritually."

Randy picked up his glass of milk. "Well, thanks to Mrs. Jensen, I'm developing strong leg muscles anyway." Then he grinned. "OK, I'll keep at it." *E.A.S.*

HOW ABOUT YOU?

Are there "Columbia Hills" in your life—problems you don't want to face? Are there problems with parents, brothers and sisters, health, school, or peer pressure? Remember that you aren't alone. God will help you meet your "Columbia Hills" and overcome them.

MEMORIZE:

"I can do all things through Christ who strengthens me."

Philippians 4:13, NKJV

 God Gives Strength

Hidden Eagles (Read Isaiah 40:25-31)

While Sandra waited for Grandma to finish making their sandwiches, she walked over to the porch swing where her grandfather was carving a small block of wood with his knife. "What are you doing, Grandpa?" she asked, sitting down beside him.

Grandpa smiled and without stopping said, "There's an eagle trapped in this wood, and I'm setting it free."

Sandra looked closely at the block in his hands and then up at Grandpa. "Huh?" she said. She screwed up her face in confusion. "I don't see anything in there."

Grandpa smiled and stopped carving for a moment. "Well, it's there all right," he insisted, turning the wood block in his hand. "When you come back from the zoo later this evening, I'll show it to you."

Sandra didn't quite believe him, but before she could say anything, Grandma called her. "Coming, Grandma," Sandra said. "See you later, Grandpa."

That evening when they all sat down to dinner, Grandpa placed a freshly carved eagle beside Sandra's plate. "There you are, young lady," he said with a wink. "There's the eagle I set free from the wood."

Sandra's eyes grew wide with excitement. "Oooh! It's so pretty," she said.

"I want you to have it, sweetheart," said Grandpa with a smile. "And whenever you look at it, I want you to remember something very special." Sandra looked expectantly at him. "You couldn't see the eagle in the block of wood this morning, but I could," continued Grandpa. "It just took some time to bring it out. In a similar way, God sees within you a very special creation. You might not see it yet. But he does. And in time the *hidden* Sandra inside you will become a beautiful sculpture in his hands."

Lost in thought, Sandra looked again at the eagle. Finally she put it down and turned to Grandpa. "Thank you," she said. "I wonder what God is going to do with me." *R.S.M.*

9
MAY

HOW ABOUT YOU?

Do you know that God has a plan for your life? Ask him to have his way in your life, and you'll be surprised by what he will do.

MEMORIZE:

"**They that wait upon the Lord shall renew their strength. They shall mount up with wings like eagles.**" *Isaiah 40:31*, TLB

Let God "Sculpt" You

Pen Pals (Read John 20:26-29)

10
MAY

Becky walked home from Sunday school with Janie, her next-door neighbor. They were talking about the lesson they had just heard. "I don't know if I really believe there's a God," Becky confided. "Do you?"

Janie's brown eyes opened wide. "Of course," she said.

Becky frowned. "Well, you've gone to church all your life," she said. "I guess that makes it easier. But . . . you've never seen God, have you?"

"No," admitted Janie, "but I still know he's real."

Becky shrugged. "How can you be so sure?" she asked. But they had arrived at home, and she turned up her walk before Janie could answer. "See you tomorrow," she called.

The next day, Becky's mother picked up the girls after school. She greeted them and then asked, "Becky, do you remember the magazine with the pen pal column in it?"

"Yes! Did anyone write?" asked Becky eagerly.

"What's a pen pal column?" asked Janie before Becky's mother could answer.

"It's a column in one of the magazines we get," explained Becky. "Kids who want to exchange letters with somebody put their name, address, age, and hobbies and stuff in it, and then other kids see it and write to them. I put mine in this month's issue." She turned back to her mother. "Mom, did I get a letter?" Her mother smiled and handed her an envelope. Becky quickly tore it open. She began reading the letter from a girl named Susan, and she let Janie read it.

At home, the girls talked about the letter before going to their separate houses. Janie looked at Becky. "I was wondering," she said, "do you think Susan is real?"

Becky looked at Janie as if she had lost her mind. "Of course she's real. I got her letter, didn't I?"

"Well, you said you didn't know if God was real," Janie reminded her, "but my dad says he wrote us a letter, too. We call it the Bible."

Becky stared at Janie. Then she grinned. Suddenly, she knew God was very real, just as Susan was. *M.P.C.*

HOW ABOUT YOU?

Do you have trouble believing in an invisible God? Look around at all the things he has done. The beauty of a sunset, the rainbow, the growing plants, the animals, and even yourself. He made them all. Read the Bible, God's letter to you, and believe in him. You don't need to see God to love him.

MEMORIZE:

"Blessed are those who have not seen [Jesus], and yet have believed." *John 20:29,* NIV

 *Believe in God*

Leaning Lisa (Read Psalm 18:1-3, 30-32)

11
MAY

"Can you drill me on some review questions for a test, Dad?" asked Lisa one evening. Dad agreed, so Lisa went to her room and came back with her schoolbooks.

Dad asked Lisa several questions. "Just a few to go," he said finally. "What's the name of the tower in Italy that leans?"

"The leaning tower of Pisa," Lisa said promptly.

"And how high is it?" asked Dad.

"About as high as a fifteen-story building in the United States," Lisa replied.

Dad looked at the next question. "Was the leaning tower meant to lean?"

"No," Lisa said. "It was supposed to stand straight."

"You know this material well," said Dad, closing the book. "I'm going to have to make up some harder questions for you. What holds up the leaning tower of Pisa?"

Lisa was stumped. "It leans but doesn't fall, but what keeps it from falling?" she murmured. "Is God standing there holding it up?" she asked with a grin.

"No," said Dad, "but that answer brings another question to mind. What leans that God *does* hold up?" Lisa thought hard. "Hint," Dad said. "God intended for this part of his creation to lean on him for support." Lisa still didn't know. "Last hint," Dad said, and he sang a few lines of a hymn about "leaning on the everlasting arms."

"Us!" Lisa exclaimed. "God made us to lean on him."

"That's right," Dad said. "God doesn't want us to be proud and to think we can handle everything on our own without him. He wants us to lean on him for support and direction." He paused. "I'm not sure what holds up the leaning tower of Pisa," he added. "Some people believe it will fall someday, but we can lean on the Lord forever, and we never have to fear falling."

"So I can be 'Leaning Lisa.' Isn't that neat?" said Lisa with a smile. "I'll try to remember that." *N.E.K.*

HOW ABOUT YOU?

Do you think you need to be tough and handle your problems alone? Humble yourself and lean on Jesus. He is there waiting to support you.

MEMORIZE:

"[God] fills me with strength and protects me wherever I go." *Psalm 18:32,* TLB

Lean on God

Memory Work (Read Psalm 37:27-31)

12
MAY

Bonnie's little sister Ann recited the entire alphabet without one mistake. "I can write my name, too," Ann said, proud of her accomplishments. "I memorized it."

"Another good thing to memorize is our phone number," Bonnie told her.

"Why?" Ann asked, giggling. "Why would I call us?"

"What if you got lost?" asked Bonnie. "Or what if there was an emergency and you needed to call Mommy from a friend's house?"

"OK," agreed Ann. "I'll learn it."

"The more you say the number, the easier it is to remember it," Bonnie told her.

Ann repeated the number over and over.

"And now you should go next door and practice calling here," said Bonnie. "Practicing it will help you remember."

"Just like with your Bible verses," said Mom, having overheard the conversation. She looked at Bonnie as she asked, "Have you learned your memory verse for Sunday school yet?" Bonnie made a face. She always put off learning her verses; it seemed boring and too hard to remember all the words. "You gave Ann a good reason to learn our phone number," Mom said. "Having a reason is an important part of memorization."

"But I don't care if I get stickers on the Sunday school memory chart," Bonnie said.

"Memorize to please God and to keep his Word fresh in your mind," suggested Mom. "Then it will be there to use when you need it."

"Like our phone number," said Ann, repeating it a few times. "Can I go next door and call you now?"

Mom nodded as she looked at Bonnie. "Follow the guidelines you gave Ann for learning our phone number, and I think you'll find learning your memory verses easier—even fun," she said. "When you practice living what the verses say, it helps you remember them." *N.E.K.*

HOW ABOUT YOU?

Is Bible memory work sometimes a chore? Having a reason to memorize, understanding the words, and practicing the truths in your life will make it easier.

MEMORIZE:

"Keep in memory what I preached unto you."

1 Corinthians 15:2, KJV

 Memorize Scripture

Drifting (Read Revelation 2:1-5)

"I'm beginning to wonder if there are any fish in this bay," said Dad, as he baited his hook with yet another worm. He and Sara had been fishing in Jabber's Bay for nearly two hours. "We'd better catch more than we have so far," he said with a chuckle, "or Mother will have us take her out for dinner." Sara laughed out loud as she looked into the pail of fish they had caught that morning. Two little fish were certainly not enough for dinner.

13
MAY

Sara and her dad had been quiet for a while when he noticed that their boat had drifted closer toward the shore. "Hmmm," said Dad as he began reeling in his line. "We better get back toward the middle of the bay. We may damage the boat if we get in too close to those rocks along the shoreline."

Sara also reeled in her line. She watched as her father rowed away from the shore. "I can't believe how quickly we drifted from the spot where we started," she said as he pulled hard on the oars. Soon they were back in the middle of the bay, fishing again.

"You know," said Dad after a while, "I've been thinking how much our spiritual lives are like fishing." Sara looked puzzled, and Dad continued, "We were so busy fishing that we didn't notice we were drifting. And as Christians, we can be so busy with things of this life that we don't notice we've drifted away from the Lord."

Sara thought in silence for a moment and then slowly nodded her head. "I guess it is easy to forget about the Lord sometimes," she agreed.

Dad watched as the water lapped against the side of the boat. "Yes," he answered softly, "sometimes it sure is easy. We need to guard against that." *R.S.M.*

HOW ABOUT YOU?

Are you so busy watching TV, playing with your friends, or doing schoolwork that you have less and less time to spend with God? If you've drifted away from time spent with God, talk to him about it. With his help, pull back from other things and spend more time on the things that please him.

MEMORIZE:

"Let us not become weary in doing good, for at the proper time we will reap a harvest if we do not give up."

Galatians 6:9, NIV

 Spend Time Every Day with God

The Garage Sale (Read Ephesians 4:22-32)

14
MAY

"When you get the garage floor swept we'll be able to set up the tables," Joey's father told him.

"OK," said Joey. "This garage sale will be a good way to clear out all this stuff and get the garage clean, won't it?" He pointed to a shelf. "What's in that box?" he asked.

His father took the box down. Setting it on the floor, they looked inside. "Looks like some of your old toys," said Dad.

"I remember this," Joey said, reaching for a baseball.

"I remember it, too," his father said, taking the ball from Joey. "I still can hear the breaking of glass from Mr. Will's window." He put the baseball back into the box.

"Well, maybe I should keep it," Joey said. He took the ball out and set it aside. "It'll be good to get rid of the rest of this junk," he said, peering into the box.

"That ball is totally worn out, Son," said Dad. He reached over and put the baseball back into the box. "You remind me of the way some people 'change' their habit patterns. God expects us to get rid of old, bad habits, and people often say they want to do that. But they still hang on to old habits, even if they cause nothing but problems."

"This old ball won't get me into trouble," Joey said, taking the baseball out.

"Yep," said Dad. "That's just the kind of thing people say when they want to keep something they shouldn't. But they need to let go of their old habits. Then they can develop new, more rewarding ones." He grinned at Joey as he added, "Keep the old ball if you want to, Son, but do get rid of bad habits."

Joey grinned back. Then he held out his hand and let the ball fall into the box. *G.G.L.*

HOW ABOUT YOU?

Do you have some old habits you should change? Ask God for strength to do it. Follow his command to put away the things that displease him.

MEMORIZE:

"Away then with sinful, earthly things; deaden the evil desires lurking within you."

Colossians 3:5, TLB

 Get Rid of Bad Habits

The Wren's Warning (Read Matthew 2:13-15; Ephesians 6:1-4)

Eva came running into the house as Mother was taking out the last batch of cookies. "Mother, come quick," she said breathlessly. "I think something's wrong with our wren. He's making a strange sound. He must be hurt."

Eva and Mother hurried out to the front yard, but when they stopped to listen to the wren, he was singing as usual. "Are you sure it was the wren that you heard?" asked Mother. "There are a lot of other birds around here."

15
MAY

"It was the wren," insisted Eva. "I saw him on that branch, and he was making a strange sound." She pointed to a branch of the big holly bush.

Mother began walking slowly across the lawn. Mr. Wren kept singing merrily. But as Mother came close to the holly bush, the wren's song changed. *"Chrr-rr-rr."* He watched Mother closely, his voice getting softer as she neared the bush. Mother stopped and quietly pointed to a nest of baby wrens deep in the branches. "The wren was talking to the babies," she said. "That's his way of telling them to keep quiet. Danger is near."

"You mean birds tell their babies things like that?" Eva had never known that before.

Mother nodded. "God teaches all birds and animals how to protect their young," she said. "He also tells us as parents to protect our children from harm. That's why we must sometimes say no to things you want to do or places you want to go." She smiled at Eva. "Many stories in the Bible show how parents protected their children," she added. "One very special story tells how God used Joseph and Mary to protect baby Jesus when he was in danger." *D.R.O.*

HOW ABOUT YOU?

Are you sad—or even angry—when your parents say no to some things? Or are you glad they love you enough to keep you from harm? They're doing the job God gave them. The job he gives you is to honor and obey them.

MEMORIZE:

"'Honor your father and mother'—which is the first commandment with a promise." *Ephesians 6:2,* NIV

 Honor Your Parents

Road Signs (Read 1 Peter 4:7-11)

16
MAY

As they traveled, Jonathan and his sister Judy watched the scenery go by. "Let's play I Spy," suggested Jonathan.

"Good idea," agreed Judy. "Maybe it will make the miles go faster. I'll start first—and I spy something red."

Jonathan looked around. "Is it that red truck?" he asked. Judy nodded, and it was Jonathan's turn.

Before long, the children got tired of their game. "How much farther?" asked Jonathan.

"I haven't been paying attention," said Dad. He glanced across the seat and grinned. "Mom hasn't been watching road signs, either. She's asleep," he added.

Dad's voice woke Mother. "I'm not asleep," she said, sitting up straight. The others laughed. "Let's stop for something to eat," she suggested. "Did anybody see any signs for restaurants?" Nobody had.

Jonathan sighed. "We all missed the signs. Maybe another one will come up before long."

"Make a note of this experience," said Dad. He pulled a little notebook and pen from his pocket and handed them to Mother. Jonathan grinned; Dad was always looking for sermon illustrations. "This reminds me of our spiritual lives," continued Dad. "God gives road signs along our way to heaven, but if we're too busy with the things of the world, we may miss God's signs."

"What are God's signs, Dad?" asked Jonathan.

"Help me think of some," said Dad. "One that comes to my mind is, 'Believe on the Lord Jesus Christ and thou shalt be saved.' That's the most important one of all."

"I know one," said Mom. "It's 'Study to show thyself approved unto God.' We certainly need to study God's Word as we travel through this life."

"'Pray without ceasing' is a good one," added Judy.

"How about, 'Forgive and ye shall be forgiven'?" suggested Jonathan. Then he pointed. "Look!" he shouted. "There's a sign that says there's food at the next exit."

Dad smiled and nodded. "You see," he said, "it pays to watch the signs." *M.P.C.*

HOW ABOUT YOU?

Are you being careful to read God's Word and to listen to teachers and preachers who help you learn about God's "road signs"? Do so—it pays!

MEMORIZE:

"Watch and pray, that ye enter not into temptation."

Matthew 26:41, KJV

 Watch for God's "Road Signs"

Parasitic Christians (Read Hebrews 10:19-25)

"We just gave Barnie a bath yesterday, but he's scratching again," said Sally. She sat beside her dog and rubbed his fur.

"Those pesty parasites!" said Mom. "Maybe he needs a new flea collar."

"Parasites?" asked Sally. "I thought Barnie had fleas."

"Fleas are parasites—they live off animals, taking from them but giving nothing in return," explained Mom. "But we'll worry about them later. Right now you need to get ready for Sunday school."

17
MAY

"Do I *have* to go today?" Sally asked. Seeing Mother's frown, she added, "After all, I'm already a Christian—I have Jesus in my heart."

Just then Dad stuck his head into the room. "You two need to hurry," he said.

"Barnie has parasites," said Sally. "They live off of him but give nothing in return—those selfish, unthankful fleas!"

"I wonder if you could be living like a parasite yourself," Mom said thoughtfully.

"What's that supposed to mean?" demanded Sally.

"I'm wondering if you're a parasitic Christian," Mom told her, "living off God—your heavenly Host—and accepting his forgiveness, protection, and eternal life without giving anything in return."

"But I don't have to give anything for those things," protested Sally. "They're free gifts from God."

"Yes, they are," agreed Mom, "but God wants you to love him, to obey him, and to worship him."

"That's true," put in Dad. "Sometimes Christians want to just take everything God has to give without giving anything back—not even appreciation."

As Barnie scratched again, Sally looked at him thoughtfully. Then she got up and hurried to get ready for church. *N.E.K.*

HOW ABOUT YOU?

Do you take everything you can from God without giving anything in return? Remember to show your commitment to God by giving him your love, time, obedience, and worship—through church attendance, Bible study, and serving him by serving others.

MEMORIZE:

"Let us hold unswervingly to the hope we profess. . . . Let us not give up meeting together." *Hebrews 10:23, 25,* NIV

 *Give Back to God*

The Human Paddle (Read Hebrews 12:5-11)

18 MAY

"Sally, please stop interrupting me," Miss Delta said loudly and firmly. Sally scowled. Several times that day Miss Delta had scolded her, and Sally was getting tired of it. After all, she had only been trying to help.

At home that evening, Sally complained to her parents about it. "I think Miss Delta just likes to pick on me. She never yells at anybody else," grumbled Sally. As she talked, she noticed her puppy Tony digging in the herb garden. Quickly she grabbed a rolled-up newspaper that was lying at the back door and ran out to the garden. *Whapp!* went the paper.

"*Ow-wow-wow!*" howled the puppy.

"I've told that puppy a million times not to dig," said Sally when she returned to the house, "and I've spanked him for it often enough, too. When will he ever learn?"

"He'll learn," Dad assured her. "It just takes time." With a thoughtful smile, he asked, "Do you suppose Tony ever wonders why that rolled-up newspaper spanks only him and nobody else?"

"He oughta know it's because he deserves it," Sally replied. Then she laughed. "Only the paper isn't spanking him. I am."

"True," agreed Dad. "You're doing the spanking; you're just using the paper as a sort of paddle to do it, right?"

"Right," Sally agreed.

"Now suppose God wanted to 'spank' you," suggested Dad. "Don't you think he would probably use a paddle of some sort?"

Sally frowned. "What are you getting at?" she asked.

"Well," said Dad, "God sometimes uses people as his paddles. Did you ever wonder if he might be trying to tell you something through Miss Delta?"

"I . . . I . . ." Sally didn't know what to say.

"Perhaps God wants to change you in some way and has been talking to you all this time, and you haven't been hearing him," added Dad.

Sally grinned as she added, "He's been talking loud, too!"

C.S.S.

HOW ABOUT YOU?

Can you think of any time God has used someone as a "paddle" on you? The people you think are picking on you—even your brothers and sisters—are often being used by God to change you and help you do the right thing. Pay attention to the "spankings."

MEMORIZE:

"When [God] punishes you, it proves that he loves you."

Hebrews 12:6, TLB

 *Let God Change You*

Sidetracked (Read Nehemiah 6:1-4)

19
MAY

As Mr. Matthews finished the Sunday school lesson, he said, "I've learned of a way you kids can do some work for the Lord. Several members of our church are shut-ins, and the pastor tells me they could use some help. Here's a list of their names. Do you see someone you'd be willing to help?"

Jeffrey looked at the list. "I could help Mrs. Johnson," he offered. "She lives near me."

The sweet old lady was pleased to have Jeffrey's help. She asked him to water her garden, as she was unable to do that. "Sure. You can count on me," Jeffrey told her. And for a few weeks, he faithfully kept his promise. But then he began to neglect the plants. There were other things that took his time.

"Look what my electric train can do, Dad," Jeffrey said one afternoon. He placed two engines on the track several feet apart and pushed some buttons. The engines raced around the track. Then Jeffrey flipped a switch. One engine ran onto a sidetrack and stopped, while the other one continued to roll along the main track. "See, Dad, I sidetracked the one and kept the other one going," explained Jeffrey.

Dad nodded. "Good," he said. He looked thoughtfully at the sidetracked engine. "It occurs to me that Christians who start out serving the Lord are sometimes like that sidetracked engine—going no place. In fact, I wonder if you're like that yourself right now, Son."

Jeffrey looked up, surprised. "Me? How's that?"

"Well, I remember that you were quick to promise to do something good," replied Dad, "and that's great! But lately you've been forgetting to do it. In other words, you got sidetracked." He paused a moment before adding, "I went by Mrs. Johnson's house today. The plants in her garden look pretty wilted."

"Oh-oh! I forgot," exclaimed Jeffrey. He looked at the two engines. "I'd rather be like the one that kept going," he said as he headed for the door. "If I hurry, I can still get those plants watered before dark." *M.R.P.*

HOW ABOUT YOU?

Have you begun to serve the Lord by doing something? Perhaps it's attending church, tithing, helping a needy person, or being kind and helpful at home. Have you kept at it? Starting out to do right is great, but keeping at it is much better. Don't get sidetracked!

MEMORIZE:

"I have stayed in God's paths, following his steps. I have not turned aside." *Job 23:11,* TLB

 Be Faithful in God's Service

Spilled Milk (Read Matthew 7:1-5)

20
MAY

"You'll never believe what Carl did in school today," announced Eric. He reached for a dinner roll and took a big bite.

"What did he do this time?" asked Dad. Eric's family was getting used to hearing about Carl every night at dinner.

"First, he got sent to the principal for having all the spelling words written on his hand during our test," said Eric. "Then when he came back, he wrote a nasty poem about Mrs. Sanderson and passed it to the kid in front of him. He got caught and had to go to the principal again!" Eric rolled his eyes. "I would never do the things he does," he added.

Just then Eric's little brother Tim bumped his glass. Milk ran all over the table and into Eric's lap. "Hey, you creep!" yelled Eric. "These are my new jeans!"

"You don't need to yell, Eric," said Dad sternly as Eric jumped up and Tim began to cry. "It was an accident. And please don't call your brother names."

"He should be more careful," declared Eric, still angry.

After the mess was mopped up and Eric had changed his jeans, Mom said, "You know, Eric, you've been telling us about all the bad things Carl does, and how you would never do those things. But I believe you have the same problem Carl has."

Eric was stunned. "What do you mean?" he demanded. "I'm not like Carl at all."

Dad nodded. "Yes, you are," he said. "The Bible tells us we're all sinners. And it warns us not to judge others when there's sin in our own lives. After all, who's to say what's worse—cheating on a test or losing one's temper?"

"Or writing a nasty poem or calling someone nasty names?" added Mother.

Eric's face turned red. "I . . . I'm sorry, Tim," he mumbled.

Dad smiled. "The difference between you and Carl may be that you know Jesus as your Savior; perhaps Carl does not. Instead of judging him, we need to pray that he'll come to know Jesus, too."

L.J.O.

HOW ABOUT YOU?

Do you easily notice the sins of others but have a hard time admitting your own sins? Acknowledge your sin to God and humbly ask him for forgiveness and help in overcoming it. And be careful about judging others.

MEMORIZE:

"Do not judge, or you too will be judged." *Matthew 7:1,* NIV

 Admit Your Own Sin

Hide-and-Seek (Read Luke 4:1-13)

". . . forty-eight, forty-nine, fifty," Dad counted. "Ready or not, here I come!"

Mark scrunched sideways into the small hole under the porch and pulled his knees up to his chest. "No!" he exclaimed suddenly as his little sister tried to wriggle in with him. "Go away. There's not enough room here, and if Dad sees you, he'll find me, too. Go find your own place."

"I wanta hide with you," said Katie. Tears filled her eyes.

"Gotcha!" cried Dad. He swooped down on them and swung Katie off the ground. Mark groaned and straightened his legs. "OK, Mark. Your turn to be the seeker," said Dad.

Mark crawled out slowly. "That's not fair," he protested. "Katie gave me away."

"You could have let her hide with you," said Dad.

"There wasn't enough room," grumbled Mark.

Dad stooped down and poked his head into the hole. "It is kind of small," he agreed.

"Yeah, and we learned in science class that two things can't be in the exact same space at the exact same time. That hole's so small that there's only room for one person, so when I'm in it, there's not room for you, Katie, and when you're in it, there's not room for me."

"You know what?" said Dad. "This hole kind of reminds me of your memory verse last Sunday."

"Huh?" Mark frowned.

"Well, what was your verse last Sunday?" Dad asked.

"It was . . . uh . . . 'Thy word have I hid in mine heart, that I might not sin against Thee,'" Mark replied, "but . . ."

"Pretend you or Katie are God's Word and the hole is your heart," Dad suggested.

Mark studied his sister. "I get it," he said. "If I really hide God's Word in my heart, there won't be room for things like fighting."

Dad smiled. "Exactly. God's Word doesn't leave space in our hearts for sin." *J.A.B.*

21
MAY

HOW ABOUT YOU?

What do you do when you're tempted to lie or call someone names or argue with others? Are there verses from God's Word hidden in your heart so that you can think about them and about how God wants you to respond to that temptation? Memorize his Word. You'll be surprised how much it helps.

MEMORIZE:

"Thy word have I hid in mine heart, that I might not sin against Thee." *Psalm 119:11,* KJV

 Memorize God's Word

A Walk in the Woods (Read Colossians 1:15-18)

22
MAY

"Would you like to come to Sunday school with me, Jill?" asked Angie as the two girls walked up the wooded hill behind Angie's house. Everyone in their science class had to identify twenty-five different wild flowers, so they had decided to go on a hike and see how many they could find.

In answer to Angie's question, Jill shook her head. "My parents believe you can get closer to God walking in the woods than you can sitting in some boring, old building reading an out-of-date book," she said. "I think that's true."

"Well, that sounds good," admitted Angie, "but we need to know what God says in his Word, too."

"My dad says it's better our way," insisted Jill. She pointed. "Look at that field—it's practically covered with flowers!"

"Wow!" Angie exclaimed. "Get out that guidebook on wild flowers that we brought from school, Jill."

"I didn't bring the book," said Jill. "Didn't you bring it?" She groaned as Angie shook her head.

"Oh, well," said Angie after a moment, "I guess that's an awfully old book anyway. It was probably written before we were even born. I bet looking at the flowers will do us a lot more good than the stuff we'd learn from such an out-of-date book."

"Wildflowers don't change!" protested Jill. "That book is still good!"

"So is the Bible," Angie said softly. "It's as important today as it was when it was first written. God doesn't change, either. And even though we like to look at his creation, we still need to learn about God through his Word—just like we need to learn about the flowers from the book." *L.W.*

HOW ABOUT YOU?

Do you think you can learn more about God by looking at his creation than you can by going to church? Do you ever use that as an excuse to skip church and go fishing or hiking? You should appreciate what God has created, but it's even more important to learn what's in his Word.

MEMORIZE:

"He was before all else began and it is his power that holds everything together."

Colossians 1:17, TLB

 Honor the Creator

A Messed-Up Garden (Read 2 Chronicles 33:1-5)

Randy went outside when he saw his friend Sean in the yard next door. "Hey, Randy, wanna play soccer?" Sean asked from his side of the fence. "Except we'll have to play in your yard. Dad spent two days working on the lawn and reseeding it, and guess what? My little brother and his friends messed it all up again."

"How did they do that?" asked Randy, looking over the fence.

Sean laughed. "Oh, they thought they were helping by spreading more seeds. But they just trampled the part he had done and made a general mess of everything. Dad had to do it all over, and now he says everybody's gonna stay off it." Sean bounced the ball. "Can you play?" he asked again.

Randy shook his head. "I can't play now. I gotta go to some silly meeting at church," he said. "All we do is sing and listen to the preacher talk. It's boring!" Randy's father was calling from the porch, and Randy hurried off.

"Poor Mr. Stevens," Randy said when he told his dad about the lawn. "He worked so hard, only to have his son ruin it."

"I know how he feels," answered Dad. "I've been working hard at planting seed, too—the seed of the Word of God. I've been talking to Mr. Stevens about the Lord for three years. He finally showed some interest. He asked a lot of questions—and Sean asked some questions, too." Randy didn't understand what Dad was trying to tell him. "Before we left for church today, I heard you tell Sean that church was boring," said Dad, "and I'm afraid that didn't help the 'seed of the Word' to grow. In fact, I'm concerned that you may have messed it up." *L.W.*

23 MAY

HOW ABOUT YOU?

Do you look for ways to plant the seed of the Word, or do you "mess up" what other people have planted by complaining about church or by showing a lack of interest in God's Word? Be a good "gardener" and show others that you are excited about your faith in the Lord Jesus Christ.

MEMORIZE:

"The seed is the word of God."

Luke 8:11, KJV

 Help Plant the Seed of God's Word

The Sensible Saguaro (Read Psalm 119:9-16)

24
MAY

"What a prickly horror!" Sherry giggled as she stood beside a huge saguaro cactus with its spiny arms reaching out and up in odd positions. "You'd think that with so many big, strong arms, this thing could at least be holding something!" she said.

"Well, it is," Dad told her. "Those arms are holding what is probably the most valuable thing in the entire region."

Sherry's brother Bob nodded. "And I know what it is," he said. "Water! Cactus plants adapt to the dry, hot climate by storing water inside their stems and leaves."

"Is that so, Mr. Smartie!" said Sherry. "Just because you took a course in biology doesn't mean you know everything."

"Bob is right this time," said Dad. "These big fellas can soak up as much as 200 gallons of water—enough to last them a whole year!"

"Yeah, that's why they're pleated like an accordion," Bob put in, eager to show his knowledge. "The pleats expand as the spongy material inside absorbs the water."

"Right," Dad agreed. "And the roots don't go deep into the earth but lie just below the surface, spreading a hundred feet in all directions. Those hairlike roots draw in every drop of rain, sending it to that hidden storage area in the arms and trunk of the cactus. That inner water supply is what keeps this cactus alive and growing."

"Really?" asked Sherry. "Well, I guess it isn't such a horror after all. In fact, this one seems to have a nice personality—like a kind old man with a very sharp beard!"

Dad smiled. "And this wise old man has some good advice for us," he said.

"About storing water?" asked Bob. "I don't really mind carrying a canteen—and I like the size of my arms the way they are!"

Dad laughed. "I wasn't thinking of your arms, Son," he said. "Let's try your heart! I hope both of you will store God's Word in your heart—that hidden place inside of you. Knowing God's Word will help you mature into Christians who are pleasing in God's sight." *T.M.V.*

HOW ABOUT YOU?

Have you been growing spiritually? If not, could it be that you are not storing God's Word in your heart? Memorizing his Word will help keep you from sin and make it easier to obey him.

MEMORIZE:

"I have hidden your word in my heart that I might not sin against you." *Psalm 119:11,* NIV

 Soak Up God's Word

Rules for Living (Read Proverbs 2:1-11, 20)

25
MAY

Abby looked up from her Sunday school lesson book. "It seems to me that the Bible is full of rules," she observed. "Doesn't God want us to have any fun?"

"We can have lots of fun and still stay within the rules," said Dad. He put his newspaper on the sofa and took off his glasses. "It may not always seem like it, but God's rules actually help you enjoy life."

Abby closed her book and looked out the window. "It's a windy day, Dad," she said, changing the subject. "Could we go try the new kite I got for my birthday?"

"Good idea," agreed Dad. "Let's go to the park and see if it will fly."

Abby ran to get the kite from her closet. Then she and Dad walked down the street to the neighborhood park where many kites dotted the sky with their bright colors.

Dad helped Abby get the kite flying. Then he put the string entirely into her hands. Abby held tightly. She laughed as she felt the wind lift and move the kite. "My kite pulls and tugs at the string as if it were alive," she called to Dad.

Dad nodded. "Think of the fun it would be to soar with the wind and not be held back," he replied. "Wouldn't the kite look beautiful? It would go much higher without the string. Why don't you let it go?"

Abby stared at her father. "But, Dad, if I do, my kite might be lost. Or it might crash and get torn. I don't want that to happen. I like my kite!" She held the string even more tightly.

"I like my kite," Abby repeated on the way home. "I can't believe you wanted me to let it go, Dad."

Dad grinned. "The string is important, right?" he asked. Abby nodded. "God's rules are something like that string, Abby," said Dad. "God gave rules to us to keep us safe and to allow us to enjoy life. When you feel like you'd rather be free of his rules, remember the string on your kite." *B.M.*

HOW ABOUT YOU?

Do you think God's rules keep you from having fun? Actually, they keep you from trouble and let you lead a happy, healthy Christian life. They teach you wisdom.

MEMORIZE:

"Incline your ear to wisdom, and apply your heart to understanding." *Proverbs 2:2,* NKJV

 God Knows Best

In the Dark (Read Psalm 119:97-105)

26
MAY

The evening service was over, and Michael went to help his mother straighten up the nursery. Rain poured outside, so when they were almost finished, Mom went to get the car while Michael picked up the few remaining toys. Just as he was ready to leave, a crash of thunder shook the building, and the power went out! "Oh, great!" he said, waiting for his eyes to adjust to the blackness. They didn't. The room was deep in the building and had no windows. He would just have to be careful.

Michael walked cautiously toward the door. Something bumped his knee. He reached down and felt a table the toddlers used. He stepped to the right. *"Ow!"* he exclaimed. His head caught the corner of a shelf, which rattled as books fell. Michael groped for the wall. *This isn't like the power going off at home,* he thought. *There you know where things are.* Though he wasn't afraid of the dark, an uneasy feeling gripped him. He edged around a long table, then straight into the stack of building blocks. They tumbled as Michael fell to his knees. *This is ridiculous,* he thought. He found the wall and moved slowly toward the door. *Where is Mom, anyway?*

The verse his class had learned that day about God's Word being "a light for my path" popped around in his head. *I guess knowing God and his Word is like a Christian's electricity,* Michael decided. *And I'd sure never want to be without it. Stumbling through the nursery in the dark is bad enough. Stumbling through life that way would be horrible!*

Then, at the end of the hall, a flashlight flickered. "Hang on, Son," called Mom. "I'm coming." *D.W.S.*

HOW ABOUT YOU?

Is it sometimes hard to "see" what you should do—what decisions you should make? Are right and wrong not always clear? As you get to know God through prayer and Bible study, his light will shine in your mind, and you'll be able to make the choices that please him. Don't stumble through life without his help.

MEMORIZE:

"Your word is a lamp to my feet and a light for my path."

Psalm 119:105, NIV

 *Use God's Light*

Detour (Read Proverbs 3:1-6)

"Uh-oh," said Mother. "We can't make our turn onto the freeway. The ramp is closed for repairs, and the sign says, 'Detour—Straight Ahead.'" She drove on down the road.

"But we're going away from the freeway," said Jenny, looking out the back window. "We have to get on it somehow, don't we?"

27

MAY

"We will if we follow the orange detour signs," said Mother. "See if you can find the next one."

"There it is," said Jenny, pointing ahead, "but we'll still be going the wrong way. I'll bet someone switched the signs. We can't go this way and get back on the freeway!"

"Now don't get excited," said Mother. "Let's just do what the sign says." She turned right at the sign. The next sign also said to go right, and the next said to go right again.

"We're going in circles!" wailed Jenny.

"Well, at least we're heading in the right general direction now," said Mother. "Oh, look—this road feeds onto the freeway. The signs were right, even though they seemed wrong." After a moment she added, "You know what? Someone else has given us directions that sometimes seem wrong to us, but we have to trust that they're good and right, too. Do you know what I mean?"

Jenny thought about it. "Dad?" she guessed.

Mother laughed. "Sometimes, maybe," she said. "But I was thinking of God. The Bible says things like 'It is more blessed to give than to receive,' and 'A soft answer turns away wrath.' That seems wrong to us, but it's true."

"How about 'Love your enemies,'" said Jenny. "That was my memory verse last week."

Mother nodded. She grinned at Jenny. "Here's one for today," she said. "'Be anxious for nothing, but in everything by prayer and supplication, with thanksgiving, let your requests be made known to God.'"

"'And the peace of God, which surpasses all understanding, will guard your hearts and minds through Christ Jesus,'" finished Jenny. "I should have prayed instead of worrying." *P.O.Y.*

HOW ABOUT YOU?

Are you learning to trust God's Word for guidance in your life? Do you trust God to lead those you have to follow—people like your parents or your teachers? God knows the way he wants you to go. Trust his directions.

MEMORIZE:

"Your laws are my joyous treasure forever. I am determined to obey you."

Psalm 119:111-112, TLB

 Trust God's Word

The Boiling Pot (Read Psalm 37:3-11)

"I just can't believe Carrie would say some of the things she said," Angie told her mother one afternoon. "She yelled at everyone in the group—Luis, Gina, and even me, and I'm her best friend!"

28
MAY

"I'm sorry about that, honey," replied Mother. She shook her head. "You know," she added, "I feel sorry for Carrie, too. She needs to learn to control her temper. I know it's given her lots of problems."

"Yeah," agreed Angie. "When Carrie gets mad, it makes such a mess of things. Luis went home mad, and Gina cried. They both said they didn't want to play with Carrie again."

"Well, hopefully they'll change their minds," said Mother, "but it will probably take time for everyone to cool off and want to be friends again."

The next morning Angie came bounding into the kitchen as Mother was making oatmeal. "Carrie called," reported Angie. "Can I go over there after breakfast? She feels bad about yesterday and wants to make up with Gina and Luis. She thinks it will help if I go with her. OK?"

Mother stopped stirring the oatmeal and looked at Angie. "Yes, of course," she said. "I'm so glad to hear that." Just then, the pot boiled over. "Oh no!" gasped Mother. She grabbed the pot and lifted it to another burner, but that only spread the gooey liquid bubbling from the pot.

"What a mess!" Angie said. Then she laughed. "Carrie has a mess to clean up, and so do you. I'm going to try to help Carrie clean up hers. Can I help you, too?"

Mother smiled. "Thanks, I need it," she said, getting the sponge. "You know," she added, "the Bible often describes anger as hot or burning. Carrie's anger boiled and spilled all over her friends like my oatmeal did all over the stove. But my mess is easier to clean than hers is." *P.O.Y.*

HOW ABOUT YOU?

Do you allow your temper to flare up and burn others? The Bible says this is a foolish thing to do. (See Proverbs 14:17.) God even warns about becoming good friends with a person who continually displays a bad temper, because you might learn his ways and get yourself into a sticky mess.

MEMORIZE:

"Stop your anger! Turn off your wrath. . . . It only leads to harm." *Psalm 37:8, TLB*

 Don't Be Ruled by Anger

Discovered! (Read Psalm 32:1-5)

29
MAY

Jesse listened when Dad said there was to be absolutely no playing close to the house because of the wet paint. But that one spot between the bush and the front of the house was ideal for hide-and-seek. And Dad was painting around the back now, so he would never know. Jesse hid behind the bush, peeking out at his friend Rob, who was searching the yard. As Rob neared the bush, Jesse ducked a little lower. He almost lost his balance but braced himself against the house.

"Found ya!" Rob called out when he saw movement in the bush.

After Rob went home, Jesse went into the kitchen and poured himself some juice. "Did you and Rob have a good time?" Dad asked, coming in from his work. Jesse leaned back against the cupboard and tried to appear relaxed so Dad wouldn't guess he had done something wrong.

"Sure did," Jesse replied, spotting some paint on his fingers and hiding them in his pants pocket.

"That juice looks good," said Dad, opening the refrigerator door.

Jesse noticed a fingerprint of paint on the juice pitcher. "I'll get that for you," Jesse offered, darting toward the refrigerator to get the pitcher before his dad saw the paint. Dad sat at the table while Jesse poured the juice.

"How did paint get on that cupboard?" Dad asked.

Jesse looked at the place where he had been leaning, and his heart thumped. "Maybe you accidentally did that when you came in for a break," he suggested hopefully.

"Perhaps," Dad said, "but I don't think so. It would make more sense to think it came from you, since the back of your pants is marked with paint." Jesse twisted and tried to see. Sure enough! In spite of his attempts to hide what he had done, he was caught. "Trying to cover up our wrongdoing only makes things worse," Dad told him. "Sooner or later you'll be discovered." *N.E.K.*

HOW ABOUT YOU?

Do you admit it when you've done something wrong? Or do you try to cover up your sins? You may get away with something for a long time, but God knows all about it. Get in the habit of being honest about your sin. Confess and forsake it, and trust Jesus to wash it away.

MEMORIZE:

"He who conceals his sins does not prosper, but whoever confesses and renounces them finds mercy." *Proverbs 28:13,* NIV

 *Confess Sin*

Storm Damage (Read Ecclesiastes 8:6-8; 9:1)

30
MAY

Ever since he was a little kid, Mark had loved the giant maple tree in his backyard. There were secret hiding places far up in its leafy branches, and at one time he had played Tarzan on a long rope swing. But one night, a wild windstorm ripped a large branch from the ancient trunk, leaving a long, white scar. It looked painful, and Mark felt a real sadness in his heart when he saw it the next morning.

"Lost a big branch this time, I see." Mark's father stepped over a pile of wet leaves to come and stand beside him.

"Makes me feel bad," Mark said. Then he abruptly changed the subject. "Dad, yesterday in school Mr. Williams told us about some doctor who helps people die when they want to. Isn't that wrong?" he asked.

"Did Mr. Williams think it was OK?" asked Dad.

Mark shook his head. "He thinks that doctor should be stopped," he said.

Dad gazed into the clear, blue sky, swept clean by the rain. His voice was quiet. "Only God should control life and death, Mark. Even before we're born, he has a plan for each of our days, and it's not for us to try to change that plan." Dad nodded toward the damaged tree and asked, "Do you think we should remove that old tree now? It's been losing branches with every big storm."

Mark spoke thoughtfully. "It still gives shade in the summer, though, and I like the sound of the wind in the leaves and, well, . . . I would miss the red colors every fall."

"Even the bare, black branches against our winter skies are beautiful, aren't they?" said Dad. Then, putting an arm around his son's shoulder, he added, "The time may come when this old tree will have to be cut down, but the Bible teaches us that human life is very special and very different. Because we're made in God's image, we belong to him. No matter what happens or how 'storm damaged' we become, we can trust that our lives—from beginning to end—are in his hands." *P.I.K.*

HOW ABOUT YOU?
Do you wonder about the value of living in pain or as a feeble, old person? God gave life in the first place, and only he knows when it should end. Leave that decision to him.

MEMORIZE:
"[Man's] days are determined, the number of his months is with You." *Job 14:5,* NKJV

 God Controls Life and Death

The Yellow Scorpion (Read Proverbs 4:14-19)

31
MAY

It was dark, and Ben was scared—not of the darkness, but of what was going to happen. He and three other boys were crawling along on their hands and knees toward Mrs. Baxter's house. "C'mon, Ben. Quit dragging. If you're a Scorpion, move like one!" Ronnie, leader of the Black Scorpions, spoke as they moved along Mrs. Baxter's fence. A few minutes later, he spoke again. "OK, Ben. Prove you're not yellow! Go ring the doorbell—and don't mess up!" he warned, squeezing the back of Ben's neck.

Ben clenched his fists tightly. Then he walked to the door and pushed the doorbell. It made a loud, buzzing sound. He heard the tapping of a cane, and then the door opened. When the white-haired woman saw the young boy, she smiled and urged him to step inside. *That's not the plan,* thought Ben. But instead of following Ronnie's scheme, he went inside.

As soon as the door was closed, Ben told Mrs. Baxter about how he was supposed to trick her into going out into the backyard so the other boys could rush into her home to steal things. "They're waiting outside by your fence. I'm really scared," blubbered Ben. "They'll say I'm a *yellow* Scorpion instead of a black one, and they'll get me for that. What can I do?" He covered his face with his hands.

Mrs. Baxter gave him a tissue. "Here, young man, blow your nose, and don't you worry. You did exactly the right thing!" she said firmly. Then she called the police.

When Ben's parents learned about the robbery gang and what had happened, they were amazed. "Ronnie always seemed so nice. We had no idea he was that kind of boy," said his mother.

"Neither did I," said Ben, "until tonight. Then I knew I didn't want to be in his gang, but I didn't know what to do. I prayed for help."

Dad nodded. "Good," he said. "God tells us to stay away from bad companions. He heard your prayer for help to do the right thing, and he answered." *S.E.D.*

HOW ABOUT YOU?
Do some of your friends influence you to do things that you know are wrong? Ask God to help you remove yourself from them.

MEMORIZE:
"Do not be misled: 'Bad company corrupts good character.'" *1 Corinthians 15:33,* NIV

 Choose Godly Friends

A Heavy Backpack (Read Hebrews 12:1-3)

1

JUNE

"Gary," called Mother as he was on his way to the door, "you forgot your backpack!"

"I don't want it today, Mom," Gary told her. "It's so heavy; it slows me down. And I'm already late." He grabbed his lunch in one hand, a schoolbook in the other, and he was gone.

Mother unzipped Gary's backpack and began piling the contents on the table. "Hmmm!" she murmured. "An empty soft drink bottle, an overdue library book, even a pair of running shoes that he doesn't need now. No wonder this backpack slows him down!"

That evening, Mother noticed that Gary didn't seem very happy. "Is anything the matter, Son?" she asked.

Gary sighed. "Jim Gordon wants me to come to his birthday party," he said, "but I still don't like him."

Mother frowned. "It's been three months now since he accused you of stealing his bike, and he's asked you to forgive him, hasn't he?" she asked.

Gary nodded. "Yeah, but it still bugs me," he said. Then he added, "Besides, I didn't get to have a party for my birthday. It isn't fair!"

"I see," said Mother. "Anything else?"

Gary hesitated. "Well," he said finally, "Pete wore the championship sweatshirt that he got when the softball team won two years ago. I missed it because I broke my leg."

"That's quite a load you're carrying," said Mother. "It reminds me of your heavy backpack."

"My backpack?" repeated Gary.

"Do you know why it felt so heavy?" asked Mother. "It's because it was loaded with things you should have gotten rid of long ago. See these?" She showed him the bottle, the book, and the shoes.

Gary looked embarrassed. "I guess it was pretty dumb to carry this heavy stuff around," he admitted.

Mother nodded. "Neither is it healthy to carry around in your heart old hurts from the past," she said. "Unload those hurts. With a light heart, you'll find it much easier to run the race Christ calls you to run." *T.M.V.*

HOW ABOUT YOU?

Do you keep remembering how people disappointed you in the past? Do you hold on to anger? Do you store up your hurts until you have a heavy weight in your heart? You'll feel much better if you forgive and forget. And you'll have much more energy to serve the Lord.

MEMORIZE:

"Let us lay aside every weight, and the sin which so easily ensnares us, and let us run with endurance the race that is set before us." *Hebrews 12:1, NKJV*

 Unload Past Hurts

Dirty Sneakers (Read Isaiah 1:16-20)

"All right!" exclaimed Jimmy, as his mom presented him with a pair of bright new sneakers. "They're just what I wanted!"

"I'm glad you like them," said Mom, "but do try to keep them clean for a while. You'll need them for when you go someplace where you need to look nice."

2

JUNE

"OK, Mom," agreed Jimmy. He ran to the chair to put the new shoes on.

Jimmy remembered to be careful with his shoes for a while, but one day when he came into the house, his shoes were caked with mud. "Jimmy! Look at those shoes!" scolded Mom.

"I'm sorry, Mom," said Jimmy. "I forgot I had them on. Old Mrs. Alberts needed help in her garden, and I guess I went a little bonkers with the garden hose."

Mom sighed, shaking her head. "It was nice of you to help her, Jimmy," she said, "but in spite of your good deed, your shoes are still dirty."

"Yeah." Jimmy sighed. Then he grinned. "It's kinda like my memory verse, huh?" he said. "It says good works are like dirty rags—in this case dirty sneakers."

Mom smiled. "Well, the Bible says that God is always willing to forgive our sins! He promises that when we confess our sins and turn to him, he will wash us white as snow. He forgives us, and I guess I should forgive you, too."

"I'll try to be more careful, Mom," promised Jimmy. He looked at his shoes. "Will you make my sneakers clean again, too?" he asked.

"Not as clean as God can make your heart," said Mom, "but I'll do my best." *N.R.*

HOW ABOUT YOU?

Does your life resemble "dirty sneakers"? Do you think that doing enough good things will outweigh the bad things you do? The Bible says it doesn't matter how many good things you do, it's never enough. Only God can cleanse your heart. Confess your sin to him today and receive his forgiveness.

MEMORIZE:

"All of us have become like one who is unclean, and all our righteous acts are like filthy rags." *Isaiah 64:6,* NIV

 Good Works Won't Outweigh Sin

Daddy's Girl (Read Matthew 22:34-40)

3

JUNE

Grandma had asked Ashley if she would like to stay overnight, since it had gotten so late before her parents were ready to leave for home. But although she always had fun at Grandma's house, Ashley didn't want to be left there. "I want to go home with you," she told her daddy.

Mother wound up the walking teddy bear that Grandma kept for Ashley to play with. Ashley loved him, and now she clutched him eagerly after he wobbled to her. "Let me take him home," she begged.

"No," Daddy said, shaking his head. "He's only for you to play with at Grandma's house."

"Grandpa has a new swimming pool for you," Grandma said. Ashley's face brightened for a moment, but then the smile faded. It was getting late, so she knew she wouldn't get to play in the pool until morning.

Ashley walked to the chair where her father was sitting. She stood, begging with her eyes as well as her voice. "I want to go home with you," she insisted.

"You're tired and could sleep in one of Grandma's big, soft beds," Daddy told her. "Then you wouldn't have to bump along in the old van, either."

"I don't care," said Ashley.

"She's a daddy's girl," said her mother with a smile. Ashley didn't say anything, but Mother was right. Neither Grandma, Grandpa, Aunt Marcy, nor anyone else could take her daddy's place.

"Well, it's nice to be special," said Daddy. "Come on then, sweetheart." He picked her up as he added, "But you know what? Our heavenly Father is a lot more special than I am, honey. I can't be with you all the time, but he can."

Ashley thought about it for a little bit. "Even if you have to leave me with Grandma and Grandpa sometimes," she added seriously.

"That's right," said Daddy. "I hope he will always be more important to you than toys or fun or anything else—even me!"

M.M.P.

HOW ABOUT YOU?

Is there someone who is extra-special to you? That's nice, but no one should be more special to you than Jesus. Make him your best friend. Take time to talk to him every day and to learn about him. Ask him to help you choose what is most important.

MEMORIZE:

"Love the Lord your God with all your heart, soul, and mind."

Matthew 22:37, TLB

 **Put God First**

The Log Bridge (Read Ephesians 2:11-18)

Amy and her brother Brent were walking along the stream, one on either side. They were using sticks to push their toy boats into the current when they heard Mother calling for them to come back to the campsite for lunch. "Let's go, Amy," said Brent. "I'm hungry."

4

JUNE

"But, Brent, the stream is too wide here to cross," wailed Amy. "I can't get over to you, and it will take me a long time to walk all the way back to the bridge."

As Brent gazed about him, he spied a fallen log that reached across the water. "Come this way, to the log over here," he said, running upstream.

Amy scrambled along the opposite bank until she, too, reached the log. She hesitated. "I'm scared I'll fall in," she whimpered.

"I'll meet you and hold your hand," offered Brent. He stepped out onto the log and edged along it until he could reach Amy's outstretched hand. Then he carefully guided her to the other bank.

Soon they were back at camp, munching on hot dogs and beans, and Amy was telling Dad all about her adventures with the boats and the log bridge. "Well, that's something like the illustration Pastor Phillips gave us last week, isn't it?" said Dad. "Remember how he pointed out that we couldn't reach God on our own because the gulf of sin was too wide, but that God provided Jesus to be our Bridge to reunite us with God?"

Mom smiled and nodded. "Amy's life wasn't in danger; the log bridge just saved her a lot of time," she said. "But our eternal lives were in danger until God provided Jesus. In our devotions this afternoon, let's be sure to thank God for saving us through Jesus."

And they did. *J.K.B.*

HOW ABOUT YOU?
Have you come to God through Jesus? Nothing we can do will get us to heaven. Ask Jesus into your life today so he can be your Bridge to God.

MEMORIZE:
"But now in Christ Jesus you who once were far away have been brought near through the blood of Christ." *Ephesians 2:13,* NIV

Jesus Is Your Bridge to God

Flying High (Read Romans 8:1-9)

5

JUNE

"Oh, no!" groaned Mark. He sat at his desk, his fingers covered with sticky glue. Slowly Mark peeled the glue off his fingers. He knew he should take a break, but instead he told himself, *I just need to get this propeller on.* Mark tried to hold the nose of the model steady, but his fingers began to shake with frustration. He heard a crunch and saw the propeller in pieces in his hands. "This is the dumbest thing!" Mark screamed. He picked up the airplane and flung it against the wall. Mark felt hot tears of shame. He hunched over his desk, laid his head on his arms, and cried.

That night, Dad sat with Mark on his bed. Dad held the mangled plane in his hand. "Son, in some ways, your life with Jesus is a lot like an airplane," he said. Mark looked puzzled. "Gravity keeps an airplane pinned to the ground. That airplane will never take off until greater laws overcome the law of gravity, right?" asked Dad. Mark nodded, and Dad continued as he moved the plane along the bedspread. "As the plane moves forward, air flows over the curved wing and air pressure under the wing pushes upward, creating lift. Eventually the lift is greater than the force of gravity, and you have . . ."

"Takeoff!" exclaimed Mark. "But what does that have to do with me?"

Dad gave him a gentle smile. "Mark, with that temper, you're like an airplane stuck on the ground," he said. "You see, the law of gravity might be compared to what the Bible calls the 'law of sin and death.' If you're controlled by the law of sin, you'll never find victory over that temper of yours."

"I . . . I guess not," murmured Mark.

"You need a higher law—a force greater than the law of sin that pins you down," said Dad, "and as a Christian, you have that! You have the Holy Spirit. When you feel your temper rising, ask for his power to help you 'fly above' your anger instead of giving in to it."

C.P.K.

HOW ABOUT YOU?

Do you have trouble controlling your temper? By losing self-control, do you hurt yourself and others? The Holy Spirit can give you power over your temper. In that difficult moment of temptation, stop and pray to him.

MEMORIZE:

"He [Jesus] who is in you is greater than he who is in the world [Satan]." *1 John 4:4,* NKJV

 Control Your Temper

Try Again (Read Matthew 13:3-8)

When Mark stopped at his grandfather's house after school, he was surprised to find Grandpa on his knees in the garden. Some new seed packages were on the ground beside him. "What are you doing?" asked Mark. "I thought you planted those same rows weeks ago."

"I did," answered Grandpa, "but the hard rains we had washed the seeds away."

"Oh," said Mark. "Well, what if it happens again? Why don't you just buy your vegetables at the supermarket? It would save a lot of work."

6

JUNE

"I know," agreed Grandpa, "but nothing tastes better than vegetables fresh from the garden." He picked up the empty seed packets. "By the way," Grandpa went on, "who's going with you on your Sunday school camping trip next week?"

"Nobody, I guess," said Mark. "I asked Scott again, but he never comes to anything."

"Well, giving an invitation is like planting seeds," Grandpa told him. "Sometimes you get results, and sometimes you don't. But if you keep on trying, it makes a difference, so why not ask someone else? It's a good way to get them to hear about Jesus. Didn't you say there's a new boy on your block?"

"Yeah," answered Mark. "His name is Brett."

"He may need some new friends," Grandpa reminded him. He handed Mark the seed packets. "Do you notice differences in what I planted this time from what I planted before?"

Mark looked the packets over. "Uh . . . let's see . . . you don't have any onions now," said Mark, "and the first time you didn't have any squash."

"Onions usually do best when they're planted in early spring. Now it's time for things that grow better later in the season, so I decided to try squash," he said. "In the garden, if one vegetable won't grow, I try another. And, for you, if one boy doesn't accept an invitation to church or camp, find one who is more likely to do so."

Mark grinned. "OK, Grandpa," he said. "I'll stop to see Brett on my way home." *M.M.P.*

HOW ABOUT YOU?

Do you give up easily if someone you invite to Sunday school or Bible club doesn't come? Ask again, and find others who need to be there, too. If you keep on trying, you may help someone else learn about Jesus.

MEMORIZE:

"After a while we will reap a harvest of blessing if we don't get discouraged and give up."

Galatians 6:9, TLB

 Keep Witnessing

Bubba's Training (Read Romans 6:11-14)

"Can't you learn anything?" muttered Cody, picking up the Frisbee. His black Labrador, Bubba, tilted his head to one side and lifted his front paw. "No, not shake! Fetch!" ordered Cody, hurling the Frisbee across the yard. Bubba raced after it. Before it spun to the ground, Bubba jumped into the air and caught it with his mouth. "Good dog!" called Cody, clapping his hands. "Now, bring it here, Bubba!" Bubba's wagging tail stopped and pointed into the air. He pricked up his ears while staring into the nearby woods. Suddenly, he dropped the Frisbee and dashed after a squirrel. "This is hopeless," groaned Cody, letting himself fall to the ground.

"What's up?" asked Cody's big sister Valerie. She sat down on the grass next to him.

"I'm trying to train Bubba. I've done everything this dog-training manual says," said Cody, picking up a book, "and sometimes he seems to get the hang of it. Then, out of the blue, he chases a squirrel."

"Bubba's a hunting dog—it's in his nature to do that," said Valerie, paging through the book.

Those words reminded Cody of his Sunday school lesson. "Kind of like it's in our nature to sin?" he asked. Valerie nodded, and Cody frowned. "Does God think we're hopeless?" he asked, hoping God didn't give up as easily as he did.

Valerie shook her head. "You know the answer to that as well as I do," she said with a grin. "God sent Jesus to save us from our sinful nature. Because of God's grace, we are no longer hopeless. The Bible is our training manual, and God wants us to learn not to sin. But when we do sin, we can ask him to forgive us, and he will."

Something pawed at Cody's back. He turned to find Bubba, holding the Frisbee in his mouth. Cody smiled as he patted Bubba's head. "Want to try again?" he asked. He gave it a fling, and Bubba bounded after it. *D.G.D.*

HOW ABOUT YOU?

Do you feel like a hopeless case, as if you'll never have victory over sin? Don't give up on yourself; God doesn't! Confess your sin to him and ask him to forgive you. Then follow him each day.

MEMORIZE:

"For sin shall not be your master, because you are not under law, but under grace."

Romans 6:14, NIV

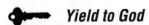 **Yield to God**

The Garden (Read John 15:1-8)

8

JUNE

"Can I have some space in the garden plot this year?" Joel had asked his parents in early spring, and they had agreed. Now it was June, and Joel looked at his part of the garden. There were so many weeds that he could hardly see his little tomato plants. He saw more dandelions and crab-grass than vegetables. Then he looked over at Mom's part of the garden. She was bending over her plants, pulling weeds out of the dirt with her hands. Neat rows of tender plants were already blossoming with fruit.

"Hi there, Joel," called Mom as she looked up from her weeding.

Joel kicked a stone with his shoe. "Hi," he said softly.

His mother stood up and walked over to him. They both stood quietly for a moment, looking at the weeds in his little plot. "Pretty messy, isn't it," said Joel.

"Mm-hmm." Mother nodded and stooped to pull up a clump of crabgrass.

"But I just weeded it last week," whined Joel.

His mother got down on her knees and pulled another handful of weeds. "You know what I was thinking awhile ago?" she asked. "I was thinking that weeds are like sin in a person's life. Weeds and sin both grow very quickly into a tangled mess." Mom held a handful of weeds and looked at Joel. "And if we don't attend to them every day, they'll grow so fast that they'll soon take over and ruin our garden—or our fruit for the Lord."

Joel looked at the weeds in his mother's hand. "Come on," she encouraged. "I'll help you. It's important to weed our gardens, but always remember that it's even more important for us to 'weed our lives'—to confess our sins every day and turn away from them so they don't have a chance to take root in our lives and grow."

Joel nodded thoughtfully. "Weeds sure can get out of hand," he agreed. Then he got on his knees and began to help his mother weed his part of the garden. *R.S.M.*

HOW ABOUT YOU?

Is your life bearing fruit for the Lord? Or is it full of "weeds" like anger, disobedience, and jealousy? Ask Jesus to help you weed out those sins so you can be fruitful for him.

MEMORIZE:

"That you may walk worthy of the Lord, . . . being fruitful in every good work."

Colossians 1:10, NKJV

 Be Fruitful for God

Window Shopping (Read 1 Thessalonians 1:6-10)

9

JUNE

As Bryan and his dad walked through the mall, Bryan talked about the soul-winning project his Sunday school class had begun. "I gathered my courage and offered Mr. Martin a tract today, but he wouldn't take it," Bryan reported. "He said he didn't even believe I was a Christian!"

"Hmmm. That's too bad," replied Dad. "Have you ever done or said anything around Mr. Martin that would make him feel that way?"

"I don't think so," Bryan answered. But then he remembered something. *Maybe Mr. Martin knows I'm the one who knocked a ball through his window,* he thought. *I was going to tell him, but the other guys said I shouldn't. They said he'd never know who did it.* "Nothing much anyway," he added as he noticed Dad studying him. Dad frowned. Just then they arrived at the sporting goods store. Pointing to a football in the window, Bryan exclaimed, "Look! There's the ball I want."

"But how do you know they sell that kind of football inside?" Dad asked.

Bryan gave his dad a questioning look. "Why, anyone knows that the stuff you see in the window is stuff they sell inside the store," he said.

Dad nodded. "Isn't that the way people judge one another, too?" he asked. "What people see in our actions is what they believe us to be like inside. It's only if they see us act like Christ that they think he's inside."

Bryan stood for a moment, looking down. Then, haltingly, he told Dad about the broken window. "I'm not going to buy a football now, Dad," he said. "I need my money to replace a window."

Later, after confessing to Mr. Martin about the broken window, Bryan handed him the money. "Bryan," the old man said, "I saw you hit that ball through my window and then run away. I must admit, I didn't think much of your Christianity when I saw that. Now I've changed my mind, though. I guess I'd like to read your piece of paper after all." *M.R.P.*

HOW ABOUT YOU?

Do your words and actions tell people that Jesus is inside? Think of the things you've said today. Would Jesus say them? What about your attitudes and actions toward others? Do they show Christ's love? If Jesus is inside, display him on the outside, and try your best to make others want what you've got.

MEMORIZE:

"Dear children, let us not love with words or tongue but with actions and in truth."

1 John 3:18, NIV

 **Display Christ**

Spiritual Muscles (Read Philippians 4:11-13)

April pushed her plate away. "Seems like we always have macaroni or rice or beans!" she grumbled. She glanced at her dad, but he didn't comment.

Mother spoke up, however. "April, you know that ever since the layoffs at the factory, we just don't have the money to eat the way we used to," she said. "Dad has tried to find another job, but there just aren't many available right now. But I think we're doing all right. This is good food."

10
JUNE

"Well, it's not fair," April retorted.

At this, Dad did comment. "I was just thinking," he said, "about the apostle Paul."

"Paul! What does he have to do with this?" asked April.

"Well, Paul was in a much worse situation than we're in," replied Dad. "He was in a dingy Roman prison. I'm sure he would have loved to have such good food as we have. But he wrote in Philippians 4, 'I have learned in whatever state I am, to be content.' You see, Paul had learned that no matter what difficulty we find ourselves in, God is in it with us."

"If God is in it, then why doesn't he just fix it?" April asked.

"Because God wants us to become stronger Christians," said Dad. "Remember those weight lifters we saw on TV the other night?" April nodded. "How do you suppose they got so strong?" asked Dad.

"Well, . . ." April thought about it. "I guess they practiced by lifting heavier and heavier weights," she said.

Dad nodded. "Life is like that, too," he said. "God wants us to accept our present difficulties and stand strong in them. In the end, we will be stronger." April thought for a moment, then lifted her fork and began eating. "Change your mind about the macaroni?" Dad asked.

"I'm still not crazy about it," replied April, "but I have decided to learn to be content with it."

"All right!" approved Dad. "Now you're building your spiritual muscles!" *D.C.C.*

HOW ABOUT YOU?

Do you grumble when difficulties come your way? God wants to make you stronger through these times. As you trust him during difficult times, he'll make you strong spiritually.

MEMORIZE:

"Is your life full of difficulties and temptations? Then be happy, for when the way is rough, your patience has a chance to grow." *James 1:2-3,* TLB

 Grow Strong through Difficulties

Under the Covers (Read Mark 4:35-41)

11

JUNE

Boom! Seven-year-old Aaron sat upright in bed as rain spattered against the window and lightning streaks made his room as bright as day. In the brief light he could see his favorite teddy bear propped in a corner. *Boom!* Another loud crash, and Aaron burrowed under his covers, a pillow pressed over his ears.

From under his blankets, Aaron peeked toward the wall where the rosy glow of a night-light usually shone, but only blackness filled the room. Cautiously, he poked the button of a little table lamp near his bed, but instead of warm, friendly light, there was nothing. Shivering, he buried himself even deeper in his bed.

Rain poured down harder outside. Aaron, wide-awake now, was wondering if he dared make a run for his parents' room when he felt a soft touch through his blanket. "Mom?" he asked in a muffled voice.

"I'm here, honey." Aaron looked out from his blanket tent and saw his mother in her fuzzy, pink robe standing next to him. Another *boom* shook the house. "Noisy, isn't it?" Mom remarked reassuringly. As she sat down on the edge of Aaron's bed, the lights came on. With Mom there and with the familiar light back on, he felt quite brave again. "Did you remember that Jesus is right here, Aaron?" asked Mom. "He was watching over you even before I came in. He controls the wind and rain, you know. We don't have to be afraid because he's with us."

Aaron felt sleepy just listening to the comforting words. His mother's hands closed around his, and he heard her saying, "Thank you, Jesus, for loving Aaron and especially for being here with him through the storm."

Through almost-closed eyes, Aaron saw his mom turn the light out and tiptoe from his room. Outside, the storm rumbled farther away, while rain dripped quietly from the roof.

"Thank you, Jesus," he whispered. "I'm so glad you're always here." Aaron yawned, snuggled under his covers, and was soon asleep again. *P.I.K.*

HOW ABOUT YOU?

Are you afraid during storms? Jesus tells us to ask for protection and then to trust him to answer. He is just like a parent who loves and watches over his or her children. Trust Jesus to take care of you.

MEMORIZE:

"As a mother comforts her child, so will I comfort you."

Isaiah 66:13, NIV

 Jesus Is Here

All in the Family (Read 1 Corinthians 12:14-25)

12
JUNE

Brent, Susan, and Amy were looking forward to a week of camping with their parents. They could hardly wait to go swimming, fishing, and hiking.

It was nearly suppertime when they arrived at their campsite. Everyone tumbled out of the van and scouted out the site. Soon Mom and Dad had organized jobs for each of them. Susan and Amy went with Dad to collect firewood and get water, while Mom and Brent set up the tents.

"The girls can't do this hard stuff," bragged Brent as he helped Mom with tent poles and stakes. "Good thing there are easy jobs like carrying wood and water for them to do."

"Don't let them hear you. I doubt they'd agree that those jobs are any easier," Mom replied, "and even if they are, you have to remember that they're younger than you. Besides, every family member's job is important. You can't look down on what anyone does."

As Brent ate his supper that night, he thought about what Mom had said. He could see that she was right. If Susan hadn't carried the wood, Mom couldn't have cooked the burgers. And if Amy hadn't gotten some water, there'd be no hot chocolate! "Thanks for getting the wood, Susan," he said. "And, Amy, thanks for carrying the water. If it hadn't been for you helping like that, we would have gone to sleep hungry tonight."

The girls looked at him rather strangely, but Mom winked and smiled as she said, "And thanks for helping set up the tents, Brent. You did a good job!" That made Brent feel great.

"You've all been good helpers," put in Dad. "You all worked cheerfully on the work assigned to you. That's what makes a family run smoothly." *J.K.B.*

HOW ABOUT YOU?

Do you think only certain people in the church are important—like the pastor or teachers? Christians make up the family of God, and each family member is needed. The Bible says every Christian has a gift from God. So find out what part you can play.

MEMORIZE:

"So we, being many, are one body in Christ, and every one members one of another."

Romans 12:5, KJV

 All Family Members Are Important

The Terrible Trio (Read Psalm 51:10-15)

13
JUNE

Mr. Bryant's Sunday school class was enjoying a talent show at their party. Now a trio began to sing. They had sung often before, so the kids knew they could sing well. But this time they sounded terrible. Jim's beautiful tenor voice was off-key. Brett hit all the right notes, but his voice was harsh and grating. And Nancy sang so softly that she could hardly be heard. The kids laughed. They were sure their friends were singing that way just for fun.

When the trio was finished, Mr. Bryant picked up his Bible. "Time for devotions," he said, "but first I want to thank all those who took part in the entertainment today." Then he asked, "What did you kids think of that trio?" He smiled at the groans he heard. "I asked the trio to sing that way on purpose. I wanted to demonstrate some things that can go wrong with our testimony for the Lord," explained Mr. Bryant. "What was Jim's problem?"

"He has such a nice voice," answered Cathy, "but he sang so many wrong notes that I could hardly recognize the melody."

Mr. Bryant nodded. "That reminds me of Christians who, although they have great potential, fall into sinful habits or errors that mar their usefulness for Christ. What about Brett?"

"He was right on key," responded Bill, "but he sounded like a . . . a bullfrog with a cold!" The class laughed, and Mr. Bryant smiled.

"I think that's like Christians who know a lot about the Bible and maintain high standards in their lives," said Mr. Bryant, "but they're overcritical and rude in their witnessing, which makes people turn them off."

"Well, what about Nancy?" asked Rachel. "She sang pretty well, though I could hardly hear her."

"That's the point," said Mr. Bryant. "Even if we have a great testimony, it doesn't do anybody much good if no one ever hears it. We need three things to be effective witnesses: submission to God, a loving attitude, and an enthusiastic spirit. If one of these is missing, our witness will probably fall on deaf ears!" *S.L.K.*

HOW ABOUT YOU?

What kind of witness are you? Make sure that sinful habits, a critical spirit, or a halfhearted attitude aren't getting in the way of the beautiful "song" God wants you to "sing" for him.

MEMORIZE:

"My mouth will declare your praise." *Psalm 51:15*, NIV

 Be a Good Witness

Brad's Choice (Read Proverbs 4:23-27)

14
JUNE

Brad and his father stood on the front porch, watching the bulldozer gouge out chunks of pavement from the street in front of their house. "They're sure making a mess," observed Brad.

Dad smiled. "Yes," he said, "but when they're finished, we'll have a better street. It's been full of potholes."

Brad didn't answer. He stood quietly thinking about something that could be messed up worse than their street—his mind. The night before, he had slept at Jimmy's house, and they had stayed up late looking at a magazine that no one should have around.

Brad hadn't known what to say when Jimmy brought the magazine out from its hiding place and suggested they look at it. He didn't want to seem like a goody-goody in the eyes of his friend. "I don't know. I . . . Dad wouldn't like it if he found out," he had murmured weakly.

"Ah, come on," Jimmy had coaxed. "Let's enjoy the pictures. Your dad will never know." So Brad gave in, and then his mind felt dirty. He had even confessed to God what he had done wrong, and he had asked God to forgive him. But what would he do if Jimmy invited him to look at such a magazine again?

"Someone sure did a lot of planning before this street project began," said Dad. "They had to consider the cost and whether it would be worth the time and money—and mess."

That's my answer, thought Brad. *I need to consider whether looking at those magazines is worth messing up my mind.* Already he knew it wasn't. *I'd rather risk not looking cool to my friends,* he decided.

That night, Brad took his Bible and wrote a prayer in the back: "Lord, when friends tempt me to do wrong, give me the courage to say no. I choose to keep my mind and heart clean." *M.S.*

HOW ABOUT YOU?

What will you say if a friend asks you to do something wrong? The Bible says to "keep your heart with all diligence." To be diligent means to pay attention. Will you pay attention to what God says instead of giving in to temptation?

MEMORIZE:

"Keep your heart with all diligence." *Proverbs 4:23,* NKJV

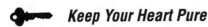 *Keep Your Heart Pure*

God and Computers (Read Job 38:4-11)

15
JUNE

"Listen to this, Ken." Doug sat on the bed while his brother sat in front of their computer. "This magazine article tells about a computer that can scan the entire *Encyclopaedia Britannica* in two seconds!"

Ken shook his head in amazement. "I bet the whole world will be run by computers ten years from now," he said.

A flash of lightning and boom of thunder made Doug jump up off the bed. "That was close!" he exclaimed.

"Oh no!" wailed Ken. "The computer's down! There must have been a power surge, and I lost the whole program!"

"Dad warned us not to use the computer when we were having a storm," remembered Doug. "Let's hope it's not wrecked!" They stared at each other in dismay.

Doug headed for the living room. "Dad," he said, "That last big bolt of lightning . . . uh . . . zapped the computer."

Dad hurried to the boys' bedroom and frowned at the blank screen. "These are sensitive machines," Dad reminded them. "They've got to be protected."

"And we were just talking about how they were going to run the world someday," said Ken. He sounded disgusted.

"They're amazing, but they're not perfect. They're just man-made machines," said Dad. "God has created man to be a remarkable creature. But because he became flawed by sin, anything he produces is flawed, too. As advanced as a computer is, it's primitive compared to the mind of God."

"Yeah. He created the minds that invented the computer, didn't he," said Doug.

"That's right," said Dad. "We can't even begin to understand God's wisdom and genius. Only he is perfect." *L.J.*

HOW ABOUT YOU?

Are you so impressed with man's achievements that you begin go feel you no longer need God? Remember that God created not just this planet but the whole universe. He created man from the dust of the earth. Man knows only what God has chosen to reveal to him.

MEMORIZE:

"Where were you when I laid the foundations of the earth? Tell me, if you know so much."

Job 38:4, TLB

 God Knows More than Man

Betty's Loneliness (Read Psalms 36:7-8; 37:3-5)

16

JUNE

Betty sat glumly on her front-porch step. The sun shone from a clear, blue sky. But deep inside, Betty felt as if a dark cloud hovered overhead. "I feel so lonesome here," she said to Rags, her new, brown puppy, as she hugged him to herself.

Just then Betty's father arrived home from work. "What's wrong, pumpkin?" he asked as he sat down beside her. "You look as if you don't have a friend in the world."

"It's almost that bad," Betty replied. "I sure don't have any friends here. I wish we hadn't moved."

"I understand how you feel," said Dad. "It's no fun being a new kid in town. But remember how we prayed and trusted God, and he helped me get a job here?" Betty nodded, and Dad continued, "Now can you trust God to help you get settled here?" He looked at the little dog resting peacefully on Betty's lap. "Think about Rags for a minute," he added. "I remember how lonesome he was, crying for his mother the first few nights you had him."

Betty smiled. "I know just how lonesome he felt," she declared, burying her face in the puppy fur.

Dad nodded. "And you gave him so much love that now he's happy to be here," he said. "Now, Betty, if you knew how your puppy felt, don't you think the Lord knows how you feel?"

"I hadn't thought about that," replied Betty slowly, "but I'm sure he does."

"And just as Rags trusts you to take care of him and make him happy, can you trust God to do the same for you?" asked Dad softly.

"I'll try," agreed Betty. "I'll trust him to give me some new friends, too." *M.S.*

HOW ABOUT YOU?

Has something happened that left you feeling lonely? Have you wished things were different? Don't forget that Jesus cares. He loves you. You can trust him to work things out.

MEMORIZE:

"Cast all your anxiety on him because he cares for you."

1 Peter 5:7, NIV

 God Knows and Cares

No Shipwreck (Read Hebrews 6:17-20)

17
JUNE

"This has been my best fishing trip, Dad," said Brad. He and his father had been deep-sea fishing on a charter boat.

As the boat sailed for home, dark clouds gathered in the sky. Soon stabs of lightning flashed, followed by loud booms of thunder. "This storm came up unusually fast," the captain told the passengers, "and the Coast Guard says we're in for some severe weather. We could try to make it to port, but it would be safer to anchor near the coastline and ride out the storm, so that's what we're going to do."

The passengers huddled in the ship's cabin as torrents of rain poured down and the lightning flashed. At last they neared the shore, and the captain let down the anchor. Still, the wind buffeted the boat about as if it were a toy.

From the cabin windows, the passengers could see the monstrous waves and the rocky coast. "I'm scared, Dad," murmured Brad. "What if we crash into those big rocks?"

Dad put his arm around Brad. "Don't worry, Son," he said. "I talked with several crew members, and they told me they've anchored here safely many times. We have a good captain. We can trust him—he knows what he's doing."

"Good," said Brad. He shivered as he peered through the driving rain. "Being in a shipwreck would be awful."

"Yes, it would," agreed Dad. After a moment he added, "But there's something even worse. It's the shipwreck of a person's soul." Brad gave him a puzzled glance. "We could compare this ship to our souls and the sea to our life on earth," continued Dad. "Life can get pretty stormy, you know, so we need an anchor, right? What would our anchor be?"

"Our anchor? Um . . . our anchor might be our faith in Jesus," suggested Brad.

Dad nodded. "Good," he agreed as he glanced out the window. "Look. The storm is letting up. Before long we'll be back in the harbor. And when it comes to the sea of life, Jesus will keep us safe and secure until we harbor in heaven, where he is." *M.R.P.*

HOW ABOUT YOU?

Have you "anchored your soul" in Jesus? Have you asked him to forgive your sins and save you? If you'll trust him, your soul will not be "shipwrecked." Instead, he'll bring you safely to heaven someday.

MEMORIZE:

"This certain hope of being saved is a strong and trustworthy anchor for our souls." *Hebrews 6:19,* TLB

 Be "Anchored" in Jesus

Rotten Oranges (Read 1 Corinthians 5:6-8)

18
JUNE

"Yuck! What is that awful smell?" Jeffrey asked as he and his dad went down the basement steps.

"Smells like something rotten," said Dad, "and I'll bet I know what it is." Dad pointed, and Jeffrey saw a large box of oranges at the bottom of the stairs. "Just as I suspected," Dad said, as he lifted two or three oranges from the top. "We left these oranges here too long. Next time I guess we'd better not buy so many at once—even if they are on sale."

"Look!" cried Jeffrey as he and Dad took out more oranges and examined them. "Mold is spreading from the bad ones to the good ones."

When they finished sorting the oranges, they went back upstairs. "Here are all the oranges that are still good," Jeffrey announced, handing a bag of oranges to Mom. "The rest are all yucky and moldy. Dad's taking them right out to the trash."

"I've heard that one bad apple spoils the barrel," said Mom. "I guess that works with oranges as well."

"And people, too," said Dad, coming into the kitchen.

"Yeah," said Jeffrey. "They catch stuff like chicken pox and colds from each other."

"That," agreed Dad, "and bad habits, too. For instance, if you're around people who take God's name in vain, you could easily pick up that habit."

"I think you might pick up such habits from television, too," observed Mom. "On many programs, God's name is sprinkled into conversation like punctuation marks."

"Which is why it's a good idea to turn such programs off," said Dad. "Turn it off before it spreads." He paused, then added, "I think the apostle Paul was talking about that kind of thing when he said leaven, or yeast, affects the whole lump of dough. Like yeast—and rotten oranges—sin spreads." *P.O.Y.*

HOW ABOUT YOU?

Do you think that by joining a rowdy group you can influence them for good? Be careful! It's more likely that you'll end up with their bad habits. Do you think TV programs won't hurt you? Be careful! Sinful habits heard and seen there may spread to you, too. Choose your friends—and TV programs—wisely.

MEMORIZE:

"My son, if sinners entice you, do not give in to them."

Proverbs 1:10, NIV

 *Avoid Bad Influences*

Rainy Day Picnic (Read Mark 4:35-41)

Danny ran to answer the phone. It was his friend Bret. "It's supposed to rain tomorrow," Bret told him. This news worried Danny because they had a Kids' Bible Club picnic scheduled.

19

JUNE

The next day, the cloudy skies became darker and darker as the morning wore on. At noon it started to sprinkle, and by the time they reached the picnic grounds, it was raining hard. To keep dry, all the kids ran under the pavilion. There they arranged picnic tables and set out the food. Before they ate, Mr. Flanigan, their teacher, thanked God for the food and prayed that they'd all learn more about God that day. But Danny silently prayed that the rain would stop.

After eating, Mr. Flanigan conducted games and Bible drills. Danny was surprised at how much fun it was—even though God hadn't made the rain stop.

When Danny's mother came to pick him up, Mr. Flanigan asked, "Did God teach you anything today?"

Danny nodded, smiling. "He taught me that I don't need to worry when things don't go like I want them to," he said. "God still lets me have fun." *C.S.S.*

HOW ABOUT YOU?

Do you worry when your plans don't work out? When rain threatens your picnic, or when you get a blister on your finger the day of your big piano recital? Jesus is in charge of everything—even the weather—and he cares. Tell him your troubles and trust him to take care of them.

MEMORIZE:

"Don't worry about anything."

Philippians 4:6, TLB

 **Don't Worry**

The Food's Getting Cold (Read Daniel 6:10, 16-23)

20

JUNE

Alec was having lunch at a fast-food restaurant with his friend Kyle and Kyle's big sister, Allison. They had just gotten their food when Allison glanced at Alec's tray. "Don't you want anything to drink?" she asked.

"Well, I would like some milk," replied Alec.

Allison set her tray on the table. "Sit here," she said. "I'll get the milk."

Kyle took a big bite of his hamburger. Alec sniffed his french fries. "Mmmm," he said. "They smell good."

Kyle tasted one of his. "They are good," he told Alec. "Why don't you eat yours?"

Alec's family always prayed before they ate, no matter where they were, but he was afraid Kyle would laugh if he did that. "Uh, . . . I'll wait for my milk," he said.

It seemed to take a long time. "Your food's getting cold," said Kyle.

Alec looked at his fries again. He was relieved to hear Allison's voice saying, "Here's your milk." She sat down, and Alec waited for her to bow her head. She didn't. She sipped her orange juice and added ketchup to her hamburger. Then she took a bite.

Alec couldn't wait much longer. He glanced at Kyle and Allison to see if they were watching. They were, but Alec bowed his head anyway. He looked at his sneakers a moment. Then he shut his eyes. "Thank you, Jesus, for the food," he prayed silently. "Amen."

When Alec looked up, Kyle was staring at him. Then Kyle turned to his sister. "Hey, Allison, we forgot to pray," he said.

Allison nodded her head. "We'll remember next time," she promised. She grinned at Alec. "You made me think of Daniel when he prayed by an open window," she said. "He didn't shut it to keep people from seeing him and putting him in the lions' den because of it. And we shouldn't be afraid to let people know we pray, either."

Alec popped a french fry into his mouth. "I didn't see any lions, but I was a little scared," he admitted. "I'm glad I prayed." *M.M.P.*

HOW ABOUT YOU?

Do you always thank God for your food? No matter where you are? Why not at least bow your head and thank the Lord silently? Knowing that you love Jesus may help someone else have the courage to thank him, too.

MEMORIZE:

"I want men everywhere to lift up holy hands in prayer."

1 Timothy 2:8, NIV

 Pray Wherever You Are

All Messed Up (Read Isaiah 61:1-7)

21

JUNE

"It's not fair!" objected Jasmine, almost in tears. "It's bad enough that Dad walked out on us. I shouldn't have to move away from all my friends, too!"

Mother sighed. "I know, honey," she said, "but I can't keep up this place all by myself. It will be cheaper for us to live with Grandma for a while. There's a very nice school not far from her house, and Grandma will be there for Davy when he gets home from kindergarten."

"But I don't know anybody in that school," wailed Jasmine.

Just then the back door opened, and Davy came in crying. "I falled," he sobbed, "and I skinned my knee, and my jeans got all messed up."

Jasmine looked at him. "Messed up is right," she agreed. "Just like my life," she added with a frown.

Mother comforted the little boy and gently bandaged his sore knee. "There," she said, "that feels better, doesn't it? Now let's see what we can do about these jeans. They're too good to throw away."

"He could just wear them ripped," said Jasmine. "Lots of kids do." Mother shook her head. "Well then, you could put patches on the knees," suggested Jasmine. "Or you could cut them off for shorts." She grinned at her little brother. "They'll be better than ever, Davy."

"Yeah," agreed Davy. "Can I have shorts, Mom?"

Mother smiled. "We'll see," she said. "One way or another, we'll make something good of your messed-up jeans." When Davy went to change his clothes, Mother turned to Jasmine. "You said your life was all messed up, just like Davy's jeans, right?" she asked. Miserably, Jasmine nodded. "And you don't know how to fix it—but God does," Mother went on gently. "If you'll trust him, he'll take your messed-up life—and mine—and build a whole new life for us. It won't be the same as the life we knew before, but it can be beautiful and good just the same. Will you trust God to fix it for you?"

Jasmine sighed and nodded. "I'll try," she promised. *H.M.*

HOW ABOUT YOU?

Does it seem that everything has gone wrong? Do you feel as things will never be the same again? That may be true—they may never be the same, but that doesn't mean they won't be good. God has promised to work all things for good in the lives of those who love him. Trust him to do that.

MEMORIZE:

"He heals the brokenhearted and binds up their wounds."

Psalm 147:3, NKJV

 God Can Make Your Life Good

Teamwork (Read 1 Corinthians 12:12-14, 18-20)

Robert jumped from the car and hurried over to the dugout, eager for the weekly league baseball game. "Robert, I want you to take right field," the coach said. And as the boys ran into the field, he called, "Remember—teamwork!"

22

JUNE

After a short time of practice, the game began. The first batter hit the ball on the second pitch and ran safely to second base. The second batter took a few practice swings and then positioned himself inside the batter's box. He struck the ball hard, sending it high into the outfield.

Robert reached for the ball as it flew toward him. *Thud!* He caught it! Robert knew he had to throw it quickly into the infield. He heard the people in the stands scream in unison. "Third base! Third base!"

Quickly Robert threw the ball. It reached Chad, the boy at second base. Chad caught it and threw it to third base. The boy at third caught it just in time to tag the runner who was sliding into third base. "Out!" shouted the umpire. The people in the bleachers responded with whistles, clapping, hooting, and hollering.

Teamwork, Robert thought to himself, and he smiled.

After the game, Robert's dad congratulated him. "I noticed that your game took a lot of team effort," Dad said as they drove home. Robert nodded. "It reminded me of the way Christians need to work together," added Dad thoughtfully. "We're all part of the body of Christ, yet each person has a different position to fill."

Robert grinned at his father. "Like helping my Sunday school class clean up the churchyard?" he asked. "Guess I'd better change my clothes as soon as I get home and get over there. I won't be very late."

Dad nodded. "Good idea," he said. "That may not seem very important to you, but we each need to do our part—whether it means witnessing in the streets, teaching Sunday school, or cleaning up the churchyard." *B.R.H.*

HOW ABOUT YOU?

Are you a faithful team member of the body of Christ? Teamwork is simply doing your part, whether it's helping a friend at school, witnessing to somebody, praying for someone who's sick, or obeying and helping at home. God honors teamwork.

MEMORIZE:

"Now you are the body of Christ, and each one of you is a part of it." *1 Corinthians 12:27, NIV*

 Christians Need Each Other

The Beauty Box (Read 1 Peter 3:1-6)

23

JUNE

Janie followed her friend Beth into the bathroom, where the girls opened a box containing partly used eye makeup, lipstick, rouge, powder, and nail polish. *What fun,* thought Janie. She had never gotten her hands on so much makeup before; her mom used very little. Beth's older sister was going to throw this away, but instead she gave it to Beth to play with.

Janie watched with fascination as Beth took a tiny brush and pressed it against her eyelashes. She didn't do a very good job, smearing her eye in the process. "Ouch!" she squealed. Then, "C'mon, Janie! Try something. You can wash it off." Janie selected a bright lipstick, but some of it ended up on her teeth and also made streaks on her nose and chin. Beth laughed, "You look like a clown!"

"Girls!" Beth's mother called. "Janie's mother was on the phone. She needs her at home to stay with Jimmy for a while." Janie grabbed a bar of soap and quickly scrubbed the bright color from her face before hurrying home.

As Janie ran up the back steps of her house and into the sunny kitchen, she saw her mother at the table. A Bible lay open before her, and to one side Janie saw a notebook and pencil. "Hi, honey!" said Mother. "Thanks for coming right away. I've been doing my Bible study while I was waiting." She smiled, and Janie felt a warm peace there in the kitchen. She realized her mother was beautiful in a special way.

"Mom, I hope I look just like you when I grow up. You're so pretty!" Janie burst out appreciatively.

"Thank you, honey. What a nice thing to say." Rising, Mother took Janie's chin in her hand and gently wiped away a red streak. "We all hope to be beautiful, Janie," she said. "Remember the Bible tells us that real beauty comes from the heart. That's why I try to spend time reading God's Word every day, so he can give me his beauty."

"Not something you can buy from the store, I guess," Janie said with a little smile. *P.I.K.*

HOW ABOUT YOU?

Do you complain about yourself when you look in the mirror? Girls often think cosmetics would make a big difference. For older girls, a little makeup might make them prettier to some people. But it's more important—for both boys and girls—to be pleasing to the Lord and to be beautiful inside for him.

MEMORIZE:

"Let the beauty of the Lord our God be upon us." *Psalm 90:17,* KJV

 *Reflect Jesus' Beauty*

Fire! Fire! (Read 1 Timothy 4:8-16)

24
JUNE

Six-year-old Tony tiptoed into the kitchen, got several matches and a bag of marshmallows, and hurried outside. Choosing a sandy spot, he piled up some paper and sticks. Then he started a small fire. "We'll roast marshmallows," he told his friend Matt.

"Yummy!" exclaimed Matt. He glanced toward the house and added, "Are you sure you're s'posed to do this?"

"It's OK," said Tony. "I can handle this little fire." But even as he spoke, a gust of wind blew pieces of burning paper onto a nearby shed roof, setting it on fire.

"Look!" yelled Matt in horror. "Fire!"

"Fire! Fire!" screamed Tony, rushing into the house.

Soon fire engines came roaring down the street. They put out the blaze, but not before the shed was burned up.

"I'm . . . s-so . . . s-sorry, Mom," said Tony, between sobs. "I'll never play with fire again."

That night Eric, Tony's older brother, was talking about some of his friends. "These kids are only twelve or thirteen years old, just like me," he said, "but they're dating already. You should hear them brag about kissing and stuff, Dad. They say it's OK to fool around because everybody's doing it—but it's not, is it?"

Dad shook his head. "If all the kids on our block played with fire, would that make it OK?" he asked.

Eric laughed. "No way!" he replied. "They'd probably burn down all our houses, like Tony burned our shed."

"Well, 'kissing and stuff,' as you call it, is like playing with fire. It can easily get out of control," Dad told him. "Before you know it, you could be doing things that the Bible says are for a husband and wife only."

"Yeah, and getting bad diseases or other problems, like a lot of kids in high school are doing," added Eric. "Right?"

Dad nodded. "Look at the trouble Tony caused because he disobeyed us and played with fire," he said. "Disobeying God about sex can have far worse results. You need to promise God that you'll keep your body pure for the one you'll marry someday." *M.R.P.*

HOW ABOUT YOU?
Do you want God to bless your life now and in your future married life? Then keep your body pure, giving your special love only to the one you marry. You'll always be glad you did.

MEMORIZE:

"Keep yourself pure."

1 Timothy 5:22, NIV

Going Back in Time (Read 1 John 1:5-10)

"What do you mean it's time for lunch?" Darlene asked her cousin Beth, as they talked on the phone. "It's already two in the afternoon. We've eaten lunch."

"It's two there in New York, but here in Colorado it's noon," Beth replied. "We're in a different time zone."

25
JUNE

"Oh, that's right!" exclaimed Darlene. "Well, Mom's motioning for me to get off the phone anyway. Have a nice lunch. Bye."

Darlene hung up the phone and raced out into the backyard, where her dad was working. "Give me a hand," he said as he pulled a few weeds. "Please take these weeds and dump them in the compost heap."

"Yuck!" exclaimed Darlene, turning back toward the house. "Forget it."

"I asked you to help me," said Dad.

"I don't want to," Darlene said over her shoulder. "I'm going to play with Jenny."

When Darlene found herself sitting alone in her room a few minutes later, she wished she had obeyed Dad, but it was too late now. She was being punished.

"Have you thought about what you did?" Dad asked, when he came in.

Darlene nodded sadly. "Yes, and I wish we could go to Colorado," she said. "Beth said it was only noon there, so the time I got in trouble wouldn't have happened yet. We could eat lunch, and then when it got to be two o'clock, we could have the weed conversation, and I would obey."

Dad smiled and shook his head. "We can't go back in time," he said. "We can't make things that have happened unhappen."

"I wish we could," said Darlene with a sigh, "because I wish I had never said I wouldn't help you."

"Honey, even though we can't go back in time, we can be forgiven for the wrong we've done," said Dad. "You don't need to move to another time zone for that. When you let God know you're truly sorry, he will forgive you, and I will, too." *N.E.K.*

HOW ABOUT YOU?

Do you sometimes wish you could go back and have another chance? You can't go back, but you can be forgiven for the messes you've made. Confess to God what you have done. And as much as possible, make it right with other people, too.

MEMORIZE:

"**If we confess our sins to him, he can be depended on to forgive us and to cleanse us from every wrong.**" *1 John 1:9*, TLB

 ***God Forgives***

Everyone's Welcome (Read John 6:37-40)

A visit to the Statue of Liberty followed by a picnic and games! Leslie was excited about the trip being planned by Miss Webber, her Sunday school teacher. "But this won't be quite all play," Miss Webber had said. "In class next Sunday, I'm going to ask for some of the information about the statue." *How odd,* thought Leslie. *Doesn't sound like Sunday school material to me. Oh, well . . .*

26
JUNE

The day of the outing arrived. The weather was beautiful, and everyone was able to go. The tour of the Statue of Liberty was very interesting, and the picnic and games were great fun. Leslie had a wonderful time.

True to her word, Miss Webber quizzed the class the next day. When she asked about the poem inscribed on the statue, and about the kind of people invited to come to America, Leslie raised her hand. "It said something about those who are poor and wretched and want to be free," she said.

"That's right," agreed Miss Webber. "For many years, all kinds of people came and began a brand-new life in a brand-new country." She paused, then asked, "What invitation did Jesus give that is similar to those words on the Statue of Liberty?"

After thinking a moment, Leslie raised her hand again. "Is it our memory verse?" she asked. "Come to me, all you who are weary and burdened, and I will give you rest."

Miss Webber nodded. "When you come to God through Jesus Christ, accepting him as your Savior, you begin a new life—just like immigrants begin a new life in a new land," she said. "One important difference is that there are now laws limiting the number of people who are allowed to come to the United States. But there are no restrictions in the number of people who may come to Christ. Everyone is welcome." *G.W.*

HOW ABOUT YOU?

Have you accepted the invitation to have your sins forgiven? Who you are doesn't matter. The color of your skin doesn't make any difference. There are no reasons why you cannot be saved if you want to be. Jesus' invitation is for you—just as you are. Come to him today.

MEMORIZE:

"Come to me, all you who are weary and burdened, and I will give you rest." *Matthew 11:28,* NIV

 You Can Be Saved

Fish Story (Read James 1:12-15)

27

Joshua shook his head sadly. "I can't believe it," he told Dad. "Andy says he's a Christian, but last Saturday he got caught drinking. He must be really weak to get suckered into that."

"So alcohol doesn't appeal to you at all?" Dad asked.

"No way!" Josh answered. "I don't have any problem staying away from that stuff!"

"I'm glad," said Dad. "Now, are you all packed for our fishing trip?"

"You bet!" exclaimed Josh. "I can almost feel a three-foot northern at the end of my hook."

"You packed my trout flies, didn't you?" asked Dad.

"Trout flies?" repeated Josh. "What for? We're fishing for northerns. You know you won't hook one of them with a trout fly!"

Dad grinned. "I can see you know a lot about fishing bait," he said, "but how much do you know about Satan's bait?"

"Satan's bait?" asked Josh.

Dad nodded. "Satan is sort of like a fisherman," he explained. "He knows that different people are tempted by different things, just like different fish are caught with different lures. So he dangles just the right temptation in front of each of us."

"Like what?" asked Josh.

"Well, Satan knows Andy can be tempted with alcohol," Dad explained, "so that's what he used as bait to catch him and draw him away from the Lord. But what does Satan use to hook you, Josh?" Josh thought for a moment, then shrugged. "Why did you get those bad grades last quarter?" prompted Dad.

"Oh, that! Well, I spent too much time playing ball with my friends instead of studying," Josh said sheepishly. "But ball isn't a bad thing, is it?"

"No—unless it keeps you from doing something you should be doing," said Dad. "When that happens, even harmless things become part of Satan's bait." *K.R.D.*

HOW ABOUT YOU?

Are you aware of your weaknesses? What does Satan use to tempt you? Maybe it's alcohol, not doing your best at school, having a bad temper, or watching the wrong things on TV. Be aware of your weak spots and ask the Lord to help you avoid the lure Satan is dangling for you.

MEMORIZE:

"But each one is tempted when he is drawn away by his own desires and enticed."

James 1:14, NKJV

 Watch Out for Satan's Lures

Just Kidding (Read Ephesians 4:25-32)

Mike entered the house, raindrops glistening on his hair. His brother Steve met him at the door. "Mike, you borrowed my bike," said Steve. "Did you put it away?"

Mike shrugged. "Naaah. A little rain won't hurt it."

Steve dashed out to rescue his bike. Soon he returned, dripping wet. "You did too put it away, Mike," he grumbled.

Mike laughed. "I was just kidding," he said.

28
JUNE

When they all sat down at the supper table, Mike grinned at his sister Nicole who had spent a lot of time styling her hair. "Your hair still looks like a haystack," he told her.

"Mom, Mike is insulting me again," complained Nicole, while he protested that he was just kidding.

Later, Mike watched Nicole take a big bite of her salad. "There was a worm on that lettuce," he told her. "Did it taste good?" He laughed as she jumped up, spitting the salad into a napkin. "Just kidding," he teased.

After supper, the rain had stopped. "I'll teach you how to throw a curve, Mike," suggested Dad.

"Great!" exclaimed Mike. "I'll get my ball and glove."

When Mike returned to the living room, thumping his baseball into his glove, Dad was sitting in his easy chair reading the newspaper. "I want to read my paper just now," he said.

Mike coaxed, but Dad read on. Mike glared at his father's head protruding above the paper. "You lied to me, Dad," he said angrily. "You said you'd teach me to throw a curve."

Dad slowly lowered the newspaper and looked directly at Mike. "But, Mike, I was just kidding," he said. Mike looked startled. "I've heard that phrase quite a lot lately," continued Dad, "but actually, you said it even better just now. If I don't play ball with you, I will have lied." Mike was embarrassed. He knew what Dad meant. "What are you going to do about it, Mike?" asked Dad. "I think you need to ask God to forgive you and then tell Steve and Nicole that you're sorry. What do you think?" Slowly, Mike nodded his head.

V.C.M.

HOW ABOUT YOU?

Do you do a lot of "kidding"? Be careful. Be sure you don't use that term to excuse yourself when you lie or say unkind things. Be sure you don't cause others unhappiness by what you call kidding. When that happens, it's time to confess it to God. Receive forgiveness from him and from those you have hurt.

MEMORIZE:

"Be kind and compassionate to one another." *Ephesians 4:32,* NIV

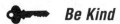 *Be Kind*

Billy's New Home (Read Psalm 139:5-11)

29

JUNE

Billy sat straight up in bed. *What's that noise?* he wondered. He and his family had moved to a new house, and now he slept in a strange, new room. Somehow, he didn't feel safe the way he had back in his old, familiar home. Billy heard the noise again. He did not want to sleep in this new room! He jumped out of bed and bolted down the stairs to find his mother.

"What's that noise, Mom?" he asked fearfully.

Mom listened for a moment. "There's a bit of thunder in the distance," she said. "It won't hurt you."

Billy knew Mom was right. The noise did sound like thunder, and it wasn't even close. There was nothing to be afraid of, but Billy was still scared. "I don't like my new room," he said.

Mom put her arm around Billy. "Sometimes it's hard to get used to a new house," she told him. "You don't feel safe here yet." She pointed to the little dog who sat at her feet. "I think Spunky still feels a little strange here, too. Why don't you take him to your room with you for company?" she suggested.

Billy looked at the puppy. "OK," he agreed. "Come on, Spunky. I'm here with you, just like I always was, and I'll take care of you."

Mom smiled. "When you get in bed, remember that we didn't move away from God. He's right here with you just like he was with you at our old house—even when it's dark and there's a storm outside. You can ask him to take care of you."

Billy went back to bed. When he heard the noise again, he pulled the blanket over himself and Spunky. "You aren't scared when you know I'm near. You know I'll take care of you and keep you safe, don't you?" he said as he stroked the puppy's head. "I'm not scared, either, when I remember that God is near. He'll take care of me and keep me safe." Then Billy closed his eyes and went to sleep. *K.E.C.*

HOW ABOUT YOU?

Do you remember that God is always with you, even when things seem scary or new? No matter how far you go, you can never move away from God. He is with you everywhere, all the time, anytime you need him.

MEMORIZE:

"Yea, though I walk through the valley of the shadow of death, I will fear no evil: for thou [God] art with me." *Psalm 23:4,* KJV

 God Is with You Everywhere

Tent Pegs (Read Psalm 46:1-3, 10-11)

Richard helped his dad smooth the big tent that lay on the ground. "I sure like camping!" he said.

Dad smiled. "Let's stretch this out and put a peg in the ground on this side and one on the opposite side," he suggested.

Richard stuck the peg into a loop on the side of the tent and pounded it into the ground with the hammer. Then he put one in on the opposite side. Dad straightened the center pole, and the tent stood by itself. "Can I go in it now?" Richard asked.

30
JUNE

"Not yet. It could collapse on you," said Dad. "We need to anchor the tent with pegs all around it." Finally the tent was secured, and they put the sleeping bags inside.

"The wind has gotten a little gusty," observed Dad a little later as they had evening devotions, "but see how secure our tent is now, Rich? The tent pegs hold it in place." He smiled at his son. "You know, there is Someone who holds us steady, too."

"I know," said Richard quickly. "It's Jesus."

"Right." Dad nodded. "Even though bad things may come into our lives, we can always count on Jesus to hold us steady."

P.O.Y.

HOW ABOUT YOU?

Many children's lives have been shaken by divorce, death in the family, crime, or loss of income. Have any of these happened to you? Trust Jesus. He loves you. He will always stay with you and help you.

MEMORIZE:

"God has said, 'I will never, *never* fail you nor forsake you."

Hebrews 13:5, TLB

 God Keeps You Secure

A Life That Counts (Read Psalm 139:13-16)

1

JULY

Steve and his Uncle Duane were hiking in the Rocky Mountains of Montana. Hoisting himself up onto a ledge of crumbling granite, Steve collapsed on a small patch of mossy grass. He rubbed his aching legs. "I've got to catch my breath," he panted.

Uncle Duane swung down his orange backpack and winked at Steve. "No problem," he said cheerfully. "We don't want to get back to the house too soon. They might put us to work!"

Steve grinned. "Yeah," he agreed. He picked up some stones. "Hey! Look at this!" he cried. Uncle Duane knelt beside him, and they looked at a stone that Steve held in the palm of his hand. Chips had been removed at regular intervals, and the rock came to an unmistakable point. "A real arrowhead," said Steve. "I'll bet it's Shoshone."

"Sure looks like it to me," agreed Uncle Duane. Steve shook his head with wonder.

Later, the two sat by the cool spray of the waterfall. Steve dug the arrowhead from his pocket. He held it up so that the light glinted off its edges. "You know," said Uncle Duane, "a Shoshone brave carefully fashioned that arrowhead, and he had a plan for it. In the hands of that hunter, it was useful."

Steve looked at Uncle Duane. He was sure his uncle was leading up to something. "We can learn from that," continued Uncle Duane. "We're far more important than a simple arrowhead, but to be useful we must put ourselves into the Master's hands . . . the hands that made us."

Steve smiled at his uncle. "You mean God, right?" he said. He looked at the arrowhead. "I'll keep this arrowhead as a reminder of that." *C.P.K.*

HOW ABOUT YOU?

Is it hard to imagine that God could use you for an important task? You are precious to God because he made you. You will be very useful as you put your life in his hands. Speak to him in prayer. Read his Word. Be willing to be what he wants you to be and to do what he wants you to do.

MEMORIZE:

"For I know the plans I have for you, . . . plans to give you hope and a future." *Jeremiah 29:11*, NIV

 *Seek God's Will*

An Important Position (Read Romans 12:3-8)

As Matt and his parents walked home from a baseball game, Matt's teary eyes and slumped shoulders told his parents that something was wrong. "Coach Nichols won't let me play first base anymore," Matt blurted out. "He says I'd help the team more if I played right field instead of first base." He kicked a small stone as hard as he could in disgust.

2
JULY

"There's nothing wrong with right field," Mom replied. "You do have one of the strongest throwing arms on the team."

Matt shrugged. "Yeah, but the guys have a saying—'right field equals left out.' The ball never gets hit to that side of the outfield. I might as well sell peanuts and popcorn while I'm out there." Nothing Matt's folks said could convince him that right field was a good position for him to play.

The next day Matt was helping his Dad plant geraniums in the front yard. "Hey, Dad," said Matt as he packed soil around each plant, "some of those little shrubs we saw while we were hiking Mount Major would look nice planted here with the geraniums."

"You're right, Son," agreed Dad, "but they wouldn't grow well here. They're suited to grow in the higher elevations." He paused, then added, "You know, God didn't intend for all plants to thrive in the same location. Each plant species has its own niche, or role, in the plant kingdom. That principle applies to people, too. None of us can do everything perfectly, but the Lord has blessed each one of us with unique talent."

Matt frowned. He wondered just what Dad was getting at, and he soon found out. "You see," continued Dad, "your niche on the ball team might be right field. Perhaps Coach Nichols thinks you can develop to your greatest potential out there. Give it a chance! And perhaps God has a lesson for you in this, too. Maybe he wants you to see that every position on a team is important—whether it's on a baseball team or Christ's 'team' on earth, his church."

L.M.M.

HOW ABOUT YOU?

Do you feel bad because you can't do something well? Don't be discouraged. God has blessed you with unique abilities. Why not thank him for what you can do? Use the gifts he has given you to the best of your ability, and you will honor him.

MEMORIZE:

"**God has given each of us the ability to do certain things well.**" *Romans 12:6,* TLB

 You Have Special Talents

The Drooping Daisies (Read 1 Peter 4:7-10)

3
JULY

"Can you watch Scotty while I get supper ready?" said Mother, getting up from the sewing table. "Your father should be home from work any minute."

"Oh, Mom," moaned Shari, standing up and stretching, "we've been working on my sewing project all afternoon! I haven't played all day." Just then her father walked into the kitchen. "Dad, watch Scotty—I'm going outside," said Shari, letting the screen door slam shut behind her. She ran out to her flower garden next to the garage.

Shari hadn't checked the flowers since the week before, and her eyes grew wide at what she found. Her beautiful daisies were drooping, looking at the ground. She ran back to the house. "My daisies look so sad," Shari wailed. "I've got to water them!"

"Shari, please set the table," called Mother, but Shari was already on her way to water her flowers.

Shari noticed her mother was unusually quiet during supper. Suddenly, Scotty accidentally spilled his milk. "Shari, please get me a towel," said Mother.

"Why me?" grumbled Shari. "Scotty spilled the milk." Mother looked at Shari with sad eyes. Then she got up from the table and left the room. Shari was shocked. "What's wrong with Mom?" she asked.

Dad frowned. "Mother needs your help to 'hold up her head,' Shari, just like your daisies did," he said. Shari looked puzzled, so Dad explained. "I think you tend to take Mother, and all that she does for you, for granted. But she can't 'hold her head up' without some help from you. She shouldn't have to always listen to you grumble or ask you more than once to do things."

Shari felt bad. She stood up slowly and went to get a towel. "I'll clean the table," she said.

"Good," approved Dad. He stood up, too. "We'll work together and do the dishes," he added.

As Shari wiped the last plate, Mother walked into the room. As she looked around the clean kitchen, a smile spread across her face. "Thank you," she said, giving Shari a hug. Shari smiled, too.

D.A.V.

HOW ABOUT YOU?

Do you expect your parents or other adults to always be strong and keep doing things for you? They get tired, too. Instead of grumbling about the work around your house, pitch in and work together. You'll be making it easier for someone in your family to "hold up" his or her head.

MEMORIZE:

"Carry each other's burdens, and in this way you will fulfill the law of Christ." *Galatians 6:2,* NIV

 *Help Willingly*

A Parent's Love (Read John 3:16-21)

4
JULY

One day when Sara went to play on her swing, she saw a little bird in the grass. The bird flapped its wings but did not fly. *That poor bird is hurt,* thought Sara. She wanted to help, so she tried to catch the bird. But each time she got close, it fluttered out of her reach. It led her way over to the front of the house, then flew up and perched on a wire high above her. Sara was surprised. *That bird can fly! Why does it want me to think its wing is hurt?* she wondered. She decided to ask her mother about it and went into the house.

"If that bird wasn't hurt, why did it let me get so close to it?" Sara asked after explaining what had happened.

Mom smiled. "There are baby birds in the maple tree. The mother bird wanted to lead you away from her babies," she explained.

"But wasn't she afraid I'd catch her?" asked Sara.

"Maybe," said Mom, "but she'd rather have you come after her than get too near her family. Parents love their children so much that they'd die to keep them safe."

"Oh, wow!" exclaimed Sara. Then she thought of something. "Jesus *did* die for us, didn't he?"

Mother nodded. "Yes, he did," she said. "He willingly died for us so we could have our sins forgiven." Sara felt warm inside. She knew Jesus must love her very much to die for her sins.

Sara went back to her swing. She heard the chirping of the baby birds way up in the tree. She could see the mother feeding them in the nest. "You're a good mother, little bird," said Sara. "You love your babies the way God loves me." *K.E.C.*

HOW ABOUT YOU?

Do you appreciate how much Jesus loves you? He gave up his life so you could go to heaven. Have you accepted this great gift? If not, do so today. Then let your life show that you love God, too.

MEMORIZE:

"For God so loved the world, that he gave his only begotten Son, that whosoever believeth in him should not perish, but have everlasting life."

John 3:16, KJV

 Accept Jesus' Love

A Little or a Lot (Read Mark 12:41-44)

5
JULY

Nancy jingled her coins together. She liked hearing the tinkling sound they made. She called it her "Sunday school song" because she jingled the coins before Sunday school class each week. She earned her own offering money, but lately she hadn't been able to find many jobs, so her offerings became smaller and smaller. Today there were no quarters or dimes—only a few nickels and pennies.

When Logan, the boy sitting next to Nancy, saw her plunk her coins into the offering plate, he giggled. "Is that all you have?" he asked. Nancy felt her face grow hot, and she squirmed in her chair. Ducking her head, she didn't answer Logan, but as she watched her classmates give their money, she noticed that everyone had more to give than she did. *Is my offering enough?* she wondered.

Back home, Nancy talked to her mother about it. "How do you know if your offering is good enough?" she asked. "My Sunday school offering was the smallest in the class."

Mother raised her brows. "I think," she said, "that your first mistake was to compare offerings. We're to give to Jesus, not to impress others. Tell me, what did Jesus think about your offering?" Nancy hunched her shoulders and let them drop. Mother was quiet for a minute. Then she asked, "Nancy, at your birthday party last month, your friends gave you presents, didn't they? Were some gifts smaller than others?" Nancy nodded. "And are you mad at the kids who gave you the smaller presents?" asked Mother.

"Of course not!" Nancy answered. "Sally's present was small, but she's my best friend. Her present was little because her family has been sick a lot—they still owe a lot of money to the hospital. I know . . ." Suddenly she smiled. "Oh, I know what Jesus thought about my offering now!" she declared. "He was happy with it because he knew it was the best I could give."

Mother smiled. "That's right," she agreed. "What matters the most is what is in your heart." *B.K.G.*

HOW ABOUT YOU?

Are you ever afraid that your best is not good enough? You can't witness well enough? Pray like someone else? Give as much money? Remember, Jesus sees your heart, and it's your love for him and your desire to serve him that's most important.

MEMORIZE:

"The Lord does not see as man sees; for man looks at the outward appearance, but the Lord looks at the heart."

1 Samuel 16:7, NKJV

 God Accepts Your Best

The Oak Tree (Read James 4:6-10)

6 JULY

"And this giant oak is the landmark for which Oak Park is named," intoned the tour guide. John listened attentively. He loved history and soaked up information like this.

Back home, he told his mother about the tour. "That big oak tree survived the Civil War, a flood, and six fires," he told her. "It kept on growing, even though the odds were a hundred-to-one against it."

"That's interesting," said Mother. After some thought, she added, "You know, you're like that tree."

John was surprised. "I am?" he asked. "I didn't survive a war or fire or nothin'."

Mother smiled. "No," she agreed, "but I still think you're like that tree. The oak is one of the slowest growing trees in the world, but it's also one of the hardiest. It survives things a normal tree would die from. Now you, John, are a Christian. You may grow slowly in Christ, but you do grow steadily. And you survive attacks from Satan."

John thought about some trouble he had gotten into the week before. "But I keep doing wrong things," he said, embarrassed.

"I know." Mother nodded. "Satan sometimes succeeds in getting you to do wrong. But the fact that you feel bad when you sin shows that you're continuing to grow."

"Really?" John smiled. "That's pretty neat," he said.

"God doesn't give up on you, Son," Mother told him, "so don't you give up, either, even when 'growing' gets tough!" *N.R.*

HOW ABOUT YOU?

Do you ever feel that Satan's attacks are too much for you? The Bible says that you have the power to resist the devil. Don't be discouraged if you make mistakes; confess your sins. God will forgive you and help you to overcome them as you trust him. Remember, God isn't finished with you yet.

MEMORIZE:

"Resist the devil and he will flee from you." James 4:7, TLB

 *Resist Satan*

Why the Sky Is Blue (Read Psalm 104:1-6, 10-19, 24-31)

7

JULY

Dad rowed the boat to the edge of the lily pads. It was the best place on the lake to catch fish, but the fish didn't seem to be very hungry. As Billy sat in the boat with his father, he watched his little red-and-white bobber closely, waiting for it to go down. The sky and trees along the shore were reflected on the calm water. Birds were singing, and a frog hopped off a lily pad and splashed into the lake. The bobber wiggled as the ripples spread under it.

"It sure is nice out here with the blue sky and water and the green grass and trees," Dad said. "It's all so peaceful. It makes me forget all about the office."

Billy turned to his dad. "We've been studying about colors in our class," he said. "Scientists say that blue slows down the heart rate and green helps prevent eyestrain. That makes them restful colors."

Dad smiled. "Do you suppose that's why God made so much blue and green in nature?" he asked as he checked his line. But the fish still weren't biting. "Just imagine what it would be like if the sky were bright red or all the leaves were black."

Billy laughed at the word picture Dad had painted. "We learned that red is supposed to raise blood pressure, so I bet that wouldn't make people feel very good," he said. After a moment he added, "God sure is smart."

"God is very wise," Dad agreed. "We see a great deal of his wisdom in nature—even in the colors he chose."

Billy looked at his fishing line. "You know what else scientists say?" he asked. "They say orange makes you hungry." He grinned at Dad. "I wish God had made these bobbers. Instead of red and white, I bet he would have made them orange to make the fish more hungry." *J.K.C.*

HOW ABOUT YOU?

Do you notice how God has created things to work together? Don't take the things around you for granted. See what you can learn about God through what he has created.

MEMORIZE:

"How many are your works, O Lord! In wisdom you made them all; the earth is full of your creatures." *Psalm 104:24,* NIV

 Appreciate God's Creation

Phony Things (Read Matthew 23:23-28)

8
JULY

"I don't see what's so bad about wearing furs," stated Joanie as she and her sister came down the stairs.

Tenderhearted Hannah frowned. "Wearing furs is unnecessary!" she cried. "It's downright cruel."

Their brother Rick looked scornful. "Arguing about furs on a hot day like this," he muttered, shaking his head in disgust. He went out for a swim at a friend's house.

That evening, the subject came up again. "Dad, people can just as well wear fake furs as real ones, can't they?" pleaded Hannah. "Most people can't tell the difference, anyway."

Dad smiled. "This family will make do with fake furs—if they have furs at all," he said. "The price of real ones makes sure of that."

"Well, I'd want the real thing, not a fake," insisted Joanie.

"It's time for family devotions," Dad told her, "so let's read about some other fakes, shall we?" The children looked at him curiously as he opened the family Bible and began to read from Matthew, chapter 23. (See today's Scripture.)

When he finished reading, Dad looked around the table. "There are still lots of hypocrites—fake Christians—around today," he said. "Often we can't tell the difference between them and the real thing. Why do you suppose that is?"

After a moment, Rick volunteered an answer. "Because they put on such a good show," he said. "They go to church, give money, do 'good' things, and in general look really good to other people."

"But they've never accepted Jesus as Savior," added Mom.

Dad nodded. "I hope," he said, "that we don't have any fake Christians in our own family. As we bow our heads to pray, let's all examine our hearts and make sure that we have truly trusted in Jesus." *H.M.*

HOW ABOUT YOU?

Are you a real Christian? You may go to church every Sunday and know all the right words to say, yet you've never accepted Jesus as your personal Savior. Most people may not be able to see that you're really a fake, but you can't fool God—he knows the difference. If you've never accepted Jesus, do so today.

MEMORIZE:

"On the outside you appear to people as righteous but on the inside you are full of hypocrisy and wickedness."

Matthew 23:28, NIV

 Be a Genuine Christian

If It Feels Good (Read Ecclesiastes 5:18-20)

9
JULY

Drops of rain still glittered on the lawn, and the wet grass felt good to Jon's bare feet. Careful to keep off the planted rows, Jon inspected the garden. The ground was muddy, but he liked the way it felt on his toes.

"We have to leave in five minutes," called Mother. "Come and get ready." Jon hurried through the kitchen to the bathroom. "Jon," Mother scolded, "you're making tracks on my clean floor."

"Sorry," mumbled Jon. Quickly he grabbed a towel and rubbed his feet with it. The mud left streaks on the towel. At least Mother didn't see that before they had to leave!

As they started out, a little, blue van sped around them, almost hitting a green truck. Jon read aloud the bumper sticker on the van: "If it feels good, do it."

"I guess it feels good to him to take chances," said Mother with a frown.

Jon nodded. "Bet it won't feel good if he has an accident," he said.

"I bet not," agreed Mom. Then she said, "When you played in the mud this morning, did it feel good?"

"Well, yes," admitted Jon. "But I didn't mean to make more work for you. Honest."

"I know," said Mother, "but it will still be your job to scrub the floor when we get home. That may not feel so good."

Jon had a question. "Is everything that feels good wrong?"

"Of course not," said Mother. "It's fun to eat, sing, run, and play. It also feels good just to talk or to listen to a story. Actually, it wasn't even wrong to play in the mud, though you should have been more careful about tracking it in. But God warns us about doing things just because they feel good. Some things will always be wrong. God knows we won't feel good after we do wrong, but we will after we do right."

"I get it," said Jon. After a moment he asked, "Mom, how do I get the mud out of a towel?" *M.M.P.*

HOW ABOUT YOU?

Have you heard the saying "If it feels good, do it"? That's not what God says. Follow his teaching, no matter how it feels at the moment. Don't think that God doesn't want you to have fun. He's given you many things to enjoy, like friends and sunshine. Doing right things will make you feel good.

MEMORIZE:

"Trust . . . in the living God, who giveth us richly all things to enjoy." *1 Timothy 6:17*, KJV

 **If It's Right, Do It**

A Mushroom's Message (Read Psalm 1:1-6)

10

JULY

"Look, Grandpa!" exclaimed Lisa, pointing to the ground. "Another mushroom!"

Lisa was visiting her grandparents for the weekend. She and Grandpa were on a nature hike, and Grandpa was looking for mushrooms. "Oh, that's a nice big one!" he said, bending down. He plucked the funny-looking growth and put it in his bag. "Let's see . . . nine, ten . . . that makes eleven," he announced. "We'll enjoy these in Grandma's stew tonight."

"I've got an idea, Grandpa," said Lisa as she swatted a mosquito. "Let's dig some up by the roots and put them in your garden. Then you won't have to come so far to get them."

Grandpa laughed. "I'm afraid they wouldn't do too well in the garden," he said. "They're quite different from other vegetables. Most vegetables enjoy lots of sunlight and good, loose soil to sink their roots into, but mushrooms prefer dark, moist conditions, and they don't have real roots or leaves at all."

Lisa nodded. "Yeah, they're funny," she said.

Grandpa smiled. "Mushrooms depend on other plants for food," he told Lisa. "God designed them to simply absorb food that other plants have made. They can't manufacture food and grow on their own." Then his voice grew quiet. "It reminds me of salvation," he added. "We can't achieve that on our own, either. Only by accepting Christ and depending on him can we truly live and grow." *S.L.K.*

HOW ABOUT YOU?

Do you often feel empty inside? Do you feel that you just can't cope with the problems in your life? You were created by God to find satisfaction and strength in him alone. Make sure you know him through his Son, Jesus.

MEMORIZE:

"Your fruitfulness comes from me." *Hosea 14:8,* NIV

Depend on Christ

A Mushroom's Message (continued from yesterday)

(Read Acts 17:1-4, 10-12)

11
JULY

"How did you like Sunday school today, Lisa?" asked Grandpa, as they drove home from church.

"OK," answered Lisa. "But it was different from my church. This one didn't have as many pretty decorations."

"There's more to a church than decorations," said Grandpa. "What about the Bible teaching?"

"Well, some of the things the teacher said today were different," Lisa said slowly. "For one thing, she mentioned that Jesus had brothers and sisters. I always thought he was Mary's only son." She sighed. "And my other teacher told us that Christians don't go right to heaven when they die, but this teacher says they do. Who do I believe?"

"That's a good question," said Grandpa. He thought for a few minutes, then he said, "I believe you accepted Jesus as your Savior last year, right?" Lisa nodded, and Grandpa continued. "Do you remember the mushrooms we picked yesterday?"

"Sure," said Lisa, surprised at his question. "What about them?"

"Well, yesterday they were a good example to us—they showed how we need to depend on Christ for salvation, like they need to depend on other plants for their food," replied Grandpa. "They also can serve as an example of us as Christians—but this time they're a bad example. But we should study God's Word on our own, too—we need to ask God to help us understand passages that aren't clear to us."

Lisa sighed. "But that's hard," she said.

Grandpa smiled. "Yes," he agreed, "but remember, as a Christian you're never alone. God will reveal his Word to you as you depend on him. I can help you, and so can other Christians, but the important thing is that you know Jesus. Human teachers may be wrong sometimes, but God is always right—so check to see if what your teachers say agrees with God's Word—the Bible."

S.L.K.

HOW ABOUT YOU?

Do you believe everything you hear in church and Sunday school? Be careful! Even the best human teacher is wrong sometimes, and you need the challenge of finding things out for yourself in God's Word. Study and find all the wonderful things God has for you!

MEMORIZE:

"Now we believe because we have heard him ourselves, not just because of what you told us." *John 4:42*, TLB

 Study God's Word

God's Creation (Read Psalm 139:13-18, 23-24)

12
JULY

As Timothy rode home from vacation church school with his mom, he began to hum a song they had sung that day: "Jesus Loves Me, This I Know." Timothy stopped singing and looked at his mom. "Does God really love me?" he asked.

"Oh yes," Mom assured him. "God loves you very much."

"Why?" asked Timothy. "Why does he love me?"

"Well . . ." Mom pointed at a picture Timothy held in his hand—a picture of flowers, grass, and trees. He had drawn and colored the picture with great care while in class. "That picture is special to you, isn't it?" she asked. "Why do you like it so much?"

Timothy looked at his picture. "I made it," he said proudly.

Mom nodded, "It's like that with God," she said. "He loves us because he made us. That makes us very special to him."

Timothy smiled. "God likes me the way I like my picture," he said happily.

"He loves you even more than you like your picture," Mom told him.

"Even more," Timothy repeated. "That's a lot, isn't it, Mom?"

"Yes, it is," said Mom.

When he got home, Timothy put the picture on his bedroom wall where he could see it every morning when he woke up. And every morning it reminded him that he was special to God.

K.E.C.

HOW ABOUT YOU?

Do you have something that is very special because you made it and it belongs to you? Remember that God made you and he loves you very much. That's why he sent Jesus to earth—to save you. Do you love him in return? Have you accepted him into your life? If not, do so today.

MEMORIZE:

"For God loved the world so much that he gave his only Son so that anyone who believes in him shall not perish but have eternal life." *John 3:16,* TLB

 God Made and Loves You

A Mist (Read James 4:13-17)

Starr stretched and yawned, then jumped eagerly from the top bunk and hurried to get dressed. As she tied her shoes, she read a plaque on the cabin wall: "What is your life? You are a mist that appears for a little while and then vanishes."

"Let's go, troops," yelled a cheery voice from outside. "We have many miles to cover on our morning hike."

"How can our counselor be so cheerful at six o'clock in the morning?" asked Ashley, one of Starr's cabin mates.

"I don't know," Starr answered, "but Mr. Jim's cheerfulness has a way of rubbing off onto me. Let's go."

Starr and Ashley joined the other campers as they gathered in front of the dining hall. "Good morning," said Mr. Jim, smiling. "Are you ready for our adventure? We'll fix ourselves some breakfast a little way down the trail." And they were off. "Stay right on the trail for a while," advised Mr. Jim. "The grass is soaked from the mist last night."

"It's not misty now," observed Ashley. "Isn't it funny how it just disappears?" Mr. Jim nodded.

After the hikers had stopped and eaten breakfast, Mr. Jim gathered them together for a devotional time. He referred to the mist again. "As Ashley said, the mist is here for a short time, and then it disappears," he said. He glanced around the group. "Did you know that your life is like that? The book of James says you're a 'mist that appears for a little while and then vanishes.' That's a serious thought, isn't it? But tell me—what did the mist do while it was here?"

"It soaked the ground," someone replied.

Mr. Jim nodded. "Right. And in a way, we 'soak' our environment, too," he said. "For example, do you know anybody who 'soaks' you with joy?"

Starr spoke up quickly. "You do," she said. "You always soak me with your cheerfulness. You make me feel happy."

Mr. Jim was surprised. "Why, thank you!" he said. "Today let's all try to 'soak' those we meet with God's love." *K.A.B.*

HOW ABOUT YOU?

Are you a "mist for Jesus"? After you've been with your friends or family, will they be soaked with God's love? Ask God to fill you with his love. Than ask him to show you whom to "soak" with it.

MEMORIZE:

"What is your life? You are a mist that appears for a little while and then vanishes."

James 4:14, NIV

 "Soak" Others with God's Love

Weeds of Life (Read Galatians 5:22-26)

Grandma Nelson was working in her garden when Sarah stopped in on her way home from school. "Grandma, this is the most wonderful flower garden in the whole world!" exclaimed Sarah enthusiastically.

Grandma looked up from her weeding and smiled. "I'm glad you like it," she said. "I enjoy it, too—and working in the flower beds always reminds me of the Christian life."

14
JULY

"It does?" asked Sarah. "Why?"

"Well, think about it," replied Grandma. "I need to work out here often. In nice weather, I spend some time each day hoeing, watering, weeding, or transplanting. The weeds would just take over if I'd let them."

"It seems like a lot of work," observed Sarah.

"Yes," agreed Grandma, "but it's worth it. Now think about our Christian life. Why do you think working with these flowers and weeding them reminds me of that?"

"Well," said Sarah slowly, "I guess it's because you have to take care of it every day to keep it really nice. It's sort of like we always have to read our Bibles and pray and stuff."

"Why do we need to do that?" asked Grandma.

"Well, I think it helps me act more like Jesus wants me to," said Sarah.

"That's right," agreed Grandma. "I have to weed and water my flower bed to keep it beautiful. I always picture the time I spend with God as his weeding and watering time for my life. Weeds in my spiritual life grow as quickly as weeds in my flower bed."

"Weeds in your spiritual life?" asked Sarah. "Do you mean sins?"

Grandma nodded. "Life is often difficult," she explained. "People may hurt us deeply; we might get mad at someone; maybe a pet or someone we love dies. When such things happen, we can become angry, bitter, and unforgiving. Those attitudes, and many other things, always remind me of weeds with very long roots. When we let God weed out those bad attitudes, we can grow in him." *R.J. C.*

HOW ABOUT YOU?

Do you ever let anger and resentment grow in your heart? It's easy to do, but Jesus really wants you to be free of those kinds of "weeds" so that your life can be a beautiful "garden" that produces the fruit of the Spirit.

MEMORIZE:

"See to it that no one misses the grace of God and that no bitter root grows up to cause trouble." *Hebrews 12:15,* NIV

 Don't Let Sin Grow

Repair Needed (Read Acts 2:42-47)

15 JULY

Alan joined his father on the cabin roof. "I'm glad we bought this cabin, but it sure needs a lot of work," he said. "It's falling apart."

Dad nodded. "That's why we were able to get it so cheap," he replied. "We'll need to replace a lot of boards up here. Be careful when you walk—they may not hold you."

Just as Dad finished speaking, Alan heard a creak beneath his foot. Before he had time to react, the wood splintered and gave way and Alan's leg plunged through the roof up to his knee. He swore before he realized what he was saying.

As Dad bandaged the slightly sprained knee, Alan offered an apology. "Uh . . . Dad . . . I didn't mean to say what I did up there. It just kinda slipped out all by itself."

Dad looked up. "Usually the words that slip out are those we use a lot." Alan looked down without speaking. He knew his father was right. "There's something else I need to ask you about because there may be a connection," continued Dad. "This morning I saw Mr. Peters, your Sunday school teacher, and he tells me you haven't had your lesson done lately."

Alan fidgeted in his chair. "Well, I've been kinda busy," he mumbled. Then he frowned. "Why is it so serious if I skip stuff like Sunday school lessons or devotions sometimes?" he asked. "I'm still a Christian, and that's the important thing, isn't it?"

Dad looked up at the gaping hole above them. "Well," he said, "our spiritual lives are a lot like this cabin. If we neglect regular maintenance like Bible study, for instance, we can become 'structurally' weak, too. Then it becomes easier to take on the ways of the world without even realizing it."

"The ways of the world?" asked Alan.

Dad nodded. "Like using words we shouldn't," he said, "and watching questionable movies—all sorts of things. The list is endless."

Alan nodded slowly. What his father said made sense. *A.J.S.*

HOW ABOUT YOU?

Are you maintaining your spiritual life? Do you regularly go to Sunday school and church? Do you take time for daily devotions? People in the early church worked regularly at spiritual maintenance. You need to do that, too.

MEMORIZE:

"They joined with the other believers in regular attendance at the apostles' teaching sessions and at the Communion services and prayer meetings." *Acts 2:42,* TLB

 Maintain Your Spiritual Life

Just a Little Old Y (Read Hebrews 6:9-12)

16

"Mom!" called Mark as he dashed into the house. "Jeff's going to ride his bike to his grandma's house this afternoon. Can I go with him?"

"Did you forget that you have to go to puppet practice later so you'll be ready for the Sunday school program tomorrow morning?" Mom asked.

Mark groaned. "Aw, I'd never be missed in the program," he said. "I have only three or four little lines in the whole thing. Can't I skip it?"

"Those three or four lines are important," said Mom. "There will be other times to ride your bike. Besides," continued Mom, "I have a little job for you before you leave for practice. You need to write a note to Grandma and thank her for the candy and cookies she sent."

"All right," Mark answered slowly. He grabbed some paper and sat down to type. *Thank ou for the cand,* began Mark's note. He stopped typing and looked at it. He touched the Y key, but nothing happened. He tried again and again. "Mom, the Y won't work."

"Let me try it," said Mom. She hit the key time after time, but it would not print. "Oh, well," she said at last, "I guess the Y isn't all that important. It isn't needed as much as other letters, and there are twenty-five other letters you can use. Why don't you just type your note with them?"

"Mother!" protested Mark. "How can I write *you* or *candy* without the Y? It may not be used as often as some letters, but it's just as important!"

"Hmmm," murmured Mom. "Reminds you of people, doesn't it?"

"People?" repeated Mark. "What are you talking about?"

"The puppet play," replied Mom. "One member may not seem very important—especially when he doesn't have much to say. But without those few words, the play wouldn't be as good, would it?"

"I suppose not," admitted Mark.

"When we have a job to do, God wants us to do our part—at church, at home, or wherever we are," said Mom, "and he wants us to do the best we can!" *M.M.P.*

HOW ABOUT YOU?

Do you ever feel that the things you do at church aren't needed? Do you leave it to others to invite friends, answer questions, and join in singing? Are you helpful at home and at school? Always do your part. It is important.

MEMORIZE:

"Whatever your hand finds to do, do it with your might."

Ecclesiastes 9:10, NKJV

 *Do Your Part*

My Will or My Won't (Read Matthew 21:28-32)

17
JULY

Jason popped a juicy, red strawberry into his mouth before putting another handful into his bucket. "Why did Mom and Dad have to get that divorce, Grandpa?" he asked with a sigh. "I just don't like Frank, and I wish he hadn't married Mom. If he hadn't come around, maybe Mom and Dad would have gotten back together."

"I know it's a hard adjustment for you, but the Bible says we must honor and obey those in authority over us," Grandpa reminded Jason. "You know," he added, "I think maybe you need to forgive your parents for getting a divorce and forgive Frank for marrying your mom. We need to forgive if we expect to be forgiven, you know."

Jason brushed away a tear. "I guess I'm a lost cause, Grandpa," he said. "But I just can't help the way I feel inside."

"Jason, did you *feel* like helping me pick berries this morning?" asked Grandpa.

Jason shook his head. "Not really," he said. "I wanted to go swimming."

"Well, are the berries in your row getting picked?" asked Grandpa.

"Sure, my bucket's almost full," said Jason, holding up the pail of sweet, juicy fruit.

"You see, Jason," Grandpa explained, "your will and your feelings aren't always the same. God wants us to serve him with our will, not our feelings. I don't think Jesus really felt like going to the cross. Do you?"

"I guess not," said Jason slowly, "but he went anyway."

"Right," said Grandpa. "So, are you telling the Lord that you don't feel like forgiving Frank and your folks, or that you will not?"

Jason thought for a moment. "OK, Grandpa, I see what you're saying. Maybe I can't change my feelings, but I can change my will."

Grandpa nodded. "Your will doesn't have to be your won't!" he said. "Right now I *feel* like having some strawberry shortcake," he added, "and since we're done picking this row, I think I will!"

Jason grinned, and they headed for the house. *J.R.L.*

HOW ABOUT YOU?

Have you ever felt guilty because you didn't feel like obeying your parents or your teacher? Or because you didn't like the boy or girl who sits across from you in school? Ask God to forgive you, and then *make up your mind* to do the right thing, whether you feel like it or not.

MEMORIZE:

"If you are willing and obedient, you will eat the best from the land." *Isaiah 1:19,* NIV

 Decide to Do Right

The Vine (Read Matthew 7:15-23)

"I wish the zinnias would last longer," said Jenny with a sigh, as Mother dumped the dead bouquet into the trash.

Mother smiled. "We can cut more," she said.

"But why did they die, anyway?" Jenny asked. "We put them in water."

"Yes, we did," her mother said, "but they need more than water. They need the nutrients they get when they're attached to the plant. We can't give them that."

18
JULY

Dad, who had just come in from the field, overheard the conversation. "You're growing up on a farm, but you've just discovered that for flowers to stay alive they have to be attached to the plants?" he teased. He grinned at Jenny. "They're just like people," he added.

"Like people?" asked Jenny. "What do you mean? I'm not attached to a plant."

"Tell you what. Let's have our family devotions now, even though it's not our usual time," suggested Dad. "Is that OK with everybody?" It was, so Dad got out his Bible and read from John 15. "'I am the vine; you are the branches. If a man remains in me and I in him, he will bear much fruit; apart from me you can do nothing.'"

Jenny's eyes opened wide. "Just like the zinnias," she said.

Dad nodded. "I think Jesus is really telling Christians that they are helpless if they don't abide in him—if they don't live in his will and follow his teachings. But this is a good warning for the unsaved, too. So many people try to please God in their own way instead of simply trusting in Jesus. But he says that apart from him, all their efforts are worth nothing. They will die in their sins."

P.O.Y.

HOW ABOUT YOU?

Are you "attached" to Jesus? You need to be, and you can be by accepting Jesus as your Savior. It's only when you are a part of him that you can do anything truly worthwhile.

MEMORIZE:

"No branch can bear fruit by itself; it must remain in the vine. Neither can you bear fruit unless you remain in me."

John 15:4, NIV

Stay "Attached" to Jesus

A Cup of Cold Water (Read Mark 9:41; 10:42-45)

19
JULY

Greg let the door slam behind him. "I don't want to go to the nursing home with our class," he said.

"Why not?" asked Mother.

"Everyone else has something important to do," he told her in disgust. "Ann and Sara will sing. Andy is going to read from the Bible. Katie will play a hymn." He scowled as he added, "I'm not good at anything."

"Isn't there something Miss Young asked you to do?" asked Mother.

"Well, yes," Greg admitted. "But it's nothing important." He paused. "All I get to do is serve lemonade."

"Anything we can do for Jesus is important," said Mother, "and Granny Brown will miss you if you don't go." Granny Brown, who was not really Greg's grandma, had lived next door for many years. Greg sighed, but he agreed to go.

At the nursing home, the music and entertainment were enjoyable. Then Andy read in a loud, clear voice: "'Anyone who gives you a cup of water in my name because you belong to Christ will certainly not lose his reward.'" Greg was surprised to hear that, but he didn't have long to think about it because soon it was time for refreshments. Greg poured lemonade, and Miss Young served the cookies. She made it seem important.

Granny Brown was first in line. "My, it's good to see you, Greg," she said. "You were my best errand boy."

Greg smiled. "I miss living next door to you, too," he told her. "Your cookies were the best." Granny wanted all her friends to meet Greg. Each of them had something to tell him about their grandchildren, and he told them about his new dog, Skipper. All too soon it was time to go home.

"Mom, Granny Brown said hello," Greg called as he dashed into the house. "I had a good time after all."

"Just doing something for others makes you feel like you've been rewarded, doesn't it?" asked Mother.

"Yes, it does," Greg agreed. "And all I did was to give them cups of cold water—with lemon juice and sugar in it." *M.M.P.*

HOW ABOUT YOU?

Would you like to do something important? Even though some tasks may not seem important to you, do them as if you were doing them for Jesus. They're important to him.

MEMORIZE:

"Whoever wants to be greatest of all must be the slave of all."

Mark 10:44, TLB

 Serve God However You Can

A Lesson of Love (Read Romans 12:9-18)

20

JULY

"Mom, the twins are fighting again," Cole said as he ran into the kitchen. "What should we do?" Cole's little brothers had just turned two, and they didn't like sharing anything. They were constantly fighting over trucks, blocks, shovels, and Mom's lap. "Was I selfish like that when I was two years old?" Cole asked.

"Sometimes," said Mom. "Little children often go through a stage where they don't like to share—experts say it's a way of becoming independent. But they have to learn that we're happier when we share and love one another." She smiled at Cole. "Sometimes it's still tough for you to be kind to others," she reminded him gently. "Like when I'm busy with household chores and I can't do what you want. Or when you're waiting for your turn at bat during baseball practice. Right?"

"Yeah," admitted Cole with a nod. "I wish we could do something to help them learn about sharing and loving."

"Let's try," suggested Mom. "Follow me." They walked out to the backyard, and Mom asked Cole to give each of his little brothers a big hug. "Cole is showing you love," she told the two little boys as Cole wrapped his arms around each toddler. "Now, can you give love, too?" she asked them a moment later. They didn't move. They hadn't learned to talk much, but their pleading eyes told what they were probably thinking: *Do we have to, Mom?* "Can you give love?" prompted Mom. "Show each other love."

The toddlers looked at each other. Then they took slow steps toward one another, put their heads on each other's shoulders, and exchanged hugs. Cole and Mom clapped and cheered. Big smiles spread across the twins' faces. They knew they had done something good.

"You know, Cole," said Mom as they returned to the kitchen, "we learn in the Bible that God wants us to love one another. Sometimes it's hard, and we think, *Do we have to, God?* But he keeps urging us to take slow steps toward each other in kindness and love. Let's be sure to obey him and try to love others." *R.J.P.*

HOW ABOUT YOU?
Do you find it hard to show kindness and love to some people? Is God urging you to reach out to someone? He will help you if you ask him.

MEMORIZE:
"Be devoted to one another in brotherly love." *Romans 12:10,* NIV

 Show Love to One Another

Twists and Turns (Read Job 23:8-14)

21
JULY

"Are we ever gonna get to Grandma and Grandpa's?" asked Kevin. "It seems like we've been driving on these winding mountain roads forever!"

"Yeah," agreed Cindy. "I can't wait to see their new house and swim in the lake. It'll feel great after being cooped up in this car so long—we've been in the car an awful lot during the past few months." Dad and Mom had been speaking in many different places, raising support to go out to the mission field.

Dad slowed for a curve. "Yes," he said, "but we're getting close to our full support now, and we should be able to leave by next summer, Lord willing."

Kevin frowned. "Sometimes it seems like we'll never get there, either," he mumbled. "First, the field we were going to was closed to missionaries. Then Mom got sick, and after that our car kept breaking down." He sighed. "If God is leading us, why does everything seem to go wrong?"

Dad began to speak, but Cindy interrupted him. "Look!" she exclaimed. "We're coming to Cedar Drive—Grandma's letter said that's the road they live on."

Dad slowed down and turned onto the narrow crossroad, and soon Kevin called out, "Hey! I bet that's the lake Grandpa and Grandma live by!" But the road made a sharp turn and then another. Soon Kevin saw the lake again—but this time it was behind them. "That lake must not be the right one," he said. However, the road turned again and again, and almost before they knew it, they saw the lake before them as they pulled into Grandma and Grandpa's driveway.

Soon they were all relaxing by the water. "This is great," said Dad, "but the winding road we took to get here reminds me of something I started to say earlier. As we obey God's leading, it may seem that the way is full of twists and turns—that it's not leading us to our goal at all. But if we keep following God, we can be sure he'll bring us to the place he wants us to be." *S.L.K.*

HOW ABOUT YOU?

Have you tried to follow God's will in your life and gotten discouraged when obstacles or delays came up? Remember, he knows where he is taking you, and he knows the best way to get you there. Be patient, and keep trusting him!

MEMORIZE:

"He knows the way that I take; when He has tested me, I shall come forth as gold."

Job 23:10, NKJV

 Trust God's Leading

Good-Looking Lure (Read Luke 4:1-14)

Holly searched through the tackle box until she found the shiny, red lure Dad wanted. "Is this the one?" she asked.

Dad took it from her hand. "Yup." He grinned. "This is the one. As soon as Mr. Fish sees this, I have no doubt he'll gobble it up."

"And then we'll catch him and gobble him up, right, Dad?" Holly beamed with excitement.

22
JULY

Dad nodded as he tied the lure to the fishing line and cast it into the pond. "We sure will," he said. "Now all we have to do is wait."

"How long do we have to wait?" Holly asked.

Dad shrugged. "Oh, maybe a few minutes, or maybe a little—hey! I think we've got a bite, Holly!"

"Oh, goody!" Holly clapped her hands. Soon Dad reeled a big, blue fish onto the shore. "Wow!" exclaimed Holly. "Are we going to eat it tonight?"

Dad nodded. "Why not?" he said.

As they drove home a little later, Dad asked, "Do you know why that shiny thing you gave me is called a lure?"

"Unh-uh." Holly shook her head.

"It's called that because it lures—or tricks—fish into thinking it's something good to eat," explained Dad. "But when they grab it, they're caught." Holly looked up at Dad and remained still. She knew he had something else on his mind. "Did you know that Satan often uses lures to trick and trap people?" continued Dad.

"He does?" Holly's eyes widened in surprise, and she shook her head.

"Yup," said Dad. "He often tricks people into thinking sin is harmless—even fun. Maybe he calls your attention to somebody who's gotten away with shoplifting or with telling a little lie, and he makes you think you should try it, too. Or maybe he uses a TV show to make things like smoking or drinking look attractive. Once you're hooked—once you've gobbled the lure—only the Lord Jesus can rescue you." *R.S.M.*

HOW ABOUT YOU?

Are you aware of the things Satan uses to lure you into sin? He lures all of us—he even tried to lure Jesus into sin. He wants you to think sin is good. Don't let him fool you. When you're tempted to do something that would not please God, ask God for strength to say no.

MEMORIZE:

"Resist the devil, and he will flee from you." *James 4:7,* KJV

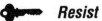 *Resist Satan's Lures*

She Made Me Thirsty! (Read Psalm 63:1-8)

23

JULY

"Mommy, Lisa made me thirsty!" cried Matthew. "She gave me potato chips."

Lisa laughed. "You didn't have to eat them, Matthew."

Matthew pouted. "She made me want them, Mommy," he insisted. "That's why I ate so many. Lisa said they were so good, and she kept eating 'em and eating 'em."

"Were they good, Matthew?" asked Mother.

"Yes." Matthew nodded. "But now I'm thirsty."

With a smile Mother poured two glasses of juice. "Did you know that Christians are supposed to be like potato chips?" she asked as she handed each of the children a glass.

"Mom! That's silly. How could anybody be like a potato chip?" asked Lisa.

"Yeah!" agreed Matthew. He grinned at his big sister. "I'd *sure* be thirsty if I ate a giant potato chip like you."

"She'd make you thirsty, wouldn't she?" said Mother, giving him a little chuck under the chin. "That's exactly how you're supposed to be like a potato chip, Matthew. You're supposed to make people thirsty for Jesus."

"Mom, how could we do that?" asked Lisa.

"Well, because the potato chips are salty, they make you thirsty," explained Mother. "Jesus said *Christians* are the salt of the earth, so we should make people thirsty for him."

"I still don't know how we can do that, though," said Lisa as she took another handful of potato chips.

"Matthew said you made him want the potato chips by telling him how good they were, right?" asked Mother. "And he could also see how much you enjoyed them."

"I think I get it!" cried Lisa. "If we tell our friends how wonderful Jesus is, and if they can see that we're happy as Christians, we'll make them thirsty for Jesus. They'll want what we have, just like Matthew wanted the potato chips!" *M.L.D.*

HOW ABOUT YOU?

Are you a salty Christian? Do you tell your friends about Jesus? Do they see that you enjoy learning about him in church and Sunday school? Does your life show that you love him? To make your friends thirsty for Jesus, you need to praise him with both your lips and your life.

MEMORIZE:

"You are the salt of the earth."

Matthew 5:13, NIV

 Make Others Thirsty for Jesus

The Hike (Read Psalm 33:4-12)

24
JULY

"I think I see the end of the trail, Mom!" Andrew shouted with relief. The family had been hiking the steep Treetop Trail for two hours, and Andrew was glad to collapse on a large, flat rock. As he rested, he gazed at the view below.

Andrew's younger brother, Michael, plopped down beside him. "Wow! This is awesome!" he exclaimed. "Hey, look, Dad! You can see for about a thousand miles, I bet!" Michael pointed to a tiny house in the distance.

Dad came to look. "I'd say that's more like twenty miles away than a thousand," he said with a smile.

"Well, it's still totally awesome!" Michael repeated.

Mother sat down beside him. "You boys are always saying something is awesome. Do you know what the word means?" she asked.

Andrew shrugged. "I don't know," he said. "I guess it just means something extra important."

"I looked it up in the dictionary after I heard you use it one day," said Mom. "There were a few definitions, and they all had to do with something sacred or sublime. One was 'a reverent wonder.' I like that."

"I like to use the word *awesome* to describe God," said Dad. "Psalm 33 says that we are to stand in awe of God. We are to respect him and recognize that he is in control of the entire world." Dad paused and looked around. "Being on this mountain makes you feel pretty tiny, doesn't it?" he added.

"You can say that again!" exclaimed Andrew.

"So it is awesome because God made it, and it gives us just a glimpse of his greatness," continued Dad.

The boys sat quietly for several minutes. Then Mother added quietly, "Yes, it's God who is truly awesome!" *D.A.F.*

HOW ABOUT YOU?

Would your friends describe a new bicycle or a spectacular fireworks display as awesome? Maybe you even do that yourself. If you want to see something truly awesome, look around you at the world God created. Think of his great power and glory. Stand in awe of him.

MEMORIZE:

"Let all the earth fear the Lord: let all the inhabitants of the world stand in awe of him."

Psalm 33:8, KJV

 God Is Truly Awesome

The Way In (Read Romans 5:1-2, 6-11)

25
JULY

"I'll be back for dinner, Mom," called Zachary, as he pulled his beach towel off the clothesline. "I'll be swimming with Micah at the country club."

"Be careful." Mom smiled and waved good-bye. "You may invite Micah over for cheeseburgers later if you'd like."

The boys had a great time swimming. Before they knew it, the afternoon was gone, and they headed to Zac's house for dinner. The aroma of burgers on the grill made the boys realize that they were even hungrier than they thought. "Yum! When do we eat?" asked Zac.

Dad gave the hamburgers a final flip before adding the cheese. "As soon as this cheese melts," he answered. "Why don't we give thanks for this meal, and then they should be ready." Everyone bowed their heads as Dad prayed. "Thank you, Father, for this beautiful sunny day, for our friends, and especially for your Son, the Lord Jesus. We ask you to bless this food. In Jesus' name, amen."

As Dad passed the food, Micah said, "We hardly ever pray at our house. There's a lot I don't really understand about it. Like why are you especially thankful for Jesus?"

"If it weren't for him, we wouldn't get to go to heaven. Right, Dad?" answered Zac.

Dad nodded. "Think of it this way, Micah. We don't have a membership at the country club, but Zac often goes swimming there. How does he get in?"

"Well, since my dad owns the country club," replied Micah, "Zac can get in because he's my friend."

"So he gets in free because he knows you, the son of the owner, right?" asked Dad. Micah nodded. "That's how it is with heaven," continued Dad. "We get to go to heaven when we know Jesus, the Son of God. And you know what, Micah? You can know him, too."

D.L.R.

HOW ABOUT YOU?

Do you know Jesus? Is he your personal friend? It's only through him that you can have access to God. It's only by knowing him that you may enter heaven. If you have never asked Jesus to be your Savior, why don't you ask him today?

MEMORIZE:

"Jesus answered, 'I am the way and the truth and the life. No one comes to the Father except through me.'"

John 14:6, NIV

 Jesus Is the Way to Heaven

God Calling? (Read Luke 16:10-13)

As Dr. Jensen talked about his "call" to the mission field, Kevin wondered what it would be like to receive a call from God. Dr. Jensen referred to it as a "strong urge to serve God," but Kevin still wondered how he would know if God ever called him to do something.

Dr. Jensen told about how he fixed a truck with the help of his thirteen-year-old son, Joel. It was especially interesting because they just didn't have any of the right tools, and Joel came up with one crazy idea after another. When they least expected results, the engine began to roar.

26
JULY

"I'd like to have been there when Joel and his dad fixed the truck," Kevin said on the way home from church.

"That would have been interesting," agreed Dad. "It was rather sad that they didn't have any decent tools to work with, wasn't it?"

Kevin nodded. "You should have been there with your supply of tools," he said. In Dad's business, he had tools to fix just about anything.

During the next few days, Kevin often thought about the lack of tools on the mission field. He had some money saved that he could use. Still, that would mean giving up the bicycle he wanted to buy. His thoughts went back and forth for some time. Then one evening, he talked to his father about it.

"Dad," Kevin said, "would the money I saved for a bike be enough to buy tools for the missionaries?"

Dad thought about it. "At my cost, that money would buy quite a lot of tools, and I'd like to throw in a few extra, if that's what you really want to do," he said after a moment.

Kevin nodded. "It is," he said. "I don't know why, but it seems a lot more important to help the missionaries than to buy a new bike." Even as he spoke, Kevin wondered if he was beginning to understand what it would be like to receive a call from God.

E.M.B.

HOW ABOUT YOU?

Do you wonder what God plans for your life? Have you thought you might like to be a missionary or pastor? Before God calls you to do something big, he will probably call you to do little things. Any time you feel a strong desire to do something good, God may be calling. How will you answer?

MEMORIZE:

"It is [God] who saved us and chose us for his holy work not because we deserved it but because that was his plan long before the world began."

2 Timothy 1:9, TLB

 Listen for God's Call

Who Says? (Read Isaiah 55:8-11; Hebrews 4:12)

27
JULY

As Leslie helped her mother in the kitchen one afternoon, she said, "Guess what, Mom? I got to witness to Cathy today."

"Great!" exclaimed Mother. "What did you say?"

"Oh, you know—I told her she had to get saved, or she wouldn't go to heaven," replied Leslie.

"What Scripture verses did you use?" asked Mother.

Leslie shrugged. "I didn't use any, but it doesn't really matter, does it?" Then she added, "Can we eat pretty soon?"

Mother nodded. "We're almost ready," she said. "Would you please call Jason in for me?"

Leslie opened the door. "Jason!" she yelled. "Come on in!"

A few minutes later, Mother asked, "Where's Jason?"

"I guess he never came in," answered Leslie. "I'll go call him again." This time she went all the way out to the sandbox. "Jason, I told you to come in!" she scolded.

"Yeah, yeah," replied Jason, without looking up. "I'm coming." But five minutes later, there was still no sign of Jason.

"It's not like him to disobey me like this." Mother went to the door and called loudly, "Jason, come in right now!"

"OK, Mom," replied Jason.

As Jason entered the kitchen a few moments later, Mother asked sternly, "Why did we have to call you three times? I want you to help Leslie set the table."

Jason looked surprised. "But Leslie didn't say *you* wanted me," he explained. "I thought she just wanted me to play a game or something."

As he left to wash his hands, Mother looked at Leslie. "Now that's an example of why it's important to quote the source of your message," she said. Leslie was puzzled. "What do you mean?" she asked.

"You said you didn't use any Scripture when you talked with Cathy about salvation today," explained Mother. "I'm glad you witnessed to her, but don't forget that the salvation message is God's, not yours. You need to tell people what the Scripture says, not just give your opinions." *S.L.K.*

HOW ABOUT YOU?

Do you look for opportunities to witness to unsaved friends? That's great! But be prepared with some Bible verses to back up what you're saying. Better yet, mark your Bible, and have your friends read for themselves what God says about salvation. Let them see that the message is from God himself.

MEMORIZE:

"Preach the word."

2 Timothy 4:2, KJV

 Use God's Word in Witnessing

The Birthday Party (Read Mark 12:28-34)

Melissa and her two friends, Danielle and Becky, were celebrating Melissa's birthday at the roller-skating rink. Melissa and Danielle were having a wonderful time, but Becky acted bored. Even before it was time to leave, Becky took off her skates and sat on the sidelines, pouting.

28
JULY

After skating, the girls returned to Melissa's house for cake and ice cream, and her two friends each gave her a present. "I made this myself," Danielle said shyly as she handed Melissa the gift. It was a cross-stitched bookmark with flowers and the words *Friends Forever* on it.

Becky snickered when she saw Danielle's bookmark. Then she handed Melissa a large box. It contained a beautiful Spanish doll for Melissa's doll collection.

Later, when Danielle and Becky had gone home, Melissa sat on her bed and looked at her two presents. "Did you have a nice time?" Mom asked from the doorway.

"Yes," said Melissa. She held up the bookmark. "I love this bookmark Danielle gave me. She really seemed to enjoy herself." Then Melissa picked up the doll. "I'm sure this was very expensive, but I'm not sure I really like it. Becky acted as though she didn't even want to be here." Melissa sighed. "Do you understand how I feel?" she asked.

"Yes, I do," said Mom. "And God understands how you feel, too—he feels the same way about our gifts."

"What do you mean?" asked Melissa.

"Well, there are several places in the Bible that tell us God wants us to obey him with a loving, willing heart," Mom explained. "If we bring him offerings or do good works with a bad attitude, he actually despises our gifts and good works." She gave Melissa a hug. "Come on," she said. "Let's have some more cake." *L.J.O.*

HOW ABOUT YOU?
Do you do all the right things without feeling any love for God? God wants you to obey him, to do kind things for others, and to give him your offerings. But more than that, he wants you to love him.

MEMORIZE:
"God loves a cheerful giver."
2 Corinthians 9:7, NKJV

 Obey God with Love

Not All Potatoes (Read Romans 12:4-13)

29

JULY

Julie pedaled her bike slowly down the road to Grandpa's house. It was a bright, sunny afternoon, and she wasn't surprised to find him working in his garden. When he saw her, he looked up with a smile. "How's my special Julie today?" he asked.

Julie felt tears well in the corners of her eyes as she walked slowly over to where Grandpa was weeding. "I really feel miserable," she admitted. "I can't do anything as good as my sisters. Lynn always makes straight A's. I studied as hard as I could for my English test, but I got a B. And Lydia's a super-good softball player. I struck out today."

Grandpa put his arm around Julie's shoulder. "You have talents, too," he assured her. "Maybe you don't appreciate the things you do well because you're too busy trying to be like your sisters." He pointed to his garden. "Do you see these carrots and potatoes and beans?"

Julie nodded. "Sure," she said.

"I'm going to make some of them into a vegetable soup," Grandpa told her. "But what if all the vegetables in my garden decided they wanted to be potatoes?"

Julie grinned. "That couldn't happen," she said, "but if it did, I guess you'd have to make potato soup."

"But I wouldn't like that as well," said Grandpa, "I like the taste of all the different vegetables in my soup." He smiled at Julie. "I think, honey, that sometimes we forget that we're not all meant to be potatoes. Just as God gives each vegetable a different taste, he gives each of us a different gift."

"So I shouldn't worry about grades?" asked Julie.

"Well, you should study hard and try to make good grades, and you should do your best at sports or whatever else you try to do," replied Grandpa. "But you should also ask God to show you your special talents so you can use them to serve him. After all, the world would be a pretty boring place if all of us were potatoes!"

K.E.C.

HOW ABOUT YOU?

Do you know that God has given you special talents? They may be different from those of your friends and family. Maybe God has given you a talent in the area of music or art or helping sick people get well. Serve God with whatever talents he has given you.

MEMORIZE:

"We have different gifts, according to the grace given us." *Romans 12:6,* NIV

 Use Your Talents for God

Dark Glasses (Read 1 Corinthians 13:9-13)

30
JULY

Sandy had spent the afternoon at the beach with her girlfriend. "We had such fun!" she declared when she got home. She plopped down in a chair and described the good time she'd had swimming, building sand castles, and looking for shells on the beach. She looked around the room. "Why is it so dark in here?" she wanted to know.

Her brother let out a whoop. "Because you're still wearing your sunglasses, silly," he told her, laughing. Sandy laughed, too, and removed the glasses.

Her father smiled. "I just thought of something, Sandy," he said. He reached for a Bible and opened it. "Put those glasses back on and come here a minute. I'd like you to read some verses for me." He pointed to the text with his finger.

Sandy looked at the Bible. "You mean with my glasses on?" she asked. Her father nodded.

Sandy held the Bible a little closer. The page wasn't very clear, but she managed to read it. "'For now we see through a glass, darkly; but then face to face: now I know in part; but then shall I know even as also I am known.'" She stopped reading and grinned at her father. "Seeing through a glass darkly describes me all right," she said.

"It describes all of us," said Dad. "When your cousin, Jason, died last month, we all were very upset and even angry, weren't we?" Sandy's expression became sad, and she nodded. "And we all had questions—we wanted to know *why*, didn't we?" Again, Sandy nodded, and her father continued softly, "In this life, we see the events occurring around us as though we had dark glasses on. Things are unclear, and we wonder why. But when we meet the Lord in Glory, we won't have questions like that anymore. We'll truly understand that God does all things well."

Sandy took her glasses off and looked at them, lost in thought. After a while, she slowly nodded her head and smiled. *R.S.M.*

HOW ABOUT YOU?

It's easier to trust God when you see things clearly, isn't it? But God appreciates faith that trusts him when things *don't* seem clear. Ask God to help you trust him, regardless of how things may appear. God loves you so much. He *can* be trusted.

MEMORIZE:

"For now we see through a glass, darkly; but then face to face: now I know in part; but then shall I know even as also I am known." *1 Corinthians 13:12*, KJV

 Trust God Even in Hard Times

Help for Mom (Read Psalm 27:1-10)

31

JULY

"Tim, if you're going over to play with Greg, wear your sweatshirt," said Mom firmly.

"All right," agreed Tim. It was a July morning. Nobody needed a sweatshirt, but neither Mom nor Tim wanted anyone to see that he was black and blue. Besides, if Tim objected, Mom might start hitting him again. That usually happened only when she was drunk, though.

Soon Tim and Greg were making roads for their trucks in Greg's sandbox. Before long, they were wiping sweat from their faces. "Isn't it too warm for a sweatshirt?" asked Greg's mother when she came outside. "At least roll up the sleeves. Here . . . your hands are dirty. I'll do it for you."

"No . . . no, don't," protested Tim.

But Mrs. Hall had already seen his arm. "Why, Tim!" she gasped. "What happened?"

"I . . . uh . . . I fell." It was true. In her anger Mom had knocked him to the floor and kicked him. "I'm all right. Honest," he said.

"Tim, you recently had a very black eye," said Greg's mother, "and you didn't want to talk about that, either." She paused a moment. "Does someone beat you?" she asked gently.

"Uh . . . well, just if I deserve it," mumbled Tim.

"No," said Mrs. Hall sadly. "Boys and girls often need to be punished, but you do not deserve to be beaten."

Tim brushed a tear from his face. "Don't tell anyone. Please don't," he begged. "Mom says someone will take me away if anyone finds out. She's always sorry when she does something like this."

"Tim," said Mrs. Hall, "your mother needs God's help to quit what she is doing. Let me call Pastor Brown and ask him to go with us to talk to her about it. We want to help her and you. Maybe you can stay with us for a while—just until she gets the help she needs." Fearfully, Tim agreed. He didn't know what would happen next. But he knew God and his friends would help. *M.M.P.*

HOW ABOUT YOU?

Have you or a friend been hurt badly—not just spanked, but actually hurt—by an angry adult? Don't keep it a secret. Tell someone who loves God and will help—someone like your pastor, your Sunday school teacher, or a grandparent. Remember that adults sometimes need help, too.

MEMORIZE:

"When my father and my mother forsake me, then the Lord will take me up."

Psalm 27:10, KJV

 Ask for Help When Needed

Little by Little (Read Psalm 119:9-16)

Kevin groaned. "Ten whole verses! That's too many. I'll never be able to memorize ten whole verses!"

His father looked up from his dinner and smiled at him. "Sure you will," he encouraged. "Ten verses are not very much to memorize." Kevin slumped in his seat and said nothing.

"Of course you can learn them," added Mother. "We can all do it together for our family devotions." Kevin stopped listening. All he could think about was what a huge challenge it was.

As they finished eating, Dad asked, "Do you remember our vacation last year to New York City?"

Kevin looked up at his father and nodded. "Yeah," he answered. "New York was fun, and so were all those places we stopped along the way—like that zoo in Ohio and the battlefield at Gettysburg. Can we go again?"

Dad chuckled. "Well, we'll see," he said. "If we did, do you think you'd like to drive straight through from here, without stopping?"

Kevin frowned and shook his head. "Uhn-uh," he answered. "That wouldn't be near as much fun."

"Well," said Dad, "here's something to think about. Just as our trip to New York was enjoyable because we took our time and didn't rush, memorizing the Bible can be pleasant if we also take our time with that. We don't have to memorize all ten verses in one night, you know."

Kevin thought about what Dad said. *Maybe it won't be so hard after all,* he thought to himself. *Yeah, maybe it will even be fun.*

R.S.M.

HOW ABOUT YOU?

Do you memorize God's Word? Why not set a goal to memorize at least one verse of Scripture each week for the next year. That may sound like a lot of verses, but if you do it a little at a time, it won't seem like much at all.

MEMORIZE:

"I have hidden your word in my heart that I might not sin against you." *Psalm 119:11,* NIV

 Memorize God's Word

In God's Hands (Read Matthew 10:27-31)

2

AUGUST

Beth lay back on her inflatable raft. She wished Daddy could play in the pool, too, but he was sick in bed. "I'm going to pop your float," her brother, Don, threatened. "You'll sink!"

"So what," Beth said, not letting his words bother her. "My life jacket will support me."

"What if I take the life jacket?" Don teased.

"It still won't matter," Beth insisted boldly. "This is the shallow end, and the water only reaches my waist."

"I might pick you up and dunk you under," taunted Don.

"No problem. I'll still be OK," Beth replied, grinning as she pointed to Mom sitting at the side of the pool.

"You're no fun," Don accused, and he swam away.

At lunchtime, Mom informed the children that she was taking Dad to the hospital for some tests and that Grandma would be coming to watch them. "What do they think is wrong with Daddy?" Beth asked.

"The doctors aren't sure yet," replied Mom. "But you know Dad hasn't felt good for a long time."

"I don't want anything to be wrong with Daddy," Beth whispered sadly.

"I don't either," Mom said, giving her a hug.

"I'm scared," said Don. "What if it's really serious?"

"Sometimes I'm scared, too," admitted Mom, "but we need to know that, whatever it is, Daddy—and each of us—will still be OK because we're in God's hands." Both children shuddered at the thought of something terrible being wrong. How could that ever be OK? "Earlier today you were teasing your sister in the pool, Don, but she knew that no matter what you did, she'd still be OK because I was there. She knew I would take care of her. As Christians, we can have absolute confidence that we're still OK, too, because God is watching, and he'll take care of us. No matter how hard the circumstances, we're safe in his hands. No matter how painful the outcome, in the end we'll be rejoicing in heaven with him." *N.E.K.*

HOW ABOUT YOU?

Has something happened that makes you feel very sad or scared? Is someone you love very sick? Has one of your parents lost a job? Did your parents divorce? Stay close to Jesus and trust him to watch over you and love you, no matter how difficult the circumstances.

MEMORIZE:

"Fear ye not therefore, ye are of more value than many sparrows." Matthew 10:31, KJV

 *Trust Jesus*

Christmas Every Day (Read Luke 2:1-7)

3 AUGUST

"We have a record-breaking 104 degrees in Lakefield this afternoon," the weatherman reported on Saturday afternoon.

"Wow!" Benji sighed. "That sure is hot! It feels like we're living in a furnace. Can we go to the town pool for a while?"

But Dad shook his head. "I drove past the pool this morning, and it's packed!" he said. "I have a better idea. Let's go for a ride." So they piled into the car and drove for some time. Finally Dad stopped right in front of a place called Noelle's Christmas Palace.

Mother laughed. "What a great way to forget the heat!" she said. "A Christmas store!"

"Jingle Bells" played over the loud speaker. Everywhere Benji looked there were Christmas ornaments, trees, and wreaths. In one corner, a lady was handing out punch and Christmas cookies.

While his parents were checking out Christmas cards, Benji walked over to a manger scene so real-looking that he could almost imagine himself in Bethlehem! For a long time, he stood there, thinking about the events of that night long ago.

"Come on, Benji," called his dad after a while. "Let's go."

On the way home, Benji was thoughtful. "Wouldn't it be nice if Christmas lasted all year?" he said.

"In a way it does," said Dad. "What is Christmas, Benji?"

"Well, it's when we remember the night God sent his Son to earth," replied Benji.

"Yes, exactly!" agreed Dad. "And isn't that something we should celebrate all year?"

"I guess so," Benji agreed slowly. "We shouldn't just thank God at Christmastime for sending Jesus. We should thank him every day!" Then he grinned slyly at his mother as he added, "So can we put up the Christmas tree when we get home?"

Mother laughed and shook her head. "We'll save that for December," she said, "but let's be sure to remember the real meaning of Christmas all year long." *L.W.*

HOW ABOUT YOU?

Are you thankful for God's "Christmas gift" every day of the year, not just in December? Thank him right now for sending his Son to earth to die for you. There could not be a better gift than that!

MEMORIZE:

"Thank God for his Son—his Gift too wonderful for words."

2 Corinthians 9:15, TLB

 Remember God's Gift All Year

The Amazing Cleanser (Read 1 Corinthians 6:9-11)

4

Dad pushed the kitchen door open with his elbow, holding his dirty, greasy hands high in front of him. "Please turn on the faucet, Jake," he said. "I've been working on the car, and I don't want to touch anything."

Jake quickly turned on the water. "You'll never get those hands clean," he said, handing Dad a bar of soap.

"Sure I will," said Dad, "but not with soap. Under the sink there's some special hand cleanser that's made for getting off grease and oil."

Jake reached under the sink and pulled out the can of hand cleanser. Dad sank his fingers into the goo and rubbed it over his hands. He worked it in well, scrubbing between his fingers and around the nails with a soft brush. When he was finished, he rinsed his hands under the warm water. "What do you think?" asked Dad. He held up his hands for Jake's inspection.

"That's some amazing cleanser!" exclaimed Jake. "Those were the dirtiest hands I've ever seen!" Dad grinned as he dried his hands.

That evening Dad and Jake listened to a news report about a prisoner who had turned his life over to Christ. The prisoner claimed to have been changed. "Did you hear all the awful things that guy did?" asked Jake. "Now he says he's different. I think that's a joke!"

"Well," said Dad, "if he's really sorry and has put his trust in Jesus, God has forgiven him."

"But after he did all those horrible things he can't just say he's sorry and be forgiven, can he?" protested Jake. "Doesn't he have to show that he's changed?"

Dad smiled. "If a person truly repents and trusts Jesus, God will cleanse him and change him," he said. "Jesus died on the cross for our sins. He shed his blood, and that blood is powerful enough to cleanse even the most sinful of souls." Dad held up his hands. "It's lots more powerful—and amazing—than that 'amazing cleanser' I used on my hands." *J.A.P.*

HOW ABOUT YOU?

Has your soul been made clean, or does it need a "scrubbing"? Do you feel like you've done some terrible thing? All sin is terrible in God's sight. Confess your sins to him and ask Jesus to wash them away. He promises to do that.

MEMORIZE:

"The blood of Jesus Christ His Son cleanses us from all sin."

1 John 1:7, NKJV

 *Jesus Washes Sin Away*

Penny's Diary (Read Titus 3:1-8)

5

AUGUST

"Ohhhh!" squealed Penny when she opened the birthday present from her sister. "A diary. Oh, goody! Thanks loads, Cathy." Her sister smiled and nodded.

"Read your book to me," begged Kenny.

Penny laughed. "I can't. See . . . the pages are all empty." She flipped through them so he could see. "This is a book for me to write down everything that happens in my life," she explained.

"Write down that I cut my finger," Kenny said importantly. "And that I got a new truck."

Penny grinned. "This is supposed to be the story of *my* life, Little Brother, not yours," she told him. "Then when I'm old and gray, I'll read my diary and remember all the stuff I did."

"Well, what if you don't like what you did?" asked Kenny.

"Then I'll rip those pages out," said Penny.

Kenny thought about that. "I want a book, too," he decided.

Dad smiled at the conversation. "You know," he said, "in a way, our lives are like a book with empty pages. We fill in a new page each day."

"That's true," agreed Mom, "and we look back over the pages, too. Some are filled with happy memories that make us laugh again. Of course, there are always a few sad pages in every life, but even those can bring good memories as we recall how God helped us through a difficult time."

Dad nodded. "God has given us the responsibility and privilege of deciding what will be printed on our 'life pages,' and we can't tear any out," he said. "We need his help to choose wisely." *H.M.*

HOW ABOUT YOU?

What kinds of things are you "writing" on the pages of your life? When you look back, will you see that you've been kind, obedient, and loving? Now, while you're still young, ask God to help you live in such a way that there won't be any pages you'd want to tear out when you look back.

MEMORIZE:

"That those who have trusted in God may be careful to devote themselves to doing what is good." *Titus 3:8,* NIV

 Fill Your Life with Good Things

Nature-in-Waiting (Read Romans 8:19-25)

6

AUGUST

Joshua rushed outdoors to see why Grandpa's dog, Blackie, was barking so loudly. He found Blackie jumping higher and higher, trying to reach a squirrel up in the apple tree. "Shame on you, Blackie," said Joshua as the squirrel loudly scolded from his perch in the tree. Joshua pulled the dog away.

Joshua decided to find Grandpa. As he headed for the toolshed, he saw Smokey, the cat, hiding in the grass and staring at some birds pecking at seeds on the ground. "Get away from those birds, Smokey," warned Joshua.

Hearing his grandson's voice, Grandpa came from the shed with two rakes. "How about helping me clean up the garden?" Grandpa asked. Joshua took a rake and followed Grandpa. "I can tell an owl was up in this tree the last few nights. Here's the fur and bones from some small animal the owl had for dinner."

Joshua frowned. "Grandpa, why do some of the animals eat each other?" he asked. "It seems so cruel."

Grandpa nodded. "Well, God's Word says that nature is groaning because of sin in the world," he said. "Ever since sin came into the world in the Garden of Eden, animals have suffered right along with people."

When Grandpa and Joshua carefully raked dead sticks and leaves from the flower bed, they saw tiny green shoots peeking above the ground. Grandpa pointed. "New life," he said. "It reminds me that someday God is going to make a brand-new world where animals won't be afraid of one another or harm one another. It's going to be more wonderful than we can imagine." He grinned at Joshua and added, "God rules over nature, in spite of sin."

C.E.Y.

HOW ABOUT YOU?

Do you feel sad that some animals have to kill others for food? Or that bigger animals often pick on smaller ones? A better day is coming for those who know Jesus. When you see new plants springing up, thank God that someday he will make all things new.

MEMORIZE:

"The wolf and lamb shall feed together, the lion shall eat straw as the ox does."

Isaiah 65:25, TLB

 God Will Make a New Earth

Love like Muffie's (Read Luke 6:27-35)

Two-year-old Becky toddled about the living room, chasing after Muffie, the dog. When she finally caught up to her, Becky reached out a chubby hand and pulled Muffie's fluffy, brown tail. Muffie did not bite or even growl. She just moved away and lay down by the fireplace. Becky followed. She tugged on the animal's ear and said, "Nice doggie." Muffie still did not growl or bite. Instead, she licked the back of Becky's hand with her big, rough tongue.

Mother, who sat across the room, was watching. "Becky, be nice to Muffie," she said.

"Why does Muffie put up with all that torture?" asked Megan, who was sitting beside her mother. "Most animals would bite someone who was always pulling on them. Muffie doesn't even growl at Becky."

"Muffie loves Becky, just as she loves the rest of our family," Mother answered. "Becky is still too young to realize that she's hurting the dog, and we all need to help teach her not to mistreat Muffie or any other animals. But no matter how many times Becky mistreats her, Muffie puts up with it. We're fortunate to have a faithful dog who is so loving and patient with Becky."

Megan nodded. "Muffie is a good dog," she agreed.

"She's a good example of how we all should treat others—even those who don't treat us well," observed Mother. "Even when others are mean or unkind, we need to do as the Bible instructs and show them love. God says to do to others as we would have them do to us. That may not always be easy, but if we have God's love within us, we can show love to everyone—even our enemies."

"Love like Muffie's?" asked Megan.

"Something like that—and even greater love than that," said Mother. "Only God can give us humans the kind of love he requires." *W.E.B.*

7
AUGUST

HOW ABOUT YOU?

Do you treat others the way you would like to be treated? Are you kind to them—even to those who are unkind to you? The verse below is called the Golden Rule. Follow it—it's one of God's commands.

MEMORIZE:

"Do to others as you would have them do to you."

Luke 6:31, NIV

 Follow the Golden Rule

Pretender (Read Isaiah 29:13-16, 20-21)

8
AUGUST

Steve and his sister Barbara had found an interesting insect out in the garden. "Look," said Barbara, "it's praying!" Sure enough, the insect's forelegs were folded together as if in prayer.

"Let's catch it and see if we can find out its name," suggested Steve. He quickly ran and got a jar. After capturing the insect, the children searched through Steve's book about bugs and found its picture. "It's a praying mantis," announced Steve.

"Does it really pray?" asked Barbara.

Steve laughed. "Of course not!" he said. "Bugs don't pray!"

"What are you going to feed it?" asked Barbara.

Steve looked at his book. "It says here they eat other insects," he said. "They like to eat their prey alive."

"Gross!" exclaimed Barbara, wrinkling up her nose.

"'If you put a small piece of meat on a string and move it in front of a praying mantis, he will think it's alive and eat it,'" read Steve from the book. So they tried it. Sure enough, the mantis lunged for the piece of hamburger Steve put on the end of a string. The children were laughing about its actions when Mother entered the room. "See our praying mantis," said Steve. "My book says here that he's a vicious creature. The female will even eat her husband if she gets hungry enough."

"Why, you little hypocrite," said Mother, looking at the insect. "You look so holy with your forelegs folded like that, but you're a pretender, not holy at all."

Barbara giggled. "That would be a good name for him," she said, and Pretender he became.

Whenever Steve looked at Pretender, he felt a bit funny inside. He knew he was a pretender himself. Everybody probably thought he was a Christian, but he knew he really wasn't. He had never asked Jesus to forgive him and take over his life. When he went to bed that night, God seemed to be whispering to him, *Haven't you been a pretender long enough, Steve? Don't you want to be a real Christian?* This time Steve said yes to Jesus. *M.H.N.*

HOW ABOUT YOU?

Have you said yes to Jesus and asked him to take over your life, or are you a pretender? If you are, don't you want to change that and become a real Christian today?

MEMORIZE:

"These people . . . honor Me with their lips, but their heart is far from Me." *Matthew 15:8,* NKJV

 Don't Be a "Pretend Christian"

The Hidden Spot (Read Psalm 32:5-7; Proverbs 28:13-14)

9

Tommy glared at the blue scribble marks on the wall he was painting in the family room. His little sister must have gotten her hands on his markers again. He glanced over his shoulder to where his dad was painting the trim around the window. If Dad saw the marks, he would make Tommy scrub them off before continuing. That would take so long, and Tommy wanted to go outside and play ball with his friends. Quickly, he zipped the paint roller over the marks. *There! Nobody will ever see them*, he thought. Soon he finished the wall and raced outside.

After supper that evening, Dad called Tommy into the newly painted room. "Do you see anything wrong with the wall you painted today, Tommy?" he asked. Tommy looked it over. He gasped as he saw those same blue marks again!

"How can that be?" asked Tommy in astonishment. "The paint completely covered those marks this afternoon!"

Dad smiled. "The ink from the marker bled through the coat of paint you put over it," he explained. "It would have been much easier to just clean off the marks before you painted. Now it will take a lot more work." Tommy sighed with frustration. "You know, those marks are a lot like sin," added Dad. "Sometimes we try to cover up our sin by 'painting' a bright coat of deceit—like a lie—over it. We can hide it for a while, but eventually it will show up in our lives. Can you think of a Bible verse that tells us how we can clean up our 'spots,' Tommy?"

Tommy thought for a minute. He nodded. "First John 1:9 says that if we confess our sins, God will forgive us and make us clean."

"Exactly," said Dad, "and if you keep yourself clean on the inside, no dirty spots will show up on the outside, either. Now . . . let's get to work on the spots on this wall." *E.C.O.*

HOW ABOUT YOU?

It's easy to tell a little lie to keep from getting punished or to get your own way, isn't it? You may think nobody will ever know or that it won't hurt anything, but God knows, and it hurts him. Remember, you can't hide anything from God. So don't try to cover your sin. Confess it and receive forgiveness.

MEMORIZE:

"There is nothing concealed that will not be disclosed, or hidden that will not be made known." *Luke 12:2*, NIV

 God Sees Everything

Bonuses (Read Luke 6:30-38)

10

"Everybody's frowning at me," said David. "I wish they'd smile instead of scowling at me all the time."

"I have just the remedy," said David's mother. "I have a wonderful experiment for you to try—and you'll get bonuses from it, too."

"Bonuses?" asked David. "What's bonuses?"

"A bonus is something good you get in addition to what you have earned—it's something extra," explained Mother.

"Bonuses," repeated David. He liked the sound of that.

"Here's what you do," said Mother. "Every day you think of one or two things you can do for other people. Then you do them. Try it for a week and see what happens—see what bonuses you get."

David thought for a moment. Then he said, "Just what *are* the bonuses . . . and who gives the bonuses to me?"

"In a way, they come from God," said Mother. "The Bible says, 'Give, and it will be given to you. A good measure, pressed down, shaken together and running over. . . . For with the measure you use, it will be measured to you.' The bonuses are surprises from God, but they come through people. They don't necessarily come from the people you help, but the bonuses do come."

David decided to try it. That week he polished his dad's shoes; he washed his uncle's car; he even got the dog's leash and took his dog for a walk—after all, dogs are God's creatures, too.

All that week, as David gave, people started smiling at him. He felt happier than before. The Bible verse was true—he was getting more than full measure for everything he had given to others.

"How do you like your experiment?" asked his mother.

"It's neat," declared David.

"Whenever God promises something, he does it," said Mother with a smile. "And you know what? All week you've been acting like Jesus would. He went about doing good—and so have you!" David smiled, too. *C.J.Z.*

HOW ABOUT YOU?

Does it seem to you that you're always in trouble? That you get raps on the knuckles instead of pats on the back? Do they doubt you instead of having faith in you? If so, maybe you need to try "giving of yourself" to them.

MEMORIZE:

"Freely you have received, freely give." *Matthew 10:8,* NIV

 Do Things for Others

Unfinished Projects (Read Philippians 1:6, 9-11)

11
AUGUST

"Can I get this?" Charlie asked, showing a model airplane kit to his mother. "It would be so neat to put it together."

"You mean it would be neat to start putting it together," Mom corrected. "Then you'd let it sit, unfinished, like all the other projects lying around your room."

"Aw, Mom," protested Charlie, "I'm still working on them."

"It sure doesn't look that way," said Mom with a frown.

"But I am!" insisted Charlie. "Some of the models are waiting to dry before I do the next step. And my bike is still apart because Dad wants me to wait till the part it needs goes on sale. And the puzzles I've started . . . well, I like to do them a little each day. I'll get them done."

Just then some people from their neighborhood came along. Charlie looked down at the floor while Mom chatted with them. "Why didn't you say hello to the Gordons?" Mom asked after their neighbors moved on.

"I don't know," Charlie replied. "I never know what to say to adults. I feel embarrassed and tongue-tied. They make me nervous."

"Maybe you could work on learning to speak to them," suggested Mom.

"I'll try," Charlie said with a sigh. "I've even asked God to help me," he added. "He's helped me with other problems, but not this one. I'm beginning to think God is going to keep me this way."

Mom looked at the model airplane kit Charlie was holding. "OK, you can have that," she said. "I'll trust you to finish the work you've started in your own good time. And let's trust God to finish the work he started, too. You see, when you accepted Jesus as your Savior, God began a good work in you, and he's still working. God hasn't stopped shaping you or helping you to talk to adults. He's working in the time frame that he knows is best for his project to turn out just right." *N.E.K.*

HOW ABOUT YOU?

Do you get discouraged when you lose your temper? When you feel too shy to be friendly? When you forget to read your Bible? Keep on working on these and other areas of your life and ask God to help you. Remember that he is working and won't stop until you are just the way he wants you to be.

MEMORIZE:

"God who began the good work within you will keep right on helping you grow in his grace until his task within you is finally finished on that day when Jesus Christ returns."

Philippians 1:6, TLB

 God Is Working on You

A Good Snake (Read Genesis 1:21-25, 31)

12
AUGUST

"Katy, look what I found in the woods!" Scott approached his sister, carrying a cage. Something was moving inside.

"Oh no! Get that out of here!" screamed Katy.

Scott laughed. "It's only a garden snake," he said. "It can't hurt you."

"Daddy! Daddy!" Katy dashed behind her father, her eyes filled with fear. "Kill it!"

"Don't be afraid." Dad put his arm around Katy. "What Scott says is true; garden snakes aren't poisonous. We don't kill something just because we don't like it. All animals are God's creatures, so we learn to treat them with respect."

"Why do people hate snakes?" asked Scott.

"I guess because they remind us of evil," replied Dad. "Satan, as a serpent, tempted Eve to sin. And sometimes we hear of snakes harming farmers' poultry and livestock."

"Maybe if they'd quit biting people we'd like them better," put in Katy. "After all, people can die from snakebites."

"That's true," said Dad. "God has given some snakes built-in protection from enemies. Deer have antlers, porcupines have quills, skunks have spray, and many snakes have venom."

"Sometimes shoes are made from snakes' skin," said Katy.

Dad nodded. "Their skin can be used for many good purposes," he agreed. "And snakes can rid our property of mice and insects that carry germs. Many years ago the bubonic plague, caused by infection from rats and fleas, killed a fourth of Europe's population. Had there been more snakes, the epidemic might have been averted."

"See, Katy," said Scott, "there are good things about snakes as well as bad."

Scott and his sister studied the squirming captive. "I wonder how long it is," said Scott. "Will you get a tape measure, Katy?"

"OK." She ran toward the house. "But I won't hold its tail!"

J.E.R.

HOW ABOUT YOU?

Do you remember that God created everything? Plants? Animals? People? God made them all for a purpose—and he made everything good. Treat all of his creation with respect.

MEMORIZE:

"The Lord works out everything for his own ends—even the wicked for a day of disaster."

Proverbs 16:4, NIV

 Every Creature Serves a Purpose

The Big Picture (Read 1 Peter 1:6-8)

13

AUGUST

It had not been a good week! First, Jenny's dog died. Then her friend moved away. To top it off, on Saturday Jenny discovered that her favorite dress had accidentally been bleached in the washer. By the time Mother returned from her afternoon shopping trip, Jenny was feeling absolutely terrible. She told Mom all about it.

"Things certainly have seemed to take a turn for the worse lately, haven't they!" said Mom as she put a big square package on the table. Jenny just nodded her head and turned to stare out the window. "I bought a picture to hang on the wall," said Mom, motioning toward the package. She smiled at Jenny. "Would you like to see it?" Jenny really didn't care at the moment, but she put on a smile and walked over to the table.

"Would you get me a pair of scissors from the drawer, please?" her mother asked. Jenny got the scissors and gave them to her mom. She was surprised when, instead of taking the picture out of the package, her mother cut a small hole in the center of the wrapping. "How do you like my new picture?" asked Mom with a smile as she held the package up for Jenny to look at it.

"I can't see it—it's still in the package!" replied Jenny.

"Yes," her mother answered, "but you can see the picture through this hole, can't you?" Jenny shook her head. She was puzzled. Surely Mom knew she couldn't see the picture!

Mom smiled at Jenny. "Sometimes life is like this package, honey," Mom said. "At times, all we can see is a small hole in the package that covers the big picture of our lives. But we can trust God to use everything in our lives to make something beautiful." Then she unwrapped the package. It really was a beautiful painting! *R.S.M.*

HOW ABOUT YOU?

Are you troubled by things that have happened in your life and don't understand how they fit into the "big picture"? Trust your days to God. When he "unwraps the package," things will look different.

MEMORIZE:

"Trust in the Lord with all thine heart; and lean not unto thine own understanding."

Proverbs 3:5, KJV

 God Is in Control

The Tattered Bible (Read Psalm 119:24-33)

14
AUGUST

"It's getting dark. We'd better hurry," said Grandpa, as he and Jim walked along the path. The two had been exploring the woods near Grandpa's summer cabin.

Jim pointed ahead. "Look! There's a fork in the path," he said. "There aren't any trail markings, but the path to the left looks overgrown with weeds. The one to the right is all trampled down as if lots of people have gone that way, so I think we should take it." Grandpa nodded in agreement.

That evening, Jim sat by the fireplace with his grandparents. "Jim," said Grandpa, "would you hand me a Bible, please? It's time to read a chapter."

When he went to the bookshelf, he noticed two Bibles—one looked shiny and new, and one looked worn and tattered. Even some of the gold lettering was worn off the leather cover. "Here, Grandpa," said Jim as he handed his grandfather the shiny, new Bible. "This one is cleaner than the other one."

"OK, I can read from this one," agreed Grandpa. "I got this Bible as a birthday gift last month, and I haven't used it much yet. I usually prefer to use the old one."

"Why?" asked Jim.

"Bring it here, and I'll show you," replied Grandpa.

Grandpa showed Jim how some pages in the old book were marked with notes taken in Sunday school classes or church services. Many verses were underlined, and the margins were filled with comments. "This Bible has been with me for thirty-five years, Jim," said Grandpa. "It's been well used, and it's easier for me to find passages dealing with specific topics."

"So isn't this new Bible as good?" asked Jim.

Grandpa smiled. "It's just as good," he said, "but these Bibles remind me of the fork in the path on our hike today. Because the path on the right was well worn—well used—it directed us, just like a well-used Bible directs me. All Bibles are fine, but they help you only if they're used, not if they're left on a shelf. Now, let's start reading." *T.K.M.*

HOW ABOUT YOU?

Do you read your Bible daily, or does it lie on a shelf for weeks without being used? Take it down and start reading it every day. Mark the verses that speak to you. God gives you his Word, the Bible, to guide you in all you do—but it guides you only if it's opened and used.

MEMORIZE:

"Show me your ways, O Lord, teach me your paths."

Psalm 25:4, NIV

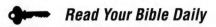 *Read Your Bible Daily*

Junior High Blues (Read Psalm 37:3-6)

"It's hard to believe you're already old enough to be in junior high this year, Chad," said Mother as they drove home from shopping for school clothes.

"Don't remind me," Chad said miserably. "I wish I could stay in my old school forever."

"Why is that?" asked Mother.

"Easy," replied Chad. "My class last year was the oldest one in school. There weren't any bullies to bug us or call us names."

"Sounds like you have the junior high blues before you even get there," observed Mother as they waited for a light.

"Well, this year my class will be the youngest again, so all the bullies will pick on us," explained Chad.

"Remember your tricycle, Chad?" asked Mother as she watched a little girl on a tricycle cross the street with her mother. "How come you don't ride it anymore?"

"Ride my tricycle?" asked Chad in surprise. "Wouldn't that be a sight!" He grinned at the thought. "I'm much too big to ride that thing now."

Mother smiled as the light turned green and they went on. "Remember, Chad, how you prayed every night that you could take the training wheels off your first bike?" she asked.

Chad laughed. "I guess I did, didn't I?" he said. "Well, after all, a kid doesn't want to be a baby forever."

"You do," said Mother. "At least when it comes to school."

"Oh! Well, school is different," Chad said defensively.

"Somewhat different," agreed Mother as they turned into their own driveway. "But just as you went from your tricycle, to a bike with training wheels, to a bike without when the time was right, you'll go from elementary school to junior high to high school. Whenever you fell off your bikes, you had Dad and me to pick you up. And we'd often pray about your problems, too. Well, your father and I are still here for support, and you're never too big to pray. Don't worry so much about next year; just enjoy today." *R.K.M.*

HOW ABOUT YOU?

Do you worry about going to a new school? moving to a new place? graduating? Pray about the new events coming up in your life, but don't spend your time worrying. Enjoy today and, trusting God, look forward with confidence to the years ahead.

MEMORIZE:

"Do not worry about tomorrow." *Matthew 6:34,* NKJV

 Don't Worry about the Future

Toys and Things (Read Romans 14:12-13, 19-21)

16

Sherri's friends, Susan and Jenny, had come over to play, but when Jenny picked up a toy Sherri wanted, Sherri became very angry. "Give it to me!" she demanded, grabbing at the toy. When Jenny didn't let go, Sherri slapped her on the arm. That worked! Jenny let go of the toy; she also got up and went home. "You're just a big baby," Sherri called after her.

Susan looked doubtfully at Sherri for a moment before joining in. "Yeah, a big baby."

After Jenny left, Sherri said, "I don't like Jenny much."

Then the girls began to talk about several of their classmates—about what funny clothes they wore, how stupid they were, how ugly.

After a little while, Sherri's mother looked in. "Time for Susan to leave," she announced. "And Sherri, pick up all those toys, and then I want to talk to you."

Susan left, and without picking up the toys, Sherri went to her room. Soon she heard a piercing scream. She rushed back to the family room and saw that her little brother, Scotty, had stumbled over one of the toys and cut his head. The cut was bleeding badly, and Sherri felt terrible.

When Scotty had been taken care of, Mother sat down with Sherri. "I'm sorry," whispered Sherri. "It's all my fault that Scotty got hurt. I should have put the toys away."

Mother nodded. "Yes, but I'm even more concerned about something else," she said. "Wasn't Susan saved at Kid's Club just a few weeks ago?" Sherri nodded. "Well, not only did you cause Scotty to stumble, but I'm afraid you may have caused Susan to stumble in her new life as a Christian," said Mother. "I saw the way you acted today, and I heard some of your conversation. I'm afraid your words and actions were not pleasing to the Lord."

Sherri blushed as she remembered her behavior that afternoon. "I think an apology is in order, don't you?" Mother asked. "To Susan, and to Jenny, too?" Slowly Sherri nodded. "It's a serious thing," added Mother, "when we cause someone else to sin." *H.M.*

HOW ABOUT YOU?

Are you careful to be a good example to other Christians—especially to new ones? It's important to live so that you do not cause anyone else to fall into sin. Ask God to help you do that.

MEMORIZE:

"Live in such a way that you will never make your brother stumble by letting him see you doing something he thinks is wrong." *Romans 14:13*, TLB

 Don't Cause Others to Stumble

New Glasses (Read Psalm 119:9-18)

Sara skipped down the sidewalk toward Grandpa's house. Her new glasses felt strange, but she thought she looked very grown-up wearing them. She was amazed at all the things she could see! For example, the trees had individual leaves even when she wasn't up really close. She could also see the unique bark pattern on the tree trunks. When she focused her eyes on the stop sign at the far corner, the previously fuzzy letters were replaced by sharp, clear ones. She laughed in delight. Sara picked up her pace as she got closer to her grandparents' house. She saw Grandpa working in his front yard. Even from where she was, she could see the cable stitch in the blue sweater Grandma had knit for him.

17

AUGUST

As Grandpa led Sara into the house a little later, he said, "We have one excited little girl here, Grandma." Happily Sara told Grandma all she could see with her new glasses.

Grandma smiled. "God has many wonderful things in his world for you to see," she said. "I can remember when I got my first glasses, too."

"And I can remember when I got my spiritual glasses," added Grandpa.

"Spiritual glasses?" Sara asked. "What are they?"

Grandpa smiled. "Well, when you ask Jesus to come into your life, he opens your spiritual eyes," he explained. "You begin to see—or to understand—his Word and his plan for your life."

"And that's wonderful," added Grandma. "To see and understand the things of God is the most wonderful sight of all." She looked at Sara. "Do you plan to wear those glasses every day?" she asked. "Or will you leave them lying on the shelf sometimes?"

Sara laughed at the silly question. "Of course I'll wear them every day," she said. "What good will they do otherwise?"

Grandma nodded. "Use your spiritual sight every day, too," she advised. "Otherwise it will do you no good." *P.O.Y.*

HOW ABOUT YOU?

Do you exercise your spiritual sight every day by seeing what God has in his Word for you, or just on Sundays? The things from God's Word are even more wonderful than things you see in nature. Don't miss out—ask him today to open your eyes and help you to understand his teaching.

MEMORIZE:

"Open my eyes that I may see wonderful things in your law."

Psalm 119:18, NIV

 God Gives Spiritual Sight

Not Whitewashed (Read Psalm 51:1-12)

"Look, Keith, I didn't *mean* to hurt your stupid bike! You don't have to get so mad!" Justin was defending himself as his younger brother stared at the scratches on his bicycle.

"What's going on out here, boys?" asked Dad as he walked up.

"Justin took my bike and messed it up!" exclaimed Keith, anxious to get in the first word.

"Well, somebody left a big rock on the sidewalk," Justin put in quickly. "Besides, look what happened to my white shirt when I fell. It's got grass stains on it!"

"Well, Keith," said Dad, looking at the bike, "I think we can touch up this paint so it'll hardly show. I'll help you with it, OK?" Keith looked relieved as he nodded. Then Dad turned to Justin. "Let's see. . . . I think I have some paint that should work fine on that stain on your shirt, too."

"Paint?" asked Justin. "What do you mean? Mom will have to wash it to get it clean. We can't paint it—that would just cover it up."

"But wasn't that what you were just trying to do?" asked Dad. "Instead of accepting your responsibility and apologizing, you tried to make excuses. You even made yourself a victim by complaining about your shirt. You were trying to 'paint over' or 'whitewash' what you did."

"Well, I guess I should have been more careful," admitted Justin.

"The Bible tells us to confess our sins to each other," said Dad, "and also to forgive each other. If you admit you were wrong and ask Keith to forgive you, I'm sure he'll be willing to do that."

Before Justin could speak, Keith said, "Sure, I'll forgive you, Justin. I just wanted you to be more careful."

Dad smiled. "When we do wrong—when we sin—it's important to also confess it to God and ask him to forgive us," he said. "Then the sin is washed away—kind of like Mom will wash away this stain on your shirt." He grinned at the boys as he added, "It's a lot better to be washed white than to be whitewashed." *L.F.W.*

HOW ABOUT YOU?
Do you sometimes make excuses or blame others when you've done wrong? Wouldn't it be better to take responsibility and receive forgiveness? God will forgive—and others usually will, too.

MEMORIZE:
"Wash me, and I shall be whiter than snow." *Psalm 51:7,* KJV

 Confess Sin; Receive Forgiveness

Time Capsule (Read Luke 12:13-21)

It was Brownville's one-hundredth birthday, and Gayle stood on tiptoe, stretching to see the town officials on the platform as they unlocked the time capsule that had been created and stored one hundred years ago. Then the mayor presented several papers and mementos from the capsule.

"Wouldn't it be fun to have a time capsule for our family?" Gayle asked on the way home. "I'm going to start one—I'll put in family treasures for future generations."

As soon as she got home, Gayle found a box. She took some coins and a dollar bill from her wallet and placed them in the box. Then she packed in a neon shirt, a cassette tape, and one of her favorite cartoons from the newspaper. Next she added her old, worn teddy bear, an old pair of swimming goggles, a report card, some jewelry, a Frisbee, and a family photo. "That about does it," Gayle told her parents. "When the next generation sees this, they'll get an idea what their ancestor—that's me—was like. I'm going to call this 'Gayle's Treasure Box Time Capsule.'"

"Those are nice earthly treasures," Mom commented. "I'm sure they'll be interesting to future family members. But if you want to make a statement about your life, I think you're missing the most important thing."

"A pair of Rollerblades!" Gayle guessed, thinking of her favorite sport.

Mother shook her head. "I was thinking about something that makes your life important and worth living, even without any of the other things in the box," she said.

Gayle knew what her mother meant, and she was really embarrassed. "But I can't put my Bible in there," she said. "I need it."

"What about writing out some favorite verses," Dad suggested. "Or including a short testimony about what Jesus means to you? After all, these earthly treasures will get old and outdated, but what really matters will last forever." *N.E.K.*

HOW ABOUT YOU?

What is your most important treasure? Be honest now. If it's some earthly thing—such as money, clothes, toys, good grades—you need to remember that such things will pass away. Ask God to help you please and serve him. Store up treasure that lasts.

MEMORIZE:

"Lay up for yourselves treasures in heaven, where neither moth nor rust destroys and where thieves do not break in and steal." *Matthew 6:20,* NKJV

 Store Up Heavenly Treasure

Not Afraid (Read Psalm 61:1-4)

20
AUGUST

"Oh, look!" exclaimed Lana, as she and her family toured the outdoor farm section of the museum. "Aren't those baby chicks peeking out from under that mother chicken?"

"Yes, that's where they go when something frightens them," replied her father.

"Me see, too," begged Jonathan, Lana's little brother. Grabbing his hand, Lana pulled him over to the fence and showed him the mother hen and chicks.

"Can I have one of them babies?" he asked.

"No, sweetie," Mother spoke up. "They would be very lonesome if we took them away from their mother." As she spoke, big drops of rain began to spatter around them.

"How far is it to the car, Dad?" asked Lana, as she hunched down into her jacket.

"This is a big place, kiddo—it's a long way to the parking lot," replied Dad, looking at the sky. "I think we're in for a downpour. Let's go over to the pavilion and wait it out there." The family ran to the pavilion and huddled with the rest of the people who were trying to stay dry.

"Look what I've got in my purse," said Mother as Jonathan scrunched close to her. She pulled out a small envelope and opened it. As she pulled the contents out, it opened up into a thin raincoat. Putting it on, she pulled it down around Jonathan to keep them both dry. All that could be seen of Jonathan was his head sticking out of the raincoat as he huddled close to Mother.

"Look at Jonathan, Dad. He looks like a baby chicken," said Lana with a laugh.

"They were 'fraid!" protested Jonathan. "I not 'fraid."

"Well, if you were, Tiger, that would be just the place to be," said Dad. He smiled at Jonathan. "That reminds me of Jesus. He wants us to get as close to him as we can. Then we don't have to be afraid."

"Like the little chicks aren't afraid when they're close to their mother?" asked Lana.

"That's right," Mother said. "Isn't it nice that Jesus loves us so much?" *M.L.D.*

HOW ABOUT YOU?

Are you sometimes afraid? Do you know what to do about it? Where to go for help? If you're a Christian, you don't have to be afraid because Jesus will never leave you. When you feel afraid, talk to him about it, remembering that he's right there with you. Trust him.

MEMORIZE:

"When I am afraid, I will trust in you." *Psalm 56:3,* NIV

 Jesus Takes Care of You

The Woodpecker Tree (Read 2 Corinthians 6:14-18)

21 AUGUST

Robert and his family got up early to join a special nature walk with the camp guide. "Enrique!" Robert called, as he spotted a boy who had become his friend during the week. Enrique ran over, and the boys sat together on a rock ledge beneath a tall tree until the guide arrived.

"Before we start our nature walk, I want to show you our famous woodpecker tree," said the guide.

"Woodpecker tree," said Enrique to Robert. "I have never heard of a woodpecker tree. I don't think we have them in my country."

The guide overheard Enrique and laughed. "Well, look up, boys," he said. "You're sitting under one right now."

When the boys looked up at the tall tree, they saw that nearly all the upper trunk was covered with holes. "Wow!" said Robert. "I see why you call it a woodpecker tree."

"Don't all those holes hurt the tree?" asked Enrique.

"If you mean will the tree die because the woodpecker makes holes in it, no," replied the guide, "but the tree will always be scarred. There will always be holes in it."

"That sounds like the sermon my dad preached last week," said Enrique.

"Really?" asked Robert. "What did he say?"

"I remember it in Spanish," said Enrique, "but I'll try to say it in English. Dad said that when someone sins, that person can stop doing wrong things and be forgiven by God." Enrique paused, trying to find the right words. "That would be like chasing the woodpeckers away, I guess," he said, "but the scars from the sin would still be there—like the woodpecker holes are still there. Did that make sense?"

Robert nodded. "Sure does," he said. "And I think it's a good thing to remember." *P.O.Y.*

HOW ABOUT YOU?

Do you think it doesn't matter so much if you do something wrong because God will forgive you anyway? It's true that God will always forgive your sins, but bad things you do now or bad habits you acquire (such as using drugs, smoking, being unkind, or lazy) can cause lifetime scars.

MEMORIZE:

"God has bought you with a great price. So use every part of your body to give glory back to God because he owns it."

1 Corinthians 6:20, TLB

 **Sin Leaves Scars**

Grandpa's Sheep (Read John 10:2-5, 14)

22
AUGUST

"Oh, look!" exclaimed Megan as Mother parked the car at Grandpa's farm. "Grandpa has sheep now! Let's pet them."

The children climbed out of the car and raced toward the sheep pen. "I'm first," yelled John. But the sheep darted for the farthest corner of the pen. "We scared them," said John in disgust. "This time let's walk, not run."

"Help me pull some grass," suggested Megan. "That will bring the sheep to us." John agreed, and they each pulled an armful of grass and slowly carried it toward the sheep. All at once the flock spun around and dashed away. Megan dropped her grass. "I give up," she said.

As John threw his grass on the ground, the children saw Grandpa coming to meet them. They ran to give him a hug. "Grandpa, why do you have those baby bottles? asked Megan, when she saw what he was carrying.

"Two of my lambs need these," replied Grandpa. "I feed them because their mother died."

"I wish I could feed a lamb," said Megan, "but your sheep don't like us. They run away."

Grandpa smiled. "Watch," he said, as he led the children to a small pen beside the barn. "Here, Fluffy. Here, Snowball," he called as he opened the pen. Two lambs scampered out and followed Grandpa across the lawn.

"They play follow the leader," said John.

Grandpa nodded and handed the children the bottles. "You can hold the bottles for them," he said.

Megan giggled as she fed one of the lambs. "This one dances while he eats," she said. "Mine's praying," said John. The one in front of him was on its front knees. "But why wouldn't your sheep eat the grass we pulled?" John asked.

"They didn't hear my voice, so they ran," explained Grandpa. "Sheep follow their shepherd and tend to run away from other people." He smiled at John. "It always reminds me that we should be like them—we should run away when Satan calls us to follow him. We should love Jesus and do what he says." *M.M.P.*

HOW ABOUT YOU?
Whom do you follow? The Bible says that if you know Jesus, you'll follow him. Are you doing that?

MEMORIZE:
"My sheep listen to my voice; I know them, and they follow me." *John 10:27, NIV*

 Follow Jesus' Teaching

Too Good to Be True (Read Romans 5:6-10)

Everyone was already eating when Steven got home. He hadn't meant to stay so long, but their baseball game went into extra innings. "You're late!" Dad scolded as Steven slowly took his place at the table.

"Sorry," mumbled Steven.

23
AUGUST

"We'll talk about it later," said Mother, passing him the potatoes. Steven nodded. He already knew what his punishment would be. He had been warned that if he were late again, he would have to spend the evening in his room. He felt bad about that because Grandma was coming over after dinner, and he loved to spend time with her.

Steven felt lonely in his room that evening, but he knew he deserved the punishment. Soon his brother Scott appeared in the doorway. "You can go downstairs now, Little Brother," Scott said quietly.

"I can? Did Mom and Dad say I could?" asked Steven.

Scott nodded. "Yes. I'm taking your punishment for you because I know how much you like to play games with Grandma," he said. He left, and Steven heard his door close.

Steven sat still for a while, not knowing what to do. *Should I really go down?* he wondered. *No*, he decided. *I can't believe Scott is really taking my punishment. That sounds too good to be true.*

Much later Grandma came into Steven's room. "Why did you stay up here alone and miserable?" she asked. "I've been waiting to see you, but now it's time for me to leave."

"Is Scott really taking my punishment?" Steven asked. Grandma nodded. "Oh no!" groaned Steven. "I missed all the fun because I didn't really believe him."

Grandma looked serious. "This reminds me of someone else who took punishment for you," she said. "Jesus died for your sins. Have you accepted what he did for you?" Steven nodded, and Grandma smiled. "I'm so glad of that," she said. "Many people don't believe that Jesus took the punishment they deserve, and then it does them no good." She put an arm around Steven and gave him a hug as she got ready to leave. *K.F.G.*

HOW ABOUT YOU?

Did you know that Jesus took the punishment for your sin? Have you accepted what he did for you? If you don't accept it, it does you no good. Trust him, and accept him as your Savior today.

MEMORIZE:

"While we were yet sinners, Christ died for us." Romans 5:8, KJV

 Jesus Took Your Punishment

The Warning (Read Psalm 19:7-11)

24
AUGUST

"There Sarj goes again," said Randy with a sigh. "He's always barking."

"This bark sounds different than usual," observed Mother. "Maybe one of you boys should check it out."

"Aw, Mom, we're busy," protested Josh. "Besides, Sarj barks at everything—squirrels, people walking by, cars. You name it, and he barks at it."

The barking continued for some time, but no one checked to see why Sarj was so persistent. When the dog finally stopped barking, Josh said, "See—it was nothin'."

Later that afternoon, Josh and Randy decided to go for a long bike ride. When they walked into the garage, their mouths fell open. "Where are our bikes?" gasped Randy.

"They have to be here somewhere," replied Josh hopefully. But the bicycles were nowhere to be found.

"I just can't believe it!" cried Randy. "Who would have enough nerve to come into our garage and take our bikes right from under our noses in broad daylight?"

"Yeah! What a jerk!" Josh exclaimed. "After all the work on our paper route, saving our money—and now this!"

The boys rushed into the house, slamming the door behind them. "Our new bikes are gone!" they yelled. "Someone stole them!" After telling their story, everyone hurried out to see for themselves.

As Dad returned to the house to call the police department and report the loss, he stopped to pat Sarj. "Didn't we hear Sarj barking a couple of hours ago?" asked Dad. "He was trying to warn us, and we didn't listen to him."

That evening, Dad read aloud from Psalm 19. After reading the eleventh verse, he looked up. "Warnings are important," he observed. "Today Mother warned you boys to check on Sarj. You didn't. Sarj warned us about the thieves, but we didn't listen. Now we see that God uses his Word, not only to teach and bless us, but also to warn us. Let's be sure to listen to him." The boys nodded.

E.J.B.

HOW ABOUT YOU?

Do you listen when your parents ask you to do something? Do you listen to God when he tells you in the Bible what he wants you to do? He knows what is best for you. Listen to him and obey his commands.

MEMORIZE:

"By [God's laws] is your servant warned; in keeping them there is great reward."

Psalm 19:11, NIV

 Heed God's Commands

The Warning (continued from yesterday) (Read Luke 6:27-37)

After their bicycles were stolen, Randy and Josh asked all their friends and neighbors to be on the lookout for the missing bikes. And they prayed—not only for the return of their bikes, but also for whoever had taken them.

As they were praying one evening, Randy's thoughts wandered. *I wish I could get my hands on the person who would take something after we worked so hard for it,* he thought. *He'd have a black eye and a bloody nose and . . .* He opened his eyes just then, and they fell on the words of the motto hanging on the wall: "Forgive and you will be forgiven." Randy struggled with his thoughts and feelings. He knew he'd like to get back at the person who had taken his bike, but he also knew it was wrong. Perhaps God was warning him by showing him this verse. "Lord, help me to forgive," he prayed.

25

AUGUST

Then one evening, a man and a tall, thin boy came to the house with a red bicycle. "My son Todd, here, has something to say to you," said the man.

"I . . . I think this is your bike," murmured Todd. "I was afraid to bring it back because I scratched it, and I was afraid you'd call the police. I'm sorry. I'll pay for it."

"Yep, that's mine all right," said Randy. He felt a bit of the old anger rising up as he looked at the long scratch. Quickly he again asked the Lord to help him to forgive.

"I saw a man put a blue bike in his truck, and when I came along, he took off," explained Todd. "That's what gave me the idea to take this one. I was just going to ride it for a while, and then, well, I . . ."

Dad took over. "Thank you for having enough courage to bring it back," he said. "We do appreciate it." Dad looked at Todd's father. "We'll leave any punishment in your hands," added Dad. "Right, Randy?"

"Right," agreed Randy. The anger was gone, and he happily pushed his bike into the garage. *E.J.B.*

HOW ABOUT YOU?

Do you find it difficult to forgive someone who has wronged you? It isn't easy. You need to ask God to help you do what you can't do on your own.

MEMORIZE:

"Forgive, and you will be forgiven." *Luke 6:37,* NIV

 *Forgive Others*

Clean Windows (Read Proverbs 15:1-4)

26
AUGUST

"You're always messing up this room," grumbled Judy, as she pushed her sister's things off the dresser.

"I am not, and leave my things alone!" ordered Mary.

"Then keep your stuff off my side of the dresser," answered Judy.

"My things were not on your side."

"Were, too!"

"Were not!"

Judy and Mary were at it again, and Mother reluctantly headed for their room. "I'm tired of the constant fighting that goes on between you two," she said sternly. "You are sisters and should show respect for one another. Follow me."

Judy and Mary followed their mother into the back hall and watched as she got out some rags and some window cleaner. "Now," she said, "you are going to clean the living room window thoroughly. Mary will wash the outside, and Judy will work on the inside. And don't you dare smile at each other! You must scowl all the time. I want you to do your quarreling while this window is between you."

Judy and Mary found it hard to scowl when they had to. Mary tried to hide her dimples, but it was hard to do. As they worked, both girls found it harder and harder to scowl at each other. Slowly their faces turned red; then they burst out laughing. How foolish their fight seemed now!

This was what Mother had been waiting for. She called the girls into the kitchen, and they sat at the table while she got them some lemonade. "You know, girls," she said, "you are really disobeying God when you get angry and shout nasty things at each other. He wants us to be kind and forgiving. You need to learn to talk over your differences and work out a solution. Now, shall we first talk to the Lord about this and then discuss the things that are bothering you?" The girls looked at each other and nodded. *C.B.*

HOW ABOUT YOU?

Are you feeling angry toward your brother or sister? Toward your parents or a friend? Ask God to show you if there is anyone with whom you should talk things out. If someone comes to your mind, go to that person and discuss the problem—and then pray with them.

MEMORIZE:

"**Watch out that no bitterness takes root among you, for as it springs up it causes deep trouble.**" *Hebrews 12:15*, TLB

 **Don't Fight**

The Woodcarver (Read Psalm 103:11-14, 22)

David held the bat steady. He just had to get a hit! He was the last hope for the Tigers. If he made an out, his team would lose the game and be disqualified from the tournament. The ball flew toward him, and he swung as hard as he could. The ball bounced weakly to the pitcher. A moment later, the game was over.

27

AUGUST

David felt terrible. "I really blew it!" he moaned, as he rode home with his dad and his older brother, Sam.

"Everyone feels like that now and then," said his father. "Remember, the Lord understands. After all, he made you!"

That afternoon, David and Sam went to a woodcarving show. They wandered around, admiring carved ducks, fish, and flowers. "Look at that Canada goose," David exclaimed. "That's my favorite so far! And look—it won! The tag says 'Jim Bailey, Grand Prize Winner.'"

"I wonder if the carver did that from one piece of wood," murmured Sam.

"If you look closely at the neck, you can see where two pieces of wood were glued together," said a man standing behind them.

Sam studied the carving. "I wonder what kind of wood it's made of," he said.

"White pine," said the man. "Winter-cut, air-dried for two years."

"You know a lot about this goose," said David.

The man nodded. "I'm Jim Bailey," he said with a smile.

"Oh," said Sam. "That explains it."

The boys had a good time, but on the way home David again mentioned his failure in the ball game. "Hey, listen," said Sam. "Mr. Bailey knew all about the goose because he made it, right? Well, remember Dad said the Lord understood how you felt about the game because he made you. He's your Creator! He knows all about you—even how you feel."

"That's a good way to think about it," David agreed. "I'm glad we went to the woodcarving show." *L.W.*

HOW ABOUT YOU?

Do you feel as if no one understands you? Do you wish you had someone with whom you could discuss your fears, your problems, your discouragements? The Lord made you! You are his creation. He knows exactly how you feel, and he wants you to talk with him.

MEMORIZE:

"For he knows how we are formed, he remembers that we are dust." *Psalm 103:14,* NIV

 The Lord Understands

A Strong Hand (Read Psalm 71:12-16)

28

AUGUST

"Wow, Dad! Did you see those fish?" Nathan's eyes sparkled as he lifted his face out of the water and adjusted his snorkeling mask.

"I sure did! Those little blue ones look just like some of the fish we've seen in aquariums at the pet store."

"And I almost touched one of those yellow-and-black striped ones." Nathan was bubbling with excitement.

Dad looked at the setting sun. "Well, it's getting late," he said. "We'd better start swimming back to shore. Are you ready?"

"So soon?" asked Nathan. "OK . . . let's go. Bet I can beat you back."

But it was farther to the shore than Nathan realized, and after a while he called to his father. "Dad, can we rest a minute?" he asked.

Dad stopped swimming and shook his head. "If we do, this current may take us too far offshore. Here"—he stretched out his arm for Nathan to grab—"Hold on to me, and I'll pull you along." Soon they reached shore, tired but safe.

As they loaded their snorkeling gear into the car, Dad turned to Nathan. "It's a good thing I was with you to pull you along, isn't it?"

"Uh-huh," agreed Nathan. "I sure was getting tired."

Dad smiled. "You know, I think living the Christian life is sometimes a little like swimming," he said. "Once in a while you may get a little weary of doing things you know are right. Where do you suppose you can get encouragement and help then?"

"From you," Nathan answered promptly.

Dad chuckled softly. "Good," he said. "I'll help all I can. I've also learned that if I ask the Lord for *his* help, I sometimes feel as if he says to me, *Here, . . . I'll pull you along.* As we struggle against the current of temptation or with difficult things in our lives, he often uses other Christians to help us. He also teaches and comforts and encourages us through his Word and through his Holy Spirit. We need to learn to depend on him. *R.S.M.*

HOW ABOUT YOU?

When you get tired and discouraged as you try to live for the Lord, do you look to other Christians for encouragement? They can be a lot of help to you. Be sure to ask the Lord himself to help you do what is right. He will always reach out his hand and help you when you depend on him.

MEMORIZE:

"Fear not, for I am with you. . . . I will strengthen you; I will help you; I will uphold you with my victorious right hand."

Isaiah 41:10, TLB

 Get Help from God

When God Said No (Read Isaiah 55:8-13)

As Eric's parents came slowly up the front walk, he opened the door. "Is Gramps OK?" he asked anxiously.

"Your grandfather isn't suffering anymore," Dad told him quietly. "He died this afternoon—he's home in heaven now." Eric swallowed hard, forcing back tears. He walked away while Dad was still explaining.

29

AUGUST

In his room, Eric hunched over on his bed. "It's not fair," he muttered. "It's just not fair." He looked up as Dad came in. "I don't get it," Eric said. "I prayed all day for Gramps. God could have healed him, but he didn't even hear me."

"God always hears, but sometimes the answer is no," said Dad gently. "It was time to let Gramps go." He paused, then added, "You know, Eric, Gramps had been missing Grandma an awful lot lately. They're together in heaven now, and someday we'll see them again." Eric turned away from Dad's quiet words.

Dad sat down beside Eric. "When you ask Mom and me for something we can't buy you, or when you ask to do something we can't let you do, it sometimes makes you angry," Dad reminded him. "You know we love you and want what's best for you, but you also want your own way." Eric squirmed; his temper was a problem. "When you get over being mad, we talk about it, and we go on loving each other. We're a family, even though we disagree," continued Dad. "Well, that's how it is with God, too. When we don't get our own way, we sometimes get angry and shut him out. But when you get over being angry, I believe you'll see how much God loved Gramps and how much he loves you."

"But I'm going to miss Gramps so much," Eric said miserably. He pressed his face against his dad's side. He didn't care if he was acting like a baby.

"Hey, it's OK to cry," Dad said gently. "We can sit here and cry together. I'm going to miss Gramps like crazy!"

Eric slipped his arm around his dad and hung on tight. *J.L.B.*

HOW ABOUT YOU?

Have you lost someone you love? Do you worry that your parents or grandparents may die? Tell God about your hurt and fears. He will comfort you and give you peace. Share your hurt with someone you love, and let him or her comfort you, too.

MEMORIZE:

"Blessed are those who mourn, for they shall be comforted." *Matthew 5:4,* NKJV

 Let God Comfort You

Incredible Love (Read 1 John 4:9-15)

30 AUGUST

"I'm glad I brought my sunglasses and sunscreen today," said Mandy, as she sat on the beach. "The sun is so bright!"

Dad nodded. "It's turning this day into a scorcher!" he agreed. "An article I read recently said that the sun sends out such enormous streams of light and heat that if there were two billion earths instead of only one, there would be enough for all of them."

"Really?" asked Mandy. "That's incredible!"

Dad nodded. "The sun was created by an incredible God—a generous God who never does things in a small way," he said. "In this day of shortages, at least we won't run out of sunshine!"

Mandy wiped her forehead. "That's good, but I am about to run out of something, Dad—and that's time! I'd better be getting home. I have to help Aunt Carrie at the day care center this afternoon."

"Good," Dad said as they turned to leave the beach. "Maybe you can bring a little sunshine there?"

For five hours that afternoon, Mandy found herself rocking babies, changing diapers, warming bottles, serving crackers, picking up toys, reading stories, drying tears, stopping fights, and much more. She came home exhausted and discouraged.

"Well, Mandy, how did you do in spreading sunshine to the children today?" asked Dad. "Did you pour forth a lot of warmth and light?"

"I tried," replied Mandy with a sigh, "but I just didn't have enough hands. I could tend to them only one at a time, but some want more attention than that."

Dad smiled. "You did your best, and that's all any of us can do, Mandy," he said. "Only God can do better. His love is as incredible as his amazing sunshine—he loves each one of us as if there were only one of us to love!" *T.M.V.*

HOW ABOUT YOU?

Do you think of the billions of people on earth and feel that God's love can't possibly reach every one of them? God does love those billions, and God loves *you,* personally and completely. He loves you so much that he sent his Son to die for you. Have you accepted his gift of love?

MEMORIZE:

"How great is the love the Father has lavished on us!"

1 John 3:1, NIV

 God's Love Has No Limits

This Old Planet (Read Deuteronomy 10:12-14)

31
AUGUST

"Mom says we're going to have a picnic supper at the park," announced Alecia, when her father arrived home one Saturday afternoon. "Can we go soon?"

"We want to have time to play on the swings before we eat," added Vicky.

"There should be time for that," said Dad, "but before we go, we have to wash and wax the car."

The girls frowned. "Why?" asked Vicky. "It's not that dirty. And besides, it's such an old car."

Now it was Dad's turn to frown. "Well, it may be old, but it's the only car we have," he replied. "And God calls us to be good stewards of all we've been given. By washing and waxing the car and taking care of it, hopefully we'll have it for a good, long time."

The girls grudgingly got out the soap and car wax while Dad pulled out the hose. They washed and waxed the car until it shone brightly. "There!" Dad said proudly. "It looks almost as good as new."

Alecia nodded and smiled. "Can we go now?" she asked, and soon they were on their way.

At the park, Dad pushed Alecia and Vicky on the swings. Then, surrounded by trees and flowers, they all enjoyed their picnic lunch.

"It's so beautiful here," said Mother.

"We should be very thankful to live on this planet," Dad agreed. "God has given us a wonderful home."

When they had finished eating, Alecia helped Dad carry the trash to a garbage can. "Look at this," Dad said. "The can is full, so people have been dumping trash next to it. It's a shame the way so many people treat this old planet."

"It may be an old planet, like our old car," Alecia said with a giggle, "but it's the only home we've got right now. God wants us to be good stewards of our planet, too."

"You're right," Dad said. "I'll get a trash bag out of the car, and we'll clean up this mess." *D.B.K.*

HOW ABOUT YOU?

Do you or your family or friends throw wrappers or cans or bottles on the ground? What do you do when you find trashy messes that other people have made? God calls us to be good stewards of our earthly home. Cleaning up shows him you care.

MEMORIZE:

"**The earth belongs to God! Everything in all the world is his!**" *Psalm 24:1, TLB*

 Take Care of God's Earth

Poisonous Mushrooms (Read 2 Peter 2:1-3, 18-19)

1

SEPTEMBER

"Raise your arms toward the sky and then draw them in, placing your palms together," Martha instructed her sister, Helen. "Now sit and be at peace with yourself. Take a deep breath of this fresh air, feel the grass beneath you, and meditate on nature." The girls, who were camping with their family, were trying out a type of meditation one of Martha's classmates had talked about. They had never heard of meditating this way before—they only knew they were supposed to meditate on Scripture and on God's love. This must be like that, they decided. After all, God created nature.

"I'm picking mushrooms for supper," their brother, Bill, called, breaking their concentration. He stooped to pick one. "They look just like the ones we've eaten before."

Helen wasn't so sure. "They could be poisonous," she said. "I'll ask Mom."

"Honey," Mother told Bill a moment later, "leave the mushrooms alone. I'm not at all sure I can tell the difference between the poisonous ones and the good ones—they look so much alike." Reluctantly Bill agreed to leave them alone.

Martha and Helen walked away and returned to their meditating. "What are you girls doing?" Mom asked.

"Meditating on the earth, peace, and our oneness with the universe," Martha replied. She told Mom about her classmate. "She said it makes you feel peaceful and powerful," Martha finished. "We weren't sure if it was a good thing to do, but we thought we'd try it."

Mom shook her head. "Honey," she said, "sometimes it's hard for young Christians to tell the difference between Christianity and false religions—just like it's hard to tell the difference between good or poisonous mushrooms. If you aren't sure a religious practice is right, don't get involved in it. Some practices may appear harmless but can still be very wrong for you. I think this is one of them. This puts emphasis on nature and on you instead of on the Bible and God." *N.E.K.*

HOW ABOUT YOU?

Can you identify false religions? Rather than risking the chance of getting mixed up in the wrong activity, stick to what you learn in the Bible and at your Bible-believing church.

MEMORIZE:

"For false Christs shall arise, and false prophets, and will do wonderful miracles so that if it were possible, even God's chosen ones would be deceived." *Matthew 24:24,* TLB

 Beware of False Teaching

A Few Little Flowers (Read Ephesians 5:8-11, 15-17)

2

Tommy was having trouble deciding what to get his mother for her birthday. As usual, he asked his best friend David for help. "I know what you can get her," David said, as he led the way to Mrs. Monroe's flower garden. Tommy passed by old Mrs. Monroe's house on his way to school every day. She had the most beautiful flowers in the neighborhood. "This is what I got my mom for her birthday," said David.

Tommy was a little confused. "Do you mean you stole Mrs. Monroe's flowers?" he asked.

"Don't make it sound so terrible," answered David. "She has so many flowers she'll never notice any are missing. Go ahead. Take some."

"Maybe tomorrow," Tommy said reluctantly. "I have to get home for dinner now."

Tommy knew his mother loved flowers. Still, he knew it wasn't right to steal even a few little flowers. *Stealing is a sin*, his conscience told him. So he decided to ask for his dad's advice. "Dad," he began, "do you think Mrs. Monroe would mind if I took some of her flowers for Mom's birthday?"

"I don't know," said Dad, not bothering to look up from his newspaper. "Why don't you ask her?"

Ask old Mrs. Monroe? Did he dare? Tommy decided to do it. It took all the courage he had to walk up to Mrs. Monroe's front door. A shiver passed through his whole body as he knocked. When Mrs. Monroe finally answered the door, he blurted out his request in one breath and waited for her response. He was astonished to see a wide smile appear on Mrs. Monroe's wrinkled face. "You must love your mother very much," she said. "Don't you think she'd be proud if you earned those flowers by helping me in my garden? Come back tomorrow, and we'll work out the details over a piece of chocolate cake."

Tommy breathed a sigh of relief as he waved good-bye and ran home. He was glad he had talked to Mrs. Monroe. *L.L.G.*

HOW ABOUT YOU?

Do you stand up for what you know is right? Do you think for yourself, or do you go along with others? God lets us choose between good and evil in our lives. Don't let the evils in the world cause you to do wrong.

MEMORIZE:

"Anyone, then, who knows the good he ought to do and doesn't do it, sins."

James 4:17, NIV

 Do the Right Thing

Clouds without Water (Read Ecclesiastes 5:2-7)

3
SEPTEMBER

Lance stood at the window, watching a dark cloud vanish into the distant sky. "That cloud sure wasn't any help," he said. "I was hoping it would rain so I wouldn't have to mow Mrs. Smithwick's yard today." Lance sat down and flicked on the television. "Oh, well, I'm not going to anyway."

"Mrs. Smithwick is expecting you at two o'clock, isn't she?" asked Lance's father.

"Yeah, but it doesn't matter," said Lance. "The grass will still be there tomorrow. Besides, this is one of my favorite shows."

Dad stood at the window, watching the cloud, which had just about disappeared on the horizon. "That cloud seemed to promise a lot, but it didn't come through," he said. "And I think there's another waterless cloud right here in this room."

Lance looked around. "In the house?"

Dad nodded. "Sometimes people are like that cloud," he said. "They talk a lot and make promises, but when it's time to fulfill the promises, they just never get around to it." He looked sternly at his son.

Suddenly the television show didn't seem all that interesting to Lance. "I guess you mean me," he said. "And if I don't do what I promised, I guess Mrs. Smithwick won't think any more of me than I do of that thundercloud." He jumped up and flicked off the TV.

Dad gave him a smile. "Good decision, Son." *S.L.S.*

HOW ABOUT YOU?

Do you say you'll do things and then try to get out of them? Have you ever made a promise that you really didn't want to keep? You don't have to make promises; but if you do make them, you should always keep them. Then you will not only please people, but you'll please God, too.

MEMORIZE:

"It is far better not to say you'll do something than to say you will and then not do it."

Ecclesiastes 5:5, TLB

 *Keep Your Promises*

A Doll and a Monkey (Read 1 John 1:5-10)

"I found out how to catch a monkey," Curt told his sister, Cathy. "All I have to do is find a good-sized gourd, make a hole in it just big enough for a banana, and put one in it. I'm going to try it this afternoon before I go to the village with Dad. Won't it be fun to have a pet monkey?"

Cathy nodded, but her thoughts were not on monkeys. The missionary girl was thinking about the visit they'd had from the important Spanish lady and her little daughter, Rosita, a few days before. Rosita had brought a beautiful little doll, and they had played with it together. When Rosita and her mother were ready to leave, Cathy noticed that Rosita had forgotten her doll. But Cathy did not say anything about it. Instead she hid it beneath the clothes in her trunk.

4

SEPTEMBER

Much to her relief, nobody had mentioned the doll since. Cathy was sure that if Mother saw her playing with it, she would punish her and make her send it back to Rosita. So she kept it hidden, but all the while she was feeling miserable and guilty.

Cathy was almost finished with her afternoon chores when she heard an awful commotion outside. She ran to look. There she saw a monkey with its paw in Curt's gourd, jumping around, trying to get free, and screeching all the while. Cathy felt sorry for the howling creature. "Let go of the banana, and you'll be free!" she called. But the monkey would not let go of his prize. Curt would no doubt catch him when he got home from the village and make him his pet.

Cathy remembered Rosita's doll in her trunk. A little voice told her, *If you let go of Rosita's doll, you can be free of your guilty feelings and be happy again.*

Cathy hesitated only a moment; then she ran into the house to get the doll. "Jesus, forgive me," she breathed as she pulled it out of its hiding place. "I'll give it back." *M.H.N.*

HOW ABOUT YOU?

Do you feel bad because you are hiding some sin? There's a way to feel good again. Confess your sin, and you will be forgiven.

MEMORIZE:

"He who conceals his sins does not prosper, but whoever confesses and renounces them finds mercy." *Proverbs 28:13,* NIV

 Confession Is Better than Guilt

Undeserved Gift (Read Romans 10:6-13)

5

As Joanna was playing in the yard at her grandmother's house one day, she heard an ice-cream truck come down the street, ringing its bells. Joanna was sure her grandma wouldn't buy ice cream before lunch, but she decided to play a joke. She whistled loudly to get the driver's attention. The ice-cream truck stopped, and the man got out expecting to sell something. But no one came to buy.

"That was unkind," Grandma said, coming out of the house. "It was wrong for you to stop that man and make him think he was going to get business. I'm ashamed of you. Now come with me." They approached the truck, and Joanna apologized to the ice-cream man. Then Grandma bought an ice cream bar for each of them.

Joanna felt ashamed. "No thanks," she said when Grandma handed her the treat.

"But I bought this for you," Grandma said.

"I'm not hungry," replied Joanna, pushing it away. She looked at the ground. "I don't deserve it after the trick I played."

"That's true," agreed Grandma. "But I want you to have it anyway—it's a gift from me."

Reluctantly Joanna took the ice cream bar and began to eat. It tasted so good and refreshing on such a hot day! She was glad she had accepted Grandma's gift.

"There's another undeserved gift you need to accept," Grandma told Joanna. "We're all sinners, but Jesus died on the cross to pay the penalty for our sin. He offers forgiveness and the gift of eternal life. Don't push away the gift God offers, Joanna. Accept it."

N.E.K.

HOW ABOUT YOU?

Have you accepted Jesus as your Savior? No one deserves the gift of eternal life, but it's for anyone who wants it—it's for you. Tell Jesus you're sorry for your sin. Thank him for dying for you. Ask him to be the Lord of your life, and accept eternal life with him.

MEMORIZE:

"The gift of God is eternal life in Christ Jesus our Lord."

Romans 6:23, NKJV

 Accept Jesus' Gift

Making Friends (Read Acts 4:9-13)

Peter banged the door open as he raced into the house after the first day at his new school. "Mom!" he yelled. "Guess what? I made some friends today, and they're coming over in a minute to play baseball!"

"That's great!" replied Mother. She followed Peter into the living room. "Just be sure to come inside in time to get ready for the special youth services at church."

6

SEPTEMBER

Peter hesitated at the bottom of the stairs. "Oh," he said slowly, "I don't think I'll go after all." He looked at Mother anxiously. As she waited, his gaze shifted to the carpet. "See, Mom, I'm trying to fit in with the guys," explained Peter, "and I don't think any of *them* go to church."

"Well," said Mother, "we'll talk about this when Dad gets home." Peter sighed. He knew what Dad would say. "By the way," continued Mom, "who was the boy I saw you talking to yesterday? The one with the leg braces?"

"Oh, that's Andy," replied Peter. "I like him; he's my friend. But some of the kids at school make fun of him, so then a lot of the others avoid him, too. It's kind of sad."

"I agree," Mother said. "It's a shame that the kids at school would miss out on a friend like Andy just because of what others think." She frowned as she added, "But isn't that what *you* want to do, Peter? You want to miss out on spending time at church with your best friend, Jesus, because your new friends might not approve of him."

Peter blushed. "I guess you're right, Mom," he admitted at last. "I'll tell the guys I'm going to the service tonight."

Just then Jeff and Mike arrived, dragging their mitts and bats. "Let's get goin', Pete!" said Mike. "We've gotta leave early for a special meeting at church."

"Really?" Peter exclaimed. "I was planning to go, too!" He and his mother shared a little smile. *C.Y.P.*

HOW ABOUT YOU?

When you're with your friends, do you talk about Jesus, or do you keep your friendship with him a secret? Are you afraid others will laugh if they find out you're a Christian? No earthly friend is ever as important or precious as Jesus. Let your love for him be seen.

MEMORIZE:

"In the same way, let your light shine before men, that they may see your good deeds and praise your Father in heaven."

Matthew 5:16, NIV

 Please God, Not People

A Sweeter Smell (Read Luke 6:27-36)

7

SEPTEMBER

"That stupid Stanley," grumbled Travis, as he slammed the back door. "He pushed me on purpose, and I told him what I thought about it."

"Travis," began his mother, giving him the you-know-better-than-that look. "What happened?"

"Stanley pushed me and made me fall right into one of his mom's rosebushes," explained Travis. "Boy, was she mad at him—I hope she gives it to him good!"

"Oh, but you smell just like a rose," teased his sister.

But Mother frowned. "I can see why you're angry," she sympathized when she saw his scratches, "but I think you need to ask yourself how Jesus would want you to behave toward Stanley." Travis just shrugged.

After dinner that evening, Travis played football at his friend Kevin's house. Mother was reading when she heard the door open later that evening. "Travis!" she exclaimed as he came in. "What in the world happened? You smell terrible!"

"Kevin's place doesn't have any roses, but it sure does have skunk cabbage," replied Travis. "I fell into some—but Stanley got it even worse." He grinned as he thought about it. "I tried to be nice to him, Mom," he continued. "I really tried, but there are some people you just can't be nice to. You should have heard him."

"Perhaps Stanley doesn't know any better," said Mother, "but you do. You know what God says about loving your enemies."

"But, Mom, you can't be nice to everyone all the time," protested Travis.

"If your heart is right, you can," insisted Mom. "Tell me, what happened when you fell into the skunk cabbage?"

"I smelled like skunk," said Travis.

Mother nodded. "Yes, you did," she said. "You trampled on skunk cabbage plants and smelled like skunk because that's the odor that is deep down in them. But earlier when you landed in the roses and trampled on them, they gave off their sweet scent because that's what they are deep down. If God's love is deep down inside you, it should be obvious, even when you're trampled down." *S.S.*

HOW ABOUT YOU?

What "comes out" when you are knocked down or laughed at? Is it anger and a desire to get even, or is it God's love? When you have trouble with people who aren't nice, ask Jesus to help you show his love to them anyway. Ask him to help you love them as he does.

MEMORIZE:

"A man's heart determines his speech." *Matthew 12:34,* TLB

 Show God's Love

No Benchwarmers (Read Exodus 20:1-6)

8

Zack bolted into the kitchen where Mom and Dad were already at the table. "Sorry I'm late," said Zack. He tossed his football helmet down and went to wash his hands. When he returned, he grinned at his parents. "In scrimmage today I ran the ball for a twenty-yard gain," he said. "I faked left, then I cut to the right. . . ." He grabbed a melon off the counter and zigzagged across the kitchen to demonstrate.

Zack sank down in his chair with a happy sigh. "I love football," he said. "Coach says you gotta make it number one in your life if you really want to be good. He says it can't be just talk. It's got to be practice, practice, practice. Otherwise, when the big game comes, you'll end up being a benchwarmer—a guy who just sits out the game on the bench."

"Hmmm," murmured Dad. "Practice, practice, practice. That's kind of like what the Lord expects of you. Only he expects you to give *him*—not football—first place in your life."

"Huh?" asked Zack. "What do you mean?"

"Well, it takes just as much practice to become the person God wants you to be as it does to become a good football player," explained Dad. "God must be number one in your life. As the coach would say, it can't be just talk, or you'll end up sitting out the game."

Zack frowned. "But I really love football!" he protested. "Are you saying there's something wrong with that and God expects me to give it up?" He didn't like that idea at all.

"There's nothing wrong with football unless you put it ahead of God," Dad assured him. "How is football going to fit into God's plan for you? What importance are you going to give it? Those are questions you need to pray about." He grinned at Zack. "In the game of life, God wants you to be busy playing—or maybe I should say working—for him. He doesn't want you to end up being a benchwarmer." *L.J.*

HOW ABOUT YOU?

What's the most important thing in your life? Is it sports or clothes or hanging out with your friends? God wants the number one spot in your life. Give him the best of your time, your talents, and your energy.

MEMORIZE:

"Seek ye first the kingdom of God, and his righteousness."

Matthew 6:33, KJV

 Give God First Place

The Tiger and the Bike (Read Matthew 6:7-13)

9

SEPTEMBER

Terry's shoulders slumped as he trudged home. When he reached his driveway, he saw his dad working on the car. Glancing up, Dad said, "You look unhappy."

Terry nodded. "I am," he said. "You know that new bike they were giving away at Horne's Department Store?" Dad nodded and Terry continued, "Somebody else won it. I can't believe it. I prayed so hard, Dad! I need that bike. Why did God let somebody else win it?"

Dad looked thoughtful as he wiped his hands on a rag. Before he could reply, Terry's little brother, Ricky, came bounding out of the house. "I saw a tiger on TV, and he did lots of tricks! Can I have a tiger, Daddy?" asked Ricky eagerly. "I could teach my tiger to do tricks, too."

Terry rolled his eyes. "You can't have a tiger, silly," he said. "A tiger is a wild animal. He'd eat you."

"He would not!" shouted Ricky. "I'm going to get one, and I'll ride on his back and teach him tricks. You'll see!"

"You can't have a tiger," Terry repeated.

"Yes, I can!" insisted Ricky.

Dad held up his hands for quiet. "Why don't you go play in the backyard, Ricky," he said, "and just pretend you have a tiger." Ricky left, and Dad turned to Terry. "You're older than Ricky, and you understand things better. You know lots of reasons why he shouldn't have a tiger for a pet, right?"

"Right," agreed Terry.

"But Ricky doesn't understand that. He just know he wants a tiger," said Dad. "Maybe that's a little like God and you and the bike. You know you want that bike, but maybe God knows it isn't best for you to get it right now. You don't understand the reason, but that doesn't mean God doesn't have one."

Terry sighed. "So I should trust God because he knows what's best, just like you know what's best for Ricky?" he asked. Then he grinned. "And I suppose I have to ride a pretend bike, huh?"

Dad smiled and nodded. "I guess so," he said. *K.E.C.*

HOW ABOUT YOU?

Do you willingly accept God's answer to your prayers, even when it's not the answer you would like? Trust him always. He knows what he's doing—even when he tells you no.

MEMORIZE:

"Your Father knows exactly what you need even before you ask him!" Matthew 6:8, TLB

 God Knows What's Best

No Big Deal? (Read Proverbs 6:16-19)

10

SEPTEMBER

"My catcher's mitt is missing!" exclaimed Paul as he ran into the kitchen. "Donnie probably took it. He's always taking things that don't belong to him."

Just then Donnie entered the room, and hearing his older brother's comment, he said, "I didn't *take* anything, Paul."

"Do you have Paul's mitt?" Mother asked.

"Yes," admitted Donnie, "but I just *borrowed* it. It's not like I stole it. It's no big deal!"

"It is to Paul," Mother said firmly. "Now go and get your brother's mitt and return it to him." Silently Donnie did as he was told. But when he came back with the mitt, Mother had left the room, so he didn't bother to say he was sorry.

Later that morning, Donnie brought a shirt to Mother, who was putting clothes in the washing machine. "I need this washed," he told her. "Look, it has stains on it."

Mother looked at the place where Donnie pointed. "It's really not too bad, Donnie," she said after a moment, "and I've already got a big load. This can wait till next time."

Donnie frowned. "But, Mom, it's dirty," he argued, "and I want to wear it."

Mother looked at the shirt again. "All right," she said, "I guess there's room for one more shirt." As she threw it into the washer, she looked thoughtful. "You know, Donnie," she added, "the way you feel about this shirt is something like the way God feels about your sin. You may think it's no big deal, but God hates all sin." Donnie felt guilty and looked down as Mother added, "I heard that you didn't even apologize to your brother. I think you need to do that, and I hope you'll tell God you're sorry, too." *W.E.B.*

HOW ABOUT YOU?

The Bible says God hates every sin—even the ones you might think are no big deal. The good news is that if you're sorry for your sin, you can confess it and be forgiven. Be sure to do that as soon as you're aware of any sin in your life.

MEMORIZE:

"If we confess our sins, he is faithful and just to forgive us our sins, and to cleanse us from all unrighteousness."

1 John 1:9, KJV

 No Sin Is Small

Too Many Suckers (Read Colossians 3:5-10)

11

Julie was helping her mother in the garden. She didn't want to—in fact, she had put up quite an argument, and Mom had almost had to pry her away from the TV. But now she was here, picking red, ripe tomatoes. It was a warm, sunny day, and every once in a while she would pop a cherry tomato in her mouth, savoring the juicy warmth when it split open.

Julie glanced at her mom and saw her pinch off a small stem of the tomato vine. Puzzled, she watched as Mom plucked off a few more. "Why are you breaking off parts of the tomato plant, Mom?" Julie asked. "Won't that hurt it?"

Mom straightened up and walked over to Julie. "No, I'm just pruning it—removing the suckers," she replied.

"Suckers!" Julie exclaimed. "What are they?"

"Look here," Mom directed, and she reached to the center of Julie's plant. "See this stem with the blossoms?" Julie nodded. "And see this small sprout growing just below it where it joins the main stem?" Julie nodded again. "Well, if we let that sprout grow, it robs the stem with the blossoms of some nutrients. But if we snap it off, bigger and better fruit can develop." Mom snapped the sprout off as she spoke.

"Oh," said Julie as Mom resumed her pruning.

"That's more or less what I was doing with you this morning," Mom added a minute later. "I was removing something that robs you of a lot of time—TV. And I was helping you develop something better, like good work habits. I want you to grow up knowing how to use your time wisely, so you can accomplish good things." Sarah frowned and said nothing.

"And you know what?" continued Mom. "God does the same with us. He helps us get rid of things that stop us from bearing good fruit—so it must be a good thing to do, don't you think?"

J.K.B.

HOW ABOUT YOU?

Are there things in your life that rob you of the ability to grow in the Lord and bear good fruit? Like laziness? A bad temper? Not reading the Bible or praying? Ask the Holy Spirit to prune these out of your life so the fruit God expects will have a chance to grow.

MEMORIZE:

"He cuts off every branch in me that bears no fruit, while every branch that does bear fruit he prunes so that it will be even more fruitful." *John 15:2, NIV*

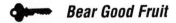 **Bear Good Fruit**

A Night Walk (Read Psalm 119:105, 113-117)

12

SEPTEMBER

Dad and Amy decided to walk over to the lake to see the moon's path on the water. To get to the beach, they had to take a narrow trail through the woods. There were branches and roots that could trip up the unsuspecting traveler, even in the daytime. "Make sure you use the flashlights," Mom cautioned, as Amy and Dad left the campsite.

Amy followed her dad along the path and heard the soft *"whooo"* of an owl. She was shining her flashlight toward the treetops, hoping to catch a glimpse of the bird, when her foot caught in a root and she fell down.

"Amy, are you all right?" Dad asked anxiously, as he spun around to help her up. "What happened?" Amy got up, and as Dad brushed her off, she said she tripped on a root. "Didn't you see it with your flashlight?" asked Dad.

"Well, I was pointing my flashlight up at the trees to see if I could spot the owl," replied Amy. "I guess the light didn't do me much good that way, huh?"

"No, I guess not," said Dad with a smile.

They continued their walk, and soon the beach was in sight. The water was still and calm, and the moonlight made a beautiful reflection on the water. It was breathtaking. After enjoying it in silence for a while, Dad spoke. "The moon gives a beautiful light," he mused, "and I've been thinking about a verse in Psalms—one that talks about God's Word being a light. We have to look to the Bible to know how to walk and follow God's path. If we get too caught up in all the interesting things around us and forget to shine the light of God's Word on our way, we can trip and fall in our Christian walk."

"Like I fell when I used the flashlight on the trees instead of on the ground, huh?" asked Amy, remembering how it hurt when she fell. She would listen more carefully to what God had to say in the Bible. *J.K.B.*

HOW ABOUT YOU?

Do you take time to read your Bible? When you need to decide something important, do you look for answers in God's Word? Be sure to ask Mom or Dad to explain things you don't understand. The more you study God's Word, the better God's light can shine on the paths of your life!

MEMORIZE:

"Thy word is a lamp unto my feet, and a light unto my path."

Psalm 119:105, KJV

 Use God's Light—the Bible

A Fish Story (Read 1 John 2:15-17, 26-28)

13

SEPTEMBER

Brent and his dad were fishing along the bank of the lake at which they were camping. Sometimes they used big, fat earthworms. Other times, they would cast out one of Dad's fancy lures, which had brightly colored feathers and shiny "spoons" concealing the hooks. Dad explained how the fish were attracted by the sound and sight of the lures traveling through the water, looking like insects or other food.

It was nearing dusk, and they had quite a stringer of fish. They were also having a good time talking together, something they didn't always have time for at home.

"I saw this really neat tape at the music store the other day," Brent told his father. "It looked really awesome—I liked the pictures on the tape jacket. I might save up from my paper route to get it next week."

"What kind of music is it?" asked Dad.

"I don't really know the group that sings on it—they're new," replied Brent, "but the kids at school were talking about how great it is. I never heard the songs, though."

"I think you should check it out before you buy it, Son," said Dad. "It may look neat on the outside, but you know how bad some music is. We've talked before about how listening to bad messages can tempt you and cause you to have thoughts that are displeasing to God." Dad reeled in his fishing line and carefully detached a fish from the lure. "This fish thought the lure looked pretty tempting, too," he pointed out, "but look where it got him!"

Brent laughed. "Yeah, I guess you're right," he said. "I better do some more checking before I spend my hard-earned money on something that might hurt me in the end." *J.K.B.*

HOW ABOUT YOU?

Do you sometimes want something that looks interesting at first glance but is really a temptation to sin? All of us can sometimes be confused by things that look good. We need God's help to keep from sinning. Ask him each day for wisdom, even in the little ordinary decisions you must make.

MEMORIZE:

"The Lord can rescue you and me from the temptations that surround us." *2 Peter 2:9,* TLB

 *Keep from Sin*

The Fire (Read James 3:1-6)

14

Susan and her father were sitting lazily in their lawn chairs near the tent. Dad was trying to read, but Susan kept interrupting with her chatter.

"Mandy says the police took Erin's father to the station," Susan said now. "She told me he was drunk and banged into another car. Mandy says he gets drunk every weekend."

Dad stopped her. "Hey, Susan, hold on a minute," he said. "How do you know that what Mandy is saying is true? And even if it is, should you be repeating it like this? Either way, you could really be hurting Erin's father by saying things like that."

Susan felt guilty and couldn't look her dad in the eye, so she gazed off to one side. Suddenly, she stood up and pointed. "Dad, look! Over there at that other campsite! Those leaves are on fire!"

They raced over to the empty campsite, grabbing a couple of towels from the line as they went. A log had rolled out of the fire pit, and the dry leaves in the area had caught fire. Susan and Dad stomped and beat at the spreading flames until they had the fire contained.

"Whew! That was a close one!" Dad exclaimed. "I wasn't sure we were going to be able to handle it."

Susan was breathing hard, but she grinned at him, glad of their success. Dad tousled her bright, golden hair and smiled at her. "You know, we call you a chatterbox," he told her, "and most of the time it's fun for us. But we want you to learn to be careful that your chatter is just that—fun, not harmful. God says in the Bible that the tongue is like a fire, and you saw how fast that fire got out of control. The things you say can build and spread just as fast, so you need to take care."

Susan nodded. It was going to be hard because she loved to talk, but she made up her mind to watch what she said more closely from now on. *J.K.B.*

HOW ABOUT YOU?

Do you have a problem with your tongue? Do you ever lie? Swear? Gossip? Tease someone or put someone down? God says there are better ways to use your speech. You should be praising God and building up other people with what you say. Ask God to help you control your speech.

MEMORIZE:

"Keep your tongue from evil and your lips from speaking lies." *Psalm 34:13,* NIV

 *Guard Your Tongue*

Hidden Gems (Read Psalm 119:17-24)

15
SEPTEMBER

The sun had just poked its head over the tops of the trees when Susan and her mother went for a walk in the woods. Susan walked ahead, turning back to Mom now and then and chattering as much as the chipmunks. "I didn't understand what Dad read in the Bible this morning," she said. "Some parts of the Bible don't seem to have anything important to say to me, so how come we have to read it all?"

Mom thought about that for a minute, trying to find a way to explain. Meanwhile, Susan was looking at the bushes along the path. Her eyes had spotted something intriguing.

"Mom, look at these bushes. Are those some kind of berries?" she said.

Mom stopped and peered into the bushes. When she lifted aside some of the leaves, she saw a cluster of blackberries. "Mmmm!" she exclaimed. "Wild blackberries! They sure would taste good on our cereal—or with some milk and sugar! Let's get a bucket and pick some."

Susan ran back to camp to get a pail, and soon they were gathering the ripe, luscious fruit. "I'm glad your bright eyes noticed these," Mom told Susan. "All I saw was some green bushes. I didn't see what was hidden under the leaves." A moment later she added, "Maybe that's the answer to your question a while ago. When we read the Bible, we don't always see the little gems of wisdom that might be hidden in a passage, just like I didn't spot those berries. But if we take time to study and search, God can always reveal something in his Word to help us or to teach us something about himself. That's why we read all the parts of the Bible, even the ones that seem unimportant to us at first. Does that make sense?"

"Kind of," Susan replied. She grinned. "I guess with my 'bright eyes' I might even be one of the first to spot God's little gems, huh?" Mom laughed and agreed. *J.K.B.*

HOW ABOUT YOU?

Do you sometimes like to skip over parts of the Bible? That's when it might be good to study it a little more carefully or to ask for help from your parents or pastor. And don't forget to pray first, asking God's Spirit to show you what you need to learn from his Word.

MEMORIZE:

"Open my eyes to see wonderful things in your Word."

Psalm 119:18, TLB

 Look for God's "Gems"

The Storm (Read Psalm 46:1-11)

It was the last day of the camping trip, and everyone wanted to spend it at the beach. So they loaded the van with towels, swimsuits, and food, and drove around to the large, sandy shore on the other side of the lake.

For several hours the children swam, floated, and built sand castles. Dad and Brent tossed the Frisbee, and Mom helped Sue and Amy practice their swim strokes. They were so busy having fun that the storm took them by surprise. As they hurried to pack up their things, there was a flash of lightning and a loud clap of thunder. "This storm is moving in fast," said Dad. "We'd better hurry!"

16
SEPTEMBER

Everyone scrambled to get the gear. "Run to the van!" shouted Mom at the next flash of lightning and roll of thunder. A strong wind began to blow, and they all took off. They had just crammed everything and themselves into the van when the heavens opened and sheets of rain pounded the roof of the van.

Lightning continued to flash, and Amy turned a frightened face toward her father. "Is the lightning going to get us?"

"No, honey, we'll be all right in the van," Dad assured her. "It has rubber tires, and rubber doesn't conduct electricity. That makes a car a good place to be in an electrical storm—it's better than our tent!" He paused. "Would you feel better if we prayed together?" he asked Amy. She nodded, so Dad asked God to keep them safe.

After a while, the lightning and thunder seemed to be past. "Hey, the sun's coming out again!" exclaimed Susan.

Mother nodded. "The weather can surely change quickly, can't it?" she said. "It reminds me of life—stormy times can come up quickly in life, too. And we can go to God with any kind of trial or trouble, just like we could go to our van for protection from the rain and lightning."

"That's right," agreed Dad. "And let's always be sure to trust him to cause the sun to shine again in our lives, too." *J.K.B.*

HOW ABOUT YOU?

Have there been storms in your life? God wants you to turn to him when you're frightened and lonely. He'll be your refuge. Trust him when trouble comes. He'll care for you and help you through it—and the sun will shine again!

MEMORIZE:

"God is our refuge and strength, a very present help in trouble." *Psalm 46:1,* KJV

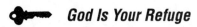 *God Is Your Refuge*

God's "Everlasting" (Read Psalm 103:15-18)

17

"'As for man, his days are like grass. . . .'" The minister read from his well-worn Bible, one hand resting on the big box covered by a blanket of flowers.

Kathy stood quietly in the warm sunshine, half listening to the solemn words. Deep inside she felt sad and lonely. Grandma—dear, funny grandma whom she loved so much—had died.

The day was hot, and Kathy wished she were back at the cottage on Lake Michigan with its golden beaches and the little sandpipers. She remembered the telephone call that had ended their vacation and brought them hurrying to the city. But before they had arrived, Grandma was gone.

The minister finished, and people began to move toward their cars. Only relatives remained, talking softly around the flower-covered box. Kathy wandered off a little way. "Dust to dust." The minister's words echoed again in her ears.

A bit of yellow in the grass caught Kathy's downcast eyes. A broken blossom had dropped from the flower blanket. As she gently lifted the flower, she knew the blossom would soon die, too, but she remembered some other words the minister had read from the Bible: "from everlasting to everlasting." God was everlasting, and in a way, she and Grandma were, too. They had both accepted Jesus as Savior, and he had given them everlasting life!

"Honey, we're ready to go." Dad smiled down at her.

"Oh, Dad, I loved Grandma, and I know that God loves her—and someday we'll see her again, won't we?"

Dad nodded. "We sure will," he said. "There's more to life than just what we have here. Jesus' death on the cross has made it possible for us all to be together again. That's God's Good News for us, Kathy, and that's why we can smile even at a time like this." The warm, tender words were like a blessing in Kathy's heart.

"Dad, I'll sure miss Grandma," Kathy said, "but God's everlasting makes it easier to say good-bye to her." Kathy slipped her hand in her father's, and they walked to the car. *P.I.K.*

HOW ABOUT YOU?

It makes you sad to think about your loved ones dying, doesn't it? It seems hard to say good-bye, but if you love Jesus and they do, too, God promises that you'll be together again someday.

MEMORIZE:

"And so we will be with the Lord forever."

1 Thessalonians 4:17, NIV

 Life Is Everlasting

A Scary Tower (Read Psalm 27:1; Isaiah 41:10, 13)

18
SEPTEMBER

"Mr. Robinson asked me to give my testimony at youth meeting Sunday night," Rachel told her mother as they walked along the path in the woods. "But I'm too scared. I'm going to tell him I can't."

"Why don't you think about it a while longer," Mom suggested. She pointed. "Look. There's the old fire tower I wanted you to see. Let's climb it."

Rachel looked at flight after flight of stairs that led to the top of the tower. "I don't know. . . ." She hesitated. The top of the tower rose above the highest tree. "It looks scary."

"I'll be behind you to make sure you won't fall," Mom assured her. So Rachel began climbing with Mom close behind. The higher they climbed, the more Rachel's knees trembled. But she could feel the presence of her mother, whom she knew was ready and able to support her if she needed help.

Finally, they reached the top. Rachel carefully sat down on the top step. Only then did she look out over the forest. The setting sun had left behind brilliant colors that clung to clouds on the horizon. "Awesome!" exclaimed Rachel.

"Was it worth being scared?" Mom asked.

"It sure was," said Rachel. "Besides, even though I was scared, I knew you were with me."

"You know, Rachel," said Mother, "I was just thinking that if you let fear keep you from sharing at the youth meeting, you may miss something as awesome as this. Just as I was with you and ready to help you on these stairs, God will be with you and ready to help when you speak at the youth meeting. You can do it."

Slowly, Rachel nodded. "I think I can," she said. *K.R.A.*

HOW ABOUT YOU?

Are you afraid to do something that you believe God wants you to do? Is there someone you should invite to church or talk to about Jesus? God will be there with you, and he may have a special blessing for you if you do it, even though you are afraid.

MEMORIZE:

"For God has not given us a spirit of fear, but of power and of love and of a sound mind."

2 Timothy 1:7, NKJV

 Don't Be Afraid to Serve God

Deaf, Yet Hearing (Read Mark 8:13-21)

19

SEPTEMBER

Carol could hardly wait for the children's choir to sing. This was the first Sunday they would sign the words as they sang. Carol watched the choir director, but she also looked out at Toby, a young, deaf boy sitting in the front row. It was exciting to sing in a way that a deaf person could understand, too. Toby was watching attentively, and Carol felt warm inside. Later, when Pastor Glenn spoke, she again noticed Toby carefully watching the interpreter.

Later that afternoon, Carol's brother wanted her to help him with an experiment. "Oh, I'm sick of your dumb experiments!" she grumbled. "They're silly and don't work, and most of them don't even make sense." But even though Carol refused to help, her brother kept pleading. "Get away from me," Carol said crossly. Then she added some other mean comments.

Mother looked at her sadly. "I was just remembering that you told us how eagerly your friend Toby listened to God's message to him this morning," she said. "Even though his ears didn't work, he still heard. But I'm not sure you heard the message."

Carol scowled. "I'm not deaf," she said. "Of course I heard Pastor Glenn."

Mom raised her brows. "Well, Pastor Glenn spoke about how Christians need to build each other up and be there for each other," she said. "After the service, I saw Toby hug some people and help a woman in a wheelchair. I think his actions showed that, even without physically hearing, he heard with his heart. Judging from the way you've been speaking to your brother, I wonder if perhaps the message stopped in your ears."

Carol blushed. She knew Mom was right. Hearing God's message with one's ears was not the most important thing. Responding with one's heart was. *N.E.K.*

HOW ABOUT YOU?

When you hear Christian messages, do you just let the words go "in one ear and out the other"? Listen, understand, and respond with your heart.

MEMORIZE:

"**Be ye doers of the word, and not hearers only.**" *James 1:22,* KJV

 Hear with Your Heart

What Standard? (Read Deuteronomy 4:1-2, 5-9)

20

SEPTEMBER

"Jerry," called Dad from under the raised hood of the car, "would you bring me the other toolbox from the shed, please? I forgot that these bolts are metric."

Jerry went into the toolshed. After a few moments he came back, carrying a blue, metal box by its handle. "We learned about metric measures in school," he told Dad, "but I'm still confused about it."

Dad pulled a socket wrench from the box and ducked back under the hood. "Metric," he grunted as he loosened a bolt, "is a type of measurement, like inches and feet. Most countries use the metric system as their standard of measurement, but we, unfortunately, use two standards of measurement." He stood upright again and tossed the wrench back into the box. "That causes quite a bit of confusion at times—you have to remember which kind is used on the particular item you're trying to fix."

Jerry leaned over the side of the car to watch his father work. After a while, Dad grinned and wiped his hands on a rag. "How about some lemonade?" he suggested.

A few minutes later, as they were drinking their lemonade, Dad said, "People would avoid a lot of confusion about many different things—like how to live our lives, for example—if we all followed only one standard of measurement."

Jerry looked at his dad, puzzled. "What do you mean?" he asked. "Whether we use metric measurements or not isn't that important, is it?"

Dad took another sip of lemonade and smiled. "I was thinking of a different kind of standard," he said. "You see, God gave us the Bible as his standard by which we can measure our lives, to see if we are living as we should. On the other hand, there are lots of books that offer people other standards of conduct. It's easy to get confused when you're using more than one standard of measurement." *R.S.M.*

HOW ABOUT YOU?

What standard are you using as you live the Christian life? By using only God's standard, the Bible, you will always be sure of how God wants you to live.

MEMORIZE:

"The grass withers and the flowers fall, but the word of our God stands forever."

Isaiah 40:8, NIV

 The Bible Is God's Standard

The Square Wheel (Read Galatians 6:4-10)

21
SEPTEMBER

Becky charged out of the house, slamming the screen door behind her. "I don't belong in this family!" she yelled angrily, running past the open garage door.

"Hold it!" Becky stopped and turned to face her father. He was sitting at a worktable in the garage, holding a small, wooden car with a missing wheel. "What's this I hear?" he asked.

Becky's cheeks burned. "Mom always gives me jobs to do," she complained. "Jessica has to do hardly *any* work just because she's smaller than I am."

Dad looked at the hole he had drilled for the wheel. "Hand me that block over there," he said. Becky did so, and her father quickly attached the block to the tiny car, saying, "Here. Give it a test drive."

"But it has a square wheel," protested Becky. She pushed the little car across the table. "It won't work with a square wheel. You need to round the corners."

Dad nodded. "That's right. And wheels are like people."

"Huh?" grunted Becky.

"They all affect each other," explained Dad. "How many people are in our family?"

"Four," murmured Becky.

"And who's been complaining about her share of the work?" asked Dad.

Becky hung her head. "Me," she mumbled.

"Your complaining is hurting all of us," Dad told her.

Becky blushed. "You're saying I'm like a square wheel," she said slowly. "I'm sorry." After a moment she added with a sigh, "But I *still* hate housework!"

"Maybe you could talk about happy things while you're working," Dad suggested. He put his arm around her shoulder as they walked into the house. "And you could sing some of the songs you've learned during Bible class. God has given you a beautiful voice to share with us."

Becky hugged her father. "OK, Dad," she agreed. "I'm going to be a good worker, not a square wheel anymore!" *D.A.L.*

HOW ABOUT YOU?

Do you complain when you have to help with chores? Do you come right away when it's time to work? If you come quickly and do your jobs cheerfully, your parents will be pleased, and so will God. Also, you'll be doing your part to make the "wheels" of your family run smoothly.

MEMORIZE:

"Let us not get tired of doing what is right." Galatians 6:9, TLB

 *Work Cheerfully*

Late Arrival (Read Proverbs 3:11-18)

22

SEPTEMBER

"I don't see why Stewart's dad wouldn't let him come with us to release the pigeons," Bill told his father as they loaded a crate of cooing homing pigeons into the back of the truck. "It isn't fair. His dad got all mad over *nothing!*"

"Nothing?" asked Dad, as he backed out of the driveway.

"Well, it was just because Stewart didn't come straight home from school yesterday," said Bill.

"You think it was OK for Stewart to let his parents worry about him?" asked Dad.

"It was only for about half an hour," replied Bill.

"God gave parents the responsibility of caring for their children," said Dad. "He also gave children the responsibility of obeying."

After they had driven about ten miles into the country, they stopped and released the pigeons. "See you later, guys," Bill said as the birds began to circle higher and higher.

"They'll probably beat us home," said Dad. "They'll fly in a straighter path than we can drive."

When Bill and his dad arrived at home, they went right to the little building where the pigeons lived. "You were right, Dad," said Bill. "They beat us home." He went inside and looked at the birds, eating and drinking after their flight. "Hey, I don't see Big Red!" he exclaimed. Big Red was Bill's favorite bird. "What if a hawk caught him?"

"He'll probably be along soon," said Dad.

"I think I'll wait here a while," decided Bill.

For what seemed like a long time, Bill stood gazing into the sky. Finally he saw a dark speck against a white cloud. The speck got closer, and at last Big Red landed on top of the loft, hopped down to the little swinging door, and pushed through.

"Good boy!" murmured Bill as Big Red began eating with the other pigeons. "I was worried about you." And then Bill thought of something else. *Hmmm,* he thought, *now I think I understand how Stewart's parents felt when he didn't come home from school on time. S.L.S.*

HOW ABOUT YOU?

Do you sometimes think your parents expect too much of you? Do you resent the restrictions they put upon you? Your parents love you and want only the best for you. When you obey and respect them, you are giving them honor, just the way God wants you to.

MEMORIZE:

"Listen, my son, to your father's instruction and do not forsake your mother's teaching." *Proverbs 1:8,* NIV

 *Obey Your Parents*

A Matter of Timing (Read 2 Corinthians 5:18-21; 6:1-2)

23

SEPTEMBER

Jason's knuckles turned white as he gripped the back of the pew in front of him. For the first time in his life, he had really listened to the evening sermon. "Now is the time to come to Jesus," Pastor was saying. "Later may be too late." But Jason just didn't want to give in. The other kids might laugh, and besides, he was still so young. There would be plenty of time later. The service closed, and Jason had not made a decision for the Lord.

The next day Jason played soccer in gym class. He was the best soccer player in his class, and he was sure his team should win easily. But Jason just wasn't himself. He kept thinking about the message of the night before. The game started, and soon the other team was ahead, two to nothing.

"We'll catch up," said one of Jason's teammates.

There was just over a minute left to play when Jimmy, one of Jason's teammates, came from out of nowhere and stole the ball. He darted left and right and beat the goalie for a goal. It was now two to one.

Mr. Berg, the gym teacher, was looking at his stopwatch and holding his whistle in his mouth to signal the end of the game. Then Jimmy again made a terrific steal and slanted a perfect pass to Jason, who was standing open in front of the goal. "Kick it in!" Jimmy shouted.

"Tie the score!" another teammate yelled. But Jason swung his leg and kicked a little late. The ball rolled uselessly off to the side of the goal just as Mr. Berg blew his whistle.

"Your timing was off today, Jason," Mr. Berg said later.

"Yeah," mumbled Jason. With good timing he could have tied the score for his team. Suddenly he thought of something else. *What if I have bad timing and wait too long to accept Jesus as my Savior?* The other boys had left the locker room, but Jason stayed behind and bowed his head to quietly tell the Lord of his decision to accept him right away. *A.A.S.*

HOW ABOUT YOU?

Have you made Jesus your Lord? Will you bow down before his mighty name now, while the timing is right? Don't wait until you're older; *now* is the time to accept him.

MEMORIZE:

"I tell you, now is the time of God's favor, now is the day of salvation." *2 Corinthians 6:2, NIV*

 Don't Wait to Accept Jesus

Within the Limits (Read Colossians 3:20-25)

"Dad, can I sleep over at Brandon's house tomorrow night?" asked Jimmy, as he and his father played catch in the backyard. "He's a new kid at school."

Dad shook his head. "You know the rule, Jimmy," he said. "You can't go to someone's house until Mom and I have met him and his family."

24
SEPTEMBER

"Aw, come on, just this once?" begged Jimmy. "You'll like him. He's a nice guy." Dad again shook his head.

Jimmy was unhappy. "Why do we have to have so many rules?" he grumbled.

Just then a couple of boys rode by on their bicycles. Jimmy's dog, Sheba, barked at them and ran along the edge of the lawn, stopping abruptly where her yard met the neighbor's yard. Jimmy grinned. "Good girl!" he called to the dog. "We've got Sheba well trained, haven't we, Dad?"

"Yes," said Dad. "She knows just where her boundaries are, and she doesn't go one step beyond them. Staying within the limits keeps her safe, doesn't it?" Jimmy nodded as he patted his dog. "It's sort of like God's rules and like the rules in our family," continued Dad. "We may not always like them, but they're there to protect us. OK?"

Slowly Jimmy nodded. *T.K.M.*

HOW ABOUT YOU?

Do you get frustrated with some of your family's rules? Discuss them and figure out how each one provides limits or protection for you. Then thank God for the boundaries he provides through your parents.

MEMORIZE:

"You children must always obey your fathers and mothers, for that pleases the Lord."

Colossians 3:20, TLB

 Follow Family Rules

Stamped "Different" (Read Romans 12:9-18)

25
SEPTEMBER

Walt and his friend Lon were walking through the mall, looking in various stores while they waited for Walt's parents to finish shopping. After a while, they sat on a bench in the middle of the mall to rest.

Soon an older couple sat down next to them. They wore unusual clothes and spoke in a language neither Walt nor Lon understood. Walt frowned and stood up. "Let's get going," he said. The boys strolled off, and when they were out of hearing distance, Walt added, "I don't like foreigners. You can't understand their language, and they dress funny. I think when foreigners come here they should try to be like us and stop being so different." He pointed to a store window. "Look!" he said excitedly. "A store for stamp collectors! It's new!" Walt and his father collected postage stamps and kept them in a big album.

The boys peered through the window at the display of stamps. Lon noticed the prices and his eyes widened. "Some of those stamps are awful expensive!" he exclaimed. "Why do they cost so much? They're nothing but a little piece of paper." He shook his head in disbelief.

"Some stamps are valuable because there weren't many of them printed," Walt explained, "or because they have unusual pictures on them. And some of the most expensive ones are those that were misprinted. They're valuable because they're different from other stamps."

Just then the foreign-speaking couple passed by the stamp store, and Walt gave them a sour look. Lon frowned. "If it's so great for stamps to be different, why do people have to be all the same?" he asked. "Maybe being different is what makes them interesting, too." Walt looked at the foreign couple. His face colored as Lon added, "Besides, remember our Sunday school lesson? About how God loves everybody and we should, too?"

Walt stopped to think. Maybe Lon had a point. He nodded his head and entered the stamp store. *D.B.K.*

HOW ABOUT YOU?

Do you judge people by the color of their skin? By the country they come from or by the language they speak? It's important to remember that God made everyone. He says to love one another, not to love only those who are like you.

MEMORIZE:

"Be devoted to one another in brotherly love. Honor one another above yourselves."

Romans 12:10, NIV

 Value Everyone

Sowing and Reaping (Read Galatians 6:7-10)

26

SEPTEMBER

"Yuck! Tomatoes!" Ginny complained, as she watched her mother in the kitchen. "I wish you were canning green beans. I hate tomatoes."

"I can't can green beans when we didn't plant any this year," said Mom. "We planted tomatoes, and tomatoes grew. So that's what I'm canning."

The phone rang and Ginny answered it. "You're kidding! Oh no!" she groaned. She listened a few minutes. "No fair," she protested. She finished the conversation in a whisper and then hung up the receiver.

"What was that all about?" Mom asked, continuing her work with the tomatoes.

"It's just a big mess," Ginny mumbled. She didn't want to go into detail, but she could see that Mom was going to ask for more information. "Tara told Sandy that I think BettyAnn is a stuck-up brat. Sandy told Sue, and Sue told other kids. Somehow word got back to BettyAnn. Now BettyAnn is inviting everyone to her birthday party but me."

"Where did Tara get the idea that you didn't like BettyAnn?" asked Mother. She had to repeat the question before Ginny answered.

"Well, . . . I said it to her," admitted Ginny, "but I didn't think she'd tell anybody else." She moaned. "I want to go to the party! BettyAnn's parents are renting ponies and giving everyone rides. I heard they're having clowns, too!"

Mom handed Ginny a pan of tomatoes. "You can wash these for me," she said, "and while you work, think about this: We planted tomatoes last spring, so tomatoes are the crop we're reaping. The Bible teaches that we reap what we sow—in life and actions as well as in the garden. You cannot expect nice things to come about as a result of your unkind words."

"I guess not," said Ginny with a sigh. Sadly she began to wash the tomatoes. *N.E.K.*

HOW ABOUT YOU?

Do you sow kind, Christlike words and actions? Or do you sometimes say mean things and do unkind things? Remember that you reap what you sow. Sow kindness and bear good fruit for Jesus.

MEMORIZE:

"**Whatever a man sows, that he will also reap.**" *Galatians 6:7,* NKJV

 *Sow Good Things*

The Big Blow (Read Matthew 7:24-29)

27
SEPTEMBER

"Dad!" cried Billy. "Look at this!" He pointed to the TV set. The evening news was showing clips of a raging coastal storm. "Look, Dad. I think that's the beach where we go every summer for our vacation," added Billy. They watched silently as a big wave came onto shore and removed a large amount of sand from under a house. Soon the entire building was swept out to sea. "Just like the Bible says," said Billy after a moment, "Never build your house on sand."

"How right you are," agreed Dad. Then he motioned toward the sofa. "Mother and I have something to share with you—let's all sit down." Billy obeyed promptly—this sounded serious. "As you know," continued his father, "many places across our country are going through tough times as far as money and jobs are concerned. Many companies aren't doing enough business to pay their bills. Well, that's what has happened in my company, and it's going out of business."

"Wow!" was all Billy could think of to say. His heart sank, and he slumped back in his chair.

"We'll have to get along for a while on far less money," continued Dad. "We'll have changes to make—like no vacation at the beach—but God will give us strength to go through whatever we have to face. Our family is built on the foundation of Jesus Christ because each of us has accepted Jesus as Savior. Our lives and our family will not be swept away like a house built on sand."

"Jimmy Parker's family was," said Billy in a small voice. "Soon after his dad lost his job, he left them and never came back."

Dad nodded his head. "I know," he said. "The church is trying to help them."

Billy's mother smiled. "We'll stay together, Son," she said. "Remember that we have Jesus as our foundation." *H.A.D.*

HOW ABOUT YOU?

Are bad things happening to your family? Are you afraid that your family will break up because of problems your parents have? If so, put your trust in Jesus and trust him to take care of you. He is your foundation and will help you through your problems.

MEMORIZE:

"Unless the Lord builds the house, its builders labor in vain." *Psalm 127:1, NIV*

 Make Jesus Your Foundation

Soybean Surprise (Read 2 Timothy 1:6-12)

"Are we having chop suey for dinner?" asked Susie as she came into the kitchen after school. Mom nodded. "Great!" exclaimed Susie. "I'm starved! At the cafeteria today we had something they called Steak Surprise, but it sure didn't taste like steak. Patti says it's made of soybeans. Yuck!"

Mom smiled. "Well, I'm glad you're making friends at your new school," she said. "Are any of them Christians?"

28
SEPTEMBER

"I don't think so," replied Susie with a sigh. "I sure do miss my Christian friends. I'm sure everybody here thinks I'm weird—like today when I closed my eyes to pray at lunch. When I opened them, I saw Patti staring at me."

"Perhaps she thought you weren't feeling well," suggested Mom. "Did you explain that you were praying?"

"Well, no," admitted Susie, "but she wouldn't understand anyway. Yesterday when she started using swear words, I just walked away, and she called me a bad name. She apologized today and asked if I wanted to watch a video at her house tonight. I knew it wasn't a good one, so I said I had to do homework." She sighed again.

Later, at the dinner table, Susie asked for a second helping of the chop suey. Mom smiled at her. "Do you know," asked Mom, "that these bean sprouts you're enjoying are closely related to the soybeans in the Steak Surprise you disliked so much?" asked Mom.

"Really?" asked Susie, looking at her plate. "I guess when I know they're vegetables, I expect them to taste the way they do. But I don't like it when people try to fool me into thinking that beans taste like meat. It's just not honest!"

"You know, Susie," Mom said, "I wonder if that could be the answer to why you're having problems at school," she said. "Perhaps if you would come right out and tell Patti and the other girls that you're a Christian, they'd accept that and even expect you to act differently than they act. But if they don't know of your faith in Christ, they'll just continue to be surprised at your behavior." *S.L.K.*

HOW ABOUT YOU?

Do you know Jesus as your Savior? If so, have you told your family and your friends about your faith in him? If you haven't, do it right away. They'll most likely respect you more if you're honest about your faith.

MEMORIZE:

"You have kept my word and have not denied my name."

Revelation 3:8, NIV

 Tell Others You're a Christian

A Hungry Spirit (Read 2 Kings 22:3-10; 23:1-3)

29
SEPTEMBER

"You're ready to be tucked in so quickly tonight!" exclaimed Mother. "Did you read your Bible already?" She bent over Laura and tucked the blanket around her snugly.

"I'll read double tomorrow, Mom," said Laura. Smothering a big yawn, she added, "I played so hard with Kelly today, I can hardly keep my eyes open." Mother hesitated, then said good-night and turned out the light.

When Laura was ready for school the next morning, she slid onto a kitchen chair. "I'm starved!" she declared. "What's for breakfast today?"

"I was so tired this morning, I didn't have the energy to fix anything, honey," said Mother. "In fact, maybe I'll just take a vacation from cooking all day. But don't worry—I'll fix you *two* of every meal tomorrow."

"Mom!" cried Laura. "I'm hungry now!"

"But, Laura, if your spirit can fast for a day, I thought you wouldn't mind if your body fasted, too," Mother told her.

"Fast?" asked Laura, puzzled.

"Go without food," explained Mother. "You skipped your spiritual food last night—you skipped your Bible reading."

Laura blushed. "And reading the Bible is how we get spiritual food?" she asked. She already knew the answer.

"That's one way," agreed Mother. "But not eating one day and doubling it the next really isn't satisfactory, is it—for either your body or your spirit. Like your body, your spirit has to be fed regularly."

Laura shook her head. "I guess maybe I'd better feed my spirit last night's meal—*before* I go to school," she decided. She jumped up to get her Bible.

"I think my energy just climbed way up," said Mother. "I'll fix breakfast for your body while you feed your spirit." With a gentle smile, Mother reached for the frying pan. *M.L.D.*

HOW ABOUT YOU?

Do you feed your body and forget to feed your spirit? God speaks to you through his Word; will you make the very important decision to let him speak to you every day?

MEMORIZE:

"Be a good workman, one who does not need to be ashamed when God examines your work. Know what his Word says and means." *2 Timothy 2:15,* TLB

 Feed on God's Word

The Quarrel (Read Colossians 3:12-17)

"You clumsy ox!" exclaimed Jill. "Why don't you watch what you're doing?"

"Don't be so touchy," retorted Rob. "It was an accident."

The quarrel had started with Rob's throwing a paper airplane at his sister Jill. The nose of the plane poked Jill in the eye. She paid him back by pulling his hair. Soon Rob and Jill were calling each other names, which led to a nasty scuffle on the living room floor.

30
SEPTEMBER

Dad appeared in the doorway. "That's enough," he said. "Get up off the floor. I want peace in this house, starting now." Jill and Rob glared at each other. "The two of you seem to have a lot of extra energy this afternoon," said Dad, "and the garage needs cleaning. You can do that."

"And no fighting, either," added Mom, who had come into the room.

It was a quiet afternoon. While Dad and Mom worked in the front yard, Rob and Jill cleaned the garage without speaking to one another. Rob let Jill struggle to carry out several large boxes of garbage. Jill laughed to herself when Rob spilled a whole bag of potting soil on the newly swept garage floor. She didn't offer to help clean it up.

After a while, Mom and Dad came into the garage. "Hey, this looks great!" said Mom.

"Sure does," agreed Dad. He shook his head sadly. "Too bad Rob and Jill aren't at peace with one another, though."

"What do you mean, Dad?" asked Jill. "We didn't fight all afternoon."

"I know," replied Dad, "but you didn't help each other, either. You appeared to keep peace between you—that is, you didn't fight out loud. But I'm afraid you were still angry with one another and took pleasure in seeing the other have a difficult time."

Mother nodded. "When you really want to make peace with someone, you want the two of you to be friends," she added. "So who wants to take the first step at being a real peacemaker and showing a little love and forgiveness?" *L.J.O.*

HOW ABOUT YOU?

After you have a fight or disagreement with someone, do you continue to hold a grudge against that person? Or do you let go of bitterness and anger? Don't just stop quarreling out loud; really try to make friends with him or her again. That produces real peace between you.

MEMORIZE:

"Be at peace with each other."

Mark 9:50, NIV

Live Peacefully

Passing Tests (Read Job 28:12-20, 28)

1

"I'm going to fail our math test for sure," Jimmy told Alison as they walked to school. "I'm a dummy when it comes to figuring percentages."

"I'm a dummy, too," Alison said, "but I'm not going to fail. Here's why." She slid a card comparing fractions, decimals, and percentages from under the tight cuff on her sleeve. "I've got an extra card. Want it?" She pulled a card from her other cuff.

"That's cheating," objected Jimmy.

"What's worse," Alison asked, "cheating or failing?"

Jimmy took the card and looked at it. How easy it would be to cheat. His desk was near the back of the room, and Mr. Collins rarely looked around the room when they had a test. "I'm not going to do it," Jimmy said, handing the card to Alison. "I don't think you should, either. It's not right."

"You *are* a dummy," Alison replied, "and not just in math."

Jimmy struggled through the test without looking around. He didn't want to see Alison cheat.

After school, Jimmy hurried home. "How was school?" his mother asked as he entered the kitchen for a snack.

"OK," Jimmy replied, "but I think I failed my math test."

"Oh, that's too bad," Mother said, but she didn't get upset. She knew he had trouble understanding math. "Did anything make you feel good today?"

"Strange as it sounds," replied Jimmy, "I felt good about taking the test. I had a chance to cheat, but I decided to be honest."

"Good for you!" Mother sounded pleased. "Think about it," she said. "You passed a harder test—you were tempted and resisted. You knew what was right to do, and you did it! You passed God's test for wisdom. I'm proud of you." Mother was so pleased that she cut an extra-big slice of cake for Jimmy's snack. *D.G.D.*

HOW ABOUT YOU?

Do your friends sometimes encourage you to do something wrong? Do you resist the temptation to join them? God says the wise thing to do is to say no to that temptation. If you ask him, he'll give you the wisdom to make right choices.

MEMORIZE:

"If any of you lacks wisdom, let him ask of God . . . and it will be given to him." *James 1:5,* NKJV

 **Ask God for Wisdom**

Passing Tests (continued from yesterday) (Read James 5:7-11)

2
OCTOBER

As Mr. Collins returned math tests, he handed back everyone's paper except one. "Jimmy, I want to see you after class," he said. *I've failed for sure,* Jimmy thought.

"Tough luck, dummy," whispered Alison as she left the room after class. "I got a B." Jimmy didn't answer. He went up to Mr. Collins's desk.

"Jimmy, I know you have trouble with math," Mr. Collins said, "but that is no excuse for cheating." Jimmy's jaw dropped. He was shocked. "I thought you had done well," continued Mr. Collins, showing him his paper. "I gave you a C, but then I compared your paper with Keith's. Answer for answer, they're the same."

"But I didn't cheat," said Jimmy.

"Don't lie to me," Mr. Collins said sternly. "I want you to stay after school. I'll give you another test to see how you do on your own. You may go now." Slowly, Jimmy left the classroom.

Alison and Keith were waiting to hear what happened. "So you did cheat," said Alison when she heard what Mr. Collins had said. "You act like such a good-goody, but you cheated."

"No, I didn't," protested Jimmy. "Maybe Keith copied from me."

"No way," said Keith. "Who'd want to copy from you?"

"Want to use my cheat card this afternoon?" asked Alison. Jimmy shook his head. "You really *are* a dummy," Alison told him. "If you get accused of cheating, you might as well do it."

Keith agreed with her. "Everybody cheats!" he said. "And there's sure no point in being honest if Mr. Collins thinks you cheat anyway. It doesn't make sense."

"Not to you, maybe," Jimmy replied. He knew it didn't really matter so much what others thought—his parents and God expected him to be honest. His father had said an honest F was better than a dishonest A, and Jimmy agreed. But he prayed that he could do well enough to get another C that afternoon. *D.D.V.*

HOW ABOUT YOU?

Have you ever been accused falsely? Have you been teased for making right choices? Remember that what others think isn't nearly so important as what God thinks. Live to please him.

MEMORIZE:

"Blessed is the man that endureth temptation: for when he is tried, he shall receive the crown of life." *James 1:12,* KJV

 Stand Up to Temptation

Passing Tests (continued from yesterday) (Read Psalm 34:1-4, 14-17)

3
OCTOBER

Jimmy sat in a front seat to take the test Mr. Collins had prepared just for him. Mr. Collins sat at his desk, checking papers as Jimmy worked.

Jimmy struggled through the first few problems. Then something happened! Suddenly he understood how to convert decimals and fractions into percentages. What had been difficult suddenly made sense!

"Finished so soon?" Mr. Collins asked as Jimmy handed in his paper. "Well, sit down, and I'll check this right now." Jimmy watched nervously as Mr. Collins graded the paper. "This is amazing, Jimmy," said Mr. Collins after a moment. "You have only two wrong! It's the best you've done in math all year."

"I don't know how to explain it," said Jimmy, "but as I was working the problems, I finally understood what you've been teaching. Then it was easy."

Mr. Collins nodded. "I'm sorry I accused you of cheating," he said.

"That's OK," replied Jimmy. "At least now I know how to do the problems. May I go?" He couldn't wait to get home and tell his mother.

Jimmy ran all the way home. "Mom!" he yelled as he raced into the house. "I got only two problems wrong on my math test!"

Mother had his snack ready on the table. "Tell me about it," she said, "and tell me why you're late."

Jimmy told her about Mr. Collins's accusation and about taking another test. "It's strange how I suddenly knew how to work the problems even though I didn't understand them before."

Mother smiled. "Maybe it's not so strange," she said. "You studied hard, and you also told me you prayed about it. God answers prayer. You were honest, too, and didn't cheat, and now God made it possible for you to prove that to Mr. Collins. Did you thank God for that—and for helping you understand your math?"

D.D.V.

HOW ABOUT YOU?

Do you pray when things go wrong in your life? Are you surprised when God answers? He cares for even the small things in your life. Talk to him about everything, and remember to thank him when things go right.

MEMORIZE:

"Whatever is good and perfect comes to us from God, the Creator of all light, and he shines forever without change or shadow." *James 1:17,* TLB

 God Gives Good Gifts

Needlepoint (Read Romans 5:1-5)

Mother was sitting on the couch doing her needlepoint when Mark came into the room and sat beside her. He looked at her with tear-filled eyes. "Why did God let Grandpa die?" he asked. "We prayed and prayed for him, but he died anyway."

Mother was quiet for a little while before she answered. "I don't really know why the Lord called Grandpa home at this time," she said, "but . . ." She paused, then she picked up her needlework and held it up so Mark could see the underside. "This isn't very pretty on the underside, is it?" she said with a smile. Then she turned the cloth over so he could see the finished side. Mark could immediately recognize the letters of the alphabet encircling a brown-and-white teddy bear.

4
OCTOBER

Mother laid the needlework back in her lap and looked at Mark. "Sometimes things that happen to us and to those we love look like the wrong side of a needlepoint picture," she said softly. "If we could see the finished side of God's great 'needlework,' we'd see how pretty his work really is. We can trust God for that, can't we?"

R.S.M.

HOW ABOUT YOU?

Has something sad happened in your life? Though you may not understand some things about this life, you can be sure of God's great love for his children. Trust him to do what is best for you.

MEMORIZE:

"Trust in the Lord with all thine heart." *Proverbs 3:5,* KJV

 *Trust God*

Little Tugboats (Read 2 Kings 5:1-4, 9-14)

5

The breeze felt cool against Victor's cheeks as he and Uncle Pablo stood quietly on the pier watching the ships enter and leave the great harbor. "Do you see how those little tugboats can push those big ships through the water, Victor?" Uncle Pablo pointed toward a large tanker in the middle of the harbor as he spoke.

Victor shielded his eyes from the sun and looked in the direction Uncle Pablo pointed. "Uh-huh," he said.

"A person wouldn't think such a little boat could bring such a big ship safely through the harbor, would he?" Uncle Pablo asked. Victor shook his head, and Uncle Pablo continued, "Watching those tugboats makes me think about . . . well . . ." Uncle Pablo paused a moment. "Watching them makes me think about how even a small child can lead a big adult safely to the Lord Jesus."

Victor turned away from the ships to look at his uncle. "What do you mean, Uncle Pablo?" he asked.

"Well, I was thinking of something I read this morning in the Bible—'Even a child is known by his doings,'" Uncle Pablo quoted from Proverbs 20:11, "'whether his work be pure, and whether it be right.'" He looked at Victor and smiled. "By setting a good example of how a Christian should live, even a young child can show himself to be different from those around him who are not Christians. The Holy Spirit can use that kind of child to lead even an adult to Christ." Victor looked back at the tugboat in the harbor.

"Grown-ups can be very impressed by the way a child acts," added Uncle Pablo.

Victor smiled as he understood that God could use him to lead someone else—even a grown-up—to Christ. *R.S.M.*

HOW ABOUT YOU?

Do you think you're too young to be used by God to lead someone to Christ? Don't underestimate what God can do through you, even though you may be small. God is able to use anyone who is willing to be used by him.

MEMORIZE:

"Even a child is known by his doings, whether his work be pure, and whether it be right."

Proverbs 20:11, KJV

 God Can Use You

Rain and Good Deeds (Read Mark 10:35-45)

Mark and his dad chose a spot in the middle of the backyard to set up the rain gauge. Mark was proud of the hollow tube and its funnel-like top. "This is the best school project I've ever made," he said. "I hope it rains soon so my gauge will start measuring rainfall!"

Mom hung up the phone just as Mark and Dad came into the house. "Mr. Blake is afraid his garbage cans might roll out into the street," she said. "His arthritis is acting up, and it's hard for him to walk. Would you go bring in his trash cans, Mark?" When Mark groaned, she added, "This is an opportunity to serve."

6

OCTOBER

"Right," said Mark sarcastically. "But it's really a dumb little chore." He got up and went to take care of it.

When Mark returned, Mom was taking a batch of brownies from the oven. "You can run some of these over to Mr. Blake," she said. "They might boost his spirits."

"Just call me the delivery boy," Mark mumbled.

"You're serving," Mom told him.

"Aw, c'mon," protested Mark. "The things I've been doing are just little errands." He paused. "It would be neat to do something big!" he added after a moment.

Later that day, Mark felt some raindrops. "It's raining!" he exclaimed as he held open the back door. "My gauge is going to start measuring rainfall! Come see!"

Mom and Dad joined Mark in the backyard. "This is just a little sprinkle," Dad said. "It will take a lot more rain than this to make a difference in your gauge."

"Every drop counts!" Mark insisted. "All the drops will be added together, and the water will build up. You'll see."

Mom nodded. "You're right, Son," she agreed, "and do you know what? In the same way, every one of your deeds—no matter how small—will be part of a testimony that continues to grow. Every little thing you do counts, Mark. For example, the more little things you do for Mr. Blake, the more they'll join together to show him a big picture of God's love." *N.E.K.*

HOW ABOUT YOU?

Do you feel that the small things you do don't amount to much? Nothing you do for others is too simple or insignificant to count. Remember that everything you do is part of your testimony.

MEMORIZE:

"For even I, the Messiah, am not here to be served, but to help others, and to give my life as a ransom for many."

Mark 10:45, TLB

Lemonade, Anyone? (Read Romans 8:18, 28-31)

7

OCTOBER

Pete tried to stay out of the way of the movers as they carried furniture into the apartment. He hated moving, and it showed in his expression. "Why the long face?" asked one of the movers when he stopped for a moment to rest.

"I don't like this apartment," said Pete. "It doesn't have a yard for me to play in." He didn't add that he had no room of his own, either, and would have to go to a new school.

The mover nodded. "Well," he said, "if life hands you a lemon, son, make lemonade. In other words, make the best of what comes to you. It may seem like a sour lemon, but it can turn into something sweet. You'll see."

Pete sat down on the back steps and thought about what the man had said. Suddenly he noticed a boy sitting on the back steps of the next apartment. The boy had black hair and brown skin. Curious, Pete walked over to talk to him. "Hi," he said. The boy looked up. He looked as if he had been crying. "What's wrong?" asked Pete.

"I no like it here," replied the boy. "In my country back home, the soldiers kill my father. My mother and sister and me—we come to America, but I no like. I no can speak good English. American boys at school laugh when I talk."

Pete wasn't sure how to answer, but he was busy thinking. Did God send him here to help this boy? Was this the way God wanted him to make lemonade out of his lemons?

Pete sat down on the step beside his new neighbor boy. "I'll help you learn English," he said. "We'll go to school together, and we can play together."

The boy looked at Pete. After a moment, he smiled. "I get ball," he said. He ran into his apartment.

Pete felt good inside as he waited for his new friend to come back. Maybe living in an apartment was turning into something good after all! *M.H.N.*

HOW ABOUT YOU?

Do you have a "lemon" in your life—something that is hard or unpleasant? Ask God to help you accept it and see what good he wants to bring from it.

MEMORIZE:

"'For I know the plans I have for you,' declares the Lord, 'plans to prosper you and not to harm you.'" *Jeremiah 29:11, NIV*

 Make the Best of Life

In Training (Read 1 Timothy 4:6-10, 15-16)

As Jim walked toward home, he heard a familiar voice calling his name. Turning, he saw his Sunday school teacher, Mr. Myers. "Hi, Mr. Myers!" exclaimed Jim, running to meet him. "What are you doing on this street?"

"I just came from Tom Herman's home," answered Mr. Myers. "He visited our class last Sunday. When we have a visitor, I always try to meet his parents as soon as possible."

8
OCTOBER

"They just moved here," said Jim. "Tom seems real nice, but I felt pretty bad for him at school today. It was track and field day, and Tom was last in everything."

"It looks like you did all right," said Mr. Myers. "What's this? Three blue ribbons and a red one pinned to your shirt?"

"Yeah," agreed Jim. "I do OK on a lot of the events."

"Athletes get a lot of attention, don't they?" said Mr. Myers. "And they always have. Even the apostle Paul mentioned physical training in his writings."

"Really?" asked Jim. "What does he say?"

"Well, he says that although physical training has some value, it's more important to train yourself to be godly because godliness helps us in every area of our lives."

Jim thought about that. Then he said, "So you don't think he'd be much impressed with my ribbons, huh?"

Mr. Myers smiled. "Paul didn't put down physical training. He just wanted Timothy to be more concerned about being like Jesus," he explained. "You are to be congratulated on those ribbons. But if, like Tom, you didn't get any ribbons, that wouldn't be so serious. It's far more important to be like Jesus than to be good in sports. You always need to remember that what's really important in life is godly character." *R.J. C.*

HOW ABOUT YOU?

Do you put a lot of value on physical ability and training? Or are you one of those people who are not very athletic? It's great to be athletic, but it's not nearly as important as being like Jesus.

MEMORIZE:

"Train yourself to be godly."

1 Timothy 4:7, NIV

 Godliness Is of Greatest Value

A Time to Wait (Read Genesis 25:29-34)

9

OCTOBER

"When will these flowers bloom, Dad?" asked Danielle when they had buried the last bulb.

"Not until next spring," Dad answered. "You may see little green shoots in a few weeks, but they'll grow very slowly during the winter. When the spring sun comes, they'll start growing faster, and we should have some flowers."

"Spring!" exclaimed Danielle. "That's too long to wait."

Dad laughed. "You might as well forget them for a while," he said. "Concentrate on something else, and before you know it, spring will be here, and we'll have flowers."

"It seems like I always have to wait for everything," said Danielle with a sigh. "Mostly I have to wait to grow up. I'm like those flowers."

Dad smiled and put his arm around Danielle's shoulder. "Lots of kids try to grow up too fast," he said. "I know it's hard to wait for God's perfect time, but trying to hurry the growing-up process usually gets us into trouble. You're God's perfect age for you to be right now. The most important thing you can do while you're waiting is learn to know God better. Then—like those flowers—your life will blossom into something beautiful." Dad picked up the rake and handed the hoe to Danielle. "I hope lunch is ready," he said. "I can't wait for that good hot soup!"

"Dad," teased Danielle, "you just have to think of something else until it's Mom's perfect time to call us for lunch." *P.O.Y.*

HOW ABOUT YOU?

Do you "want what you want when you want it"? In the story of Jacob and Esau, Esau refused to wait. He didn't look at the consequences of the choice he was making. Don't make that mistake. Be patient as you're growing up. Wait for God's perfect time to become an adult.

MEMORIZE:

"Wait on the Lord; be of good courage, and He shall strengthen your heart; wait, I say, on the Lord!"

Psalm 27:14, NKJV

 Wait for God's Best

A Watchful Eye (Read Proverbs 3:1-8)

10
OCTOBER

The sleek, black car crept slowly down the tree-lined street as Sally and Linda walked home from Kids Bible Club. They were planning a busy weekend and didn't see the big car until it eased up to the curb. Rolling down the car window, the man called, "Can you tell me where Magnolia Street is?"

Sally and Linda stopped, looking around. Was the man in the car across the street talking to them? "Remember, we never talk to strangers," Sally whispered, grabbing Linda's arm.

Ignoring her friend's warning, Linda started toward the car. "It can't hurt to give directions," she said. "He looks nice enough. Besides, we just had a lesson on how God is watching over us, remember?"

Sally stayed on the sidewalk and watched. Suddenly the man jumped out of the car. Grabbing Linda's arm, he tried to force her into the backseat. Screaming, Linda jerked back, scattering her armload of books all over the street.

Without thinking, Sally ran to help her friend. *Lord, please help us,* she silently prayed as she swung her book bag with all her strength, hitting the man across the face. Letting go of Linda, the man fell against the car, holding his face in his hands. The girls ran to the sidewalk, screaming at the top of their lungs, as Mrs. Smith stepped out of her door. People came from all directions. The man jumped into the car, roared down the street, and left the small town.

Mrs. Smith hurried the girls inside. After calling the police and their parents, she gave them a stern lecture about talking to strangers. "Haven't your parents told you these things?" she asked.

"Y-yes. B-but our Bible club teacher said God w-would be w-watching over us," blubbered Linda.

"And he was," Mrs. Smith assured her, "otherwise you might not be here now. But just because he's watching doesn't mean you can ignore the warnings your parents give you. In fact, giving you those warnings is one of his ways of protecting you. Always remember that!" *E.L.N.*

HOW ABOUT YOU?

Do you sometimes forget the warnings of your parents or teachers? Or do you disobey, thinking no harm will come? One way God takes care of you is by providing advice and warnings from responsible people. Pay attention to them. And don't forget to thank God for his watchful care.

MEMORIZE:

"Listen to your father and mother." *Proverbs 1:8,* TLB

Listen to Parents

The Right Move (Read Jeremiah 29:11-14)

11

OCTOBER

"Which do you want first?" asked Mom when Morgan got home from school. "The bad news or the good news?"

"The bad, I guess." Morgan munched on an apple. She knew that when Mom played Bad News/Good News with her, the news was never terribly bad.

"Dad's transfer is to Dalton instead of Briggs."

"Dalton?" moaned Morgan. "That's too far to see my friends very often. And we found a house in Briggs."

"Sorry, honey," said Mom, "but maybe we'll find an even nicer house in Dalton. And your friends can come for longer visits since it's farther."

Morgan sighed. "What's the good news?"

"Kit had her kittens today. They're in the utility room," said Mom. Morgan jumped up and went to check on them. But when she looked in the box, it was empty. "Kit must have moved them," said Mom, and she and Morgan began searching the house.

"Here they are, under my bed," squealed Morgan.

"That isn't a good place for your babies," Mom told Kit. "You'd better take them back to the nice box I fixed for you."

Morgan laughed. "Kit doesn't understand you," she said. "Besides, it would be fun to keep them in my room."

"Maybe, but your room is a very busy place, with you and your friends scooting in and out so often," Mom pointed out. "The kittens would be safer in the utility room."

"Yeah, I guess so," agreed Morgan. "I wish we could explain to Kit that she didn't move them to a very good spot."

Morgan and Mom moved the kittens back to the box. "This reminds me of us," Mom said. "We thought Briggs was the best place to live, but the Lord shut the door on that idea. He must have had a good reason."

"Just like we have good reasons for not letting Kit keep her kittens under my bed, huh?" asked Morgan as she closed the door to her room so Kit wouldn't move them back. "Well, then I guess your news wasn't so bad after all—I knew it wouldn't be." *K.R.A.*

HOW ABOUT YOU?

Have you had a disappointing change in your life's plans? Are you unable to do something you wanted to do? God may have allowed those plans to be changed for some reason you don't understand. You can trust him to do what is best for you.

MEMORIZE:

"And we know that in all things God works for the good of those who love him." *Romans 8:28,* NIV

 *God Knows Best*

No VCR Needed (Read Psalm 139:1-6)

"Why are you watching the Panthers game?" Alicia asked her older brother as she entered the family room. "I thought you said you were going to watch the Hawkeyes."

"Yeah, well, I'm taping that game on the VCR to watch later," replied Ben as he munched some popcorn. Just then a car commercial came on the TV, and Ben turned on a portable radio. He grinned at his little sister. "Our high school team is playing out of town tonight, so during the commercials I tune in to see how they're doing," he told her. "Have you got a smart brother or what?"

12

OCTOBER

Before long, it was Alicia's bedtime. "Come tuck me in, Daddy," she called when she was ready to sleep.

"Shall we pray together before I tuck you in?" suggested her father when he reached her room.

"I guess so," agreed Alicia. "But aren't lots of other kids saying their prayers right now?"

Dad nodded. "Yes, I imagine they are," he said.

"Well, does God put all of us on a big VCR to listen to later?" Alicia wondered.

Dad smiled. "Sounds like you've been talking with Ben," he replied. "No, honey, God doesn't have to use a VCR. He can hear everyone's prayer at the same time."

"Well, when the commercials come on, Ben switches over to the radio," said Alicia. "If my prayers aren't very interesting, does God switch to someone else?"

"Oh, honey, God isn't like Ben or any of us," Dad said. He gave her a hug. "God is God. He can hear all the little children of the world all at the same time," he assured her. "He is greater than we can ever understand. He doesn't need a TV set or a VCR or a radio. He hears everything we say and even knows everything we think. We can never really understand how he does it, but we have faith that he does it because he is God."

"I'm glad." Alicia smiled and slipped to her knees beside her bed. "I'm ready to pray now." *R.K.M.*

HOW ABOUT YOU?

Do you ever wonder how God can hear your prayers when so many other people are talking to him at once? Do you think God may tune you out and give his attention to someone else? Don't worry; God cares about every detail of your life, and he hears all your prayers. Pray right now; God is listening.

MEMORIZE:

"You know what I am going to say before I even say it."

Psalm 139:4, TLB

 God Is All-Knowing

On Your Feet (Read 1 John 1:8-10; 2:2)

13
OCTOBER

Baby Clint toddled unsteadily from the sofa to a chair, and Brenda turned her attention back to the book she was reading. But then her little brother was off again, this time to an armchair on the other side of the living room. About halfway there, he teetered for a moment and then sat down hard. He looked surprised, as if he wondered what had tripped him. A moment later, he was pushing himself to his feet. Then he continued walking toward the chair.

"I'm surprised Clint keeps getting back up so quickly," Brenda told her mother. "Sometimes he falls really hard, but he picks himself up and keeps going."

"Some babies are determined to get where they want to go," Mother answered. She smiled as she watched the little boy. "I wish Christians were as determined to reach their goal," she added thoughtfully.

"What goal?" asked Brenda.

"Well, as Christians we should have a goal of becoming more like the Lord Jesus," replied Mother, "but like Clint, we fall sometimes—we fall into sin."

"Yeah," agreed Brenda, thinking of her struggle to break her habit of lying.

"When we fall, we get back on our feet by confessing our sin to God and anyone else we've wronged," added Mother. "We keep going by obeying the commands in the Bible."

Brenda sighed. "But I always end up falling again."

Just then, little Clint fell with a loud thud. He whimpered and crawled on his knees a little way, but then he carefully stood back up and started to walk again.

"As Clint learns to walk, he falls more than once," said Mother, "but he gets back up each time, and he'll get better and better at walking until he'll hardly ever fall. Like Clint, you and I fall—we fail to obey God—more than once. Each time we do, we have to confess our sin. As we choose again and again to do right with God's help, we'll fail him less often." *R.L.V.*

HOW ABOUT YOU?

When you disobey, lie, or do some other wrong thing, do you confess your sin and start to obey the Bible again? Or do you decide that you might as well give up? God expects you to get up and keep going. Confess your sin and, with God's help, do what you know is right.

MEMORIZE:

"If we confess our sins, he is faithful and just to forgive us our sins, and to cleanse us from all unrighteousness."

1 John 1:9, KJV

 **Confess Sin**

No Bare Branches (Read Psalm 1:1-6)

Amy and Jennifer kicked their way through piles of fallen leaves as additional bright yellow, red, and gold leaves floated like lazy butterflies from the trees. "Oh, Jen, isn't it beautiful?" Amy sighed dreamily. "Do you ever wonder what makes leaves turn from green in the summer to such pretty fall colors?"

14
OCTOBER

"I wrote a report on that just last week," Jennifer replied. "In the summer, trees produce chlorophyll, which makes the leaves green. Then when the days get shorter, other chemicals take over, resulting in the bright colors of fall."

"That sure sounds boring," groaned Amy.

"Yup, boring and dull," said Jennifer, "but true!"

"I wish the pretty leaves could stay on the trees all winter, too."

Jennifer grinned. "My resource book says the stems get weak as the days get shorter, and the leaves finally break off and drop to the ground."

"And we have to rake 'em up," Amy finished.

Jennifer laughed. "Right!" she agreed. "So enjoy it while it lasts." She looked thoughtfully at her friend. "Last week in Sunday school, my teacher compared people to trees. Mrs. Graham said the beautiful, colored leaves reminded her of the good things lots of people do in the hope of getting to heaven—finally those good deeds drop off like old leaves, leaving nothing but bare branches."

Amy wrinkled her nose. "Yeah?" she asked.

Jennifer nodded. "And she said that when we know Jesus as Savior, we constantly grow in him—like new, green leaves on a tree." She smiled. "And as Christians we can have the beautiful, colored leaves of good works at the same time—but they're not what get us to heaven."

Jennifer's eager smile and enthusiastic words impressed Amy. "That sounds so nice, Jennifer," she said quietly. "I wish I knew more about it."

"You can! Come with me next week," invited Jennifer. "Mrs. Graham is a great teacher." Amy smiled and nodded. *P.I.K.*

HOW ABOUT YOU?

Is your life filled with beautiful "leaves"—good deeds? That's great, but be sure you don't trust them to get you to heaven. They'll all drop away. Simply trust in Jesus for salvation.

MEMORIZE:

"All our righteous acts are like filthy rags; we all shrivel up like a leaf, and like the wind our sins sweep us away."

Isaiah 64:6, NIV

 Good Works Don't Save

Boundaries (Read Ephesians 6:1-4, 10-12)

15
OCTOBER

Ryan and his friends drew a large chalk circle on the driveway. "What's that for?" asked Dad, who was outside raking leaves.

"We're playing hide-and-seek," answered Ryan, "and this is the safety zone. If we're found, we're still safe if we can reach the zone before we're tagged."

After a while the children began to leave, and Ryan ran over to his father. "Dad," he said, "everyone's going over to Tom's house to watch a show. Can I go, too?"

Dad asked Ryan a few questions, then shook his head no. Ryan stuck out his lip and frowned. "Aw, Dad, what's wrong with that show? Joey goes to our church, and he gets to watch."

Dad thought for a moment. "The game you were playing can help me explain," he said. "It's as though Satan is 'it' in your life. Your mother and I protect you from him by drawing a limit on what you may do. Inside that limit is your safety zone. When we choose your boundaries, we leave out the things that are definitely bad."

"Like drinking and smoking and swearing?" Ryan asked.

"Yes. They're far away from your safety circle. But there is a whole range of activities the Bible doesn't specifically talk about. Some are better than others. Some have more bad in them than good," explained Dad. "To keep you safe, we must pick some point, draw a boundary, and say, 'This is as far as you can go.'"

"And the show is beyond my safety zone?" asked Ryan.

Dad nodded. "Other Christian parents may draw boundaries at different places, and that doesn't make them wrong," he said. "But for us, the line is here."

"And Satan can't get to me if I stay inside the boundaries?" asked Ryan.

Dad smiled. "I wish that were true," he said, "but the boundaries can't entirely keep him out. He doesn't have as much freedom within them, but you need to depend on Jesus for complete protection from Satan."

Ryan nodded slowly. "I guess I understand," he said. "I'll tell the guys I can't come." *C.Y.P.*

HOW ABOUT YOU?

Have you ever wondered why your parents wouldn't let you go to a party, dance, or movie that all your friends were attending? It's hard to be the only one staying home! But remember, the boundaries are set for your safety. Stay within them—and thank God for parents who watch out for you.

MEMORIZE:

"Your enemy the devil prowls around like a roaring lion looking for someone to devour."

1 Peter 5:8, NIV

 **Rules Protect You**

Pepper and Hilary, Too (Read 1 John 4:7-11)

"I know God loves everybody, but even he must have a hard time loving Hilary," Amber told her older sister as they raked leaves in the backyard.

"Is she that girl in your class who pushes in front of kids in the cafeteria line?" Kendra asked while she filled a garbage bag with leaves.

16

OCTOBER

"Yeah," said Amber. "She cheats, too, and she writes bad words on the bathroom walls."

"Wow, she—" Kendra was interrupted when Amber's dog, Pepper, dashed through their pile of leaves and scattered them all over. "Bad dog," Kendra yelled.

Just as Amber and Kendra got the scattered leaves raked into a pile again, Pepper returned with a dead mouse in his mouth. "Gross," Kendra said, jumping back from the dog. "Take it away." Pepper ran through the leaf pile into the alley.

The sisters decided to take a break, and they sat down on the dry leaves. Soon Pepper returned and lay down at Amber's feet. "Honestly, Amber," said Kendra, "I don't see how you can love that awful creature. Pepper is funny looking, he has doggy breath, he brings dead animals around, and he growls at Grandma every time she comes over."

"Pepper has lots of good qualities, too," insisted Amber. "And even if he didn't, I'd still love him because he's mine."

"Yeah . . ." Kendra was thoughtful. "Do you think God feels that same way about Hilary?" she asked. "Pastor Blander talked about how we're made in God's image, remember?"

Amber thought about that. "I guess you're right about God loving Hilary," she said at last, "but I can't love her."

Kendra got up and began raking leaves again. "You don't have to like the things Hilary does," she said, "but you should love her because she's made in God's image, just like we are." She grinned at her sister. "Tell you what, Amber. I'll try to find some good qualities in Pepper if you'll look for good qualities in Hilary."

R.K.M.

HOW ABOUT YOU?

Do you know some boys and girls who are mean and do bad things? Do you wonder how God can love them? He doesn't love the bad things they do, and you shouldn't, either, but he does love them. Learn to love people, not their deeds.

MEMORIZE:

"This is My commandment, that you love one another as I have loved you." *John 15:12,* NKJV

 Learn to Love Everyone

A Great Privilege (Read Romans 8:14-17)

17

OCTOBER

Brandon sat at the dinner table with his mother, father, and two older brothers. He had belonged to the family for exactly nine years now. As they held hands, Brandon's father prayed. "Father in heaven, today we celebrate the day you brought Brandon to our family. Thank you for giving us the chance to adopt him—he has brought us great joy. Bless our son in every way. In Jesus' name, amen." Brandon looked up to see his mother's smile, and he felt warm and wonderful inside.

But fifth grade had brought questions. Being adopted was a mystery, and he had been asking about it. So Brandon listened intently as his father talked about it during family devotions that evening. "Historians tell us that in Bible times many sons were adopted," said Dad. "Some believe it's quite likely that Joseph adopted Jesus as his very own son, even though God himself was Jesus' real father."

Mother smiled. "So you're in good company, Brandon," she said, giving him a hug.

"In Bible times, a man with no children would adopt a son in order to pass on all that he owned," added Dad. "That son bore his name and called him Father."

Keith, the oldest son, kicked at Brandon playfully. "Well, Big B, it looks like adoption really is a privilege!" he teased. "That inheritance part sounds good, too. I think I'd like being adopted."

Dad spoke again. "The wonderful thing is that not only did God create us, but he wants each of us to be adopted as his sons. We can call God Father when we receive Christ as Savior. What a privilege!"

Keith winked at Brandon and asked, "And what about the inheritance?"

Dad laughed. "It's far greater than our minds can fathom," he said. "The Bible says we're 'heirs of God' and 'joint-heirs with Christ.' It couldn't get any better than that!" *C.P.K.*

HOW ABOUT YOU?

Do you realize that God wants a relationship with you? He wants to be your heavenly Father. He paid a great price to give you all that he owns. Accept his offer today and become his adopted child.

MEMORIZE:

"His unchanging plan has always been to adopt us into his own family by sending Jesus Christ to die for us."

Ephesians 1:5, TLB

 You Can Call God Father

Best Friends (Read John 15:11-17)

"Mom, it's going to be so neat having Tiffany living right across the road," Kerry bubbled. "We're going to be best friends and do everything together. I invited her to my Sunday school class, and pizza is her favorite food, just like mine!"

Mom smiled as she took a pizza out of the oven. "Well, it's nice that you and Tiffany have so much in common," she said.

18
OCTOBER

Kerry nodded. "We're going to do everything together."

A few weeks later, Kerry came storming into the house. "Tiffany isn't my best friend anymore," she declared angrily.

"What on earth happened?" asked Dad.

"I went over to play with her, but she went to a piano recital with Justine," grumbled Kerry. "She didn't even tell me they were going."

"Be sensible, Kerry," said Mom. "Justine and Tiffany like piano recitals, and you don't."

"I don't care," said Kerry stubbornly. "We're supposed to be best friends, and best friends don't act like that!"

At dinner, Kerry was surprised to see spaghetti on her parents' plates, while her own plate contained only cold, leftover pizza. "This looks good, but don't I get some spaghetti, too?" she asked.

"I know pizza is your favorite food, so I decided to let you have it for every meal," Mom told her. "There's some you can have for breakfast tomorrow, too."

Kerry frowned. "I like pizza," she said, "but I wouldn't want it all the time; that would be boring." She held up the limp slice of pizza and looked at her mother suspiciously. "What are you really trying to say?" she asked.

Mother smiled. "Well, I was hoping you would see that just like it's good to have variety in the food you eat, it's good to have variety in friendships. Don't be jealous when Tiffany has other friends."

"That's right, Kerry," agreed Dad. "Remember, even Jesus didn't spend all his time with just one person. Your influence for him will be greater as you show interest in, and love toward, a number of people." *R.K.M.*

HOW ABOUT YOU?

Are you jealous if your best friend has other friends? Don't be. God wants you to show love toward that person and toward many others as well. You each need to spend time with family and other friends. Pray for all your friends like Jesus did, and make him your best Friend of all.

MEMORIZE:

"A friend loveth at all times."
Proverbs 17:17, KJV

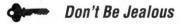 **Don't Be Jealous**

A Clean Slate (Read Psalm 32:1-5)

19
OCTOBER

When Kelley tried to open the sliding door to the patio, she could not get it open. In her frustration, she said some words she had heard her friend at school say when she was upset. "Kelley, where did you hear that?" asked Mom. She sounded shocked.

"At school," said Kelley guiltily.

"I think you know better," said Mom. "That's swearing, and if you love God, you should not talk that way."

"I-I'm sorry," murmured Kelley, and she was. She went outside, but she didn't feel like playing anymore. Instead, she found a quiet spot and asked God to forgive her for swearing.

When Kelley sat down to eat her sandwich that noon, she bowed her head to pray. She thanked God for the food, and again she asked him to forgive her for swearing.

"I'm glad to see you thanking God for your food even when you're eating alone," Mom complimented Kelley.

Kelley sighed. "I asked God to forgive me for swearing, but I still feel bad," she said as she played with her sandwich. She didn't even feel like eating.

Mom raised her brows. After a moment she said, "Set your sandwich aside for a bit and come with me." She led Kelley out to the back patio. "This is what happened, Kelley," Mom said, as she took a piece of sidewalk chalk and wrote on the concrete, *Kelley is guilty of swearing.* That made Kelley feel even worse, but then Mom walked over and picked up the garden hose. "And this is what happened when you asked God to forgive you," continued Mom. She turned on the faucet, directed the stream of water at her writing, and washed the accusing words away.

A smile formed on Kelley's face. She didn't bow her head again, but her heart said, *Thank you, Lord. E.M.B.*

HOW ABOUT YOU?
Have you failed God even after you accepted Jesus as your Savior? Have you been unkind, said something wrong, or done something bad—perhaps even without thinking? Satan will tell you it's all over between you and God, but don't believe him. Confess your sin and receive God's forgiveness.

MEMORIZE:
"I finally admitted all my sins to you. . . . I said to myself, 'I will confess them to the Lord.' And you forgave me!"
Psalm 32:5, TLB

 *Confess Sin*

A Grandpa Up for Adoption (Read Romans 8:28-32)

Randy and his friend Joe trudged down the street to the nursing home. They were going to visit Joe's grandpa. Randy felt cheated because *his* grandpa lived far away. Randy had prayed that Grandpa would come to live with them when he could no longer live alone. But Grandpa decided against it. Mother told Randy that sometimes God answers our prayers in a different way from what we want, but he does always answer.

20

OCTOBER

Joe's grandpa greeted the boys warmly when they came into his room. He was sitting in a wheelchair. A thin man in the next bed called to the boys. "You'd better get out of here as fast as you can, or they'll tie you up, too," he said. "First time in my life I've been in jail."

The boys looked at Grandpa with questions in their eyes. "He thinks he's in jail," whispered Grandpa.

"Who comes to see him and cheer him up?" asked Randy.

Grandpa shook his head. "His wife and only son both died in a car accident. Nobody comes to visit him."

Randy walked slowly over to the old man's bed. The man glared at him, and then his face softened as he reached for Randy's hand. "You're my boy," he said. Randy looked uncertainly over at Joe. "Yup," continued the old man, "my boy came to visit me in jail."

Randy didn't know what to say. He shook the old man's hand. "I'll come again," he promised with a grin. "Maybe I can bring you some cookies."

"You're my boy," said the old man again, and he seemed much happier than he'd been before.

When Randy and Joe left, Randy could hardly wait to get home and tell his folks about his new friend. "I'm going to adopt him as my grandpa, since my own grandpa doesn't live with us," he told them. "If God had answered my prayers the way I thought he should, that old man wouldn't have anybody coming to see him. Now he has me, so he won't be so lonesome anymore. I guess God knows best!" *M.H.N.*

HOW ABOUT YOU?

Do you trust God to answer your prayers the way he knows is best? Will you thank him even when you are disappointed, and wait to see what he will do? (And by the way—is there an older person that you could cheer up and be a friend to?)

MEMORIZE:

"As for God, his way is perfect." *Psalm 18:30,* KJV

God Answers Prayer

Where's Your Passport?

(Read Ephesians 2:13-14, 18-22)

21
OCTOBER

"We're pretending to travel to Europe in our social studies class," Brandon told his family. "We planned our trip, made passports, scheduled travel arrangements, and packed our bags. Today we went to Paris. Every day we travel to a new place and learn all kinds of neat things."

"That sounds like a fun way to learn," Dad said.

"We're flying back to America tomorrow," Brandon reported a week later, "but I can't find my passport!"

"Why not make a new one?" suggested Mom.

So Brandon copied information, pasted on a new picture, and added his signature. "It looks almost the same as the other one," he said, showing his new passport to his parents.

The following day, Brandon sat on the pretend class plane headed for America. After the plane landed, everyone took out their passports and lined up to reenter the United States.

"Sorry," said the student who checked passports. "You can't come into our country. This passport is not the real thing. You have no proof of citizenship."

"But I *am* a citizen," Brandon insisted. "I couldn't find the passport we made in class, so I made a new one. Come on—this one has all the right things."

"Step aside, sir. We'll have to look into this," replied Brandon's classmate. "Security!" he called.

That evening, Brandon told his family about it. "I wasn't allowed back into the U.S.," he said. "No valid proof of citizenship."

"So your phony passport didn't work?" asked Dad. Brandon shook his head. "Reminds me of Pastor Burns's sermon last week," said Dad. "He reminded us that those who haven't accepted Jesus will be turned away from heaven, even though they think they've done all the right things."

Mom nodded. "I'm surely glad we have valid proof of citizenship to get into heaven," she said. "Our citizenship is guaranteed when we ask Jesus to be our Savior. The proof is in our hearts and in God's Book of Life." *N.E.K.*

HOW ABOUT YOU?

Are you a citizen of heaven? Have you asked Jesus to be your personal Savior? Remember, doing the right things won't get you into heaven. The only way in is through Jesus.

MEMORIZE:

"**Consequently, you are no longer foreigners and aliens, but fellow citizens with God's people and members of God's household.**" *Ephesians 2:19,* NIV

 *Accept Jesus*

Pizza Party (Read Job 23:10-14)

22
OCTOBER

"I've tried to get started reading my Bible every day," said Trisha as she reached for a piece of pizza, "but I never seem to be able to keep at it. I'll read a whole lot for a few days, and then I just . . . well . . . quit again." Several of the other young people nodded knowingly. They were at a combination Bible study/pizza party, and their leader, Mr. MacRay, had been urging them to develop a time of daily devotions.

"Bible reading is a little like eating," Mr. MacRay said. "First you take a bite, next you chew it, then you swallow it, and finally you digest it."

"But how do you take a bite of the Bible?" Karen asked.

"This pizza is cut into sections, and the Bible is in sections, too," said Mr. MacRay. "Select a section each day, but don't try to take too big a bite. A bite might be just a verse or two, or it might be a chapter."

"As Mrs. Green says, 'Don't take more than you can chew,'" said Mike, imitating the school lunchroom teacher. The others laughed.

"That's good advice," said Mr. MacRay. "Chewing might be compared to thinking about what you've read."

"What about swallowing?" asked Sue. "What's that?"

"Well, when someone says, 'That story sure was hard to swallow,' it means it was hard to believe, doesn't it?" said Mr. MacRay. "Swallowing is believing—believing God's Word is true. That brings us to digestion. What happens when we digest food?"

"We just studied that in school," said Mike. "When food is digested, it's changed into something the blood can take to the rest of the body to use."

"Good." Mr. MacRay nodded. "When it comes to Bible reading, digestion would be applying God's Word to your life. It means letting God's Word make a difference in your life."

"So I guess we really need to eat four meals a day—breakfast, lunch, dinner, and a slice of our Bibles," said Mike with a grin.

S.S.

HOW ABOUT YOU?

Do you find it hard to study your Bible? Perhaps you're taking too big a bite; try starting with just a verse or two. But then think about what you've read. Think about what God wants to teach you through it. Then follow that teaching.

MEMORIZE:

"Man shall not live by bread alone, but by every word that proceeds from the mouth of God." *Matthew 4:4, NKJV*

 "Eat" Your Bible

Someone to Listen (Read Matthew 6:8-13)

23
OCTOBER

Linda looked out at the tall buildings surrounding her new home. A big lump came into her throat as she thought about the stormy divorce. Linda tried to talk to her mother about how lonely she felt, but Mother didn't listen. She always talked about *her* problems, not Linda's. Today her mother was nervous because it was her first day at a new job. *She doesn't even think about my first day at a new school,* Linda said to herself with tears in her eyes.

Linda dreaded walking into the new school, but the principal was kind and sent an aide to guide her to the sixth-grade classroom. When the bell rang for lunch, the girl sitting in front of Linda turned around. "Want to eat lunch with me?" she asked. Linda breathed a huge sigh of relief as she went with her new friend to the cafeteria.

"What does your dad do?" asked Holly.

Linda had hoped nobody would ask about her dad. "He's a salesman," she answered vaguely. "How about yours?"

Holly shrugged. "He left when I was a baby."

Linda didn't answer right away; then she said in a small voice, "My folks are divorced, too." Almost in tears, she added, "And it seems like Mom just thinks about her own problems and doesn't even hear me when I talk about mine."

"I know what you mean," answered Holly. "I was really lonely until I met my heavenly Father."

"Your what?"

"My heavenly Father—God!" replied Holly. "He always listens. I can talk to him about anything. He's with me all the time and helps me not to feel so lonely."

"Must be nice," said Linda wistfully.

Holly leaned forward eagerly. "Why don't you go to Sunday school with me to learn about him, too?" she invited. "When you don't have a dad, it's really neat to have a heavenly Father."

"Someone to listen, right?" asked Linda.

Holly nodded. "To listen and help."

"OK," said Linda, "it's a deal." *M.H.N.*

HOW ABOUT YOU?

Do you know the heavenly Father? Even if you have an earthly father, you need to know the heavenly Father, too. He loves you and is always ready to listen to you, no matter where you are or what your problem is.

MEMORIZE:

"Your Father knows exactly what you need even before you ask him!" *Matthew 6:8,* TLB

 God Always Listens

The Secret Room (Read 1 Corinthians 6:19-20)

24

OCTOBER

The day after Grandpa Joe's funeral, Matthew's parents went to help Grandma take care of Grandpa Joe's things. Matthew was excited. They were going to go into the room Grandpa Joe had always kept locked. Even Grandma was never allowed to go into it. *What did Grandpa Joe keep hidden in that room all those years?* wondered Matthew. "Why can't Grandma go in every room?" Matthew had once asked his father. "It's her house, isn't it?"

Dad nodded. "Yes," he said, "but when my stepfather moved in, he took that room for himself. To keep peace, Grandma just let him have his secret room."

When the secret room was opened and they stepped inside, they saw only some old boxes covered with dust. But when they looked inside the boxes, they discovered stacks of money! "I can't believe it!" Grandma exclaimed. "I thought we were poor. I had to do without many things, but there was plenty of money."

Matthew felt both excited and sad as the money was counted. He was glad Grandma had it, but he was sorry she didn't have it sooner. On the way home he talked to his parents about it. "That room and the money really belonged as much to Grandma as to Grandpa Joe," he said, "but Grandpa Joe kept it all for himself. That was greedy!"

Mother nodded slowly. "I'm afraid so," she said, "and they both suffered because of it."

"I believe we can learn a lesson from this," said Dad. "You see, we're like that sometimes, too. Our bodies and our lives really belong to God. He created us, and he purchased our eternal life with the precious blood of Jesus. Yet we sometimes want to keep a part of our lives for our own desires or pleasures. We don't want God to have it."

"That's true," agreed Mother. "Then, like Grandpa Joe with his secret room, we gain no real profit for ourselves or for God or for anybody else."

"Each of us needs to give his whole life over to God," added Dad. "After all, it's really his." *M.R.P.*

HOW ABOUT YOU?

Do you have a "secret room" in your life that you're holding back from God? Perhaps it's a friendship he wouldn't approve of, bad reading material, or a "sneaky" way of getting out of work. Jesus paid a great price—his blood—to purchase you. Allow him into every part of your life.

MEMORIZE:

"Do not let any part of your bodies become tools of wickedness, to be used for sinning; but give yourselves completely to God—every part of you." *Romans 6:13, TLB*

 Give God Your Whole Life

Building Temples (Read 1 Corinthians 6:12-13, 19-20)

25

OCTOBER

A new church was being built not far from where Peter lived. One day Mr. Davis, one of the workers, let him go inside so he could see how beautiful the stained-glass windows looked with the sunshine coming through them.

As Peter walked past the church on the way to school the next day, he was surprised to see pieces of colored glass all over the ground. During the night, some vandals had thrown rocks and smashed the windows. "Who could have done such a terrible thing?" exclaimed Peter in an angry voice.

Mr. Davis, standing nearby, heard him. "It's surely sad when people have so little respect for God and the things that belong to him," agreed Mr. Davis. He shook his head. "But do you know," he added, "many people do much the same thing to their bodies as the vandals did to those stained-glass windows?" Peter looked at him with a puzzled expression. "Using drugs, smoking, and drinking damages our bodies, just like stones damage glass windows," explained Mr. Davis. "Christians are the temple of the living God, just as this church is a temple for believers."

Peter picked up a piece of colored glass and turned it over and over in the sunlight. "Isn't this pretty?" he asked.

"Yes," agreed Mr. Davis, "and like this piece of glass reflects the light of the sun, we should reflect the light of Jesus."

"And we can't do that so well if we've messed up our bodies with drugs and stuff, right?" asked Peter.

Mr. Davis nodded. "That's right," he said. *M.M.K.*

HOW ABOUT YOU?

Do you belong to Jesus? Then you need to keep your body pure and free from things such as drugs, alcohol, and tobacco, so that you can truly reflect Jesus' beauty. Say no to such things.

MEMORIZE:

"Honor God with your body."

1 Corinthians 6:20, NIV

 Don't Use Drugs, Tobacco, and Alcohol

Umbrella Weather (Read Ephesians 6:10-18)

Tracy woke up one morning to the sound of raindrops on her bedroom window. Leaping out of bed, she pulled up the shade. "Oh, what great umbrella weather!" she shouted. For weeks, Tracy had saved money for her new pink umbrella. Her friend Erin, who lived next door, had one, and the girls were eager to walk to school in the rain. So before long, they were walking down the sidewalk together.

26

OCTOBER

It was raining again when they returned home. Erin stopped in at Tracy's house. "It was so much fun, Mother," bubbled Tracy as they came into the kitchen. "We kept so nice and dry under our umbrellas!"

Erin wasn't so cheerful. "The rain was fun, but school wasn't," she said with a sigh. "I couldn't get some of my homework last night, and no one would help me. Sometimes I think God doesn't care about me, either."

Tracy glanced helplessly at her mother. Although Erin had accepted Jesus as Savior, when problems came up she doubted that anyone—including God—cared for her. Tracy had often prayed that she could find a way to help her friend.

Mother pointed to the umbrellas propped open on the floor. "Erin, how do umbrellas keep you dry?" she asked.

"Umbrellas?" echoed Erin. "They just keep the rain from falling on us."

"They're a shield against the rain, aren't they?" said Mother. "Well, there's another shield you need to use, too. The Bible tells us to use the 'shield of faith' against doubts that Satan puts in our minds. You need to learn more about God, and then you'll learn to love him more and trust him when troubles come."

"Come to Bible Club with me this afternoon," suggested Tracy quickly. "And maybe every week we could do our Bible lesson together. I know that will help you put up a shield against doubting God—won't it, Mother?"

Mother nodded, and Erin did, too. "Maybe it would help," she agreed. "At least, I'll give it a try." *C.E.Y.*

HOW ABOUT YOU?

Do you doubt that God loves you and cares for you? Learn all you can about him. Listen carefully in Sunday school, Bible Club, and church. Be faithful in reading God's Word and in doing your Bible lessons. By knowing God better and remembering his promises, you'll be shielded from doubts.

MEMORIZE:

"In every battle you will need faith as your shield to stop the fiery arrows aimed at you by Satan." Ephesians 6:16, TLB

 Shield Yourself from Doubts

Heavy Load (Read Matthew 11:28-30)

27
OCTOBER

Aaron squealed with excitement as the tractor strained to pull the heavy load. It inched along, then gathered speed to the finish line. "He made it," Aaron shouted and clapped along with others in the crowd at the tractor-pulling contest.

"The next load will be heavier," Grandpa said.

Loud growls came from the big machine as the driver revved the engine. The load behind the groaning tractor dragged at a snail's pace to the finish line. Aaron shot up from his seat and shouted, "Cool!" while the crowd stood up and cheered.

But Aaron grew anxious as he watched the workers add more weights to the next load. The driver powered up the engine, but nothing happened. Again the engine roared, but the load didn't budge. The driver hunched over the wheel as if to coax the machine into one last try before time was up. Aaron's white knuckles showed his fear that the tractor would fail. He felt like he was in the contest himself, and he yelled encouragement as the tractor began to inch forward. Slowly, slowly it went, until it at last reached the finish line. The crowd went wild—cheering, yelling, and clapping as loudly as the tractor had roared.

Afterward, Grandpa and Aaron talked about the contest. "It made me think about the big contests we have in life," said Grandpa. "Sometimes our loads are almost too heavy for us to pull."

Aaron nodded soberly, thinking about the hard time he had with reading class at school. It seemed he just couldn't read as well as the other kids. But now Grandpa was smiling at him. "Way back when I was a boy like you, I found out that Jesus wants to help us pull heavy loads in life," said Grandpa, "so I ask him to help me whenever I feel like things are just too much. With Jesus beside me, the load is much lighter."

Aaron smiled back at Grandpa, knowing what he had to do. He would talk to Jesus about his reading lessons. *C.E.Y.*

HOW ABOUT YOU?

Does something in your life seem too heavy to bear? Are you having trouble with schoolwork? In your family? With friends? Jesus wants to help you in your trouble. He wants to comfort you and make your burden easier. Ask him to do that—not just once, but each time you need it.

MEMORIZE:

"**For my yoke is easy, and my burden is light.**" *Matthew 11:30,* KJV

 Jesus Lightens Loads

Dirt Is Dirt (Read Psalm 101:1-8)

"Oh, please, Mom," begged Cora Lee, "may I watch that program on television that Sally keeps telling me about?"

"No, you may not," replied Mom as she stirred the cake batter. "That is not a good program to see—it's not acceptable for a Christian."

28
OCTOBER

"I'd watch it just this once," whined Cora Lee. "Sally says it's going to be really exciting this week." She glanced at her mother. "Sally says you should let me watch a few things like that," Cora Lee continued. "She thinks I have old-fashioned ideas. She said this program gives her a taste of reality." When her mother still didn't say anything, Cora Lee added, "Besides, this program isn't *so* bad. Sally says some of the others are a lot worse."

"Please put a scoop of the dirt from the flower pot over there into this cake batter," said Mom, holding out the sugar scoop. Cora Lee looked at her mother in amazement. She could not believe her ears. "No! Wait a minute," said Mom. "Instead, get a scoop of that nice, white sand from Donny's sandbox. That's new, so it's not so very dirty."

Cora Lee continued to stare at her mother. "But dirt is still dirt!" she exclaimed.

Mom chuckled. "And you don't want any dirt in this cake?" she asked. "Not even 'clean' dirt, just to give it a taste of reality?"

Cora Lee saw the twinkle in her mother's eyes. "OK, Mom," she said. "I get the point."

"Good," said Mom. "This recipe does not call for dirt, and adding dirt would ruin the cake. Our recipe for life should not include 'dirt' either. We should take care that what we see and hear is pleasing to God, because all the things we see and hear do affect us—whether we think so or not." *B.M.*

HOW ABOUT YOU?

Do you think some things that are not good are acceptable anyway—just because some other things are worse? Remember that dirt is dirt. Avoid it. Instead, listen to and watch the things that would please the Lord.

MEMORIZE:

"I will set nothing wicked before my eyes." *Psalm 101:3, NKJV*

 Be Pleasing to God

A Special Event (Read Psalm 132:1-7)

29
OCTOBER

"Ashley, will you play games with me tonight?" Laurie asked as the two girls walked home from school.

"I can't," answered Ashley. "I have to get ready for my big class field trip tomorrow. It's a really special event—we get to see Mount Vernon, where our first president lived. We studied about him in school, and I went to the library and took out some books about him, too. Tonight I'm going to wash my hair and check my clothes and get everything ready. Oh, I can hardly wait to go!"

After the field trip, Ashley came home, bubbling with enthusiasm. She excitedly told her parents all about the good time she had. "It was so much fun to see the things and places I'd read about," she said. "I even knew some things the guide didn't mention."

At breakfast the next Sunday, Dad asked the children if they had studied their Sunday school lessons. "I didn't," confessed Ashley. "I was just too busy this week." Then when it was time to leave for church, her hair wasn't quite dry, and she couldn't find her Bible. She finally ran out to the car without it. She sighed as they turned into the church parking lot. "Church has been kinda boring lately," she grumbled. "I don't get much out of it."

"I'm not surprised," Mom told her. "You know, before you took that trip to Mount Vernon, you did everything you could to prepare for it. Then you really enjoyed it. Why don't you do the same for church?"

"But that trip was so special . . . ," Ashley began.

"Which is more special," asked Dad, "a president and his house or God and his house?"

Ashley blushed. "I . . . I'm going to do better," she promised. "After this I'll get ready for Sunday early." *M.R.P.*

HOW ABOUT YOU?

Do you get bored at church? Try preparing yourself early. Study your lesson and pray for your teacher. Get your clothes ready on Saturday night. At church, center your mind on God and pay attention to the lesson. You may be surprised to find church becoming the most special part of your week.

MEMORIZE:

"Now I have prepared with all my might for the house of my God." *1 Chronicles 29:2,* KJV

 Prepare for Church

One Size (Read Galatians 3:8-9, 26-29)

30

OCTOBER

"Oh, look, Mom!" exclaimed Sally as she picked up a pair of gloves in the store. "These would match my new jacket perfectly! But I doubt they'll have my size—they haven't had my size in anything else I wanted today." Sally and her mother were having a rather unsuccessful shopping trip.

"Well, let's have a look," said Mother. "Maybe we'll do better this time."

Sally looked at the tag and read: "'One size fits all.'" She dropped the mitten. "Oh, sure it does," she moaned. "Those things never fit me."

"Well, try one on," suggested Mom. "Maybe you'll be surprised."

With a frown, Sally picked up a mitten and slipped it onto her hand. "It fits!" she squealed in delight.

"How about that?" said Mother. "And the price is right, too. So . . . OK—you've got new gloves."

Back home, Sally told Dad about the shopping trip. "I never believe those one-size-fits-all tags, but this time it told the truth. Mom says my gloves are made of such a stretchy material that they probably do fit almost anybody." Dad smiled and nodded.

That evening, after reading a Scripture passage for family devotions, Dad said, "This makes me think of your one-size-fits-all gloves. God says salvation through Jesus Christ 'fits' everybody. There are some people who think they're too good to need salvation, and some think they're too bad to be able to receive it. But God says all those things make no difference in his sight. He offers salvation to one and all, and it's only by accepting it that anyone gets to heaven." *H.M.*

HOW ABOUT YOU?

Have you accepted Jesus as your Savior? Your national background, your good works, your family connections—these things don't make any difference to God. Everyone needs the same salvation, and it is offered to you as a free gift. Accept it today.

MEMORIZE:

"For there is no difference between Jew and Gentile—the same Lord is Lord of all and richly blesses all who call on him." *Romans 10:12,* NIV

 Salvation "Fits" All

Pure White (Read Psalm 119:1-11)

"How many eggs?" asked Shelly as her mom started blending the margarine and sugar.

"Three," answered Mother. "This recipe makes lots of cookies."

31
OCTOBER

Shelly carried the eggs from the refrigerator to the work counter. "May I crack them?" she asked, and Mom nodded. As each egg was added, Mom beat it into the cookie dough.

"Now," said Mother, "we need to add flour, soda, and salt." She measured the flour into the sifter, and Shelly measured the baking soda. She spooned the soda on top of the flour.

"I thought this flour was white," said Shelly in surprise.

"It looks white to me," said Mother.

"But look," said Shelly. "The soda is really white. Next to the soda the flour is kind of yellow-white."

"That's true," said Mother slowly. She added the salt and sifted the ingredients together. "Shelly," she said after a moment, "if I said that flour is like us and the soda is like God's Word, what would you think I meant?"

Shelly frowned. "I would think you weren't making sense," she said with a shrug.

Mother smiled. "We often think we're OK, but the Bible shows us we're not as good as we think we are," she explained.

"Oh, I get it," said Shelly. "Just like the flour isn't very white compared to the soda, our lives aren't as good compared to what the Bible says they should be."

Mother nodded. "I'm afraid that's often true," she said. "As we learn to follow God's teachings and become more and more like him, the difference becomes less and less." *P.O.Y.*

HOW ABOUT YOU?
How does your life compare to God's standard—his Word? Read it daily to see what he says, and ask him to change your actions and attitudes.

MEMORIZE:
"**How can a young man stay pure? By reading your Word and following its rules.**"
Psalm 119:9, TLB

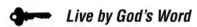 *Live by God's Word*

The Pearl Necklace (Read Colossians 4:2-6)

Shelly was staring out her bedroom window when her mother came in. "How are you feeling?" Mom asked as she sat down on the bed and felt Shelly's forehead. "I think you still have a fever."

"Why do I have to be sick today?" moaned Shelly. "My Sunday school class is putting on the puppet show at Children's Hospital, and I can't be there." Her lower lip quivered a little.

"And that makes you feel bad, doesn't it?"

Shelly turned on her back. "Sure, it does," she answered. "My teacher said we could do this for the Lord, and I really wanted to. Now I can't."

Now Mom was quiet for a while. "You can pray for the Lord to use the puppet ministry," she suggested.

Shelly thought about that. "It just doesn't seem the same," she said with a sigh.

After a moment, Mom stood up. "I'll be right back," she said. She left the room and returned soon with her strand of white pearls. She knew they were Shelly's favorites. "The most important part of this necklace is the part you can't see," Mom said.

Shelly looked puzzled. "What do you mean?" she asked.

Mom smiled. "Everyone notices the pearls," she explained, "but look at this." She carefully pulled two pearls apart to reveal the thin, white thread holding them together. "No one notices this plain and simple thread, but without it my necklace would fall apart." Still puzzled, Shelly looked at the pearl necklace and then at her mother. Again Mom smiled. "Don't you see?" she asked. "Prayer is like this unseen thread. Prayer is the strength behind everything we do for God—even puppet ministries." Mom fingered the pearls in the palm of her hand. "Even though you may be too sick to join the others at the hospital, God can still use your prayers to make the ministry fruitful for him."

Shelly took the pearls into her hand and looked at them in the sunlight streaming through her window. Then she smiled. "Thanks, Mom," she said. *R.S.M.*

HOW ABOUT YOU?

Do you sometimes feel like you can't do anything worthwhile for Jesus because you're too young or too sick or for some other reason? Do you get discouraged about that? Remember that every Christian can pray—and that's the most important thing anyone can do.

MEMORIZE:

"Devote yourselves to prayer, being watchful and thankful."

Colossians 4:2, NIV

 *Prayer Is Important*

Mickey's New Shoes (Read Matthew 23:5-7, 11-12)

2

NOVEMBER

Mickey picked up the shoe on display. "This is the one I want, Mom," he said. Mother seemed doubtful. "It's the latest," Mickey insisted. "All the guys are buying this brand. The ad on TV says the special sole reduces the pounding you get from the gym floor." Mickey shut his eyes, imagining what his friends would say if he arrived at practice wearing these. He looked hopefully at his mother, but she was moving away.

"How about this one?" asked Mother. She pointed to a shoe almost exactly like the one Mickey held.

"Yuck," he protested. "Nobody buys *that* brand."

Mother spoke quietly. "I want to buy you shoes you'll like, but I won't pay a lot of extra money for a brand name."

"But I don't want any other shoe," Mickey whined, thinking of his friends. He began to complain loudly.

Mother looked unhappy. "Let's talk about it at home," she said, hurrying him out of the store.

During dinner that night, Dad asked, "Who was at the door a while ago?"

"That old show-off, Joey," answered Mickey with a scowl. "He just came to brag about his new skateboard. He got a new one a few months ago, and now he bought another one just to impress the guys. It's sickening."

Mother looked surprised. "But isn't that what you had in mind today in the store? Impressing your friends?" Mickey stared at her, shocked, and Mom continued gently, "Just think about it, Mickey. Do you really need the brand of shoe you begged for? Or are you, like Joey, trying to use possessions to build yourself up in your friends' eyes?"

Mickey chewed his food slowly. It was true—he *had* wanted his friends' attention. He was acting like the Pharisees he had studied in Sunday school. His teacher had talked about how they tried to impress others, too. "I guess Joey and I have a lot to learn," he finally admitted. *C.Y.P.*

HOW ABOUT YOU?

Do you nag your parents for clothing with certain brand names? Do you plead for expensive shoes just because "everybody else" is wearing them? Examine your heart. Do you really need these items? It's all right to dress neatly and look nice, but you should never dress just to show off.

MEMORIZE:

"They, measuring themselves by themselves, and comparing themselves among themselves, are not wise."

2 Corinthians 10:12, NKJV

 Don't Dress to Impress

Out of Focus (Read Mark 14:32-38)

Dinner was finished, and Dan was just thinking of teasing his sister when Dad's voice changed the whole mood. "We got a call from your teacher today, Son." Dan swallowed hard as the kitchen became very quiet. Only Shane, the family dog, had anything to say as he yipped for a handout. "Shane! Quiet!" Dad commanded. Shane sat down immediately and waited. He knew his master's voice well. "Mrs. Folkema was not very happy," continued Dad, "and neither am I. She told me you cheated on a test."

3

NOVEMBER

Dan couldn't raise his eyes. "I . . . I just couldn't seem to help it," he mumbled. "Heidi wasn't covering her paper at all, and I kept thinking about being on the honor roll."

Dad cut a scrap of meat and held it out toward Shane. Shane began licking his lips hungrily. "Shane . . . stay!" Dad ordered loudly, then placed the meat on the floor in front of him. Shane thumped his tail excitedly but stayed where he was. "Why do you think Shane is able to resist temptation?" asked Dad.

Dan grinned. "Because he knows Sarah helped out with dinner tonight . . . *Ow!*" His sister's elbow made a direct hit in Dan's ribs.

"Check out Shane's eyes," said Dad, not finding Dan's remark too amusing. "They're looking at me, right?" Dan nodded. "If Shane kept staring at the meat, he'd never be able to resist it," continued Dad. "Instead, he's focusing on his master." He turned to Dan. "Whenever you're tempted, who should you focus on?"

Dan knew the answer. "On Jesus," he said. "I know that, but you make it sound so easy."

"I admit, it's not easy," replied Dad, "but when we lose our focus, we need to redirect our thoughts to where they ought to be. And you know what? I believe that when we succeed in doing that, God rewards us richly." He picked up the scrap of meat and tossed it into the air. Shane caught and swallowed it, barely chewing. He sat down and licked his lips again. It had been well worth the wait.

A.J.S.

HOW ABOUT YOU?

Do you find yourself in situations where you feel tempted to cheat or to do other things you know you shouldn't? Don't spend time thinking about something you know you should not do and wishing you could do it. Instead, think about Jesus and what pleases him. Let him be your strength.

MEMORIZE:

"And God is faithful; he will not let you be tempted beyond what you can bear."

1 Corinthians 10:13, NIV

 **Focus on Jesus**

Behind the Scenes (Read 1 Corinthians 12:14-27)

4

NOVEMBER

"Put this blue block here," Justin suggested to Sandy, his four-year-old sister. Justin was helping her build a tower with blocks. The structure was almost finished when Sandy pulled out a green block from near the bottom. The tower wobbled, and one whole section toppled. "You ruined it," scolded Justin. "Why did you do that?"

"I wanted that green block at the top," answered Sandy. "You could hardly see it down there."

Just then the telephone rang. "Justin, it's for you," called Mother.

When he got off the phone, Justin said dejectedly, "That was my Sunday school teacher. He wants me to come to a rehearsal for that skit they're going to do on youth night. He said he doesn't have any parts left in the skit, but they need somebody to help move props between scenes."

"What's the matter with that?" asked Mother.

"I don't want to help," grumbled Justin with a scowl. "I'm not good enough to be in the skit, but I'm good enough to move furniture around! Anyone can do that!"

"Well, moving the props may not seem as glamorous as acting in the play, but it's a very important job," Mother told him. "The whole production could be ruined if the props aren't in the right place." She paused, then added, "It's like the block Sandy took out of the tower you were building."

"What do you mean?" asked Justin.

"When Sandy took just one block out, the whole building came tumbling down," replied Mother. "It was an important part of the structure even though it didn't show as much as the top blocks. And the Bible teaches us that in the church, each one of us is needed, too. If we don't do our part, the church won't reach as many people for Christ as it otherwise would."

"You make it sound as if moving furniture for a skit is reaching people for Jesus," murmured Justin. He sighed. "Well, I guess I'd better call Mr. Clark back and tell him I'll be at the rehearsal."

T.K.M.

HOW ABOUT YOU?

Do you like to do only jobs that are noticed by lots of people? Do you feel as if you're not important or needed in your church? Remember that you are important in God's eyes. Do your part, even if it's not glamorous!

MEMORIZE:

"The parts that seem weakest and least important are really most necessary. . . . All of you together are the one body of Christ." *1 Corinthians 12:22, 27, TLB*

 Use Your Talents for God

A Lesson in Courage (Read Daniel 3:14-18, 24-27)

Joshua's Sunday school teacher, Miss Green, had given the class a written quiz. "Uh-oh!" Joshua whispered as he gave her his paper. "I should have put seven, not five, in this blank. The furnace was heated *seven* times hotter than usual when Daniel's friends were thrown into it."

"I'll change it for you," said Miss Green. She turned to the class. "Don't forget," she said. "Ask God to help you make right choices this week. Then be ready to tell about a choice that wasn't easy—one that took courage."

In church that morning, Joshua felt a little guilty, and he didn't really listen to Pastor Jones's sermon. Instead, he tried to think of something courageous he could do. But what?

Joshua wasn't very happy all that week, and he didn't think about courage again until Saturday morning when he went to the grocery store with his father. The cashier forgot to charge Dad for one item he bought, so he told her about it. "Dad, did that take courage?" Joshua asked as they headed to the car with the grocery cart.

"No, not really," answered his father. "It was just the right thing to do, but it wasn't hard."

Suddenly Joshua's stomach seemed to flip-flop as a guilty feeling again came over him. He had been struggling with that feeling all week. There was something he needed to do, and it would take courage.

He and his teacher were first in the classroom the next morning. "Miss Green," he began, "I . . . I . . ." He swallowed hard. "I didn't know the right answer on that blank you changed for me. I saw it on Jill's paper."

Miss Green looked serious, but she gave him a pat on the back. "It took courage to tell me that, didn't it?" she said, "but I'm so glad you did. Would you like to tell the class about it?"

Joshua shook his head. "Not really," he said. It wasn't something he was eager to tell, though he would if she wanted him to. In any case, he felt a lot better now. *M.M.P.*

HOW ABOUT YOU?

Do you keep quiet when there is something you should say? Do you do what is right even if you're scared? Ask God to give you courage to make the right choices and especially to admit when you're wrong.

MEMORIZE:

"Be strong and courageous."

Joshua 10:25, NIV

Have Courage to Do Right

"Old Sandy" (Read Ephesians 4:1-6)

6

NOVEMBER

Sandy and her brother Ben eagerly watched the videotape Dad had taken on their vacation to Yellowstone. "There's Old Faithful!" exclaimed Ben as they watched hot water burst from the ground and shoot high into the air.

"Do you remember what caused the geysers to erupt like that?" asked Dad.

Ben nodded. "The ranger said that rock deep within the earth is so hot that its gasses heat the springwater," he replied.

"Yeah, and then when that water reaches the boiling point, pressure builds, and it erupts," added Sandy.

A little later, Sandy and Ben had a disagreement over a game they were playing. Sandy angrily pushed back her chair, tipping it over as she stood up. "Oh, you just think you're so smart!"

"What did I do?" Ben asked with a knowing smirk.

"All kinds of things," retorted Sandy. "You used my bike without asking. You embarrassed me in front of my friends." The tone of Sandy's voice became sharper. "You make me so mad I could just burst!" She ran to her bedroom and slammed the door.

Ben followed behind when Mom went to Sandy's room. "You know we don't slam doors in this house," said Mom sternly. "And your outburst of anger was not pretty."

"You erupted like Old Faithful," put in Ben. He grinned and teased, "'Old Sandy.'"

"Ben," said Mom, "you go to your room. I'll talk to you later." When he had left, she turned to Sandy. "Ben does have a point."

"Well, Ben's so mean, I couldn't help it," pouted Sandy.

"We all have feelings of anger," said Mother, "but we need to deal with those feelings, not just let them build up. The Bible says we're not to let the sun go down on our anger."

"What does that mean?" asked Sandy.

"It means that before the day passes, we need to find a way to forgive whoever has offended us," said Mother. "Talk to the person. Explain what is bothering you. Don't store up angry feelings and grudges." *N.E.K.*

HOW ABOUT YOU?

What do you do with your anger? Ask God to help you deal with it by talking, forgiving, and letting it go before the sun goes down.

MEMORIZE:

"In your anger do not sin: Do not let the sun go down while you are still angry."

Ephesians 4:26, NIV

 Don't Cling to Anger

Glassblowing (Read John 15:1-8)

"I'm missing everything since I got the chicken pox," wailed Toni. "First I couldn't sing in the concert. Then I missed Betsy's party. Now I can't go on the class field trip to the glass company!" She wiped a tear from her eye.

"That is too bad," sympathized Mom. "Maybe you'll get to go another time."

7
NOVEMBER

"But I've been looking forward to the trip ever since we studied glassblowing in school," said Toni with a sigh. "A lot of places use modern machines to shape the glass, but at this company, some of the workers still do it themselves."

"It does sound interesting," agreed Mom. "What did you learn in school about shaping glass?"

"The glass has to be heated or melted until it's in a workable state," Toni said. "Then the person can blow the glass and use tools to make different shapes. And if it doesn't look right yet, the glassblower can reheat it to soften it again and blow it some more."

"Sounds a little like what God does in our lives," said Mother thoughtfully. "Sometimes he needs to return us to a workable state so he can form us into just the right shape, too."

"He does?" asked Toni. "How does he do that?"

"Oh, he uses various ways," replied Mother. "Sometimes he uses sickness." She smiled at Toni. "Maybe God is allowing you this time from your busy life for a quiet spell, to reshape you and to remind you that he wants to have first place in your life."

Toni was quiet, remembering complaints she had voiced recently about her Sunday activities taking too much of her time. And it had been a long time since she'd spent a daily quiet time with God. Well, she had time now—she'd spend some of it getting to know God better—allowing him to reshape her life. *N.E.K.*

HOW ABOUT YOU?

Do some things that are happening in your life seem frustrating and definitely not what you had planned? Perhaps God wants to use those times to do some reshaping of your life. Ask him to help you accept them and grow stronger in your Christian life.

MEMORIZE:

"Every branch that does bear fruit he prunes so that it will be even more fruitful." *John 15:2, NIV*

 *Let God Shape You*

The High Wire (Read Psalm 33:13-22)

8

NOVEMBER

"Wasn't that a great circus?" asked Billy's dad as they got into the car.

"Yeah!" Billy's eyes were wide with excitement. "It sure was—especially the high-wire act."

"Hmmm," murmured Dad. He nodded his head. "That was pretty interesting. It was pretty scary, too, when one man was riding on the other's shoulders and the man lost his balance. What did you think about when they both fell?"

"I was glad there was a net to catch them," said Billy.

Dad agreed, and they drove awhile in silence before Dad spoke again. "You know," he said softly, "that high-wire act is like life in general."

Billy was puzzled. "What do you mean?" he asked.

"Well," said Dad, "the man who was sitting on the other's shoulders was putting all his trust in his partner's ability to safely walk the rope, right?"

Billy nodded. "Yeah, but the other guy couldn't do it," he said. "If that net hadn't caught their fall, they might have even been killed!"

"Well, we're all something like that man who trusted his partner," said Dad. "We all put our trust in someone or something. Some of us put our trust in other people to help us over the dangers of life. Some of us put our trust in money or in our jobs. But when those things fail, . . . well, tragedy often follows."

Billy looked out the window as they drove along the streets. He thought about his Sunday school lesson the week before. "That's kinda like what my teacher told us," he said. "She said we should always trust Jesus to take care of us because he never fails."

Dad smiled. "That's right," he said. "The Lord Jesus can be trusted to carry us through life's troubles. He'll never lose his balance." *R.S.M.*

HOW ABOUT YOU?

Are you trusting Jesus to take care of your needs? Or are you trusting people or other things? Don't be fooled. It's possible for people and things to fail. Only Jesus will never let you down. You can trust him, not only to take you to heaven someday, but to help you each day here on earth.

MEMORIZE:

"Some trust in chariots and some in horses, but we trust in the name of the Lord our God."

Psalm 20:7, NIV

 Jesus Can Be Trusted

Mirage (Read Romans 16:17-20)

Every day several boys at school urged Bob and his friends to try drugs. The boys promised that getting high would be the best experience a kid could have. They said that drugs made life seem happy—all "fun and games." They claimed drugs created a certain power, making them able to do things never before possible. And they even offered the drugs free for the first couple of times. Although Bob knew better, he found it hard to pass up something that looked so good.

9

NOVEMBER

As Bob and his mother drove to town one day, the sky was crystal clear. He wondered how much bluer or clearer it would look if he were on drugs. As the car approached a hill, Bob thought he saw water on the road up ahead. "Where'd that water come from?" he asked. "It hasn't rained for days."

"There isn't any water," Mom said. As the car moved closer to the puddle, Bob saw that the water disappeared. "That was a mirage," Mom told him. "Sometimes light rays from the sky get bent by hot air above the pavement and make it look like the road is wet. But it really isn't."

"Wow!" Bob said. "That's neat."

"Not always," said Mom. "What if you were in the desert, thirsting for water, and you saw a refreshing lake ahead? But then you find out the lake was only a mirage."

"A trick!" Bob said. "That would be nasty."

Mom nodded. "There are things in life that look equally appealing but turn out to be major letdowns, or even harmful," she said. "Like drugs, for instance." Bob felt his face blush. "The high can be made to look like fun," continued Mom, "but it turns out to be like a mirage. Instead of being good, drugs turn out to be very harmful to your body, as well as addictive and expensive. What might appear to add a wonderful zip to life actually destroys life." She paused, then added, "Drugs are harmful, and using them is sin."

N.E.K.

HOW ABOUT YOU?

If you're tempted to do drugs, think about how deceiving the mirage really is. As a Christian, don't be tricked into something that will hurt your life and that is also illegal.

MEMORIZE:

"Your own body does not belong to you. For God has bought you with a great price. So use every part of your body to give glory back to God."

1 Corinthians 6:19-20, TLB

 *Don't Use Drugs*

Special Fruit Salad (Read Galatians 5:22-25)

10

NOVEMBER

"Betty, would you like to help me make some fruit salad for lunch?" asked Mother one day.

"Fruit salad?" asked Betty. "Sure. I love it, and it always looks so pretty." She grinned at her mother as they began to wash the fruit they were going to use. "This reminds me of my Sunday school memory verse," added Betty. "It listed the fruit of the Spirit."

"Good," said Mother. "You know, the fruit we eat provides nutrients that help our bodies carry on their everyday functions, and the Holy Spirit produces spiritual 'nutrients' that help us form good thoughts and good habits."

"Can we put nine different kinds of fruit in our salad and pretend we're putting in the fruit of the Spirit?" asked Betty.

Mother smiled. "I'm not sure we have that many," she said, "but let's try. You name them as we put them in—starting with these orange slices."

"OK," agreed Betty. She put orange pieces in a big bowl. "We'll call these love. The pineapple chunks will be joy." She opened a can and added them. "What else do we have?"

"I have some fresh peach wedges ready," said Mom, "and here's some kiwi."

Betty called the peaches peace and the kiwi slices longsuffering. "The diced apples will be gentleness, and the pear cubes will be goodness," she said. "And I'll slice some bananas and call them faith. What else do we have?"

"Grapes," said Mother, and Betty called them meekness.

Betty looked around. "We need one more, but we've used everything," she said, sounding disappointed.

Mother thought for a moment. "Raisins," she said. "We can add a few raisins." Betty promptly did so, calling them self-control.

"Great, Betty. I'm proud that you remembered all of them," said Mother, smiling. "I hope you'll always remember that just as God expects us to take good care of our bodies, he also wants the spiritual fruit to be part of our everyday lives." *L.M.W.*

HOW ABOUT YOU?

Can others see the fruit of the Spirit in your life? Does the way you talk and act show that you know Jesus? Do your family and friends know by your "fruit" that you belong to him?

MEMORIZE:

"By their fruits you will know them." *Matthew 7:20,* NKJV

 Display the Fruit of the Spirit

Conversation with Dad (Read Matthew 6:5-13)

"It's prayer time now," Mom said, closing the Bible she and Travis had been reading. They were having devotions together, just the two of them because Dad was out of town.

"You pray," said Travis. "I don't know what to say."

"I'll be glad to start," agreed Mom, "but don't you want to talk to God, too?"

Travis shook his head. "Not today," he said. Then he squirmed while Mom prayed aloud. He wished she'd hurry up. He wanted to go out and play. *Besides, God already knows everything, doesn't he?* he thought to himself. *Why does Mom have to tell him all this stuff he already knows?*

11

NOVEMBER

When Travis was playing later, he heard the phone ring. He went on playing until it suddenly occurred to him that it might be Dad calling. Travis rushed into the kitchen just in time to see Mom hang up the phone. "Was that Dad?" Travis asked her. "I wanted to talk to him. I wanted to tell him about Brian's getting mad at me at school today and ask him what he thinks I should do."

"He wanted to talk with you, too," said Mom, "but at least he knows about Brian. I told him all about what happened."

"It isn't the same as my telling him," Travis insisted. "And besides, we haven't talked today. I want to talk with Dad."

"Well, let's call him back so the two of you can talk," suggested Mom.

When Travis finished talking with Dad and had hung up the phone, Mom grinned at him. "Earthly fathers love to have conversations with their children, and your heavenly Father does, too," she reminded him.

Slowly Travis nodded. "I . . . I guess I should tell God about Brian, too, shouldn't I?" he said. *K.R.A.*

HOW ABOUT YOU?

Do you have trouble praying because you don't know what to say? You need to pray in obedience to God's instruction, but more than that, you should pray because you love God and want to share with him what is going on in your life. God loves you and wants you to talk with him.

MEMORIZE:

"Pray in the Spirit on all occasions with all kinds of prayers and requests."

Ephesians 6:18, NIV

 God Wants to Hear from You

The Unselfish Saguaro (Read Philippians 4:8-10)

12
NOVEMBER

"Look!" Bob said, pointing to a hole in the arm of a large saguaro cactus. "See that owl?" A little elf owl stared solemnly at them from inside the hole. "We learned in school that woodpeckers and flickers make most of the holes you see in these cacti. They make a new nest hole every spring. Then other birds move into the empty ones they leave behind."

Dad nodded. "Each time the cactus skin is broken by a beak or talon, a thick, gluey liquid seeps from the cactus and forms a waterproof pouch inside the arm," he said. "This liquid then hardens—a lot like a scab—and the pouch becomes an ideal apartment for desert birds."

Sherry saw big and little holes in the cactus, some low and some very high. "This saguaro is like a high-rise apartment building," she said with a laugh. "What a busy, crowded place to live."

"Just like our place," said Bob. "We've got Grandma in the spare bedroom, Lars is sharing my room, and now Julie wants to bring Robbie and move back in for a while." Lars was an exchange student from Sweden, and Julie, an older sister, was married to a serviceman who had been called for overseas duty.

Sherry remembered well the discussion they'd had about Julie's coming. "She's kidding!" Sherry had said. "Where would they sleep?" But she already knew the answer. Julie would sleep in the extra bed in her room, and Robbie . . .

"Julie can't sleep in my room—she needs to be with Robbie," Sherry had quickly pointed out. Dad didn't answer. He just looked steadily at Sherry. "You don't think you can fit Robbie's crib into my room, too, do you?" protested Sherry.

"Pray about it," suggested Dad. Sherry had tried, but she knew she was being selfish. But now Sherry looked at the old saguaro who offered a home to any creature who needed it, even though it meant having holes pecked into its walls. *I'll do it*, she thought, *even though holes get pounded into my walls, too—which they will if I know Robbie!* T.M.V.

HOW ABOUT YOU?

Are you willing to give up some comfort or convenience to help others? Ask God to make you unselfish. Remember—you are never more like Jesus than when you give.

MEMORIZE:

"Nobody should seek his own good, but the good of others."
1 Corinthians 10:24, NIV

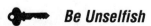 **Be Unselfish**

After Snowbunny (Read 1 Peter 5:5-11)

13

NOVEMBER

Jordan sat on the back steps with his friend Tim. He absently moved his feet back and forth, trailing a long shoestring, which his kitten, Whiskers, chased. "I don't know if I can stand it, Tim," stated Jordan flatly. "Ben may be a nice guy, but he just isn't Daddy. I wonder who ever came up with the word *stepfather!* As if someone really could just step in and replace Dad."

Tim was quiet. He had known Jordan for a long time. He knew how hard it had been for Jordan when his father had died, and again how sad Jordan felt when his cat, Snowbunny, had been run over a few weeks ago. He knew Jordan was troubled now at the thought of his mother's remarriage to Ben. But he also knew that Ben, who went to his church, was a good and godly man.

Whiskers got tired of the shoelace and jumped onto Jordan's lap, where he snuggled and purred. Jordan stroked the kitten and held him close—giving Tim an idea. "I'm really surprised you're treating Whiskers that way," Tim said. "You're treating him just as nice as you did Snowbunny, your first cat. He's not anything like she was. He's even a different color."

"So what?" demanded Jordan.

"Well, don't you miss Snowbunny?" asked Tim.

"Of course I do," said Jordan. "But since Snowbunny is gone, it helps to have Whiskers. I love him, too."

Tim put on a shocked look. "How can you love Whiskers, Jordy?" he asked. "He's not your first pet. He's a stepcat!"

Jordan looked startled. "Why do you say that?" he asked. "It's not like I'm trying to make Whiskers be the same as Snowbunny. He never could be. He's a different cat."

Tim nodded. "I don't think Ben will try to be the same as your dad, either," he said. "He's a different man, but he's kind and special in his own way, and I know he loves God a lot. Maybe you need to give him a chance." *S.F.A.*

HOW ABOUT YOU?

Do you have a stepparent, or do you know someone who does? Most stepparents try very hard to fill a difficult position. Ask God to help you to be friendly and respectful. Ask him to help you accept the changes in your family. Give a stepparent a fair chance!

MEMORIZE:

"You should be like one big happy family, full of sympathy toward each other, loving one another with tender hearts and humble minds." *1 Peter 3:8*, TLB

 Give Stepparents a Chance

Tuna Again (Read Mark 8:1-9)

14
NOVEMBER

"Yuck," said Willy, scrunching up his face with displeasure. "Tuna casserole! I wish we could order a pizza. I think I could live on pizza."

"Yeah—that's all you ever want," his sister Tricia told him. "If you're not careful, you'll turn into a pizza."

"That's better than turning into a tuna," retorted Willy. He imagined Tricia and Mom as silvery tuna fish, napkins sliding off their laps as they tried to pick up a fork in their fins. He burst out laughing.

"Does that laugh mean that you've decided to enjoy your supper?" Mom asked. She bowed her head to give thanks to God, and the children did, too.

Willy picked up his fork and toyed with the mass of noodles Mom had spooned onto his plate. Bright green peas, chunks of tuna, and noodles swam in a creamy white sauce. "I'll bet Jesus never had to eat tuna casserole," he murmured to Tricia.

"Maybe not," Tricia said, "but he did eat fish. He fed more than five thousand people with five loaves of bread and two little fish. And once he fed four thousand people with just a few loaves and fish, remember?"

Mother nodded. "The people were hungry, and Jesus gave them food," she said. "It probably seemed like a Thanksgiving feast to those people."

"Don't tell me this means we'll have tuna casserole for Thanksgiving!" joked Willy.

"That's not what I meant," said Mother, "but maybe it would be a good idea." Willy groaned. "Just kidding," said Mother, "but you know, you really should be thankful for this good food. This is what God provided for you today."

Willy ate a forkful of tuna casserole. "It is pretty good," he admitted, filling his fork a second time, "especially since I'm hungry. Thanks for cooking supper for us, Mom."

"You're welcome, Willy," replied Mother. "Eat up." *E.A.R.*

HOW ABOUT YOU?

Do you ever complain about the food at your table? Do you sometimes forget that God provides food to keep you healthy so that you're able to do his work in the world? Next time you eat, remember to thank God for the food, even if it's not your favorite.

MEMORIZE:

"Give thanks to the Lord, for he is good; his love endures forever." *Psalm 107:1, NIV*

 Be Thankful for Your Food

No Lies <small>(Psalm 33:4-9)</small>

15

"How was school today?" asked Mom, when Tony got home one afternoon.

"It was OK, I guess," answered Tony.

"You don't seem quite sure—was it a hard day?" asked Mom.

Tony shrugged. "It's just that Miss Roberts teaches that humans got here through evolution," he replied. "I said that I believe God created man, and some of the kids said I was silly. I know Miss Roberts thinks so, too, but she says it's not important whether you believe in creation or in evolution.

"It *is* important," said Mom. "God says *he* created the world—and that includes man. The very first verse of the Bible tells us that."

"Yeah, but Miss Roberts says that's only one verse. She says she believes in God, but she believes we should just be concerned about important things—like God's love and—" Tony stopped as he looked out the window. "There goes Greg—that new kid," he muttered. "He promised to sell me his bike, and I even gave him five dollars to hold it, like you said I could. But you know what he did? This morning he told me he sold it to another kid! I really wanted it!"

"Well, that's too bad," sympathized Mom. "Did he give your money back?"

Tony shook his head. "It's disgusting!" he exclaimed. "The first thing he said to me when he moved in was, 'Do you want to buy my bike?' and he promised to hold it for me. But now he says I didn't give him any five dollars. See if I ever believe him again!"

Mom looked thoughtful. "You know, Tony," she said, "you can't believe Greg because some of the first words he said to you were a lie. Now what about God? If the very first words in the Bible were a lie, do you think we could ever be sure he's telling the truth in the rest of the Bible?"

Tony thought for a moment. "You're right, Mom," he said. The first verse *is* important, and it's true. God never lies." *V.M.H.*

HOW ABOUT YOU?

Do you believe the Bible account of creation? Some people may try to convince you that it's old-fashioned to believe it—that intelligent people don't believe such things. Some may say it's not important to believe that particular part of the Bible. Just remember . . . God *never* lies. The Bible is true from cover to cover.

MEMORIZE:

"For all God's words are right, and everything he does is worthy of our trust."

Psalm 33:4, TLB

 God Never Lies

Jessie's First Steps (Read 2 Timothy 1:6-10)

16
NOVEMBER

When Mr. Brady told his Sunday school class that they would be putting on a play at the church banquet, Wesley slumped down in his seat, hoping he wouldn't have a speaking part. But Mr. Brady handed him an entire page of script!

Later, Wesley complained to his parents. "I can't get up in front of that crowd and talk," he said. "What if I goof up? I'll be so embarrassed."

His parents just smiled. "Oh, I'm sure you can do it," said Mom. "This will be a good start to help you overcome your bashfulness."

Dad nodded. "Son, you need to learn to speak out for God wherever you are," Dad told him, "and the best way to gain the confidence you need is by actually doing some speaking."

That afternoon Wesley read over his part. It was interesting, and he found he could memorize it easily. But how could he ever say it, standing in front of all those people? Mom interrupted his thoughts. "Look at Jessie," she said. "She's walking."

Wesley looked. His father was holding baby Jessie's hand as she took step after step. Then he gently let go, and Jessie took several steps alone. Suddenly, she wobbled and sat down hard. With a big grin, she let her daddy help her up, and she stepped out again.

"Big girl!" exclaimed Wesley.

Mom and Wesley grinned at each other, and Mom noticed the script he held in his hand. "The only way Jessie will learn to walk is by walking," said Mom. "It's the same with you, Wesley. You'll never get over your fear of speaking before others if you don't start doing it. And if you make a mistake, get back up and try again, just as Jessie is doing." Wesley nodded thoughtfully as Mom added, "Dad helps Jessie learn to walk, and God will help you learn to speak. Trust him." *M.R.P.*

HOW ABOUT YOU?

Do you have trouble witnessing to others or taking part in church programs? You'll never gain the confidence you need until you actually begin to do the thing that is difficult for you. Remember, you're not alone when you do any work for the Lord. He is with you to help you.

MEMORIZE:

"The Lord is on my side; I will not fear: what can man do unto me?" *Psalm 118:6,* KJV

 Speak Boldly for God

The Notebooks (Read 1 John 4:7-12)

"That Brad Cooper sure makes me sick," grumbled Eric. "He thinks he knows all about everything—he's a great big know-it-all." Eric took a heaping spoonful of lasagna and looked around the table for sympathy.

Mother sighed, and Dad frowned, but Joyce nodded knowingly. "Jill Summers is like that, too," she said. "And then there's Audrey—her clothes are simply awful. Somebody should teach her how to dress."

17

NOVEMBER

Dad reached down for a small brown package lying beside his chair. "Kids," he said, "I have something for you." Opening the bag, he brought out two small notebooks and handed one to each of his children.

"Oh, thanks, Dad!" exclaimed Joyce. She paged through it eagerly. "This will be neat for science."

"Sorry," said Dad. "These are special notebooks."

"We're tired of hearing about the shortcomings of your so-called friends," said Mother. "So each evening you are to record the names of anybody you're annoyed with and make a list of what annoys you about them."

"And then," added Dad, "list every good thing you can think of about them. You've been very critical for several weeks, so please don't leave the book empty and say you don't feel that way, because we won't believe it. Next Monday night we want to see them, so bring them to the dinner table then and we'll discuss them."

The next Monday, both Eric and Joyce looked rather sheepish as they came to the table with the notebooks, but they were smiling. "Know what I found?" asked Joyce as she opened her notebook. "My list of good things about the kids is always longer than my list of their faults."

Eric nodded. "Same here," he said.

"Good!" said Mother with a smile. "I think you'd better keep this going until you have the notebook entirely filled. That should help you break the habit of criticizing."

"Yes," agreed Dad. "Now let's look for a Bible verse that will help us." *D.R.O.*

HOW ABOUT YOU?

Are you so busy seeing the faults of some of the kids you know that you don't notice their good qualities? Do you find it hard to love some of them? Remembering that God loves you even though you don't deserve his love will make it easier for you to love others.

MEMORIZE:

"Since God so loved us, we also ought to love one another."

1 John 4:11, NIV

 *Love Others*

All for Nothing (Read Philippians 4:4-9)

18

NOVEMBER

"Hi, Mom," said Nikki. "Did you have any cavities?" Her mother had just come home from the dentist.

Mom shook her head. "Not one," she said. But then she sighed. "There wasn't a thing wrong, but I have a good-sized bill to pay anyway," she grumbled.

Nikki burst out laughing. "Oh, Mom," she said, "you're funny. You sound like you'd be happier if you had a mouthful of rotten teeth."

Mom looked startled. Then she grinned. "I'm being foolish all right," she admitted. "I know the dentist has to be paid for his work whether I have cavities or not, and I really am thankful I don't have any. I'll pay my bill gladly."

After dinner that evening, Nikki got out a script of a Thanksgiving skit. "Who wants to listen to me say my lines?" she asked.

Her brother Chad snorted. "Nobody," he told her. "We're all tired of hearing them. Besides, you know them perfectly anyway—you have for a week already."

"But what if I forget them?" worried Nikki.

"You won't," said Chad. "And I, for one, am glad the program is Sunday so we'll never have to hear them again!"

"I wonder if Allen has his lines learned," said Nikki. "If he misses his lines, I might miss the cue to start mine."

"He'll do fine, too," said Chad. "He's smart."

"I hope Barb remembers to bring the apron she said I could borrow," murmured Nikki. "The effect won't be the same without it."

Chad looked disgusted. "Yeah . . . well, I sure hope something goes wrong for you," he said. "After all, I'd hate for you to have worried like this all for nothing."

Just then Mom caught Nikki's eye. "No cavities?" asked Mom mournfully.

Mom and Nikki started chuckling. "I'm as bad as you, Mom," said Nikki. "Worse, I guess. You do have to pay a bill, but the things I'm grumbling about haven't even happened." Chad and Dad looked puzzled, but Mom and Nikki just laughed. *H.M.*

HOW ABOUT YOU?

Do you worry? Most of the things people worry about never happen. And even if they do, worrying won't change anything. Remember that God is in control and trust him. An old song says, "Why worry when you can pray?" A moment of prayer helps more than a lifetime of worry.

MEMORIZE:

"Let him have all your worries and cares, for he is always thinking about you."

1 Peter 5:7, TLB

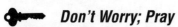 *Don't Worry; Pray*

Coats and Dresses (Read 1 John 3:16-19)

"Can you believe it, Mom?" asked Traci excitedly. "Lisa finally agreed to go to Sunday school with me next week. . . . Well, she almost agreed."

"Great!" exclaimed Mother. "What happened?"

"Lisa finally admitted the only reason she didn't want to go was because she doesn't have a dress," said Traci. "All she has are jeans. I told her that was OK, but she said she'd feel out of place in pants."

19

NOVEMBER

"I'm sure she'd be welcome just wearing what she has," observed Mother, "but I wouldn't want her to feel uncomfortable."

"Well," said Traci, "I have a solution to the problem. You know in the Bible where it says if a person has two coats, he should give one away? Well, I have more than one dress, and I want to give one to Lisa."

"You do?" Mother was surprised, but she looked pleased. "All right," she agreed. "If you really want to give one to Lisa, go ahead. Just be sure you won't mind wearing the same dress to every dress-up event."

"I really want to do just what it says in the Bible," Traci insisted. "I'll run right over and tell Lisa now."

When Traci told Lisa her plan, she was surprised at Lisa's response. "What a dumb idea!" exclaimed Lisa. "I couldn't wear your dress, Traci. Everyone in your Sunday school class would know it was yours. It would be too embarrassing!"

Traci arrived back home in tears. "I tried to do just like the Bible verse said," she sniffed, "and it didn't work."

Mother handed Traci a tissue. "I'm proud of you anyway," she declared. "I'm sure God is pleased, too. You really tried to follow the example in the Bible. And all her life Lisa will probably remember that out of Christian love you offered her one of your dresses." She paused, then added, "Now let's see what else we can work out so Lisa will be comfortable coming along to Sunday school." *R.K.M.*

HOW ABOUT YOU?

When you try to follow the examples in the Bible, do your friends misunderstand you or make fun of you? God always understands. Ask him to help you when things don't work out, and keep trying to do what the Bible tells you.

MEMORIZE:

"If you have two coats, . . . give one to the poor."

Luke 3:11, TLB

 Share with Others

Important Things (Read 1 John 5:1-5)

20
NOVEMBER

Mr. Wagner walked to the chalkboard in his boys' Sunday school classroom. "Tell me what you think should be important in your lives—the really important things," he said, "and I'll write them on the board."

The boys began to call out their answers. "Church." "Jesus." "Family." "Friends." "Bible study." "Prayer."

"All right," said Mr. Wagner. "That's a great list." He moved to another part of the board. "Now let's make a different list," he said. "What are your hobbies? How do you spend most of your time?"

The boys really got into this one. "Baseball." "TV." "Computer games!" "Football." The answers kept coming amid much laughter and excitement.

Mr. Wagner stepped back and looked at the two lists. "Hmmm," he murmured. "Tell me now, how does List Two fit with List One?"

Some of the boys giggled. Some slid down in their chairs. They could see that the way they spent their time didn't go along with what they said should be important to them. Finally Jason spoke. "Well, like we said, those things in the first list are supposed to be the most important things in our lives."

"They're supposed to be, but if we're honest, we have to admit they're not, don't we?" asked Mr. Wagner. Slowly the boys nodded. "I think it's time we say what we mean and mean what we say, don't you?" continued Mr. Wagner. "Look at the two lists and decide, honestly, before the Lord, which one you're going to change in order to make them go together." He paused, then added, "I'm not suggesting that you totally remove those things on List Two, but I hope you'll just give them places of less importance." *P.O.Y.*

HOW ABOUT YOU?

What is most important to you? Do the things you do each day show that you care for God and his Word? Jesus loved you so much that he died to save you from your sins. Do your daily activities show that you love him?

MEMORIZE:

"Seek ye first the kingdom of God, and his righteousness; and all these things shall be added unto you." *Matthew 6:33,* KJV

 Really Put Jesus First

Tiny Termites (Read John 6:5-13)

"I wish I could help with the Thanksgiving baskets," said Lori. The kids in her older brother's youth group were going to deliver the baskets of food to people who needed them.

"You did help," Mother told Lori. "You took some cans of food to Sunday school to be put in the baskets. You even did extra chores to earn money to buy that food yourself."

Lori frowned. "Big deal," she murmured.

21

NOVEMBER

"Yes, it is," said Dad. "If nobody brought food, you'd realize what a big deal it is." He smiled at the little girl. "It's a big deal to God if you did it for him," he assured her.

Lori rode along when Dad took Todd to church that afternoon. "Well, look at that!" exclaimed Dad as they drove down the street. "Looks like they're tearing the old Paulson house down. I knew someone bought the place, and I could see that it needed repair, but I wonder why they don't just fix it up."

"I heard that it was full of termites," said Todd. "I guess it was so bad they couldn't do anything with it."

"Oh, that explains it," said Dad. "That's too bad—it looked like a nice old house."

"What's termites?" asked Lori.

"Termites are insects," Dad told her. "They look something like ants."

"Ants?" asked Lori. "They're taking down that whole big building just because of such tiny little things?"

Dad nodded. "They look something like ants, but they eat wood," he told her. "If they're allowed to continue eating, they can ruin the beams that support the building, and then it becomes unsafe."

"Yeah, and then it can cost more to fix it than to tear it down and start over," put in Todd.

"Small things can make a big difference," said Dad. After a moment he added, "Things like termites. Or maybe cans of food."

"Cans of food?" asked Lori. Then she caught on. Dad was telling her again that her contribution to the Thanksgiving baskets was important. And she could see that it really was. *H.M.*

HOW ABOUT YOU?

Do you feel that the things you can do for the Lord are so small that they don't really matter? Five loaves and two fish don't sound like much, but a little boy gave them to the Lord, and he blessed them and used them. He'll bless what you do for him, too. No effort is too small.

MEMORIZE:

"It is the Lord Christ you are serving." *Colossians 3:24*, NIV

 Help Any Way You Can

The Praise Day (Read Psalm 150:1-6)

22
NOVEMBER

Justin pressed his nose against the window. It was raining again. His sister April bumped him as she walked by. "Get out of my way," she snapped.

"Leave me alone, dummy," retorted Justin. Soon the two were shouting at each other.

"What's going on in there?" called Mom from the kitchen. "Well?" she asked, entering the room. Justin felt uneasy and didn't say anything. To his surprise, April didn't either. "Praise the Lord!" Mom suddenly exclaimed loudly. It made Justin jump. Mom smiled as the children looked at her curiously. "You were complaining with loud voices," she said, "so I thought I'd praise the Lord in an equally loud voice. After all, the rain will water all the thirsty plants. I'm thankful for that, aren't you?" Justin looked at the rain streaming down the window. "I think you need to make a praise list," continued Mom. "Write down all the wonderful things God is and does. Let's have a praise day instead of an arguing day." She went to the desk drawer and got out paper and pencils. Then she returned to the kitchen.

After thinking a moment, Justin wrote, *God helped me with my math lesson.* April took a sheet of paper and wrote, *God gives us food every day.*

Justin grinned. "Hey, let's tape our pages together to make one long sheet—let's see how long a list we can make," he suggested. The list was very long and still growing when Dad came home. Mom asked him how his day went. "Terrible," said Dad. "First, I got a flat tire in the rain. It made me late for work, and then . . ."

"Praise the Lord!" interrupted Justin. Dad glanced at Mom. "We're having a praise day, Dad," explained Justin, holding up the list.

"C'mon, Dad," encouraged April. "Praise the Lord for something."

Just then Dad's stomach rumbled. He grinned. "I praise the Lord for your mom, and I'm thankful she's a good cook," he said. "Now let's thank God for our food and eat!" *C.A.D.*

HOW ABOUT YOU?

Do you complain? Do you grumble when you're bored or when you can't get your way? Are there days when nothing goes right? When that happens, make a praise list. It will make a big difference in how you feel if you deliberately make every day a "thanksgiving day."

MEMORIZE:

"With Jesus' help we will continually offer our sacrifice of praise to God by telling others of the glory of his name."

Hebrews 13:15, TLB

 Don't Complain; Give Praise

Mean Math Teacher (Read Proverbs 9:9-10; Romans 16:17-20)

Josie sighed as she sat at the dining-room table correcting her math paper. "Sometimes it seems like I can't do *anything* right for Miss Crandell," she said. "It seems like all she does is criticize. I wish I had a different teacher."

23

NOVEMBER

"Well, Josie," said Dad, who was helping her, "actually, I was glad when you got Miss Crandell for math, because I know how particular she is. You'll be able to do much better in the next level of math if you've been taught to be careful and do things right. What do you think you'd learn if Miss Crandell just told you what a good job you were doing each day, but never told you what you were doing wrong?"

"Not much, I guess," Josie grudgingly admitted.

"I don't think so, either," agreed Dad. He smiled at Josie. "She'd be like the people the Bible calls flatterers, who just tell people what they want to hear even though it isn't true."

Josie grinned. "You mean the Bible talks about math teachers?" she asked.

Dad laughed. "No, the Bible isn't really talking about math," he said, "but the principle is the same. As Christians, it's important for us to be honest with each other. Sometimes we even need to point out each other's mistakes just like Miss Crandell points out the mistakes on your papers. We need to hear the bad things as well as the good about ourselves if we're going to learn."

"I guess you're right, Dad," admitted Josie thoughtfully. "I guess I'll just have to keep trying and be thankful that I have such a 'mean' teacher." *L.F.W.*

HOW ABOUT YOU?

Do you find it hard to accept correction from others? Learn to look at it as a help rather than a criticism. Let God teach you through the help of your parents, teachers, and elders.

MEMORIZE:

"Rebuke a wise man and he will love you." *Proverbs 9:8,* NIV

 Learn from Correction

Other Mothers (Read Psalm 68:3-6)

24
NOVEMBER

"Mom," said Kristin in a troubled voice, "I feel sorry for Patti. I stopped at her house after school today. Her mother was in her bedroom, and right away she started yelling at Patti to come get the baby. So Patti got little Robbie from his crib. The poor thing had such a wet diaper—and his face was dirty!"

"What a shame!" Mother sounded sad and thoughtful.

"Patti wanted me to listen to a tape we'd been talking about," continued Kristin, "but when she turned on the music, her mother rushed into the room, angry as could be! 'Turn that off!' she yelled, and she gave Patti a hard slap on her cheek! What makes a mother act like that?"

"Well, she may have been tired or worried," Mother guessed, "but that's not a good excuse. She apparently needs a lot of help with her mothering."

On TV that night, Kristin and her mother saw a report about some little cranes that had hatched at the city zoo. But the mother crane was mean to her babies. To save the chicks' lives, they were removed from their mother. The person caring for the baby birds used a hand puppet that looked like the mother crane. Opening the "beak" of the puppet with her fingers, she picked up grain and deposited it in the large, open mouths of the chicks. "In time," the zookeeper explained, "the young cranes will be reunited with their mothers, and hopefully they will get along as a family."

"I'd say that the zookeeper and her puppet are serving as mother-helpers for those birds," Mother told Kristin. "And you know what? I think that's what Patti's mother needs."

"But how can we help?" Kristin wanted to know.

"By finding some 'other mothers' to help Patti. Your Sunday school teacher cares so much for girls; she would help Patti a lot. And I think I'll offer to keep Robbie for an afternoon every week to give Patti's mom a break. Once she knows we're here to support her, she may feel less stress and be much kinder to her children."

T.M.V.

HOW ABOUT YOU?

Do you sometimes feel your mother doesn't care very much for you? It's all right for you to ask for some extra love and care from a teacher, aunt, or good friend. And remember, if you're a Christian, the Lord is your heavenly parent and will never forsake you.

MEMORIZE:

"When my father and my mother forsake me, then the Lord will take care of me."

Psalm 27:10, NKJV

 God Won't Forsake You

From Pouting to Praising (Read Acts 16:19-25; Philippians 4:11-13)

25

NOVEMBER

"Sharon's being silly," teased Sharon's brother Mark. "She's wearing sunglasses when it's cloudy and rainy outside." Mark pointed to the raindrops on the car window. "Sunglasses are for days when the sun is out."

"The sun *is* out," Sharon said. "The sun is *always* out. Clouds might block it, but it's still there. And it's still shining." She kept her new sunglasses on.

When Sharon's family arrived home, there were several messages on the answering machine. They were from some of Sharon's friends who wanted her to go with them to get pizza. She tried to reach them, but they had already left. "Great," said Sharon sarcastically. "I could've gone out with my friends. But no! The rain had to slow us down so I couldn't get home in time. What a rotten, gloomy day!"

Mark picked up Sharon's sunglasses from the counter and put them on his face. "It's not a gloomy day," he said. "The sun is shining."

"Leave me alone!" yelled Sharon.

"Sharon!" scolded Mom. "You need to work on your attitude. I know you're disappointed, but that doesn't mean you have to be miserable and nasty."

"Tell Mark to leave me alone," grumbled Sharon.

"You're the one who said the sun always shines, even on rainy days," Mark reminded her.

"And you actually made a good point," Mom told her. "But you need to think about a different Son that's still shining even though you don't particularly like what's happening today. Not the sun in the sky, but Jesus, the Son of God. Even when things don't go your way, he's still present. You need to acknowledge his presence in your gloomy day, and you'll soon find yourself praising instead of pouting." *N.E.K.*

HOW ABOUT YOU?

Do bad times sometimes cloud your day? Remember that Jesus is still with you at those times. When you feel disappointed or afraid or lonely, when you or someone you love is sick, when you hear bad news—think about Jesus at such times and say good-bye to the gloomies.

MEMORIZE:

"I will rejoice in the Lord; I will be happy in the God of my salvation." *Habakkuk 3:18,* TLB

 *Be Cheerful*

So Much to Say (Read Luke 11:5-13)

26

NOVEMBER

Janie had spent most of the evening calling one friend after another. When Mother told her to get ready for bed, Janie asked, "Can I call Betsy real quick, first? I want to see if she's as nervous as I am about tryouts for the play."

Mother shook her head. "You've talked on the phone enough tonight. It's bedtime."

"Well, can I call Lynn for two seconds just to be sure she'll sit with me on the bus tomorrow?" begged Janie.

"Bed!" Mother said, pointing.

Janie went to get ready. "I wish I could talk to my friends," she mumbled, crawling into bed just as Mother appeared in the doorway.

"Ready to go to sleep?" asked Mother. "Have you prayed already?"

"Oh, I forgot." Janie sat up. "I really don't have anything to say, anyway, except to ask God to take care of everyone, and he already knows that," she added.

Mother sat on the side of Janie's bed. "If I let you call Betsy, would you be at a loss for words?" she asked.

"Can I call her?" Janie asked eagerly. "I do have lots to tell her—friends always have stuff to tell each other."

"Friends share their interests and feelings and activities, don't they?" asked Mother. "They share their hopes and dreams and secrets. They talk about fun and fears."

"Yeah! Friends need time to talk, Mom," said Janie, hoping to use the phone again.

"Is the Lord your friend?" Mother wanted to know. Janie nodded. "Then why don't you have anything to tell him?" asked Mother. "You think about it." She kissed Janie good night, turned out the light, and left the room.

Janie wished she could call her friends; she had so much to say. But after a minute she decided to talk to a friend she had been leaving out lately. She knelt by her bed and shared her fears and dreams with the Lord. "When I think of you as my friend," Janie prayed, "I really do have lots of things to say." *N.E.K.*

HOW ABOUT YOU?

Do you wonder what to say to God? He's your best Friend and wants to be included in every part of your life. Talk to him about all the things you would share with a true friend.

MEMORIZE:

"Abraham . . . was called the Friend of God." *James 2:23,* KJV

Talk to God

One-Way Ticket (Read Luke 16:20-26)

27

NOVEMBER

"This is a sad day, isn't it, Dad?" said Cole as he and his father drove to town. They were going to get tickets to fly to Dad's hometown to attend Grandpa's funeral. Grandpa had died after being ill for several weeks.

"Yes, it is sad," Dad agreed as he signaled for a left turn onto Main Street. "It would be even sadder if we didn't know your grandfather was saved and is now in heaven." Dad pulled into a parking space in front of the travel agency.

Cole and his father entered the office and were soon talking with an agent. "I'll need four round-trip tickets," Dad said before he gave the agent all the details.

"Round-trip—that means we're coming back, doesn't it?" asked Cole as he and his father sat in the waiting area while the agent checked flights on her computer.

"Right. If we weren't coming back, we'd get one-way tickets," Dad told him.

Cole nodded. "I guess Grandpa got a one-way ticket to heaven," he said thoughtfully.

Dad picked up a travel brochure from the rack. "That's true. That's a good thought."

Cole frowned. "My friend Brandon says he doesn't need to be saved," he told Dad. "Brandon says if he ends up in hell and doesn't like it there, he'll just go somewhere else."

"Brandon's wrong," said Dad, placing the brochure back on the rack. "Eternity is forever. If your friend Brandon dies unsaved, he will have a one-way ticket to hell. He can't get a transfer to heaven after he dies."

"Like the rich man in the Bible who went to hell and then wanted to join Lazarus in heaven," Cole remembered. "They both had one-way tickets. I'm sure glad I'm saved, Dad. And I'm glad Grandpa was, too." *R.K.M.*

HOW ABOUT YOU?

Do you have a one-way ticket to heaven? You can decide right now to accept Jesus as your Savior. Then you can be sure that your one-way ticket will take you to heaven.

MEMORIZE:

"Then [the unsaved] will go away to eternal punishment, but the righteous to eternal life." *Matthew 25:46,* NIV

 *Eternity Is Forever*

For Your Own Good (Read Deuteronomy 6:24-25; 10:12-13)

28
NOVEMBER

"Jeff, turn off that TV!" Mother called. "A program like that with its shooting, murder, and all kinds of evil is not good for you to see." Grumbling, Jeff did as he was told. Then, as he stomped out of the room, he heard his mother's familiar words, "I'm only thinking of your good, Jeff."

"I know what's good for me," Jeff muttered as he entered his room. His small dog, Swifty, was lying curled up at the foot of his bed. Seeing his dog reminded Jeff of something else he didn't like. In the paper last night he had read that no dogs were to roam freely around the neighborhood anymore. They had to be tied up when outdoors.

Jeff sighed. Swifty was going to hate being tied up. He loved to run. That was why Jeff had named him Swifty.

When Dad came home from work, he brought a collar and chain. "Here you are, Jeff," he said. "You can fasten this chain to the clothesline. Swifty will be able to roam quite far and still not get away."

"Dumb old rules," complained Jeff, but he put the collar on his dog, fastened the chain to the collar, and led his dog out to the backyard. Swifty did not like the chain. He tried to get away from it but couldn't. He ran in circles and yelped pitifully.

At last Jeff gathered his dog up in his arms. "Please try to understand," he pleaded. "If you aren't chained up, you'll be picked up, and maybe I'll never see you again. I'm doing it for your own good, Swifty."

Jeff realized he was repeating his mother's words about turning off the TV program. He knew he had acted like Swifty, angry and resentful. Shouldn't he try to understand his mother's wisdom, just as he wanted his dog to understand his?

"Trust me, Swifty," he said. "I love you and only want to do what's best for you." As he said the words, he realized his mother loved him, too. Maybe he should go find Mother and apologize.

M.H.N.

HOW ABOUT YOU?

Do you have trouble obeying the rules that God and your parents give you? Remember, they are for your good. Obey them. Someday you will be glad you did.

MEMORIZE:

"Oh, that you had listened to my laws! Then you would have had peace flowing like a gentle river." *Isaiah 48:18*, TLB

 Rules Are Friends, Not Enemies

At the Core (Read Romans 12:9-16)

When Sarah got home from school, she joined her father in the small orchard behind their house. "I'll help you pick some apples, Dad," she said.

"Good," said Dad. "How was school today?"

"OK," replied Sarah. She picked a small, red apple from a branch and placed it in her basket. "There's a new girl. Her name is Jessica. But I didn't like her much. She looks funny—all hunched over. Something's wrong with her." She saw Dad frown and hurried to change the subject. "Oooh! What a dandy!" she exclaimed, reaching for a big, red, round apple. "I think I'll eat this one."

29
NOVEMBER

"I don't think . . . ," began Dad, but then he stopped and nodded.

Sarah bit deep into the apple. "Oh, yuck!" she exclaimed, spitting it back out. It was all wormy inside.

Dad smiled and held out a gnarled, bumpy apple. Then he pulled a small knife from his pocket and cut a slice. "Here, Sarah," he offered, "try a bite of this one."

Sarah looked a little unsure, but she tasted the apple slice. "Ummm! That one's good," she said. "Much better than it looks."

"What the apples looked like on the outside wasn't as important as what was on the inside, was it?" asked Dad. "That's important to remember about apples . . . and people, too. God calls us to love everyone."

Sarah gave Dad a sheepish grin. "You mean Jessica, don't you," she said. "I guess I better find out what's on the inside of Jessica."

D.B.K.

HOW ABOUT YOU?

Do you decide how to act toward people based on the way they look? That isn't the way God judges, and it's not the way he wants you to judge. Outward beauty tells you little about what the person is really like inside.

MEMORIZE:

"Be kind and compassionate to one another." *Ephesians 4:32,* NIV

 Don't Judge People by Their Looks

Warning Strips (Read Psalm 23:1-6)

30

NOVEMBER

Thrrripth! Thrrripth! Thrrripth!

"What was that?" Alarmed, Maria sat straight up in her seat and peered out the window.

"It's OK—I strayed onto the shoulder of the road," her father answered as he shifted in his seat and adjusted the rearview mirror.

"But what was that noise?" Maria asked.

"There are little bumps on the shoulder of the road to warn drivers that they're getting too close to the edge. Driving over the bumps made the sound you heard," explained Dad. "It's OK now."

"That scared me," Maria said, leaning back.

Her father grinned. "It got my attention, too. It reminded me that I'd better pay more attention to my driving," he said. After a moment he added, "It's a good thing those warning strips are there, isn't it? Otherwise we might have ended up off the road and in the ditch." Maria looked at her father and nodded. "It may seem funny," continued Dad, "but this has reminded me that God has ways of warning us when we begin to stray away from him." Maria looked puzzled and her father explained. "For example," he said, "God has given each of us a conscience so that when we do something wrong, we feel bad about it. Then we know we need to repent and confess our sin in order to get back onto his path." Dad smiled at Maria. "God also gives us godly teachers who help us learn his truths."

Maria nodded. "My Sunday school teacher says God gives us his Holy Spirit to teach us, too!" she said.

"That's right," agreed Dad. "God uses many different ways to keep us from straying off the right path."

Maria smiled. "Kind of like his own warning strips," she said.

R.S.M.

HOW ABOUT YOU?

Have you felt the tugging of the Holy Spirit or the Word of God when you've done something wrong? Has God used parents or other people to keep you on the right path? He loves you very much, and he doesn't want you to be hurt because you have drifted in the wrong direction.

MEMORIZE:

"He leads me in the paths of righteousness for His name's sake." *Psalm 23:3,* NKJV

 God Gives Warnings

A Fake Christmas (Read John 3:14-21)

1

DECEMBER

Jesse stood at the rope barricade and stared in wonder at the Christmas tree at the mall. The shiny balls, the glittering stars, the miniature angels, and the sparkling snow all looked so beautiful. "We can get some of that snow to put on our tree," said Rodney, his older brother.

"We can?" asked Jesse. "How?"

"You just buy it," said Rodney. "It comes in a spray can and you just spray it on."

Jesse looked disappointed. "It looked so real," he said. "Who are all the presents under the tree for?"

"They're not real presents," said Rodney. "They're just empty boxes wrapped to look like presents—just part of the decorations."

Jesse could hardly believe that. He wanted to reach over the barricade and shake one.

Back home, the boys told Mother about the tree with its fake snow and presents. Mother nodded. "You know, for people who don't know about the real Christmas when God gave us his free gift, the celebration of Christmas can be just as empty as those fake presents," she said.

"What do you mean 'his free gift?'" asked Jesse.

"God gave us Jesus, his Son, to be our Savior," said Mother. "That's what we really celebrate at Christmas."

Rodney spoke up. "Well, a display at the mall is supposed to get people in the mood to buy Christmas presents, not worship Jesus," he said. "It doesn't have much to do with the real Christmas."

Jesse nodded. "It's kind of like the fake presents," he agreed.

P.O.Y.

HOW ABOUT YOU?

Do you celebrate the real Christmas? God gave his best present to you when he sent Jesus to be your Savior. His present isn't a fake. It doesn't wear out or get old, and you can't outgrow it. If you haven't received that gift yet, do so today.

MEMORIZE:

"For God so loved the world, that he gave his only begotten Son, that whosoever believeth in him should not perish, but have everlasting life."

John 3:16, KJV

 Jesus Is God's Gift to You

Picture-Perfect (Read Ephesians 2:1-9)

2 DECEMBER

"We get our school pictures tomorrow!" exclaimed Andrea one evening. "I hope mine turned out good."

"Well, how good can they be? After all, the camera just takes what it sees," teased her brother Matt. He ducked when she threw a small pillow at him.

After school the next day, Andrea came slowly into the house. "Oh, my pictures are so awful," she wailed when she saw her mother. "I fell on my bike a couple of weeks before they were taken, remember? And I got a bump on my head and skinned my nose. I sure didn't think the scratches would show in the pictures, but guess what? They do!" She threw an envelope down on the table.

"Why did you think they wouldn't show?" asked Mother.

"I covered them up good with some powder Miss Smith gave me," Andrea said, "and besides, Cheryl said they wouldn't show. She said her sister Dana had just gotten her graduation pictures, and that she had a cold sore when they were taken, but it didn't even show on the pictures." She paused, then added, "Cheryl said every hair was perfectly in place, too, even though Dana had been having trouble with her hair. But look how my hair sticks out!"

Mother smiled. "Well," she said, "I'm sure Dana's pictures were taken at a studio and were touched up by the photographer. That means that all the little blemishes—such as hairs out of place—were covered over."

That evening, Dad also heard Andrea's complaints. "So you think your pictures need a little touching up?" he asked.

Matt laughed. "Like I told her, the camera just shows what's there," he said. "You can't fool it."

Dad smiled. "This reminds me of how people like to cover up their sins," he said, "but no matter how good they think they've made themselves look, God's 'camera' shows just what's there—it shows a heart full of sin."

Mother nodded. "And only God can touch up the picture and remove the sin," she added. "He does that for us when we trust him as Savior." *H.M.*

HOW ABOUT YOU?

Has your "heart picture" been touched up? Have you trusted Jesus as your Savior? If not, there's sin there that you cannot cover over or touch up, no matter how good you try to be. Let Jesus take care of it—accept him as your Savior today. Let him make your heart picture-perfect.

MEMORIZE:

"Create in me a pure heart, O God, and renew a steadfast spirit within me." *Psalm 51:10, NIV*

 Let Jesus Make Your Heart Perfect

Open Doors (Read Psalm 31:14-16, 21-24)

Rick was glad to be spending a day with Uncle Don in the big city. The problems at home were getting too big, and there just didn't seem to be any way out. He was glad to get away from it all for a while. Rick looked forward to his first ride on the subway train, and he stood close and watched as Uncle Don put tokens in the ticket machine. Then Uncle Don pointed to the destination written on the side of the subway car. "That's where we want to go," he said, so they climbed aboard.

3

DECEMBER

The ride was a little bumpy but fun, and Rick enjoyed the *clickety-clack* sounds. Suddenly, while in the underground tunnel, the lights went out for a few moments. Then they came back on.

"Plaza station," the speaker announced a few minutes later. The subway stopped and several people stood at the door to get out. But the door didn't open. Then the lights went out again as the subway train started up and headed for the next stop. Passengers were angry and confused.

The same thing happened at the next few stops. Since the cars were all connected together with doors between, the people began to go into the next car and exit from there. Rick and Uncle Don did that, too.

"I'm glad there was a way out!" Rick said, when he and Uncle Don were up on the street. "I didn't like it when the lights went out and the doors wouldn't open."

"That doesn't generally happen," Uncle Don assured him, "but you know what? That reminds me of life. Sometimes problems come that seem too big. We can't see our way past the circumstances, and all doors to a solution seem closed. We pray but don't feel we're getting answers." Rick nodded as he thought about the problems at his home. "What we need to remember is that the Lord is going to take care of us," continued Uncle Don. "He will open a way out for us at just the right time." *N.E.K.*

HOW ABOUT YOU?

Do relationships, schoolwork, health issues, or other problems sometimes seem to be more than you can stand? Is there no way out? God will provide the door you need, right when he knows you need it. Trust him.

MEMORIZE:

"My times are in Your hand."

Psalm 31:15, NKJV

 Trust God's Timing

The Trailblazers (Read Hebrews 11:32–12:2)

4

DECEMBER

Ken and his father had gone to Uncle Jeff's farm to cut a Christmas tree. They all climbed into Uncle Jeff's truck and headed down a trail through the snowy fields until they came to the woods. "Wow!" said Ken, "these woods are thick. Good thing you've got four-wheel drive on your truck. It won't get stuck, will it?"

Uncle Jeff grinned. "Not as long as we follow the trail," he said, as he pointed to the narrow but well-marked path ahead of them. Before long they stopped. "There are some nice trees around the edge of this clearing," said Uncle Jeff. Soon they found the perfect tree and loaded it onto the truck.

"I remember when Grandpa Parker owned this farm and I helped him break this trail with a team of horses," said Uncle Jeff as they headed back down the path. "It was hard work, but we use this trail a lot!"

"You helped with it?" asked Ken. He was impressed. "Then you're a trailblazer," he declared. "We learned about trailblazing in Boy Scouts—but that was a little different kind of trailblazing than this."

Dad smiled. "I read about some trailblazers just this morning," he said. "I was reading about the great heroes of the faith—Enoch, Moses, Abraham, and others. Because they were successful in living for God through hard times, they've served as examples to other believers for many, many years."

"Yep, they were real trailblazers, all right," agreed Uncle Jeff. "We follow in their footsteps. And I can think of some more recent ones, too. For example, Grandpa Parker taught us that you don't need to have a lot of money to be happy."

"Who else?" asked Ken.

"Well, old Mr. Potts's example of faith when he lost his wife helped me when Aunt Betty died last year," said Uncle Jeff.

Ken smiled. "I know two more good trailblazers," he said. "You and Dad. You've taught me a whole lot about loving God, and you live like you mean what you say." *S.L.K.*

HOW ABOUT YOU?

Have you read about heroes of the Bible and other great men and women of God? Let their example help show you the right way to live for Jesus. Ask Christians you know and admire for their advice on serving the Lord. There may be times when you will have to blaze a trail yourself, with God's help.

MEMORIZE:

"Dear brothers, pattern your lives after mine, and notice who else lives up to my example." *Philippians 3:17,* TLB

 Follow Good Examples

Practice Time (Read Psalm 119:9-16)

5

DECEMBER

Andy was passing the kitchen door when he heard his little brother's voice. "Dad, can't I pl-e-e-ease have those shoes?"

"Now, Son, I don't know why you can't just get regular, cheaper ones," replied Dad.

"I know why," Andy announced, entering the kitchen. "The kind Scott wants are the kind Mike Justan wears. Since he's a basketball star, Scott thinks those shoes will automatically make him a great basketball player, too."

Scott fidgeted. "Well, . . . they might help," he said.

Andy laughed. "Hey! Maybe if you buy a Heroes shirt, too, they'll invite you to play on their team!" he teased.

Dad smiled. "Instead of teasing your little brother, maybe you can help him understand that effort, not a fancy pair of shoes, will help make him a good basketball player," he suggested.

Andy nodded. "Dad's right," he said. "If you practice every day, Scott, you'll get better and better, no matter what kind of shoes you have."

Scott looked a bit disappointed. "Guess I'll start practicing then," he said with a sigh as he headed for the backyard basketball hoop.

Andy grinned at his dad. "I was going to our junior high Bible study, but maybe I'll go help Scott with his basketball practice instead," he said.

Dad motioned toward Andy's Bible. "Is that the Bible we gave you last Christmas?" he asked.

"Yep . . . it's one of the nicest Bibles in class," Andy said proudly.

"Hmmm," murmured Dad. "Still looks new—as if it hasn't been used much. Just remember that merely owning a fancy Bible won't help you grow spiritually."

Andy knew what his dad was driving at. "Just like Scott needs to practice to become a good basketball player, I need to study the Bible and work at being a better Christian, huh?" he asked. He tucked his Bible beneath his arm and headed for the door. "Guess I'd better get going to Bible study after all," he decided. "I don't want to be late for 'practice'!" *A.J.S.*

HOW ABOUT YOU?

Do you want to be a better Christian? To be good at sports, you need to learn the rules and spend a lot of time practicing. The same is true for becoming better at living as a Christian should. Use your Bible often, and then put into practice the things you learn.

MEMORIZE:

"How can a young man keep his way pure? By living according to your word."

Psalm 119:9, NIV

 Study God's Word

Not a Sore Thumb (Read 2 Corinthians 6:14-18)

6

As Tyler let himself into the house after school, his little brother Zeb met him at the door. "Look what I got," said Zeb, proudly holding out his hand. His thumb was wrapped with a thick bandage. "I banged my thumb."

"That wasn't smart," replied Tyler. "How does it feel?"

"Better," said Zeb, and he went off to play.

By dinnertime, Zeb was tired of his bandage. It got in his way when he tried to use his hand. But he was afraid that if he took it off, his thumb would hurt again. Tyler grinned at him. "I see where the expression 'stick out like a sore thumb' comes from," said Tyler. "It would be pretty hard to miss seeing yours." He pushed his food around absentmindedly. "Reminds me of myself today," he added. "I stuck out like a sore thumb, too."

"How's that?" asked Dad.

"Well, first of all, the guys were telling some bad jokes before school, and I was the only one who didn't laugh," replied Tyler. "Then they discussed some of the TV shows I'm not allowed to watch, so I had nothing to say. Even in class I stood out. Our teacher asked what we thought of the ruling that nativity scenes couldn't be set up in the school. I said that since Jesus' birth is what Christmas is all about, a nativity scene should be allowed, but it seems like everybody else thinks the ruling is OK."

"Well, you may have stood out like a sore thumb to the kids at school, but not to me," declared Mother, reaching over to put an arm around Tyler. "Sore thumbs aren't the only fingers that stand out. I met our former neighbor, Julie Richards, today. Right away I saw that she's engaged to be married. She had on the biggest diamond you've ever seen. It stood out, as you would say, like a sore thumb." Mother gave Tyler's shoulder a squeeze. "I think you stood out like a diamond today. And you know what? I believe that's what God thinks, too." *H.M.*

HOW ABOUT YOU?

Do you stand out from those who are unbelievers? You should. God says to "come out from them." Take a stand for things you know are right—the things that please God. Stand out—not like a sore thumb, but like a diamond!

MEMORIZE:

"'Come out from them and be separate,' says the Lord."

2 Corinthians 6:17, NIV

 *Stand Out for God*

Sneak Attack (Read Joshua 24:14-16)

"Hey, Dad!" called J. C. as he stormed into the house. "I told Mark all about Pearl Harbor, and he said I didn't know what I was talking about. Mark said it happened in Alaska, not in Hawaii! He's the one who doesn't know what he's talking about!" J. C.'s words exploded, hot and angry.

"Settle down, Son," his father said calmly. "How do you know so much about Pearl Harbor?"

"Grandpa told me! He was right there when all the enemy warplanes flew over in a sneak attack on our military base," replied J. C. "Grandpa said thousands of people died, and a whole bunch were wounded, too—and it wasn't in Alaska!"

7

DECEMBER

"Why were you and Grandpa talking about Pearl Harbor?" asked Dad.

"When I asked him for help with a Sunday school question, he explained with one of his war stories," J. C. said. "He said the attack on Pearl Harbor happened in December 1941, and nobody was expecting it. They didn't realize what was happening until it was too late. Grandpa said we're in a spiritual warfare, and that Satan sneaks up like those planes did. He makes Christians think they have plenty of time to start serving God later—not now! Christians think they're doing well in their Christian lives, then *boom!* The war is on, and it's too late to get prepared!"

"Your grandfather is right," Dad agreed, "about both the battle of Pearl Harbor and the spiritual battle we're in. It's important to always be ready to defend ourselves as citizens of our country and also as citizens of heaven."

"Yeah," J. C. nodded emphatically. "I'm gonna tell Mark that he oughta start listening instead of thinking he knows everything."

Dad put a loving arm around J. C. "Did Satan make a sneak attack on you, Son?" he asked gently. "I know you've been trying to witness to Mark and get him to come to Sunday school with you, but you sound pretty angry with him. I don't really think that's the way to win him to the Lord, do you?" *P.I.K.*

HOW ABOUT YOU?

Do you think that you have plenty of time to serve the Lord when you're older? That's what Satan wants you to think. Don't wait. Start learning more and more about God and start serving him now.

MEMORIZE:

"Decide today whom you will obey. . . . As for me and my family, we will serve the Lord."

Joshua 24:15, TLB

 Serve the Lord

Snow and Good Deeds (Read Psalm 103:8-14)

8
DECEMBER

"Oh! It snowed last night!" exclaimed Tara as she looked out the window at the fields and trees. "Oh, it's just so gorgeous! It's so clean and white. I just love it, don't you?"

"Oh, yes! It's so be-yew-tiful!" Tara's brother Dwight clasped his hands in mock delight. "Oh, I just adore the snow," he continued. "There's nothing I like more than to have the dirt covered up—clean person that I am. I think it's simply—" His teasing was cut short by the napkin his sister tried to stuff into his mouth.

"All right, you two," said Mother with a smile. "Just get ready for school. I don't want you to miss your bus."

By dinnertime, the snow had begun to melt. "I hope it snows again tonight," said Tara as they finished eating. "It was so pretty this morning, but now everything is starting to look dirty again. I think we should have just a little snow every day to cover up the old stuff and keep things looking clean."

"That would be nice," agreed Mother.

"Oh, indeed!" began Dwight. "Oh, the sn—*auwk!*" His speech was cut short by his sister's hand over his mouth.

"Enough!" said Dad, but he smiled. "You know what this melting snow reminds me of?" Nobody ventured a guess. "It reminds me of the good deeds people do when they try to work their way to heaven," said Dad.

"Well, that's a new one," said Dwight. "Usually preachers tell us that snow reminds us that our sins are washed away and we're made whiter than snow."

"That's true," agreed Dad. "But some people believe that good deeds will get them to heaven. Like the snow covers the dirt, they think good works cover the bad things they've done. But the dirt—sin—is still underneath, showing again when the good deeds melt away. The only effective cover for sin is the blood of Jesus. Jesus can permanently take away the dirt of sin, not just cover it up for a while." *H.M.*

HOW ABOUT YOU?

Do you do good things to try to make up for, or cover over, the bad things in your life? Covering them by your own efforts isn't good enough. Invite Jesus into your life and ask him to take your sin away.

MEMORIZE:

"Behold! The Lamb of God who takes away the sin of the world!" *John 1:29,* NKJV

 Let Jesus Take Your Sin Away

Ready, But . . . (Read 2 Corinthians 5:5-9)

9

"I saw you, Dale," taunted JoAnne. "You covered your ears during the sermon."

"Only for a minute," muttered Dale. Usually he listened when the pastor spoke, but today was different. He had tried to shut out the words. He didn't think anyone had noticed because he had slumped down in the pew.

"Well, why did you do that?" demanded JoAnne. "Pastor Gray talked about Jesus coming again. Don't you want him to come?"

"Sure, someday," answered Dale.

"Sometimes I wish he'd come right away." JoAnne sighed. "Like before my math test tomorrow."

"If you'd study you wouldn't have to wish that," said Dale.

"Well, it's a good thing to wish for," insisted JoAnne. "Grandma always prays, 'Lord, come quickly.'"

"That's easy for her to pray; she's old. I want a horse first." Dale had let it slip—the main reason he hoped the Lord wouldn't come for a while. He thought, dreamed, and read about horses. Someday he hoped to have one. If the Lord returned too soon, that would never happen.

Dad, who had been quietly listening to the conversation, smiled. "You always did like horses," he recalled, "and I wouldn't be surprised if you do get a real one someday."

"But what if Jesus comes today?" asked Dale.

"Remember our camping trip?" Dad asked. "I promised we'd go, but I couldn't set an exact date because I didn't know when I'd be able to get off work. So we prepared for camping, then we went about our daily lives. We did our work and scheduled fun times, too. And when I finally said, 'We can go,' we were all glad to leave our daily schedules and take off. Nobody wanted to stay behind— even for those fun times."

Dale got the point. Being with Jesus would be better than anything here on earth—even a horse. But until that special time came, he would keep busy working for the Lord and enjoying his blessings. *B.L.K.*

HOW ABOUT YOU?

Have you wished that Jesus wouldn't come before you have time for things you want to do? That's normal. But even as God blesses you with many good things on earth, remember that nothing can compare with what awaits in heaven.

MEMORIZE:

"We . . . would prefer to be away from the body and at home with the Lord."

2 Corinthians 5:8, NIV

 Heaven Will Be Wonderful

God's Better Way (Read Romans 8:25-28)

10

DECEMBER

Sitting in front of the neighbor's Christmas tree, Jenny watched the blinking lights. *They might as well go off and stay off,* she thought. How could she be happy when God had not answered her prayer? For weeks she'd been praying that they would have a peaceful Christmas—one without Mom and Dad arguing. But last night they had the worst fight ever. Then this morning Mom and Dad went away, and Jenny did not know where. Dad had merely told her that after school she was to go to the Ryans' house next door.

When Dad's car pulled into their driveway a little later, Jenny saw that Mom was not in the car, but Grandma was. Jenny hurried home, and Dad stayed out in the garage while Grandma came into the house with her. Jenny felt sad and confused. "Where's Mom?" she asked.

Grandma sat down beside Jenny. "Honey," she said, "your father asked me to talk to you because he didn't know how to tell you." She put an arm around Jenny. "This morning your father took your mother to a clinic—a detoxification clinic," she explained.

"You mean . . ." Jenny feared she knew what Grandma meant.

"Your mother admitted she is an alcoholic, and she has gone for treatment," said Grandma. Jenny leaned against Grandma and began to cry. Grandma held her close.

As Jenny dried her tears, she said, "Grandma, I've been praying, like you taught me. But God didn't answer my prayer." She explained what she had been praying about.

"I think God did answer your prayer, Jenny," said Grandma, "but not in the way you expected. God had a better way. Your parents argued so much because your mother denied being an alcoholic. But now she's facing it and getting treatment. With the Lord's help, she will get better, and the fights will stop altogether—not just at Christmas."

Jenny sat quietly for a moment. Then she smiled faintly. "Let's go turn on the Christmas lights," she said. *E.M.B.*

HOW ABOUT YOU?

Do you think you know how God should answer your prayer? Are you willing to let him handle your problem? It may seem that God isn't answering your prayer at all, but he will answer in his own way and time. Trust him.

MEMORIZE:

"The Spirit intercedes for the saints in accordance with God's will." *Romans 8:27, NIV*

 God Answers Prayer

Accepting Help (Read Psalm 25:8-14; Isaiah 58:11)

Amy was sitting at her desk doing math homework when her little sister Lisa walked in. "I want to write numbers, too," said Lisa.

Amy smiled. Lisa was only three years old. She was too young to work math problems, but she wanted to be like her big sister. So Amy carefully wrote the numbers from one to ten on a sheet of notebook paper. Then she took Lisa's hand and helped her begin to write. "One, two . . ." Lisa pulled her hand away. "I can do it," she said.

11
DECEMBER

"OK," said Amy, and she went back to her homework. She was finishing her last problem when Lisa began to cry. "What's wrong?" asked Amy.

"My numbers don't look right," whined Lisa. Her numbers were jumbled on the paper, many of them unrecognizable.

"Let me help you," suggested Amy, bending down to take Lisa's hand again.

"No!" Lisa pulled away. "I'll do it," she insisted.

"OK," said Amy. She left the room and found her mother sorting clothes in the living room. "I tried to help Lisa write her numbers, but she won't let me," she told Mother. "She'd rather cry because she can't do it than let me help her."

Mother smiled. "I guess we all need to learn to accept help," she said, handing Amy some towels to fold. After working silently a few moments, Mother added thoughtfully, "Sometimes we're a lot like Lisa. Her numbers didn't turn out right when she didn't let you guide her. And our decisions often don't turn out right when we don't ask God for help and let him guide us through his Word and through the prompting of his Spirit in our hearts and minds."

Amy nodded as she finished folding the towels. "Yeah—I'll try to remember that," she said. "And I guess I'll go see if Lisa's changed her mind and wants help now." *K.E.C.*

HOW ABOUT YOU?

Do you ask God for help? Do you read his Word so that you may better understand what he wants and expects of you? Do you obey when you feel he wants you to act in a certain way? You'll be a happier person when you follow God's guidance.

MEMORIZE:

"I have taught you in the way of wisdom; I have led you in right paths." *Proverbs 4:11,* NKJV

 *Let God Guide You*

Potato Peelings (Read Matthew 12:34-37)

Karl trudged up the steps and pushed his way into the kitchen. His mother stood at the sink, peeling potatoes for supper. "Hi, you're late. Basketball practice went overtime again?" she asked with a smile.

"Yeah," Karl answered, unzipping his jacket and glancing toward the TV. "Hey, look who's on TV!" he exclaimed.

12
DECEMBER

On the screen, a news reporter directed quick questions to a tall, ruggedly dressed man leaning carelessly against a rail fence. "It's just one of those movie actor interviews," Mom answered. "I really wasn't listening."

Not listening! Wow! thought Karl. He recognized the actor as one of those most admired by his friends. *This guy's a cool dude, and here's my chance to hear him!* he thought.

As the interview progressed, Karl became aware of obvious discomfort in the movie star's manner. He shifted his position awkwardly, squinted nervously toward the camera, and struggled with words. Finally, there was an explosion of offensive language, which was promptly bleeped out. "That certainly was embarrassing," Mom said, frowning.

"I'll say!" agreed Karl. "He sounded really dumb!" Karl wondered what had happened to the smart-talking, smooth, wise guy of movie fame.

"Oops! Here's a bad potato!" exclaimed Mom. "No one would have guessed it just by looking at it." Mom held up a large potato she had just cut in half. The outside was clean and white, but the entire center was black and decayed.

"Yuck!" exclaimed Karl. "Pretty gross!"

Tossing the potato into the garbage, Mom said, "I think that potato gives an accurate picture of that actor, Karl. He looked pretty good on the outside, but he wasn't even capable of a decent conversation when he had no written script. He apparently has little of anything worthwhile on the inside. God warns us about people like that. As the old saying goes, you can't judge a book by its cover!"

Karl laughed. "No," he said, "nor a potato by its peel!" *P.I.K.*

HOW ABOUT YOU?

Are you swept along by the glamorous looks of so-called teenage idols? Don't be fooled. Listen carefully to discover what people are like inside. Unless they are pleasing to God, they should not be pleasing to you.

MEMORIZE:

"Whatever is in the heart overflows into speech."

Luke 6:45, TLB

 Admire Wholesome People

Accepting Help (Read Psalm 25:8-14; Isaiah 58:11)

11
DECEMBER

Amy was sitting at her desk doing math homework when her little sister Lisa walked in. "I want to write numbers, too," said Lisa.

Amy smiled. Lisa was only three years old. She was too young to work math problems, but she wanted to be like her big sister. So Amy carefully wrote the numbers from one to ten on a sheet of notebook paper. Then she took Lisa's hand and helped her begin to write. "One, two . . ." Lisa pulled her hand away. "I can do it," she said.

"OK," said Amy, and she went back to her homework. She was finishing her last problem when Lisa began to cry. "What's wrong?" asked Amy.

"My numbers don't look right," whined Lisa. Her numbers were jumbled on the paper, many of them unrecognizable.

"Let me help you," suggested Amy, bending down to take Lisa's hand again.

"No!" Lisa pulled away. "I'll do it," she insisted.

"OK," said Amy. She left the room and found her mother sorting clothes in the living room. "I tried to help Lisa write her numbers, but she won't let me," she told Mother. "She'd rather cry because she can't do it than let me help her."

Mother smiled. "I guess we all need to learn to accept help," she said, handing Amy some towels to fold. After working silently a few moments, Mother added thoughtfully, "Sometimes we're a lot like Lisa. Her numbers didn't turn out right when she didn't let you guide her. And our decisions often don't turn out right when we don't ask God for help and let him guide us through his Word and through the prompting of his Spirit in our hearts and minds."

Amy nodded as she finished folding the towels. "Yeah—I'll try to remember that," she said. "And I guess I'll go see if Lisa's changed her mind and wants help now." *K.E.C.*

HOW ABOUT YOU?

Do you ask God for help? Do you read his Word so that you may better understand what he wants and expects of you? Do you obey when you feel he wants you to act in a certain way? You'll be a happier person when you follow God's guidance.

MEMORIZE:

"I have taught you in the way of wisdom; I have led you in right paths." *Proverbs 4:11,* NKJV

 *Let God Guide You*

Potato Peelings (Read Matthew 12:34-37)

12

DECEMBER

Karl trudged up the steps and pushed his way into the kitchen. His mother stood at the sink, peeling potatoes for supper. "Hi, you're late. Basketball practice went overtime again?" she asked with a smile.

"Yeah," Karl answered, unzipping his jacket and glancing toward the TV. "Hey, look who's on TV!" he exclaimed.

On the screen, a news reporter directed quick questions to a tall, ruggedly dressed man leaning carelessly against a rail fence. "It's just one of those movie actor interviews," Mom answered. "I really wasn't listening."

Not listening! Wow! thought Karl. He recognized the actor as one of those most admired by his friends. *This guy's a cool dude, and here's my chance to hear him!* he thought.

As the interview progressed, Karl became aware of obvious discomfort in the movie star's manner. He shifted his position awkwardly, squinted nervously toward the camera, and struggled with words. Finally, there was an explosion of offensive language, which was promptly bleeped out. "That certainly was embarrassing," Mom said, frowning.

"I'll say!" agreed Karl. "He sounded really dumb!" Karl wondered what had happened to the smart-talking, smooth, wise guy of movie fame.

"Oops! Here's a bad potato!" exclaimed Mom. "No one would have guessed it just by looking at it." Mom held up a large potato she had just cut in half. The outside was clean and white, but the entire center was black and decayed.

"Yuck!" exclaimed Karl. "Pretty gross!"

Tossing the potato into the garbage, Mom said, "I think that potato gives an accurate picture of that actor, Karl. He looked pretty good on the outside, but he wasn't even capable of a decent conversation when he had no written script. He apparently has little of anything worthwhile on the inside. God warns us about people like that. As the old saying goes, you can't judge a book by its cover!"

Karl laughed. "No," he said, "nor a potato by its peel!" *P.I.K.*

HOW ABOUT YOU?

Are you swept along by the glamorous looks of so-called teenage idols? Don't be fooled. Listen carefully to discover what people are like inside. Unless they are pleasing to God, they should not be pleasing to you.

MEMORIZE:

"Whatever is in the heart overflows into speech."

Luke 6:45, TLB

 Admire Wholesome People

Caught in the Storm (Read Psalm 119:89-96)

The wind whipped snow all around the car, and the Carter family shivered in their seats. They had slid off the road and into a snowdrift. Dad stepped on the gas pedal and tried to move the car forward and then back. Nothing happened—the car was stuck.

13
DECEMBER

"Last winter I bought a shovel to keep in the car in case something like this should happen," Dad grumbled. "Then we had an unusually mild winter, and I never needed it. So I stored it away in the basement, and it's still there." He sighed. "Now we'll just have to wait for help." He flicked on the car's emergency flashing lights. It seemed like a long time before someone stopped and helped them get the car back onto the road.

"When we get home, I'm putting that shovel in the trunk first thing," declared Dad when they were finally on their way. "You never know when trouble may come."

That night at bedtime, Dad went in to tell Paul good night. "Where's your Bible?" Dad asked, looking at the nightstand.

Paul pulled the covers up around him. "I don't know," he said. "I think it's in the drawer."

"It needs to be in your heart and memory," Dad said, opening the drawer. "I've found it important to read my Bible daily, and you need to, too. I'm sorry I haven't been encouraging you to do that."

"That's OK," said Paul. "I don't have time to do much reading anyway."

"Paul," said Dad, "it wouldn't take you any longer to read a few verses than it would have taken me to get the snow shovel from the cellar and put it in the trunk. Ever since we got home today, I've been thinking about being prepared. As long as the winter was mild, I didn't bother to pack a shovel. And when things in our lives are going smoothly, we often don't read God's Word. But sooner or later we're going to be challenged—with a snowstorm or with a temptation or problem. We need to be prepared." *N.E.K.*

HOW ABOUT YOU?

Are you preparing for whatever may come your way in life? Don't wait until you have problems before you read God's Word. Read it daily so you will be ready for both good and hard times to come.

MEMORIZE:

"I would have despaired and perished unless your laws had been my deepest delight."

Psalm 119:92, TLB

 Prepare for Life with God's Word

Teddy Bear Surprises

(Read Deuteronomy 15:7-8; Proverbs 19:17; 22:9)

14

DECEMBER

"Who's going to wrap all these presents?" Angie asked her mother as they came through their front door, loaded with boxes and bags. They had just finished shopping for the last of many Christmas presents to be given to poor families in their town. Many people had already bought and delivered presents to the church. But many others had donated money for gifts, which Angie and her mother then purchased.

"Tomorrow night a bunch of people are meeting at the church to wrap these," Mom told Angie. "I just wish we'd had enough money to get a small toy for each child on the list." The gifts consisted mostly of clothing. "I bet these will be the only presents many of the children get this year."

Angie went to her room. As she started doing some homework, her eyes drifted to the collection of stuffed animals that filled her shelves. In her twelve years, Angie had collected more than a hundred stuffed bears, rabbits, dogs, alligators, kittens, monkeys, and every other type of creature imaginable. *I don't really play with them much anymore,* she thought, *and all those children have hardly any toys.*

Angie struggled for a long time with her decision and finally went out to the living room. "Mom and Dad," she said, "do you think those poor kids would like some of my stuffed animals?"

"Well, sure, Angie," said Mom, looking surprised. "Why? What did you have in mind?"

"Well, I want to keep some of my favorite ones," said Angie, "but I was thinking of taking a bunch of my stuffed animals to church tomorrow night. We could wrap one with each child's present."

"That's a wonderful idea," said Dad. "You'll help so many children have a happy Christmas."

"And God will be pleased, too," said Mom.

The next evening as they wrapped presents, Angie said good-bye to many longtime animal friends. But she smiled. She had never felt so warm in her heart at Christmastime before. *T.K.M.*

HOW ABOUT YOU?

Do you know of poor families in your town? Do you have things you could share with them? Think of one way you could give to the poor this week.

MEMORIZE:

"He who gives to the poor will lack nothing, but he who closes his eyes to them receives many curses." *Proverbs 28:27, NIV*

 Share with the Poor

Lighten Up (Read Colossians 1:10-14)

Jill and her older sister Joan were fixing a snack after school. Jill spread peanut butter and jelly on bread. Then on the way to the table . . . *splat!* The bread dropped upside down on the floor. Joan started to giggle, but tears streamed down Jill's face. "Oh, no! My sandwich is ruined," she sputtered. "This is just terrible."

15

DECEMBER

"Oh, come on, Sis. Lighten up," encouraged Joan as she started to help clean up the mess. "This isn't so bad." But Jill continued to moan about it—and about several other things that had happened that day.

When Sunday rolled around, Jill's Sunday school teacher, Mrs. Johnson, arrived a minute late and out of breath. "Everything went wrong this morning," she good-naturedly told her class as she removed her coat. Then she started to laugh. "Look at me!" she exclaimed. "I forgot to change my blouse. Oh well, you'll all just have to put up with this big rip in my sleeve for a while. This is a good joke on me."

The class laughed with their teacher, and then it was time to say the memory verse from Proverbs 17:22. "'A merry heart doeth good like a medicine'," Jill recited.

"I didn't expect to be such a good example of what that verse means," Mrs. Johnson said, "but I do try not to take unimportant things too seriously. If I can laugh about these things and let others laugh with me, we can all have a good time. It does us good to share a laugh. I can laugh about things like this if I remember that God is in control, even when things go wrong. He cares for me, so I can have a light heart, no matter what."

Jill remembered the things she had moaned about that week. If she had laughed about those things rather than becoming upset, she and Joan would have had a good time together. Jill decided that the next time things went wrong, she would remember that God always loves and cares for his children. That would help her to lighten up. *C.E.Y.*

HOW ABOUT YOU?

Are you cheerful when you're embarrassed or when everything seems to go wrong? Try to remember that God loves you and is caring for you. That's what is really important. Thinking about God's love and care will give you a merry heart and help you "lighten up."

MEMORIZE:

"A merry heart doeth good like a medicine." *Proverbs 17:22,* KJV

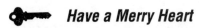 *Have a Merry Heart*

A Clever Deceiver (Read Proverbs 23:29-35)

16
DECEMBER

Shawn looked at the beer commercial on television. It showed pretty girls and good-looking young men drinking, laughing, and having fun. His folks always told him that drinking was bad, but it didn't look that way on TV. "Shawn, turn that off and do your homework," called Mom.

Reluctantly Shawn turned off the TV and reached for his books to start writing his report on ants. He looked in an encyclopedia for information. Busily he wrote down the amazing facts he found: Every ant has a job to do in the ant community. Some are nurses to care for the ant eggs and baby ants. Some are builders. Some are guards. Some are farmers, who harvest seeds and plant mushrooms. Some are cowboys, who find tiny, green aphids and milk them by stroking them for the sweet liquid they give. They even build tiny, clay barns for the aphids and protect them from insect rustlers.

As Shawn continued to study these amazing little creatures, he came upon some astounding information—some ants have drinking problems! They get an intoxicating liquid from a certain kind of beetle that comes to their nest. The beetle squirts its liquor onto the hairs of its back, and the ants lick the hairs. This causes them to become intoxicated.

What happens next? The ants that take in this substance become so drunk they don't notice that the beetles are stealing their eggs and larvae. As the ants become drunk and lazy, their work goes undone, their babies die, and the ant community becomes a ghost town.

Shawn stopped writing and looked out the window for a long time. *Are the beer ads on TV right?* he wondered. *Or are Mom and Dad right when they say drinking alcohol often ruins people?*

He knew the answer. The ants were fooled by the beetles, and many people were being fooled by the beer commercials. Shawn was determined that he would not be one of them. *M.H.N.*

HOW ABOUT YOU?

Are you taken in by the sin you see on television? Or do you think about where that sin would lead you? Drinking alcohol in any form can be dangerous and destructive.

MEMORIZE:

"Wine is a mocker and beer a brawler; whoever is led astray by them is not wise."

Proverbs 20:1, NIV

 Drinking Alcohol Is Dangerous

Grandparents' Day (Read John 20:24-29)

"Welcome to Grandparents' Day!" Mrs. Perry greeted everyone in the second-grade classroom. "We're so pleased to have you here. Just sit back, relax, and enjoy our program."

The grandparents all sat on the folding chairs while the children sang songs, recited poems, and showed pictures they had drawn. When the program was finished, the children took turns introducing their grandparents to the class. There were Grandmas and Grandpas, Nannies and Granddads, Grammies and Grampies. One boy called his grandparents, who were from Poland, Omah and Opah.

17
DECEMBER

Finally, it was Matthew's turn. He went to the front of the room and held up a picture for everyone to see. "This is my grandpa," he said proudly. "He's not here today because he's in heaven. He went there before I was born, so I don't remember him. But my dad tells me about him. Grandpa used to build furniture and stuff. He was always kind, and he gave food to people who didn't have any. I listen to tapes of Grandpa singing and playing the steel guitar. I love him a lot!" Then Matthew sat back down. A happy, little tear sparkled in the corner of his eye.

Later that day, Matthew told his parents about Grandparents' Day. Dad was quiet for a few minutes, then he said, "You know, Matthew, I love someone that I've never seen, too. Do you know who that is?"

"Jesus?" asked Matthew. Dad nodded his head and smiled. "I love Jesus, too," said Matthew.

"You love Grandpa because I tell you how good and kind he was. Why do you love Jesus?" asked Dad.

"The Bible tells me how good he is," replied Matthew. "He loves me, too!"

Dad smiled. "That's right, Matthew," he said. "We love him even though we've never seen him. But someday we'll see him, won't we?"

"Yep!" Matthew nodded. He grinned as he added, "And we'll see Grandpa, too!" *T.M.B.*

HOW ABOUT YOU?

Do you love God even though you've never seen him? He loves you—so much that he sent his Son, Jesus, to earth. Won't you give him your love, too? Then you can look forward to seeing him face-to-face someday. That will be a great joy!

MEMORIZE:

"You love him even though you have never seen him; . . . and even now you are happy with the inexpressible joy that comes from heaven itself."

1 Peter 1:8, TLB

 ***Return God's Love***

Nerve Medicine (Read Philippians 4:4-9)

18

DECEMBER

More than an hour after she went to bed, Lisa still had not gone to sleep. She tried everything she could think of to relax her mind, but nothing worked. Finally she slipped out of bed and went to find Grandma.

"Grandma, do you have any sleeping pills?" Lisa asked anxiously.

"No, I don't, and I don't think it would be good for you to take anything like that anyway, Lisa," said Grandma.

Lisa sighed. She had thought Grandma might say something like that. "I know, but I just can't get to sleep," she said.

Placing an arm around Lisa, Grandma gave her a hug. Lisa felt better just having Grandma close. "You're probably worried about the divorce hearings tomorrow, aren't you?" asked Grandma. Lisa nodded. She wished she could tell Grandma exactly how she felt, but she couldn't put her emotions into words. "It's been bothering me, too," Grandma told her. "I keep wondering how different things would be if only your father had lived the way I brought him up instead of turning away from God." Grandma was silent for a moment, and Lisa guessed their feelings were much the same.

"At a time like this, I know of only one place to go for help," Grandma continued. She picked up her Bible. "Let me read you one of my favorite Scriptures. It's Philippians 4:4-9, and I think it will help both of us."

As Grandma read out loud, Lisa noticed that the Bible verses encouraged her to pray. Most of all, Lisa liked God's promise of peace. When Grandma finished reading, she prayed that God would quiet their nerves and give them rest.

"I think I can go to sleep now," Lisa said as she hugged Grandma. "You have good nerve medicine." *E.M.B.*

HOW ABOUT YOU?

Are problems upsetting you? Where do you go for help with a big problem? The long-term peace that God gives is so much better than any nerve pills. The promise of peace is for God's children who trust in their heavenly Father.

MEMORIZE:

"The peace of God, which surpasses all understanding, will guard your hearts and minds through Christ Jesus."

Philippians 4:7, NKJV

 Exchange Worry for Peace

Hail to the Chief (Read Matthew 6:9-13)

Andrew picked up his Bible and tried once again to memorize the Lord's Prayer. "'Our Father, which art in heaven,'" he quoted, then stopped and sighed. He always had trouble with the next word. "I don't even know what that next big word means," he complained to his father.

"The word *hallowed?*" asked Dad.

"Yeah," said Andrew. "Hallowed. What does 'Hallowed be thy name' mean?"

"Hallowed means holy or sacred. When we sincerely say 'Hallowed—or holy—be thy name,' we show honor to God," explained Dad. "We should always remember that God's name is holy, and we must use it only in respectful ways."

Later that day, Andrew and his father went to see a parade. The president of the United States was coming to their city and would be making a speech downtown. Andrew was excited about seeing the Secret Service men all around, and he was eager to see the president, too. He and Dad stood close to the speaker's platform, and soon a long, black car drove up. As the president stepped out, the band played a stirring tune. Then the president was introduced amid much cheering and clapping.

"Did you notice the song the band played when the president got out of his car?" asked Dad, when he and Andrew were on their way home. Andrew nodded. "It's 'Hail to the Chief,' and it's always played when the president arrives," added Dad.

"Yeah," said Andrew. "That's neat."

"It reminds people that our president is the leader of our country and that we should honor him as such," said Dad. "If people are this careful to honor an earthly leader, how much more should we honor God? The words you asked about in the Lord's Prayer remind us of that." *C.E.Y.*

19

DECEMBER

HOW ABOUT YOU?

Do you sometimes repeat the Lord's Prayer? Have you thought about what it means to "hallow" God's name? As you say those words, think about God's holiness and how great, how strong, how kind he is. Let those words remind you to honor God with your thoughts and your life.

MEMORIZE:

"Our Father which art in heaven, hallowed be thy name. Thy kingdom come. Thy will be done in earth, as it is in heaven." *Matthew 6:9-10,* KJV

 *Honor God's Name*

White Christmas (Read Psalm 51:1-9)

20
DECEMBER

"It's still snowing, Grandpa," Jason said, looking out the window. "We'll have a white Christmas for sure." Jason had not seen much snow while he lived in the valley, but now he was staying with his grandparents in the mountains.

"As soon as I finish making this sled, you can try it out on the hill," Grandpa said as he hammered another nail.

By the time Grandpa finished, Jason had put on his new ski jacket and boots. He grabbed his cap and mittens and went outside with Grandpa. "The whole world looks so clean!"

"It reminds me of one of my favorite Bible verses," Grandpa said with a smile. "'Though your sins be as scarlet, they shall be as white as snow.'" Jason didn't know much about the Bible, but he liked to hear Grandpa talk about it. Right now, though, he was eager to experience his first sled ride.

After he got used to the thrill of gliding downhill, Jason's mind went back to the Bible verse about sin. He had a few questions he wanted to ask Grandpa. "Grandpa, you said that Dad accepted Jesus as his Savior," began Jason, while sipping the hot chocolate Grandma had served. Grandpa nodded. "Does that mean that his sins are as white as snow?" asked Jason.

"Indeed it does," Grandpa assured him.

"Then why is Dad still in jail?" asked Jason.

"Jason, when your father was young, he didn't want anything to do with Jesus," Grandpa said. "He took the wrong road and broke the law, and now he has to pay for his sins in this life—even though God has cleansed his heart."

Jason thought about that. "I don't want to wait till I'm in trouble before my sins are washed white as snow," he said after a moment.

"You don't have to," said Grandpa. "Right now you can ask God to forgive your sins and allow Jesus to live in your life." He smiled at Jason. "Then you can have a 'white Christmas' on the inside as well as on the outside. Would you like to do that?" Jason nodded.

E.M.B.

HOW ABOUT YOU?

Will you have a "white Christmas" on the inside? That's far more important than having a snow-covered landscape. Remember that a life of sin does have consequences, even though God will forgive. Accept Jesus as your Savior, now while you're young.

MEMORIZE:

"Remember your Creator in the days of your youth."

Ecclesiastes 12:1, NIV

 **Accept Jesus Now**

Danger (Read Proverbs 1:10-19)

"No-no, Padi," Renee warned the family cat. "Keep your paws out of that pail." Padi was trying to play in some water into which Renee had put a strong cleaning solution. Renee knew that when Padi licked her paws, the solution could harm her. But Padi couldn't resist, so Renee scooped up her pet, put her in the next room, and closed the door. Padi wailed, but Renee was firm. "That's the only way to keep you from danger, Padi," she said.

21

DECEMBER

Later that day, Renee met some friends at the mall. All week she had been excited about this very first time she'd be allowed to shop at the mall without her mother. But the adventure took a disappointing turn when the girls stopped to look at some earrings. "Wow! These are expensive," said Jessica, one of the girls. "But no problem—I'm going to get them free. Don't stare at me—just act natural while I slip them inside my jacket."

"But that's stealing," objected Renee.

"It's being smart," replied Jessica, and the other girls nodded. "Or are you too much of a baby?"

Renee didn't know what to do. If she stayed with the girls, she would be part of their actions, even if she didn't take anything herself. But if she left, the girls probably would never invite her to do things with them again. She'd be left out. Renee was relieved when Jessica said, "I really don't see any here I want. Let's go to a different store."

The girls turned to leave. "Come on, Renee," said one, but Renee hesitated. As she had watched Jessica fingering the earrings, it made her think of Padi and the water. The only way she had been able to keep Padi from harm was to keep her away from the temptation. And Renee knew the only way to keep herself from taking part in stealing was to keep away from these girls. "I'm going home," she said, and she turned and walked away, ignoring the laughs behind her. Tears stung her eyes, but her heart was very glad. *C.E.Y.*

HOW ABOUT YOU?

When you're with others who are planning to do wrong, do you stay with them, or do you leave as soon as possible? It's hard to be the only one to walk away, but it's the best way to avoid taking part in doing things that God forbids.

MEMORIZE:

"Do not follow the crowd in doing wrong." *Exodus 23:2,* NIV

 Turn Away from Evil

Seeing Clearly (Read 1 Corinthians 13:8-13)

22

DECEMBER

"Hey, Dad!" exclaimed Jimmy. "Look at that!" He pointed ahead toward the distant skyline of the city, which was almost completely hidden by the fog. "I've never seen fog like this before," Jimmy added, with a tinge of amazement.

Dad smiled. "Keep watching those buildings," he said. "As we get closer, the fog will seem to disappear, and the buildings will become more clear."

For the next few minutes they drove in silence, while Jimmy stared at the hazy outline of the city. Sure enough, as his father had said, the closer they got, the clearer everything began to look. Jimmy grinned at Dad.

"Do you remember the verse in First Corinthians: 'For now we see through a glass, darkly; but then face to face: now I know in part; but then shall I know even as also I am known'?" asked Dad.

Jimmy looked up at his father. "Yeah," he said. "I had that for a memory verse once."

Dad nodded his head in the direction of the city. "The fog reminds me of that verse," he said. "Sometimes we have a difficult time understanding the love and wonder of God. But as we draw nearer to him—by reading his Word, going to church, and speaking to him every day—we begin to understand him more clearly."

Jimmy looked again at the skyline and then back at his father. "That's pretty neat, Dad," he agreed.

"Best of all," added Dad, "the day is coming when we'll know him perfectly." *R.S.M.*

HOW ABOUT YOU?

Do you read your Bible and pray every day? Remember, the more you read God's Word and speak with him, the more you'll understand how much he loves you. You'll find yourself looking forward to the day when you'll see him face-to-face and know him fully.

MEMORIZE:

"For now we see through a glass, darkly; but then face to face: now I know in part; but then shall I know even as also I am known." *1 Corinthians 13:12,* KJV

 Someday You'll Know God Fully

Cleaning Out the Junk (Read Hebrews 12:12-15)

Mark and his mother were sitting on the floor with all Mark's dresser drawers beside them. Mother was helping Mark clean his drawers, and she kept wanting to throw lots of things away. "I don't know why you keep all this junk," she said. "You don't have room for all the good things you have."

23

DECEMBER

"Junk!" exclaimed Mark. "Those are important things."

"Important things?" echoed Mother, holding up a deflated basketball, a bent fish hook, and a broken kite. "These things belong in the dump."

Mark picked up the kite. "But this was my favorite kite," he said. "Remember the day Jamie broke it? He borrowed it to go to the park with his friends, and he got it caught in a tree. I still get mad when I think about it."

"I remember," answered Mother. "Maybe you need to put more than the kite in the trash."

"What do you mean?" asked Mark.

"I think you're hanging on to some miserable memories," explained Mother. "In fact, not long ago Jamie asked to use something of yours, and you reminded him of the broken kite. You know, the Bible says not to be mean and angry."

Mark was quiet for a minute as he thought about what Mother had said. "I guess you're right, Mom," he admitted. He slowly placed the broken kite in the trash can. Then he grinned. "You know what?" he asked. "Today Jamie asked if he could use my ball mitt tomorrow, and I'm going to let him." *P.J.K.*

HOW ABOUT YOU?

Are you hanging on to grudges? Did someone put a scratch on your new bike? Did your friend choose someone else first for the team? Ask Jesus to help you forgive.

MEMORIZE:

"**Stop being mean, bad-tempered, and angry. Quarreling, harsh words, and dislike of others should have no place in your lives.**"

Ephesians 4:31, TLB

 *Get Rid of Grudges*

Lifeline (Read Matthew 1:18-25)

24 DECEMBER

Amy stuffed a kernel of popcorn into her mouth. She sat forward in her seat, her eyes riveted on the TV screen. The music played. Excitement mounted. Amy took another bite of popcorn as she watched the man on the screen struggle for his life. He had fallen from his boat into the ocean. Angry waves rolled about, threatening to drown him. The man kicked and splashed, searching for a lifeline.

A shark's fin sliced through the water behind the man, and Amy's heart pounded. Closer and closer came the shark as the man fought the sea, unaware of the danger behind him. Just when it seemed the shark would surely gobble him up, a boat roared into view. A lifeline was thrown out to the man. He took hold of it and was reeled in to safety.

"Wow! That was really exciting!" said Amy. "That boat just came out of nowhere."

"Not really," said Mark, her older brother. "The boat was there all along. Don't you remember? In the beginning of the movie, the boat was sent out to take water samples in the area."

"Oh, that's right," said Amy. "I remember now. But it sure was a good thing it came when it did."

Mark nodded. "It was that guy's lifeline to safety," he said. "That was a good story."

Amy yawned. "Yeah—but not a very Christmassy one," she said.

"Nope," agreed Dad, who had watched the program with the children, "but as you think about the story, maybe you can make it seem more Christmassy by remembering that tomorrow we celebrate the day God sent us our lifeline to safety. God knew we would all drown in a sea of sin, so he sent his only Son, Jesus Christ, to save us."

"Hey, that's right," said Mark. "Jesus has been there all along, too, hasn't he? All we have to do is accept him as our personal Savior, and he'll reel us in to safety." *J.A.P.*

HOW ABOUT YOU?

Are you still "drowning" in your sin? Jesus offers a lifeline to you. He came as a baby to Bethlehem. He grew up and lived a perfect life. But he went to the cross to save us from sin. He wants to save you. Accept him now as your personal Savior.

MEMORIZE:

"She will give birth to a son, and you are to give him the name Jesus, because he will save his people from their sins." *Matthew 1:21, NIV*

 *Jesus Saves*

Crybaby Christmas (Read Isaiah 9:2-3, 6-7)

"This is my worst Christmas ever," Brittany complained to her teenage brother Logan, who was rearranging some pieces of the nativity set. "Here we are in a strange town where Dad got transferred, and the only place we could find to live is this crummy apartment. The heat isn't working right, and we don't even have a TV."

"When Mary and Joseph got to Bethlehem, all they could find was a stable," replied Logan. "At least we have a bed. They probably just had straw."

25

DECEMBER

Brittany looked at the angels in the set. "Well, Mary and Joseph heard angels singing," she said. "And the wise men brought presents."

"It was the shepherds, not Mary and Joseph, who heard the angels," Logan told her. "Besides, we had carolers last night. And when we open our gifts at breakfast, I'm sure we'll both get more presents than we deserve—especially you," he teased. He grinned at his sister, then added, "You keep saying this Christmas is the worst, but it won't be unless you let it be--unless you make it a crybaby Christmas."

"What do you mean?" asked Brittany.

"Every year I hear kids complain that they don't have enough money to buy Christmas presents," said Logan. "Or they complain about the part they do or don't get in the church pageant. A lot of times they complain, too, that they don't get every gift they want, or that somebody else got more gifts than they did. They're just crybabies!"

Brittany made a face at her brother. "Well, I'm not," she told him. "At least, I'm not going to be." She grinned as she added, "And I better not hear you complain about having to write thank-you notes!" *R.K.M.*

HOW ABOUT YOU?

Have you been complaining lately? Christmas should be a wonderful, joyful season! Rejoice in the birth of Jesus and in the gift of eternal life that can be yours because of his coming. Don't have a "crybaby Christmas" at your house.

MEMORIZE:

"And the angel said unto them, 'Fear not: for, behold, I bring you good tidings of great joy, which shall be to all people.'"

Luke 2:10, KJV

 Be Joyful at Christmas

Just Mud Dirt (Read 1 John 1:5-9)

26

DECEMBER

"Jimmy!" Mom's voice startled him as he stepped into the kitchen. "Look at your shoes!" Jimmy looked down at his feet and then at the trail of mud behind him. "Where have you been to get so dirty?" asked Mom.

Jimmy shrugged and carefully stepped backward toward the door. "I haven't been anywhere special," he said. "Just outside."

"Well, please go back outside and clean off your shoes," Mom said as she opened the door for him.

A few minutes later Jimmy walked back into the house. Mom was on her knees wiping up the last few clumps of dirt. "I'm sorry," said Jimmy.

Mom smiled. "No harm done," she said. "I know it was an accident. How about some milk and cookies?"

"Sure!" Jimmy's eyes brightened.

When he had finished his second chocolate chip cookie, Mom smiled and said, "It's pretty easy to pick up dirt on your shoes without knowing it, isn't it?"

Jimmy nodded. "Uh-huh," he said. "I don't know how they got so dirty. Honest."

Mom smiled again. "Well," she said, "at least it was just mud dirt—not sin dirt." Jimmy looked puzzled. "Getting your shoes dirty with mud is a little like getting your life dirty with sin," explained Mom. "Sometimes you don't even realize what's happened until suddenly the Lord shows you how dirty with sin you are."

"Does that ever happen to you?" asked Jimmy in surprise.

Mom nodded her head sadly. "Yes, I'm afraid it does."

"But how can you get clean again?" asked Jimmy. He was confused. He knew a person couldn't go outside and brush sin off like he could brush off dirty shoes.

Mom thought a moment before she answered. "We get clean again by asking God for forgiveness," she told him. Then she quoted 1 John 1:9. "'If we confess our sins to him, he can be depended on to forgive us and to cleanse us from every wrong.'"

R.S.M.

HOW ABOUT YOU?

Examine your life. Has sin attached itself to your life without your knowing it was happening? Ask God to show you those things from which you need to be cleansed. Then confess them, and don't repeat them.

MEMORIZE:

"If we confess our sins to him, he can be depended on to forgive us and to cleanse us from every wrong." *1 John 1:9,* TLB

 Confess Sin and Be Clean

Better than Pretending (Read Psalm 96:1-10)

At the sound of footsteps on the porch, Millie ran to greet her cousin Beatrice. Each of the girls had received a doll for Christmas, and they couldn't wait to play together with them. "Let's pretend we're missionaries," said Millie, after they finished admiring each other's new doll. "We can pretend our dolls are African children."

27

DECEMBER

Beatrice agreed, and the girls took their dolls outside and placed them on a bench under a tree—the missionaries often held church services outdoors in Africa. Millie and Beatrice imagined that Africa looked just like Alabama. And they even gave their dolls the African names of Chuma and Indosio—names that Miss Randall had used when she spoke at church.

After the girls had played awhile, pretending to teach children about Jesus coming as a baby to Bethlehem, Millie's mom called them in for a snack. "I wish we could give Miss Randall some cookies to take back to the African children," murmured Millie as she nibbled a peanut butter cookie, fresh from the oven. "I'd like to be a missionary when I grow up."

Mom smiled. "Maybe you can be, but you don't have to wait that long," she said. "You could help the missionaries right now."

"We could? How?" asked Millie.

"I've been making some dresses for Miss Randall to take back to Africa," said Mom. "You girls could do some of the hand sewing." She brought out two dresses that needed to be hemmed.

So the girls went to work. Millie and Beatrice had made doll clothes now and then. That was fun, but sewing for the missionaries was more important. Millie did her best work, and she noticed that Beatrice was making her stitches very carefully, too. When they finished, Mom said, "Think how happy two little girls will be when they get these."

Millie and Beatrice smiled. "Helping is lots better than pretending," Millie said, and Beatrice agreed. *E.M.B.*

HOW ABOUT YOU?

Do you wish you could help a missionary? Maybe you can find a missionary family with a child about your age. You could write to her or him—perhaps you could send little gifts now and then to let her/him know you care. And you can choose a missionary to pray for each day.

MEMORIZE:

"Declare his glory among the nations, his marvelous deeds among all peoples."

Psalm 96:3, NIV

 Work for Jesus Now

Boast and Brag (Read 2 Corinthians 10:12-18)

28
DECEMBER

"I can't wait to get home and show all my friends at school the picture and autograph!" squealed Amy as she climbed into the car. She and her family were enjoying a Christmas vacation trip, and they had gone to see a famous Olympic figure skater, Adele Norlund. Amy was delighted when her parents took a picture of her with Adele. Then Adele signed Amy's autograph book.

A week later, Amy rushed into the kitchen after her first day back at school. "Mom, you'll never believe what happened today!" she exclaimed, as she reached for a freshly baked cookie.

Mother laughed. "I'll bet the whole school knows that you met Adele Norlund," she said.

Amy nodded. "All my friends just about died when I showed them the picture of me with Adele," she said with a giggle. "Everybody thought it was just great!"

"It was fun meeting her, wasn't it?" agreed Mother. "I told the ladies about it at my quilting class today, too." After a few moments, she added seriously, "I wonder, does the whole school know you've met Jesus? Do the ladies in my class know I've met him?"

"Wow, Mom! I never thought about it that way before," said Amy thoughtfully.

"We often like to brag about the important people we meet, but we're ashamed to even mention the most important person in our lives," continued Mother. "If we really believe that Jesus is God's Son, and if we believe he loved us enough to die for us, then we ought to be excited about telling others of him. Instead, we're often embarrassed or ashamed to tell our friends about him." She shook her head. "Let's both try to do better, shall we?"

Amy nodded. "Sure, Mom, I'll try." *B.L.D.*

HOW ABOUT YOU?

Have you met Jesus as your Savior? If so, do your friends know that? Do you tell them about the things he has done in your life? Why not try "bragging" about Jesus today!

MEMORIZE:

"May I never boast except in the cross of our Lord Jesus Christ, through which the world has been crucified to me, and I to the world." *Galatians 6:14,* NIV

 Tell Others You've Met Jesus

The Hidden Gift (Read Romans 5:8-15)

Christmas was over, and Billy and Sally helped their parents carefully unhook the ornaments from the Christmas tree branches. They helped unstring the lights and strands of garland. Soon the shimmering and festive tree looked bare, except for the white sheet surrounding the tree stand.

29
DECEMBER

"Hey," Billy called out, pointing to a small box wrapped in green and red that was peeking out from under a fold in the sheet. "Look at that!"

"Well, what in the world?" exclaimed Mother as she bent down to pick up the box. "We must have missed this when we opened our gifts." She held the box in her hands and looked for a name. "Why, it's from Aunt Martha for me," she said in surprise. "I didn't think she had sent anything this year, and here it was under the tree all this time."

When Mother opened the gift, her eyes brightened. "Oh," she exclaimed. "How lovely!" She held up a pretty gold necklace.

"Do you know what this reminds me of?" asked Dad, after everyone had admired the necklace. No one could guess. Not even Mother. "This gift was here, all this time, waiting for Mother to receive it. But she didn't know it was there," said Dad with a smile. "God's gift of salvation is like this necklace. The gift is available, but many people don't even know it's there. And it remains hidden until someone shows it to them—like you did for Mother, Billy."

Sally and Billy looked at Dad for a moment while they thought about what he was saying. Then Billy nodded. "And when we show other people that Jesus is God's gift, they can have their present, too—the gift of eternal life," he said.

Mom and Dad smiled. "That's right," Mom agreed. "Let's all be sure to tell them about it." *R.S.M.*

HOW ABOUT YOU?

Have you taken possession of the gift of God's eternal salvation? Do you tell others where they can find God's gift of eternal life, too? He wants so much for everyone to have it.

MEMORIZE:

"The free gift of God is eternal life through Jesus Christ our Lord." *Romans 6:23,* TLB

 *Accept God's Gift*

The Dogsled Ride (Read 1 Timothy 4:6-16)

30
DECEMBER

"I don't want to go to Sunday school tomorrow," Sarah told her grandparents.

"We don't want to go either," announced her younger brothers, Jordan and Scott.

"We'll all go," said Grandpa firmly. "But right now, are you ready to go for a dogsled ride, Sarah? I have the dogs all hooked up to the sled."

"Oh, goody!" exclaimed Sarah. Dogsled rides were a special treat they enjoyed at Grandpa's house, and Sarah eagerly followed him out to the sled. "Just a minute—I guess I'll hook up Kelsey, too," said Grandpa.

"Oh, Grandpa, let's just leave him here," objected Sarah. "When we take him, the other dogs don't run as well." But Grandpa already was putting a harness on Kelsey. Sarah gave a big sigh and sat on the sled. She hated taking Kelsey. When all the other dogs were running fast, Kelsey would decide to stop and scratch at something. Before you knew it, the other dogs stopped, too, and their lines would get all tangled up.

Grandpa hopped on the runners and shouted, "Let's go!" Out of the driveway and down the snow-packed road they went. They raced to the top of the hill. Sarah clapped with excitement. Just then Kelsey spotted an old branch sticking out of the snow. He pulled the sled to the side and stopped. The other dogs tried to go on, but soon they were just as distracted as Kelsey. And, just as Sarah had expected, they all got tangled up in each other's lines. Grandpa got off the sled to straighten them out.

"Why did we even have to bring Kelsey?" asked Sarah as Grandpa worked.

Grandpa smiled. "Well, he's a lot like you," he said. "You and Kelsey both distract others from doing the right thing. I wanted you to see the problems that causes." Sarah stared at Grandpa. "Kelsey distracts the other dogs, and you distract your brothers," explained Grandpa. "When you drag your feet about going to Sunday school, Jordan and Scott don't want to go, either." He turned the dogs toward home. "We'll take Kelsey back now," he said. *C.C.F.*

HOW ABOUT YOU?

Are you a good example to your brothers and sisters and friends? Do you ever distract others from doing what is right? Think about your actions and then try to act in a way that will glorify God.

MEMORIZE:

"Be an example to the believers." *1 Timothy 4:12,* NKJV

 Be a Good Example

Inventory Time (Read Deuteronomy 8:1-6)

"Hi, Dad. What's new?" asked Kristi as Dad came in from work. "Do you have to go back to the store after dinner?" Dad was the manager at a large department store.

Dad smiled. "Nope—it's New Year's Eve," he said, "and I'm glad we're closed tonight. All week we've been so busy with Christmas present returns and exchanges—and with after-Christmas sales. We like to sell as much as possible before we take inventory next month."

31
DECEMBER

"Inventory?" asked Kristi. "What's that?"

"Oh, you know," said her brother Brent. "It's when they count everything in the store to see how well they did, and to find out what sold and what didn't, so they know what to order a lot of for the next year and what to skip—stuff like that. Isn't that right, Dad?"

Dad smiled. "That's a pretty good description," he agreed. "We do that once a year." He paused, then added, "It would be a good idea for all of us to take inventory of our lives once a year—and New Year's Eve would be a good time to do that."

"How would we do that?" wondered Brent.

"Should we count how many pairs of shoes and jeans and shirts we have?" asked Kristi. "Hey, that might be a good idea. Then maybe Mom would see that I need some more!"

"I bet she'd see that you have too many already," scoffed Brent. "Then you wouldn't get any new clothes for a whole year." He grinned at his sister.

Dad laughed. "That's not exactly what I had in mind," he said. "I'm talking about looking over the things we've done this past year and taking note of what was good and pleasing to God and what wasn't. I'm also talking about deciding, with God's help, to repeat those things that were good and to avoid the others. That kind of inventory would be worthwhile." *H.M.*

HOW ABOUT YOU?

As you look back over the past year, do you see actions that God would be pleased to have you repeat? Ask God to help you with those things again. Do you also see mistakes you've made? Ask God to help you avoid those things in the new year.

MEMORIZE:

"Remember how the Lord your God led you all the way."

Deuteronomy 8:2, NIV

 *Learn from the Past*

Index of Topics

Index of Scripture Readings

Index of Memory Verses

Psalm 119:140 *May 1*
Psalm 121:1-2 *January 14*
Psalm 126:3 *March 10*
Psalm 127:1 *September 27*
Psalm 133:1 *February 23*
Psalm 139:3 *January 31*
Psalm 139:4 *October 12*
Psalm 139:14 *April 6*
Psalm 139:23 *January 12*
Psalm 147:3 *June 21*
Proverbs 1:8 *September 22,*
  October 10
Proverbs 1:10 *April 18, June 18*
Proverbs 2:2 *May 25*
Proverbs 3:5 *August 13, October 4*
Proverbs 4:11 *December 11*
Proverbs 4:23 *June 14*
Proverbs 4:25 *January 2*
Proverbs 4:26 *April 14*
Proverbs 9:8 *November 23*
Proverbs 11:2 *April 10*
Proverbs 15:1 *March 3*
Proverbs 16:4 *August 12*
Proverbs 17:17 *October 18*
Proverbs 17:22 *February 28,*
  December 15
Proverbs 18:24 *March 23*
Proverbs 19:9 *April 23*
Proverbs 20:1 *December 16*
Proverbs 20:11 *October 5*
Proverbs 22:8 *April 5*
Proverbs 23:7 *February 15*
Proverbs 28:13 *May 29,*
  September 4
Proverbs 28:20 *April 27*
Proverbs 28:27 *December 14*
Proverbs 30:5 *February 22*
Ecclesiastes 5:5 *September 3*
Ecclesiastes 9:10 *July 16*
Ecclesiastes 10:12 *March 8*
Ecclesiastes 12:1 *December 20*
Isaiah 1:18 *January 15, March 20*
Isaiah 1:19 *July 17*
Isaiah 40:8 *January 11,*
  September 20
Isaiah 40:31 *May 9*
Isaiah 41:10 *February 8,*
  August 28
Isaiah 48:18 *November 28*
Isaiah 53:6 *January 30*
Isaiah 64:6 *June 2, October 14*

Isaiah 65:25 *August 6*
Isaiah 66:13 *June 11*
Jeremiah 18:6 *January 19*
Jeremiah 29:11 *July 1, October 7*
Jeremiah 33:3 *January 29*
Ezekiel 18:31 *February 14*
Hosea 14:8 *July 10*
Habakkuk 3:18 *November 25*
Matthew 1:21 *December 24*
Matthew 4:4 *October 22*
Matthew 5:4 *August 29*
Matthew 5:13 *July 23*
Matthew 5:16 *September 6*
Matthew 5:44 *January 20*
Matthew 6:8 *September 9,*
  October 23
Matthew 6:9-10 *December 19*
Matthew 6:20 *March 7, August 19*
Matthew 6:33 *April 20,*
  September 8, November 20
Matthew 6:34 *August 15*
Matthew 7:1 *May 20*
Matthew 7:20 *November 10*
Matthew 10:8 *August 10*
Matthew 10:31 *August 2*
Matthew 11:28 *March 15,*
  June 26
Matthew 11:30 *October 27*
Matthew 12:34 *September 7*
Matthew 15:8 *August 8*
Matthew 16:26 *April 17*
Matthew 19:14 *March 27*
Matthew 22:37 *June 3*
Matthew 23:28 *July 8*
Matthew 24:24 *September 1*
Matthew 25:46 *November 27*
Matthew 26:41 *May 16*
Mark 5:19 *January 27*
Mark 9:50 *September 30*
Mark 10:44 *July 19*
Mark 10:45 *October 6*
Luke 2:10 *December 25*
Luke 3:11 *November 19*
Luke 6:31 *August 7*
Luke 6:37 *August 25*
Luke 6:45 *December 12*
Luke 6:46 *March 19*
Luke 8:11 *May 23*
Luke 9:23 *April 3*
Luke 11:9 *January 3*
Luke 12:2 *August 9*